THE CASE OF LIZZIE BORDEN
AND OTHER WRITINGS

ELIZABETH GARVER JORDAN (1865–1947) was born on May 9, 1865, in Milwaukee, Wisconsin. Following her graduation from St. Mary's High School at Notre Dame convent, she worked as a journalist, eventually moving to New York City where she joined the staff of the *New York World* in 1890. Among varied assignments, she was dispatched to New Bedford, Massachusetts, to cover the Lizzie Borden murder trial in 1893. During her time at *The World*, Jordan rose to the position of assistant Sunday editor and became known for her column "True Stories of the News," which chronicled everyday life across the city. In 1898, she published her first collection of fictional stories; titled *Tales of the City Room*, the stories were adapted from the news and featured women reporters as protagonists.

In 1900, Jordan was appointed as editor of *Harper's Bazar* (as the magazine's title was rendered until 1929). While editing the popular women's magazine, she published collections of stories and novels, including *Tales of the Cloister* (1901), *Tales of Destiny* (1902), *May Iverson—Her Book* (1904), *May Iverson Tackles Life* (1912), and *May Iverson's Career* (1914). She also coordinated, edited, and contributed to the composite novel *The Whole Family*, which was serialized in *Harper's Bazar* from 1907 to 1908.

When Jordan concluded her tenure as editor of *Harper's Bazar* in 1913, she began working as a literary adviser for publisher Harper & Brothers. Her editorial projects included *The Story of a Pioneer* (1915), the autobiography of suffrage leader Rev. Dr. Anna Howard Shaw, which Jordan commissioned and coauthored. Jordan made another significant contribution to the suffrage cause in 1917 when she edited *The Sturdy Oak* (1917), a composite novel by fourteen American male and female writers who supported women's rights.

Throughout her life, Jordan continued to write novels, including several adapted for film. In 1938, she published a memoir, *Three Rousing Cheers*. She died on February 24, 1947, in New York City.

BROOKE KROEGER is a professor emerita at New York University, where she was the founding director of the Arthur L. Carter Journalism Institute and taught from 1998 to 2021. She was UN correspondent for *Newsday*, deputy metropolitan editor at *New York Newsday*, and for more than a decade a correspondent, editor, and bureau and division chief for United Press International at home and abroad. She serves on the editorial board of *American Journalism: A Journal of Media History*. *Undaunted: How Women Changed American Journalism* (2023) is her sixth book. She lives in New York.

JANE CARR is senior editor for ideas and planning at CNN Opinion. A scholar and writer, her work has appeared in CNN, *Slate*, *The Atlantic*, *American Quarterly*, and elsewhere. The cofounding editor of *The Brooklyn Quarterly*, she is also a former Mellon/ACLS Public Fellow and lecturer in English at New York University.

A professor in the English Department at Boston College who has received multiple awards for recovering forgotten literary works by women, LORI HARRISON-KAHAN is the editor of *The Superwoman and Other Writings by Miriam Michelson*, coeditor of *Heirs of Yesterday by Emma Wolf*, coeditor of *Matrilineal Dissent: Women Writers and Jewish American Literary History*, and author of *The White Negress: Literature, Minstrelsy, and the Black-Jewish Imaginary*.

ELIZABETH
GARVER JORDAN

The Case of Lizzie Borden and Other Writings

TALES OF A NEWSPAPER WOMAN

Foreword by
BROOKE KROEGER

Edited with an Introduction by
JANE CARR *and* LORI HARRISON-KAHAN

PENGUIN BOOKS

PENGUIN BOOKS

An imprint of Penguin Random House LLC
penguinrandomhouse.com

LIBRARY OF CONGRESS CATALOGING-IN-PUBLICATION DATA
Names: Jordan, Elizabeth Garver, 1867-1947, author. |
Carr, Jane (Jane Greenway), editor. | Harrison-Kahan, Lori, editor. |
Kroeger, Brooke, 1949- writer of foreword. |
Jordan, Elizabeth Garver, 1867-1947. Case of Lizzie Borden.
Title: The case of Lizzie Borden and other writings : tales of a newspaper
woman / Elizabeth Garver Jordan ; foreword by Brooke Kroeger ; edited
with an introduction by Jane Carr and Lori Harrison-Kahan.
Description: [New York] : Penguin Books, [2024] |
Series: Penguin classics | Includes bibliographical references.
Identifiers: LCCN 2023047227 (print) | LCCN 2023047228 (ebook) |
ISBN 9780143137603 (trade paperback) | ISBN 9780593511701 (ebook)
Subjects: LCSH: American literature—19th century. | American
literature—20th century. | American literature—Women authors. |
Journalism—United States. | Jordan, Elizabeth Garver, 1867-1947. |
Women journalists—United States—Biography.
Classification: LCC PS3519.O6 C37 2024 (print) |
LCC PS3519.O6 (ebook) | DDC 813/.52—dc23/eng/20240119
LC record available at https://lccn.loc.gov/2023047227
LC ebook record available at https://lccn.loc.gov/2023047228

Printed in the United States of America
1st Printing

Set in Sabon LT Pro

Contents

THE CASE OF LIZZIE BORDEN AND OTHER WRITINGS

TALES OF A NEWSPAPER WOMAN

I
NEWSPAPER WOMAN: SEEING "THE WORLD"

IV
COLLABORATION AND LITERARY ACTIVISM: JORDAN AS EDITOR AND ADVISER

Foreword

Elizabeth Garver Jordan's stories exemplify the adage, "Write what you know." What she knew emanated from her reporting and editing for top publications in the nation's media capital—New York City—as the nineteenth century became the twentieth. It emanated from the success she achieved among men inclined to consider the women working in their midst a nuisance. The reportage, fiction, and essays in this volume reflect the rarity of Jordan's career path in the 1890s. She rose from journalism's trenches, not from a feminized perch. She earned respect as a peer of the men in charge. The best of Jordan's work thus becomes valuable journalism history.

Jordan has a cameo in *Undaunted: How Women Changed American Journalism*, my 180-year history of women at the top of the field. She appears for her cogent reflections on what she experienced along the way. During much of her working life, women journalists numbered fewer than 250 in the United States, some 10 percent of the whole, not close to half like today. She was in the minuscule group of women reporters excused from the softer side stories and assigned to the paper's front section, where the hard news appeared. This early reportage, her fiction about women much like herself, and her essays about the woman journalist's life and lot give her work significance.

In 1893, she was twenty-eight, and three years into the decade she would spend on the staff of Joseph Pulitzer's the *New York World*. She expressed pride in her assignment to the city desk and not to the stunt girl arena, where famed investigative journalist Nellie Bly and her imitators—to their credit—carved out the only place to date where "girl reporters" could build big-bylined reputations off the women's pages. Their splashy exposés appeared illustrated in the feature sections of the paper, not among the department store and elixir ads. Jordan was spared the "I was there!" indignities that stunt work so often involved. Her early reporting for *The World* is deep, thorough, and impersonal, focused on the facts, albeit laced with empathic—the word *womanly* does come to mind—responses to what she learned.

Jordan became an editor at *The World* while still doing daily reporting. In her essay "What It Means to Be a Newspaper Woman," she speaks of the exhaustion her long days brought on. This piece and other reflections join plenty of published commentary about the impact of the newsroom's coarse, hardscrabble culture on the mental and physical well-being of journalism's women in this period.

Predictably, Jordan's initial charge as assistant Sunday editor, first under Arthur Brisbane and then under George Harvey, was to run the pages devoted to women and children; but before she left the paper in 1899, she had advanced to have charge of comics and opinion. In the 1890s, this was neither commonplace nor unprecedented. As just two examples from the *New York Tribune*, Horace Greeley entrusted Margaret Fuller with the post of literary editor a half a century earlier, from 1842 to 1844, and Nelly Mackay Hutchinson reprised the role for Greeley's successor from 1881 to 1890. Still, Jordan rates her own good-sized dot on the continuum that plots the careers of the few women who succeeded in man-like terms on the country's mass circulation dailies.

Jordan, like Hutchinson, did not have the wattage of women like Fuller in the 1840s, or Middy Morgan, Grace Greenwood, Gail Hamilton, or Mary Clemmer in the thirty years that followed, or of Bly, Ida Tarbell, or Ida B. Wells thereafter. Keep in mind that this is the case for most superb reporters and editors of any gender, right up to the present; the work is meant to be ephemeral, after all. Jordan did not have the benefit of a consistent byline to aggrandize her reputation as a reporter. As was typical for hard-news denizens, her articles went mostly unsigned. In her post as an assistant editor, achieving outside recognition would have also been difficult, especially since her name was not listed on the paper's masthead. Her name, however, does appear in 1893 articles that list the country's women journalists of special note—and that was even before *The World* sent her to cover the trial of Lizzie Borden.

Like the best of Jordan's predecessors, her networking ability was key to her success. In 1899, when George Harvey left *The World* to become editor of Harper & Brothers, he tapped Jordan to be the top editor of *Harper's Bazar.* (Women's work, to be sure, although the editor of *Ladies' Home Journal* was Edward Bok.) It was as editor of *Bazar* and from her magazine fiction that Jordan's reputation grew, starting with her city room tales, first published in magazines and then collected into a book in 1898. "These tales of a newspaper office are feminine, not because they are weak, but because they are womanly," one critic wrote in a review of Jordan's debut fiction collection. "The woman in journalism, in all her varieties, is delicately but truly portrayed."

Something else came through in reading Jordan's work. I think her reporting from 1890 to 1893 presages the next two attempts after the stunt era to bring women reporters off the women's pages. That is, the much-maligned "sob sisters" with their overwrought courtroom weepies, starting around 1907—think the Mary Sunshine role from *Chicago*—and in their wake, the more admired newspaper "front-page girls" of the 1920s, the women thought of as a "man's idea of what a newspaper woman should be."[1] The latter group—almost never more than one woman reporter per paper—would eventually do what Jordan did. Note how her "True Stories of the News" and her coverage of the Borden trial deploy the signature elements of both sob sisters and front-page girls, the two cloisters yet to come.

Elizabeth Garver Jordan deserves a place in the larger saga of journalism's women for her early hard news positioning on the staff of *The World*, for her depictions of the woman journalist's life in the 1890s and early 1900s, and for anticipating the next two movements on the boulder-strewn road to women's progress in the field. Read her reportage and essays as windows into how women found a way to thrive in a culture that offered them a reluctant, disdainful welcome. Read her fiction for its nuances and undercurrents, and for the more complete picture of journalism history that it paints.

BROOKE KROEGER

NOTES

1. Ishbel Ross, *Ladies of the Press: The Story of Women in Journalism by an Insider* (New York: Harper & Brothers, 1936), pp. xi–xii.

Introduction

In June of 1893, *New York World* journalist Elizabeth Garver Jordan spent two weeks at the New Bedford Courthouse in Massachusetts, covering one of the most famous and sensationalized murder trials in American history: the case of Lizzie Borden, a thirty-one-year-old, unmarried woman accused of murdering her father and stepmother with a hatchet in the family's Fall River home. One year after Borden's acquittal, Jordan, aspiring to expand her repertoire beyond newspaper journalism to fiction, published her first short story in *Cosmopolitan* magazine. Titled "Ruth Herrick's Assignment," the story told of an accused murderer who confesses her crime to a young woman reporter during a jailhouse interview, admitting that she poisoned her husband after suffering years of domestic abuse. In an unexpected twist, the guilty woman is acquitted, thanks to the sympathetic journalist who decides to keep the confession a secret, sacrificing the exclusive scoop that would surely make her career. The *Cosmopolitan* story caused considerable controversy. Readers took it for evidence that Jordan had suppressed her knowledge of Lizzie Borden's guilt, motivated by sympathy and gender solidarity. Jordan denied the charge, offering as proof her claim to have written "Ruth Herrick's Assignment" *before* the Fall River murders and her personal belief that Borden was indeed innocent, as the jury had determined.

Readers' conflation of the author with her fictional reporter Ruth Herrick did not dissuade Jordan from drawing on material from her own life as she went on to pursue a prolific career as a writer of magazine fiction and novels. Her popular series of May Iverson tales, for example, features a heroine whose profile resembles Jordan's: May is a convent girl turned newspaper reporter with inclinations toward suffrage activism and conflicted views on beauty culture. Furthermore, many of May's experiences and the challenges she faces as a professional woman—including the shame and trauma incurred by continually warding off unwanted sexual advances in the workplace—find parallels in episodes that Jordan relates in her 1938 autobiography, *Three Rousing Cheers*.

For readers today, Jordan's writings raise questions that make her work fascinating to read and study, including: How do writers and their audiences navigate the tenuous divide between fact and fiction? How do narrative techniques extend the cultural reach of investigative journalism and reportage? What imbues fiction with the power to influence real-world events and ignite movements for social change? A media polymath, fluent in multiple genres, Jordan explored such questions through a wide range of themes and topics. Above all, she was committed to telling unconventional stories of women's lives in women's voices.

As the first volume to compile selections of Jordan's fiction and nonfiction, *The Case of Lizzie Borden and Other Writings: Tales of a Newspaper Woman* demonstrates not only how Jordan shaped the culture of New Womanhood in her historical moment, but also how her writings were ahead of their time, giving space to women's professional successes and aspirations while disrupting silences in ways that forecasted the era of #MeToo. Jordan's fictional stories marked a shift away from women's domestic fiction of the nineteenth century; like other turn-of-the-twentieth-century New Woman writings, they offer representations of single, independent women, depicting many of the challenges professional women faced in the workplace and in pursuit of careers.[1] These portrayals—along with the dilemmas of career versus family that they pose—continue to resonate. Setting much of her fiction in the patriarchal space of the newsroom, Jordan narrates her heroines' encounters with sexual harassment, gendered violence, and toxic masculinity; in so doing, she critiqued the structural barriers limiting women's career success and gave voice to sexual trauma.

Such representations are but one example of the ways Jordan's writings can be read as progenitors of twenty-first-century feminism. Equally important is Jordan's emphasis on the primacy and intimacy of bonds between women, which often supersedes the familiar heterosexual romance plot. Featuring women characters who engage in dialogue with each other about work and social issues, Jordan's fiction presents contemporary readers with narratives that easily pass the Bechdel test and testify to the centrality and necessity of female friendships, collective action, and professional networks.[2]

Jordan's reliance on the support of woman-centered communities was bred in her youth. Born on May 9, 1865, in Milwaukee, Wisconsin, she was the elder of two daughters of William Francis Jordan and Margaretta Garver Jordan. In 1884, she graduated as valedictorian from St. Mary's High School at Notre Dame convent, a Catholic girls' high school, which would provide the setting for some of her early fiction. Educated by nuns, Jordan maintained close relationships with her teachers, who encouraged her to enter the novitiate. Despite being a self-described "high-spirited and irrepressible young person [who was] usually in trouble," she seriously considered becoming a nun. Her parents, however, advised her to first pursue secular interests and nurtured her talents as a pianist and writer.[3]

Following graduation, Jordan made a practical decision to enter business college in order to learn shorthand, which would prove useful when her father's connections helped her get her first job in journalism editing the woman's page of *Peck's Sun*. She later worked as secretary to the Milwaukee superintendent of schools while reporting for papers including the *St. Paul Globe*. At the end of the 1880s, she moved to Chicago where she freelanced for the *Chicago Tribune* and other papers.

Jordan's commitment to newspaper work had clearly solidified by 1890 when she made a tenacious decision to relocate once again, this time to New York City—a move made possible by her father, a successful businessman, who provided her with the financial resources to pursue a writing career before losing his wealth in the Panic of 1893. Yet, Jordan was adamant that "the next move on life's chess-board . . . was to be made by me, not by Father." Knocking on the door of the *New York World*'s managing editor, she submitted an "application with [her] first breath."[4] Her audacity earned her a job in the newsroom of Joseph Pulitzer's *World*.

As the epicenter of turn-of-the-twentieth-century American

journalism, New York was the key to her breakthrough as a national reporter, and the *New York World* was the city's premiere daily newspaper for a mass audience. In these years, Pulitzer was locked in a fierce competition with William Randolph Hearst. According to Jean Marie Lutes, Pulitzer succeeded by "appeal[ing] to a multiethnic, cross-class audience" and "speak[ing] to the needs of the most vulnerable members of urban society: immigrants, women, the working poor, even the barely literate."[5] His blood sport with competitors for readership thus helped pave the way for women like Jordan to make names for themselves at a time when other papers (such as the *New York Times*) still refused to hire women as reporters.

Because *The World*'s quest for circulation dominance included attracting a female readership, working for Pulitzer opened up opportunities for Jordan to tell stories about women and other marginalized people without being confined to the kinds of items covered by the woman's page. Initially siloed in *The World*'s Brooklyn satellite office, Jordan gained national attention when she secured her first major interview with president Benjamin Harrison's wife, Caroline Scott Harrison, while she was vacationing in Cape May, New Jersey, with her daughter and grandchild, Baby McKee. Jordan posed questions about a variety of human interest topics, ranging from the domestic arrangements of Mrs. Harrison's new seaside cottage to her views on women entering the professions and their "mannishness of manner and costume."[6] The interview was considered a significant scoop because the First Lady rarely spoke to reporters and due to the public's insatiable interest in Baby McKee, whose first ocean bath Jordan records in the article.

Impressed by Jordan's ability to fuse sentimentalism with clear-eyed storytelling, *The World* dispatched her to report from the remote communities of Appalachia, where she produced the front-page feature "A Mountain Preacher" (1890). She was soon transferred to hard news beats, including two notorious murder trials. The first came in 1892, when medical student Carlyle Harris was tried and convicted (and later executed) for the murder of his wife. Placing a woman reporter in titillating proximity to violence fueled the gritty sensationalism on which *The World* staked its reputation in the era of yellow journalism.[7] Many of Jordan's later achievements resulted from her accomplishments as a true-crime reporter, especially her coverage of the Lizzie Borden murder trial in 1893.

Jordan's reporting on Borden's trial is remarkable for its future-fiction-writer's eye for detail and the way her narrative techniques popularized conventions of the true-crime genre familiar to audiences today. She noted everything from the curl of the defendant's bangs to the "gasp that swept the courtroom like a great sigh" when the jaw of Andrew Borden's skull—brought forth as evidence—"sagged back and forth in a grisly suggestion of speech."[8] One of but a tiny cohort of women journalists assigned to the trial, Jordan brought a literary mind to her understanding of the public's obsession with Borden's alleged crimes. Often analogizing the court proceedings to works of fiction, Jordan alludes to nineteenth-century mystery writers such as English novelist Wilkie Collins, known for his "sensation novel" *The Woman in White*, and Edgar Allan Poe, an American short story writer and master of the gothic tale. She was especially attuned to the trial's captivating effect upon women spectators. Observing that "fully 80 per cent" of those queued to get into the courthouse "were women and little girls," she describes the female spectators as "a sort of self-constituted jury . . . [who] attend the trial every day, never missing a session."[9]

These women became secondary characters in her reportage, part of the milieu that—in combination with her finely detailed accounts of Borden's affect, comportment, and dress—allowed her to round out a portrait of the defendant. In Jordan's reporting, Borden appears as a complex woman of a particular place and time, rather than a monstrous villain or an angelic ingénue, as she was simplistically portrayed in other media reports. Covering the Borden case reinforced Jordan's understanding of the power of a woman's story—and she would spend the rest of her career harnessing it.

During the Progressive Era, women's issues were part of a wider constellation of reform efforts intended to better US society. As reformers and writers, women brought attention to a variety of social and political issues—including race relations, immigration, labor, industrialization, and poverty in both rural and urban environments—with the goal of bringing about seismic, progressive change. Against this backdrop, Jordan applied her investigative and narrative skills to tenement conditions in New York City; the resulting series of articles was published under the title *The Submerged Tenth*, sharing much in common with the influential work of photojournalist Jacob Riis, whose exposé "How the Other Half Lives: Studies Among the Tenements" had appeared in *Scribner's* in 1899. During her time at *The World*, Jordan also became known for her column "True Stories of the News," which chronicled everyday life among the city's downtrodden, and rose to the position of assistant Sunday editor. By the end of her decade at the paper, she was responsible for editing *The World's* comics supplement (home to the cartoon figure of "The Yellow Kid," from which derived the term "yellow journalism") and its editorial forum.

Jordan helped to transform journalism at a moment when troubling the divide between fact and fiction in reportage was not just encouraged—it was, particularly for women, expected. As Lutes demonstrated, women reporters did not simply adopt the same approaches to journalism employed by male reporters. Instead, they achieved the status of front-page girls by playing up the spectacle of their femininity and becoming the story themselves—perhaps none more famously than fellow *World* star Nellie Bly, who went undercover in a madhouse and manufactured journalistic stunts such as her seventy-two-day trip around the globe. Jordan was not a "girl stunt reporter" in the same vein as Bly, but she knew the potency of spectacle on and off the page, and she deployed various narrative devices to make visible stories of women in her own profession, as well as those rendered outcasts by illness, criminality, or extreme poverty.

As a result, Jordan's work, first as a reporter and then as a storyteller in other genres, provocatively complicates today's understanding of journalistic "objectivity." It foregrounds, for example, modern-day assertions that standard journalistic practices marginalize experiences of those who by dint of race, gender, class, disability, or other identity markers, are left out of what counts as "fact." In chasing an ideal of "objectivity," critics argue, traditional journalism demands that journalists ignore their own humanity and operate blind to the ways in which the implicit biases and newsroom power dynamics shape decisions about newsworthiness as well as who gets to speak and who constitutes a credible source.[10] The ethical pursuit of neutral reporting thus fosters a pernicious "both-sides-ism" that continues to relegate certain points of view to the margins—or silences them altogether.

Jodi Kantor and Megan Twohey's 2017 Pulitzer Prize–winning reporting for the *New York Times* on the allegations of sexual assault against Harvey Weinstein offers one high-profile example of how getting silenced women to speak can challenge mainstream media narratives and create symbiosis between journalism and activism. By titling the behind-the-scenes account of their reporting, *She Said: Breaking the Sexual Harassment Story that Helped Ignite a Movement*, Kantor and Twohey invoke journalism's connection to activism—in their case, the social media groundswell galvanized by their reporting, followed by inevitable backlash—and issue a critique of "both-sides-ism." In addition to recounting a groundbreaking period in investigative journalism, their book serves as a potent reminder that neutrality is not, in fact, an achievable ideal in a patriarchal society systematically engineered to validate "he said" over "she said." This contemporary example is of particular relevance to Jordan, who followed her decade of work as a reporter with fictional stories about women in the newsroom that set a precedent for #MeToo.[11] Importantly, Jordan developed her understanding of how to mobilize print culture as a means of literary activism at the beginning of her career, while working as a journalist for the Progressive Era press.

Jordan's status as a token woman in the male-dominated newspaper industry was itself enabled by her whiteness and middle-class background, which gave her access to a mainstream audience largely unavailable to women journalists of color as well as immigrant and working-class women. Black investigative journalists such as Ida B. Wells, for example, were confined to the African American press. The stakes of Black and white women's reporting also differed. Wells risked her life in pursuit of racial justice, as she worked to expose the surge of Jim Crow violence.[12] Jordan's framing of her stories reflects her own privilege and exposes the blind spots of white feminism, especially when considered in relation to her later work as a women's magazine editor and suffrage activist.[13] Like many of her allies and contemporaries who rose to leadership positions, she accrued enough power to ensure that women from similar backgrounds were well represented in print culture, but her efforts rarely extended to those who were marginalized by race.

While working at *The World* as an editor, Jordan began to write fiction, making productive use of the time she spent in the newsroom waiting for reporters to file their stories. In a time when literary realism prevailed and writers such as Mark Twain, Theodore Dreiser, Stephen Crane, and Sui Sin Far (the pen name of Asian American writer Edith Maude Eaton) moved between journalism and imaginative prose, Jordan, too, saw fiction as another means to convey slices of everyday American life. In 1898, she published her first collection of fictional stories. Titled *Tales of the City Room*, the stories were adapted from the news and featured women reporters as protagonists. Jordan's fictional alter egos reported to America's reading public in ways that journalism could not; fiction provided opportunities to depict certain realities of women's lives, such as domestic violence and sexual harassment, thus pushing the limits of what might be considered taboo to print in the daily paper.

Despite being a prolific writer of magazine fiction, much of it reprinted in the form of novels and story collections, Jordan's place in literary and cultural history thus far has rested on her editorial work—which explains, in part, why she has often been overlooked. What critic Sarah Blackwood has described as the "carework" of editing is often gendered and is, by definition, nearly always unseen, even as published words hold traces of the evidence of that labor.[14] In 1900, Jordan was appointed as editor of *Harper's Bazar*, the popular women's magazine still in print today. She held the position for thirteen years, regularly penning the magazine's editorial columns.

Jordan's years at *Harper's Bazar* amplified her mastery of middle-class literary taste and her persistent elevation of women's voices in public and professional life. In the first two decades of the twentieth century, she published multiple collections of stories and novels featuring women characters, including *Tales of the Cloister* (1901), *Tales of Destiny* (1902), *May Iverson—Her Book* (1904), *May Iverson Tackles Life* (1912), and *May Iverson's*

Career (1914). She expanded into other genres as well, collaborating, for instance, on an experimental "composite novel" (a
term she coined with William Dean Howells for a collaboratively
authored work of fiction) called *The Whole Family*. Jordan coordinated, edited, and contributed to the composite novel, which
was serialized in *Harper's Bazar* from 1907 to 1908 and included
as contributors Howells and Henry James (with whom Jordan
maintained a friendship and correspondence), alongside equally
prominent women writers such as Elizabeth Stuart Phelps and
Mary E. Wilkins Freeman. In 1913, she made her first foray into
playwriting with *The Lady from Oklahoma*, which was produced on Broadway; the play offered a humorous depiction of
American women's obsession with makeovers, representing Jordan's enduring interest in the possibilities and perils of fashion
and beauty culture. Later, she was to make herself over yet again,
drawing on her ability to create intrigue and suspense—honed
during her time as a true-crime reporter—to publish popular
golden age mystery novels such as *The Lady of Pentlands* (1924).[15]

After Hearst acquired *Harper's Bazar* in 1913, Jordan remained employed by the magazine's former publisher, Harper &
Brothers. As a literary adviser to one of the country's leading
publishing houses, she reprised her role as editor but was also
much more; she operated as a cultural power broker and arbiter
of literary trends, wielding considerable influence over the print
marketplace especially in the years leading up to World War I.
Jordan shaped the work of male literary giants like Henry James
and Sinclair Lewis, whose first novel, *Our Mr. Wrenn* (1914), she
is credited with accepting for publication. At Harper & Brothers,
she was responsible for bringing the work of women novelists
such as Zona Gale and Dorothy Canfield Fisher to the public in
addition to commissioning and coauthoring Rev. Dr. Anna Howard Shaw's memoir of her life as a suffrage leader, *The Story of a
Pioneer* (1915).

Synthesizing editorial labor and literary activism, Jordan chan-
neled her wide-ranging connections and professional reputation
as an editor to become a well-known suffragist. Like Shaw, Jordan was an effective orator and organizer who campaigned and
fundraised for the women's movement. Her media savvy was crucial to the successful effort by women in New York State to

secure the right to vote in 1917, three years before the ratification of the Nineteenth Amendment. One of her most important and innovative contributions to the suffrage cause was *The Sturdy Oak* (1917), a composite novel by fourteen American male and female writers who supported women's rights. Working with the New York State Woman Suffrage Party, the leading organization pursuing a statewide referendum to give women the vote, she solicited the authors and edited their contributions.

The novel, which appeared serially in *Collier's Weekly* in the run up to election day, was also published in book form by Henry Holt & Co. Exemplifying her ability to advance radical ideas while appealing to the masses, Jordan's preface sets the stage for the novel. The ensemble work may be "devoted," as Jordan phrased it, to the "Suffrage Cause," but *The Sturdy Oak* was "first of all a very human story of American life today."[16] As a suffragist, Jordan knew her goal (passage of the New York State referendum) depended on appealing to male voters across the ideological spectrum. Jordan the editor knew this as well. Constructing a rollicking good story from familiar tropes of magazine fiction—such as marital conflict (in this case, over suffrage) between an upper-class white couple—and publishing it in a popular magazine would guarantee a reading public and exert a wider literary influence, whether or not readers shared her politics.

Published in 1938, Jordan's memoir, *Three Rousing Cheers*, documents her vibrant social milieu, key moments in her extraordinary literary career, and her friendships with some of the most influential writers of her time, many of whom became her traveling companions during her journeys abroad. In it, she chronicles how she fashioned for herself an unconventional life, one that did not follow the expected path for middle-class, white women of marriage and childbearing. An independent woman who supported herself and members of her family after her father experienced financial setbacks, she made her home with fellow career women whom she claimed as kin. At the same time that she became editor of *Harper's Bazar*, she embarked on a "brilliant" experiment, moving in with two women she identifies as her "adopted sisters": Harriet Beardslee Prescott (head of the catalog department at the Columbia University Library) and Martha Hill

Cutler (an art student and later a leading designer).[17] As Sharon Harris discusses in her biography of Jordan, her most romantically passionate partnership was with renowned children's book novelist Frances Hodgson Burnett, best remembered today as the author of *The Secret Garden* (1911). This relationship was sustained over the course of twenty-five years through intimate weekends spent together at Burnett's home on Long Island, summer vacations in Bermuda, and loving correspondence in which Burnett refers to Jordan as "Beloved" and "Querida" (the Spanish word for "dearest," usually signifying a female romantic partner, which they had chosen as a special name).[18] Harris's findings not only shed new light on Jordan's life, but also compel reevaluations of her oeuvre, which can be read through the lenses of lesbian history and queer studies.

Since her death in 1947, at age eighty-one, Jordan's impact on American culture—like that of many popular women writers and editors—has remained largely unexamined beyond a small group of scholars. Karen Roggenkamp and Jean Lutes have demonstrated Jordan's importance to journalism history and the ways that newspapers and belles lettres influenced each other, while June Howard has focused primarily on Jordan's career as an editor. As the selections of her writing in this volume show, Jordan's various roles as journalist, fiction writer, editor, and activist were interdependent, rather than distinct endeavors.

In all these arenas, Jordan provided models of professionalism and political engagement as alternatives to traditional domesticity, strongly influencing the concept of New Womanhood at a moment when women were in the process of defining the terms of modern femininity. At the same time, as a proto-influencer at the helm of one of the nation's leading women's magazines, she fostered a print and media culture that embraced nuance, encouraging women to express and explore a range of seemingly contradictory views. In her role as editor of *Harper's Bazar*, for instance, Jordan espoused positions that may appear paradoxical—for example, advising readers to safeguard their femininity by wearing long skirts, while fiercely defending women's right to the vote. Jordan's ideological inconsistencies are evocative of contemporary debates about "bad feminism."[19]

Stylistically, Jordan's writings are of literary importance for the way they toe the line between mass culture, the principles of realism championed by Howells (her friend and collaborator), and modernism's imperative to "make it new." Just as the composite novels she edited demonstrate an interest in formal inventiveness, her solo-authored writings are laced with metacommentary and other experimental techniques that are often associated with modernist and postmodernist literature. Her troubling of the lines between fact and fiction and blending reportage with a variety of narrative devices anticipated innovations of narrative nonfiction and literary journalism that came later in the twentieth century, from the male provocateurs of 1960s and 1970s New Journalism to the essayistic eye of Joan Didion and Rebecca Solnit. In drawing directly upon her personal experiences while trying out a variety of narrative voices and personae, Jordan's work can also be read as a precursor of contemporary autofiction represented by women authors such as Rachel Cusk, Elena Ferrante, and Sheila Heti.

Jordan was an extraordinarily versatile and prolific writer whose oeuvre included novels (in genres ranging widely from Bildungsromane to mysteries), biography, and autobiography as well as reportage, essays, newspaper columns, short fiction, and drama criticism, much of it published and reviewed in the leading newspapers and magazines of her time. Yet, other than the two composite novels that she edited (*The Whole Family* and *The Sturdy Oak*), her writings have, until now, remained out of print. Tracing Jordan's path from the 1890s through the first decades of the twentieth century, this edition brings together nonfiction and fiction from her long and varied career. In the pages that follow, readers will find, for example: samples of Jordan's coverage of the Lizzie Borden trial in the *New York World* as well as other journalistic writings; advice columns she wrote to guide young women interested in pursuing journalistic careers; magazine fiction as well as excerpts from her collection of short stories *Tales of the City Room* (1898) and her series of May Iverson stories; and two excerpts from *The Story of a Pioneer* (1915), a memoir of the early women's movement that she coauthored with suffrage leader Rev. Dr. Anna Howard Shaw. A brilliant media strategist, Jordan employed literary skill, editorial acumen, and a carefully cultivated professional persona to shape the public discourse on women's roles and rights. *The Case of Lizzie Borden and Other Writings* illuminates how her work continues to resonate with feminist thought and activism in the twenty-first century.

JANE CARR *and* LORI HARRISON-KAHAN

NOTES

1. For other examples of New Woman writings, see *The Women Who Did: Stories by Men and Women, 1890–1914,* ed. Angelique Richardson (New York: Penguin Classics, 2006).
2. The Bechdel test is a set of criteria applied to film, televisions, novels, and other forms of media to assess whether the work is sufficiently feminist. The three primary criteria of the Bechdel test are: 1) at least two women are main characters 2) these women must talk to each other and 3) their conversation must be about something other than the male characters. The test is so named because it was popularized by American cartoonist Alison Bechdel in her comic strip *Dykes to Watch Out For.* For more on the Bechdel test, see "Chapter 7: The Bechdel Test," *Introduction to Women and Gender Studies: An Interdisciplinary Approach 2e Student Resources,* ed. Melissa J. Gillis and Andrew T. Jacobs (Oxford University Press, 2019), https://learninglink.oup.com/access/content/gillis-jacobs2e-student-resources/gillis-jacobs2e-chapter-7-the-bechdel-test?previousFilter=tag_chapter-07.
3. Elizabeth Garver Jordan, *Three Rousing Cheers* (New York: D. Appleton-Century Company, 1938), p. 6.
4. Jordan, *Three Rousing Cheers*, p. 17.
5. Jean Marie Lutes, *Front-Page Girls: Women Journalists in American Culture and Fiction, 1880–1930* (Ithaca, NY: Cornell University Press, 2006), p. 35.
6. "In Her New Cottage," *New York World,* June 28, 1890, p. 5.
7. Yellow journalism refers to a kind of sensationalized journalism popularized during the late nineteenth century as a means of attracting readers and increasing circulation. See Joseph W. Campbell, *Yellow Journalism: Puncturing the Myths, Defining the Legacies* (New York: Bloomsbury, 2001).
8. Jordan, *Three Rousing Cheers*, p. 120.
9. "Lizzie's Dark Day," *New York World*, June 9, 1893, p. 1.
10. The concept of objectivity in journalism has had an unstable

meaning over the course of American history. In the late nineteenth century, according to Bill Kovach and Tom Rosenstiel in
their book *The Elements of Journalism* (New York: Three Rivers
Press, 2001), journalists pursued "realism," rather than objectivity. The advent of objectivity, then defined as the application of the
scientific method to reporting, came in the early decades of the
twentieth century, often attributed to Walter Lippmann and Charles
Merz's criticism of American coverage of the Russian Revolution.
As the century progressed, Cold War tensions shaped and informed how journalistic objectivity was understood in America;
between 1949 and 1987, the Federal Communications Commission required holders of a broadcast license to devote some of their
airtime to discussing controversial matters of public interest, and
to air contrasting views regarding those matters (this was called
the "fairness doctrine"). As the Iron Curtain fell and efforts to di-
versify newsrooms continued and grew, critics argued for a more
nuanced understanding of objectivity, contending both that it
erased a human element from journalism and that it was often
weaponized against women and journalists of color. In a 2022 lecture, for example, journalism professor Kathleen McElroy noted
instances of Black journalists being barred from covering the murder trial of O.J. Simpson in the 1990s; in the late 2010s, then-
Washington Post journalist Felicia Sonmez was blocked from
covering stories related to #MeToo or sexual assault after disclos-
ing that she was a survivor. In the wake of the protests that swelled
after the murder of George Floyd in 2020, Pulitzer Prize–winning
journalist and writer Wesley Lowery published an influential essay
in the *New York Times* outlining how Black journalists were leading a reckoning over objectivity, writing: "The views and inclinations of whiteness are accepted as the objective neutral. . . . We
also know that neutral 'objective journalism' is constructed atop a
pyramid of subjective decision-making: which stories to cover,
how intensely to cover those stories, which sources to seek out and
include, which pieces of information are highlighted and which
are downplayed. No journalistic process is objective. And no individual journalist is objective, because no human being is" ("A
Reckoning Over Objectivity, Led by Black Journalists," *New York
Times*, June 23, 2020). Many contemporary journalists and media
critics reject an aspirational ideal of objectivity in favor of the
pursuit of fairness, truth-telling, support for democracy, and/or
the disclosure of any bias; meanwhile, debate continues over the
acceptability of journalists, for instance, covering political or social issues in which they themselves are active. Journalism professor

Anita Varma has written eloquently in favor of a model of "solidarity" journalism, returning the profession to a public service mission. Writing for Harvard's NiemanLab in 2021, she elaborates: "Solidarity for social justice moves journalism in a better direction . . . Objectivity as an aspirational ideal ends up encouraging journalists to avoid addressing what matters." ("Solidarity Eclipses Objectivity as Journalism's Dominant Ideal," https://www.niemanlab.org/2021/12/solidarity-eclipses-objectivity-as-journalisms-dominant-ideal/).

11. See Lori Harrison-Kahan, "The Seeds of #MeToo Started Growing 100 Years Ago," CNN, November 2, 2019, https://www.cnn.com/2019/11/02/opinions/me-too-movement-history-jordan-michelson-harrison-kahan/index.html.

12. See Ida B. Wells, *The Light of Truth: Writings of an Anti-Lynching Crusader,* ed. Mia Bay (New York: Penguin Classics, 2014).

13. On white feminism, see Mikki Kendall, *Hood Feminism: Notes from the Women That a Movement Forgot* (New York: Penguin Books, 2021); Kyla Schuller, *The Trouble with White Women: A Counterhistory of Feminism* (New York: Bold Type Books, 2021); and Rafia Zakaria, *Against White Feminism: Notes on Disruption* (New York: W. W. Norton, 2021). On Black women and suffrage activism, see Martha S. Jones, *Vanguard: How Black Women Broke Barriers, Won the Vote, and Insisted on Equality for All* (New York: Basic Books, 2020).

14. Sarah Blackwood, "Editing as Carework: The Gendered Labor of Public Intellectuals," *Avidly,* June 6, 2014, https://avidly.lareviewofbooks.org/2014/06/06/editing-as-carework-the-gendered-labor-of-public-intellectuals/.

15. Thank you to Sharon Harris for drawing our attention to this aspect of Jordan's career.

16. Elizabeth Garver Jordan, Preface to *The Sturdy Oak* [1917] (Athens, OH: Ohio University Press, 1998), p. xvii.

17. *Jordan, Three Rousing Cheers,* pp. 170, 146. For Jordan's description of Prescott and Cutler's professional roles, see Jordan, *Three Rousing Cheers,* p. 170.

18. *Jordan, Three Rousing Cheers,* p. 308. Thank you to Sharon Harris for sharing the manuscript of her forthcoming biography with us.

19. See, for example, Roxane Gay, *Bad Feminist: Essays* (New York: Harper Perennial, 2014).

Suggestions for Further Reading

Ashton, Susanna. *Collaborators in Literary America, 1870–1920*. New York: Palgrave Macmillan, 2003.

Belford, Barbara. *Brilliant Bylines: A Biographical Anthology of Notable Newspaperwomen in America*. New York: Columbia University Press, 1986.

Canada, Mark, editor. *Literature and Journalism: Inspirations, Intersections, and Inventions from Ben Franklin to Stephen Colbert*. New York: Palgrave Macmillan, 2013.

Chapman, Mary. *Making Noise, Making News: Suffrage Print Culture and U.S. Modernism*. New York: Oxford University Press, 2014.

Chapman, Mary, and Angela Mills. *Treacherous Texts: An Anthology of U.S. Suffrage Literature, 1856–1946*. New Brunswick, NJ: Rutgers University Press, 2011.

Conforti, Joseph. *Lizzie Borden on Trial: Murder, Ethnicity, and Gender*. Lawrence, KS: University Press of Kansas, 2016.

Danky, James, and Wayne A. Wiegand, editors. *Women in Print: Essays on the Print Culture of American Women from the Nineteenth and Twentieth Centuries*. Madison, WI: University of Wisconsin Press, 2006.

Doan, Laura L., editor. *Old Maids to Radical Spinsters: Unmarried Women in the Twentieth-Century Novel*. Champaign, IL: University of Illinois Press, 1991.

Edelstein, Sari. *Between the Novel and the News: The Emergence of American Women's Writing*. Charlottesville, VA: University of Virginia Press, 2014.

Fahs, Alice. *Out on Assignment: Newspaper Women and the Making of Modern Public Space*. Chapel Hill, NC: University of North Carolina Press, 2014.

Freeman, Elizabeth. "The Whole(y) Family: Economies of Kinship in the Progressive Era." *American Literary History*, vol. 16, no. 4 (2004): 619–47.

Garvey, Ellen Gruber, and Sharon M. Harris, editors. *Blue Pencils &
Hidden Hands: Women Editing Periodicals, 1830–1910*. Boston,
MA: Northeastern University Press, 2004.

Gerzina, Gretchen Holbrook. *Frances Hodgson Burnett: The Unexpected Life of the Author of* The Secret Garden. New Brunswick,
NJ: Rutgers University Press, 2004.

Gilmore, Leigh. *The #MeToo Effect: What Happens When We Believe
Women*. New York: Columbia University Press, 2023.

Glaspell, Susan. *Trifles*. New York: Samuel French, 2010.

Harrison-Kahan, Lori, editor. *The Superwoman and Other Writings
by Miriam Michelson*. Detroit, MI: Wayne State University Press,
2019.

Howard, June. *Publishing the Family*. Durham, NC: Duke University
Press, 2001.

Jones, Martha S. *Vanguard: How Black Women Broke Barriers, Won
the Vote, and Insisted on Equality for All*. New York: Basic Books,
2020.

Jordan, Elizabeth Garver. *Three Rousing Cheers*. New York: D. Appleton-Century Co., 1938.

Jordan, Elizabeth Garver, editor. *The Sturdy Oak: A Composite Novel
of American Politics*. New York: Henry Holt and Company, 1917.

Jordan, Elizabeth Garver, editor. *The Whole Family: A Novel by
Twelve Authors*. New York: Harper & Brothers, 1908.

Kantor, Jodi, and Megan Twohey. *She Said: Breaking the Sexual Harassment Story that Helped Ignite a Movement*. New York: Penguin Press, 2019.

Keyser, Catherine. *Playing Smart: New York Women Writers and
Modern Magazine Culture*. New Brunswick, NJ: Rutgers University Press, 2011.

Kilcup, Karen L., editor. *Soft Canons: American Women Writers*. Iowa
City, IA: University of Iowa Press, 1999.

Kroeger, Brooke. *Undaunted: How Women Changed American Journalism*. New York: Knopf Doubleday Publishing Group, 2023.

Lutes, Jean Marie. *Front-Page Girls: Women Journalists in American
Culture and Fiction, 1880–1930*. Ithaca, NY: Cornell University
Press, 2006.

Neumann, Johanna. *Gilded Suffragists: The New York Socialites Who
Fought for Women's Right to Vote*. New York: New York University Press, 2017.

Petty, Leslie. *Romancing the Vote: Feminist Activism in American Fiction, 1870–1920*. Athens, GA: University of Georgia Press, 2006.

Riis, Jacob. *How the Other Half Lives: Studies Among the Tenements
of New York* [1890]. New York: Penguin Classics, 1997.

Robertson, Cara. *The Trial of Lizzie Borden*. New York: Simon & Schuster, 2019.

Roggenkamp, Karen. "Elizabeth Jordan, 'True Stories,' and Newspaper Fiction in Late-Nineteenth-Century Journalism," *Literature and Journalism: Inspirations, Intersections, and Inventions from Ben Franklin to Stephen Colbert*, ed. Mark Canada (New York: Palgrave Macmillan, 2013): 119–141.

Roggenkamp, Karen. *Narrating the News: New Journalism and Literary Genre in Late-Nineteenth-Century American Newspapers and Fiction*. Kent, OH: Kent State University Press, 2005.

Roggenkamp, Karen. *Sympathy, Madness, and Crime: How Four Nineteenth-Century Journalists Made the Newspaper Women's Business*. Kent, OH: Kent State University Press, 2016.

Ross, Ishbel. *Ladies of the Press: The Story of Women in Journalism by an Insider*. New York: Harper & Brothers, 1936.

Rouse, Wendy. *Public Faces, Secret Lives: A Queer History of the Women's Suffrage Movement*. New York: New York University Press, 2022.

Schofield, Ann. "Lizzie Borden Took An Axe: History, Feminism and American Culture." *American Studies* vol. 34, no. 1 (Spring, 1993), 91–103.

Scutts, Joanna. *Hotbed: Bohemian Greenwich Village and the Secret Club that Sparked Modern Feminism*. New York: Basic Books, 2022.

Todd, Kim. *Sensational: The Hidden History of America's "Girl Stunt Reporters."* New York: HarperCollins Publishers, 2021.

Wells, Ida B. *The Light of Truth: Writings of an Anti-Lynching Crusader*. New York: Penguin Classics, 2014.

A Note on the Texts

Elizabeth Garver Jordan (1865–1947) was a stunningly prolific writer in multiple genres as well as a newspaper, magazine, and literary editor who had a significant influence on American print culture in ways that remain invisible, as is often the case with editorial labor. This volume is representative rather than comprehensive; it contains work from her early career as a newspaper reporter through her mid-career as a fiction writer and editor. The works contained herein were published between 1890 and 1915 and are thus in the public domain. We hope that readers of this volume will seek out Jordan's later works, including her suffrage composite novel *The Sturdy Oak* (1917), her mystery novels, and the regular columns she wrote for newspapers such as the *Philadelphia Inquirer* and the *Los Angeles Times*.

Capturing the first twenty-five years of Jordan's varied professional life, the works included here were chosen for their historical and literary value, as well as their relevance to contemporary issues and readers. We also curated the volume with an interactive reading experience in mind, choosing selections that would allow readers to explore the interplay between Jordan's journalism, fiction, and editorial activism.

In making editing decisions, we have prioritized readability and fidelity to the original texts. Throughout, we have silently corrected obvious misspellings and typographical errors. We have also adjusted some peculiarities of punctuation and capitalization that would create confusion for readers.

The selections in this volume were drawn from newspapers, magazines, and books that employed different conventions for typography, accents and diacritical marks, and punctuation (especially in regard to the spelling of compound words). In some cases, in order to create greater consistency across the volume, we silently regularized the text; we did so only when the conventions employed by the original source did not appear to represent a deliberate, artistic choice on Jordan's part and when such edits would not alter meaning. In most cases, we have also standardized contemporary American spellings in order to create consistency across the volume. References to time that used periods in the original text have been regularized to use colons (for example, 1.30 has been changed to 1:30).

The newspaper articles in the first section of this book were transcribed from microfilmed issues of the *New York World*. In a few cases where the quality of the original text significantly affected legibility, we used brackets to indicate our best guess. We also eliminated nineteenth-century typographical features such as the use of periods after newspaper headlines, sub-headlines, and section headings.

All notes are by the editors of this volume.

The Case of Lizzie Borden and Other Writings

TALES OF A NEWSPAPER WOMAN

I

NEWSPAPER WOMAN: SEEING "THE WORLD"

In November 1890, toward the end of her first year on the staff of the *New York World*, Elizabeth Jordan began writing a column titled "True Stories of the News." Her job was "to dig up all the facts back of the news leads and write each story as [if it were] fiction, hung on its news hook."[1] In Jordan's hands, emotion and sympathy became conduits to a truer form of realism than traditional reportage allowed, especially in stories involving girls and women like "Jessie Adamson's Suicide" (1890), "The Happiest Woman in New York" (1891), and "A Strange Little East Side Girl" (1891). In pieces such as these, Jordan supplied rich narrative context for the kinds of terse news vignettes—a two-line item about a young woman's suicide, for example—that were easy to ignore when perusing the news of the day.

By devoting space and giving voice to urban society's most vulnerable members (immigrants, women, disabled people, and the working poor), Jordan made marginalized lives visible to readers and helped the newspaper attract a cross-class, multiethnic audience. Like a number of other Progressive Era journalists, including Jacob Riis, whose documentation of squalid tenement conditions opened the eyes of many middle- and upper-class New Yorkers, she further contributed to a culture of reform by encouraging readers to take action and aid the less fortunate. This is evident in the way "Put Yourself in His Place" generated altruistic interest in the fate of a homeless family; in her follow-up article, "The Silver Lining of the Cloud," Jordan, in turn, documented her readers' generous donations and offers of employment for the father. Later, many of these human-interest pieces provided material for her fiction, as exemplified in this volume by the similarities between "The Happiest Woman in New York" and her 1902 short story "In the Case of Hannah Risser."

In 1890, Jordan had further solidified her growing star power with a front-page story titled "A Mountain Preacher," which displayed her reportorial mettle as well as her range as a journalist. For this article, *The World* assigned Jordan to travel—partially on horseback—to Tennessee and Virginia to report on remote Appalachian communities. More so than in her other articles, Jordan herself becomes a character in "A Mountain Preacher," as she incorporates her journey to Appalachia as a crucial part of the story, making it a fascinating blend of reportage and immersive narrative techniques associated with New Journalists such as Joan Didion and Tom Wolfe in the 1960s and 1970s. Contemporary readers may be especially attuned to the way Jordan "others" rural people, emphasizing the primitivism and backwardness of their lifestyle, for a readership of cosmopolitan city dwellers. For instance, she renders the speech of multiple characters in dialect, including that of the article's main subject, Rev. Joseph C. Wells, as he laments the devastating effects of industrial modernity in the form of coal and iron on his community.

In *Ladies of the Press* (1936), Ishbel Ross wrote that Jordan "combined the best features of the stunt age with sound writing."[2] Jordan's experiential, emotionally grounded reportorial style reflected the empathetic dimensions of stunt reporting but diverged from sensationalism's bombastically maudlin tones. As Jordan described in her 1938 memoir, *Three Rousing Cheers*, the "best literary criticism I have ever received" came from a nun at her convent school, who advised her pupil to "[l]et [her] readers shed their own tears."[3] It was a line Jordan later imported into more than one of her popular short stories, and it guided her newspaper writings as well. For her, emotion and human interest were pathways into insight about the news and the stories that most headlines left untold, not their own readerly payoff or punch line.

In an antecedent to the true crime genre that has thrived in recent years in the form of television docuseries and podcasts, Jordan applied her brand of emotional realism to coverage of
high-profile murder trials in the early 1890s, most notably the
1893 trial of Lizzie Borden, who stood accused of murdering her
father and stepmother. Jordan's coverage of the Borden trial
changed the trajectory of her career and irrevocably altered how
Americans think about crime stories, whetting an obsession with
understanding the psychology of accused criminals. Public pre-
occupation with Borden's alleged crime focused more on her social and sexual inscrutability as an unmarried woman accused of
fiendish brutality than on the truth of what actually happened.
The four samples of Jordan's Lizzie Borden coverage included
here illustrate how Jordan resisted the speculative, ghoulish sensationalism embraced by some of her primarily male counter-
parts, focusing instead on what *was* knowable about Borden and
the details of her legal case.

In roughly twenty articles, Jordan tracked the daily proceedings of the trial. As was the convention of the time, most of her
reports were published unsigned, but in "This Is the Real Lizzie
Borden," a profile of the defendant included in this volume, Jordan gets a tagline—a sign that she had achieved the status of a
celebrity reporter. "There are two Lizzie Bordens," writes Jordan
in this feature story—one the "very real and very wretched
woman who is now on trial for her life" and the other "a journalistic creation, skillfully built up by correspondents and persistently dangled before the eyes of the American people. . . . This
last creature is a human sphinx, a thing without heart or soul."[4]
Jordan's writings on Borden offer a considered critique of the
lurid fascination that often drives the narrative when women are
accused of violent crimes.[5]

As Cara Robertson points out in her book, *The Trial of Lizzie
Borden* (2019), the New York newspapers were not initially
granted slots to cover the trial, which took place in New Bedford,
Massachusetts, and *The World* had to ask the chief justice of the
Massachusetts Supreme Court to intercede on their behalf to secure in-person access to the proceedings. Thus, Jordan's coverage
of the Borden trial was more than a plum assignment to a sensational case; it also crucially conveyed her paper's faith in her

journalistic prowess.[6] Being publicly known and identified as a journalist at the pinnacle of professional achievement—and being able to deploy, shifting gears at a moment's notice—was to become a defining aspect of her later career as a magazine and book editor, novelist, and suffrage activist.

Jordan's skill and daring, as well as her sound judgment about what made for good and newsworthy stories that would capture reader interest, earned her the respect of her superiors at *The World*. In 1897, she was promoted to assistant Sunday editor, an extremely rare position for a woman. As the last two pieces in this section suggest, Jordan was not simply focused on her own success; she was committed to supporting fellow professional women and increasing their presence in the field of journalism. In these magazine articles, "The Newspaper Woman's Story" (1893) and "What it Means to be a Newspaper Woman" (1899), she dispenses advice to women interested in newspaper careers, documenting her own experiences and sharing practical guidance.

These selections—which were published at different moments in the decade that defined Jordan's journalistic career, for publications that drew different readerships (*Lippincott's* was a general-audience publication, while *Ladies' Home Journal* was aimed at the women's market)—exemplify Jordan's use of varied forms of print culture to expand women's influence in the public sphere. Writing in *Ladies' Home Journal* on the cusp of a new century, as she was poised to begin the next chapters in her career as a magazine editor and author, Jordan predicted that "the newspaper woman of the twentieth century will be a new type, and much will be expected of her. . . . She must stand or fall by the same tests as are given to the man at the desk beside hers in the city room."[7]

"A MOUNTAIN PREACHER"

(1890)

THE REMARKABLE POWER OF
THE REV. JOSEPH C. WELLS, OF BIG STONE GAP

WHY IT WAS THAT A "WORLD" CORRESPONDENT
WAS SENT THITHER TO TELL HIS STORY

AND IT IS WELL WORTH THE READING BY THE
SINNERS AS WELL AS THE SAINTS AMONG US

Idolized by All About Him—"In Five Minutes," Says State Senator Mills, "He Will Have a Thousand of Us Crying"—He Has Baptized Over Two Thousand of His Primitive Neighbors and "Brung a Heap of Sinners to the Mourners' Bench"—But He Has Lived on $30 a Year Salary, and Has Earned Absolutely Nothing Except the Little Log Cabin He Built for Himself, His Faithful Wife and His Ten Children—Now He Must Go Away, Driven Further by the March of Civilization—His People

[SPECIAL TO THE WORLD.]

BIG STONE GAP, Va., Nov. 17.—There is much that is romantic in the heart of the Virginia mountains, if it can be called romantic to step back 100 years and meet the mountaineers on the plane of 1700. Shut in on all sides as they are, theirs is naturally a narrow, contracted life. They know little and care less about the outside world. At rare intervals an illustrated newspaper finds its way into their log cabins and is carefully, almost prayerfully, tacked to the wall, where it hangs until it is yellow and blurred with age. Occasionally a whiff of news comes over the mountains, to be received and stolidly discussed long after it has been forgotten in the haunts of men. The people are true-hearted and clannish and stand by one another when necessary, but the wild and rugged life they lead tends to make each feel sufficient unto himself. They are firm friends, but not at all demonstrative. They are not apt to choose a leader, and it is very rarely that one of their number awakens to find that his fame has spread through the narrow little region which is his world, that the inhabitants of the hills around flock to him for sympathy and advice, and that he is looked upon as a guide, philosopher and friend by all the neighbors within a radius of thirty or forty miles.

Precisely this experience, however, has come to the Rev. Joseph C. Wells, called "The Orator of the Mountains," by the people of Wise, Lee, Scott and Letcher counties.[1]

Readers of THE WORLD may remember the following paragraph which appeared in the issue of Oct. 4 and which was probably the first mention ever made of the old minister in the columns of a newspaper.

High-salaried ministers will be interested in the life story of Rev. Joseph C. Wells, a noted Baptist preacher, who attended the Clinch Valley Association in Wise County, Va., which has just adjourned. He furnished this outline of his ministerial career: "I have never been to Bristol, the nearest town to me, nor did I ever see a steam car until a few months ago, when the South Atlantic and Ohio train began to run in front of my house, but I had seen and travelled almost every hog-path in four adjoining counties. For thirty-five years I have been roaming over these mountain counties pleading for my Saviour. I have never received $30 a year, all told, for my ministerial work. Often have I gone thirty miles to preach a funeral sermon and received not a cent for it, nor did I expect anything. When I was converted I could not read, but I felt that I must learn to read the sacred Scriptures. I worked all day in the fields and at night I studied with my mother. She taught me to read."

The little story, which says so much in such small space, could not fail to attract attention. Here is a man who in complete unconsciousness of the fact that he has been doing anything unusual, has given his best years to unrewarded work among his fellow men. His is a story of self-sacrifice, of toil without recompense and of privation. There are no stirring incidents in his life, and one day's history is the history of all days. He tells it briefly to the writer and much of it may be summed up in the pathetic statement of his boyhood: "I didn't go no wha', 'n I never seed nothin' o' nobody."

But to those who can read between the lines, there cannot fail to be an absorbing interest in the story of the life of Joseph Wells, quaint and uneventful as it is. It has been lived among scenes of which we know nothing, and which we can only imagine; its force comes out in contrast to the scenes amid which we live and of which we do know. In the nineteenth century there are comparatively few of us who are laying all our treasures up above; even our ministers of the gospel, hard-working and zealous though they are, recognize a duty to themselves and to their families which the demands of their work cannot put aside. There may be those among them who are capable of a lifetime of labor for the sake of their Master alone; no doubt there are; but the one who assumes it voluntarily, lives it constantly, and neither asks nor desires recognition or lightening of the burden, must see the day when that recognition comes.

And thus it is that the Virginia mountaineers have singled out their master and that the management of the New York WORLD has seen fit to send a member of its staff to the mountains to see the noted minister himself, and to get from his own lips the short and simple story of his life.

HIS QUIET HOME

The little log cabin where Mr. Wells now lives is hardly more than a stone's-throw from the one in which he was born fifty-eight years ago. As he says, he has never been away from these counties even to visit Bristol, the nearest town. He knows absolutely nothing of the outside world. The great questions of the day do not perplex him, for he has never heard of them. He has never ridden on the train. He has never attended an entertainment of any kind; he has never heard a musical instrument played upon; his only idea of music is the camp songs of the mountaineers. He knows nothing of free-trade, he is sweetly oblivious to any meaning in the names of Reed[2] and McKinley.[3] He could not talk for two minutes on the tariff, but in five minutes he can have a thousand people alternately crying, praying and shouting, as he preaches and exhorts.

He is entirely uneducated, being barely able to read and write, but his power over his congregations is marvelous, and the mere announcement of his intention to preach in a certain place at a certain time is sufficient to fill that place to overflowing. Among his auditors and warmest friends are the most noted men of this State, many of whom come miles to hear him preach and are said to be affected to tears by his sermons.

A FRIEND IN NEED

There is not a house in all the mountains that has not known him in its time of need. In sickness, in death; in affliction of any kind he has been at once the guide, the counsellor, the friend. He has baptized the children of the mountaineers, married them, preached their funeral sermons. Night after night he has walked or ridden miles over the mountains, through Winter snows or Summer rains, to nurse the sick or bring comfort to the dying. Through it all his family has made sacrifices with him, and his wife, especially, has borne more than her share of the burden. On her rested the care of the little home and of the meager crops. It was she who clothed and fed the children, for during his long life of toil and hardships her husband never received an average of $30 a year, all told, for his ministerial labors. A twenty-mile tramp over the mountains to marry a couple would be repaid by thanks—on a few rare occasions by a $1 bill. Funerals were conducted gratuitously; it was all the mountaineers could do to buy a simple coffin for their dead. Sermons and visits and meetings and revivals—all went to swell that treasure which is to be laid up above, but which does not lessen the grinding poverty below or keep the children from asking for bread when there is none to give them. The old minister has today in the way of worldly goods exactly what he began life with thirty-five years ago—a little one-room cabin and a few pieces of furniture. He has brought up ten children, six of whom have married and settled near him in the mountains. One is away at work, and the remaining three, two sons and a daughter, live in the cabin with the old people.

NOT WORKING FOR MONEY

Mr. Wells has not been working for money—a very evident fact, and one which more than any other won him the place he holds. His continued self-sacrifice, indifference to recompense and his faithfulness in following what he considers his life-work, are too sincere for question, even by those who are not apt to take much philanthropy for granted.

These facts I learned from the people of Big Stone Gap when the orator's name was mentioned.[4] He has very rarely come here, especially since the boom began, bringing in its wake railroads, factories and the other adjuncts of so-called civilization against which his mountain spirit rebels. But he is highly honored in the land, and any native will sing his praise for an hour at a time. To see the prophet in his own country I hired horses and a negro guide, and against the advice of the entire population started—I being a woman—over the mountains.[5] During that ride other reasons for the old minister's infrequent visits to the Gap forcibly presented themselves. We had been told that the roads were impassable and we demonstrated the fact. Up and down we rode, through ravines and over hills, our horses in mud to their knees. Four times we forded a river, the water of which came almost to the saddles. Again and again we were nearly pitched down some steep incline until, as the guide remarked frankly, "Ef de horses hadn't bin sensiblar dan we wah no tellin' what mout hab happened."

But all things have an end, and the sun had not yet set when we forded the river for the last time and drew up before the cabin of the noted mountaineer. A wilder, more picturesque location could hardly be imagined. The little hut cannot be called ornamental, but it nestles in the tiny bowl-shaped Powell's Valley, just at the foot of Powell's Mountain. Behind towers Stone Mountain, and all around range upon range of spurs extend, shutting in the cabin and making the spot about as isolated as can be fancied. A low rail fence runs round the house, and an old gate swings back

and forth in the mountain breeze. In front of the house, which
faces the mountains and not the alleged road, is an impromptu
porch and summer kitchen where a stove stands and from which
there came, at this time, suggestive reminders of supper. The
building is constructed of hewn logs, the chinks being filled with
plaster.

IN HIS LITTLE CABIN

A rap at the door brought a pleasant-faced little old woman to
the entrance. She wore a stuff dress, gathered up round the bottom, coarse shoes and a bandanna tied over her hair. The brown
eyes behind her horn-rimmed glasses twinkled merrily, and her
smile as she surveyed the stranger at her gate was very kind,
though her expression was mingled with considerable surprise.
Yes, Mr. Wells lived there. Perhaps I would come in? I would.
The guide placed himself in a picturesque attitude near the door
and awaited directions. I had determined to remain all night if
possible; if not, to seek some quicker means of suicide than a return trip over the mountains at that late hour.

I walked in. The cabin, as before stated, boasted but one room,
which was at once kitchen, dining room, sitting-room and bedroom. At the furthest end stood two beds, separated by a rude,
old-fashioned cupboard, whose open door showed a small array
of delf cups, saucers and plates.[6] Near the center of the room was
the table, and a smaller one occupied a corner. The floor was
bare and unpainted, and the log walls were hidden behind white
cloth and old newspapers, which served as ornaments and to
keep out the draft. There were two windows, an unusual luxury
in a mountaineer's home, both hung with red calico curtains,
and a small shelf against the wall accommodated an old clock.
These, with a few chairs and a trunk, filled the abode. The charm
of the place—for there was a charm—lay in the quaint old fireplace. The side of the room opposite the beds was entirely taken
up by a great brick fireplace, in which several huge logs were
burning. Outside it was growing dark quite rapidly, but the blaze
illuminated the cabin and threw the most fantastic lights and
shadows in the corners.

THE OLD MINISTER

Stretched at full length before the fire and basking in the warmth lay the figure of an old man. Fifty-eight is by no means venerable, but Joseph Wells looks fully fifteen years older. His flowing gray hair and long white beard do not add so much to his aged appearance as his shrunken, bent form and the seams and lines left in his face by a life of privation, drudgery and chronic invalidism. There is something about him, uncultivated though he is, that claims respect and confidence. His eyes have the expression of a dreamer's. He looks like one who has lived among the mountains and away from the world; in fact he looks as one expects him to look after hearing of the life he has led. He was dressed in a suit of rough, dark "store clothes" about the first he has ever worn I inferred from something he said later.

He was sick. He was suffering from the "janders," he told me as he rested himself on his elbow and looked at me.[7] Had them for "a right sma't time—nigh onto five weeks." Stay all night? Certainly I might stay all night. They hadn't much, but everything there was mine—"of you uns 'low ye can make shift with whut we hev." The guide and horses could be accommodated yonder—further up the mountain. Yonder they went, and I removed my wraps which Mrs. Wells—"Betsy," her husband called her—carefully deposited in the trunk before mentioned. Then the chairs were drawn up before the fireplace. "Lize," the unmarried daughter, brought in a great plate of apples to sustain life until supper was ready, and mine host, who had revived under the influence of a visitor, sat erect and gently asked me several questions in a manner very different from the direct and uncompromising fashion of the typical mountaineer. Name, age, previous and present condition of servitude, all came out, after which I turned the tables and became the grand inquisitor. That worked beautifully. There was nothing to conceal in the model life led in such lonely parishes, and in a short time the old man was launched into an autobiography, which loses much of its charm in being repeated on cold paper, away from the mellow firelight and without the accompaniment of Betsy's and Lize's footsteps and the soft tinkle of bells as the cows came down the mountainsides. It is given in the soft, Southern dialect of the speaker,

because he told his story in his own way better than another
could tell it for him. I am a shorthand writer and this is exactly
what he said. They had never heard of stenography before and
watched me with absorbed interest:

"I wah born jist among these maountins loss'n a quarter mile
frum this heah haouse," began the minister reflectively. "Pap
deeded me this heah land, 'n' a few yeahs ago I built this little
haouse 'n' come t' live in it—the only move we uns ever made.
Pap were a maountin' man too, 'n' we lived like they all do, hun-
tin' and farmin', 'n' working fo' a livin' in a spot wha' I recken a
livin's as hard to git as 'tis anywha' on airth. My mother wah a
woman thet spent a right sma' o' time talkin' to her chil'len
abaout relig'n 'n' the plan 'o' salvation. I rec'lec' the fust remembrance I hev' o' hearin' about Christ. It wah Sabbeth, 'n' she wah
combin' my ha'h 'n' tellin' me about Christ 'n' haow he wah put
to death. I rec'lec' the thoughts I hed whilst she wah talkin' to
me. I didn't und'stand why he died, but the thought wah thet if
I'd bin thah 'n' bin a man I'd a died fightin' fo' him. I wah only
six o' seven at thet time.

"I spent my early boyhood on the fahm right a heah, helpin'
pap 'n' aimin' to look fo' myself jist as soon's I could. I didn't go
no whar, 'n' I never seed nothin' o' nobody. I hadn't no schoolin',
'n' I spent my idle hours shootin' in these heah maountins. I wah
a moral boy until I wah sixteen. Then I fell into sin. I got led into
bad associations 'n' tuck up with wicked boys. I done everything
'twas bad 'n' I walked in sin almost foah years. I hedn't no rel'g'n
and didn't 'low 't I wanted any. I aimed t' hev a good time.

"When I wah more'n eighteen I went to Big Stone Gap 'n' he'rd
a man named Bishop preach on the Judgment Day. Hit like to
scared me t' death; I 'lowed I'd die right thah. I tuck a shiverin' 'n'
shakin' in my seat, 'n' peace left my soul. Hit opened my eyes 'n'
I aimed to do diff'rent, but fo' mo'n a yeah I roamed the moun-
tins 'n' hed no hope. I made every maount a prayin' place, 'n'
every valley raound heah seed my doubts 'n' sufferin's. One night
I went to baid 'n received the blessin'. All o' a sudden everything
looked cleah, 'n' peace 'n' joy filled my soul. Hit seemed like I
could tell the whole world how to be Christians. I tuck to
preachin' right off, but I couldn't read o' write.

GAINED HIS EDUCATION AT THE FIRESIDE

"I went to work to oncet, 'n all the eddication I hev I got at the fiah side from my mother. She larned me to read, 'n when I went into the fields with the plough I studied while I worked, 'n at night she he'rd my lessons. Soon's I could read I learned the Bible most by heart. That 'n Pollock's Poems 'n History o' this country 'n books on religion 's all I ever read. I wah baptised in the rivah heah, 'n the fust exhortation I evah made wah from the banks. All the people cried—dun'no why.

"I kept on workin' with Pap 'n' preachin' n' studyin', 'n' three years later I wah ordained—'n' sense thet time I've roamed these mountains workin' 'n' prayin' fo' my Savioh. They hain't a hog-path in these fo' counties thet I don't know, 'n' hardly a tree or rock. Sometimes I hed a horse 'n' rode, 'n' ef they needed it heah I walked. I hev bin away weeks to onct, in storms 'n' winds, sick 'n' well. They expected me, 'n' I couldn't quit or leave 'em. My chist's always bin bad, 'n' that made it a little hard; but I nevah stayed to home yit when I was called aout. I hev babtized about two thousand people, mo' er less, 'n' I've always hed three o' fo' churches to pastor to onct, some twenty miles from home. I hev been called a powerful exhorter. We can't jedge our own works, but I cert'nly hev brung a heap o' sinners to the mourner's bench.

"I didn't jine the army, but foah abaout a yeah I worked with Clarke Riley, chaplain o' Hawkin's Kentucky Regiment, as home missionaries. We uns went raound among the maountins here, him preachin' an' me exhortin'. He was mighlity tuck up with me an' I with him, an' we done well together, but he hed to go back home. Well, I've gone up these maountains ever since, baptizin' an' marryin an' funeralizin' the dead an' visitin' the sick. I felt the way pointed out to me 'n' I follyed hit. I couldn't hev left hit. My lungs hev bin mightily effected lately an' I haint bin so much good."

Just then Mrs. Wells came into the house, briskly waving her apron at a couple of small chickens that followed her.

HIS LOVE STORY

"If I didn't forgit to tell you uns about Betsy!" exclaimed her husband, with a half-quizzical, half-loving look at her as she warmed her hands at the fire and glanced at us with her bright eyes. "I married her in 1850, when I wah eighteen an' she wah a few months younger. There hain't much difference in us. She wah a Kentucky gal—Betsy Blair—an' I seed her when she came here to the maountains, a-visitin' her sister. I tuck a notion to her the fust day I seed her a-standin' in the road. Yes, I tuck a notion to her."

"I reckon he did," corroborated Betsy, proudly. "'N we've worked along together all these yeahs. Many's the night he's come home 'n' I've washed his shirt so's he could git out agin in the mornin'. He only hed one in them days, 'n' he hain't much better off naow."

"She's done her part, so she has," added the husband. "Fer we didn't git much money. She uset to hoe the corn an' take the babies out in the fiel's with her. Yes, $30 a year would more'n cover what we got. The biggest heap o' money I ever got in my life wah $75 thet the sinners o' Lee County put in a purse and give me t' preach t' 'em fo' a yeah. They hed he'rd me somewhah an' they wanted me to come to a special place 'n' preach t' them. 'N' I did; 'n' that seemed like a right sma't o' money. I've of'en went nigh onto twenty miles to marry a couple 'n' got nothin' fur it. At most I would git a dollar. I didn't expect nothin'. That wan't whut I wah workin' fo'."

Here the odor of supper became more pronounced, and as the voice of Betsy cleft the air in an invitation to "draw up," two stalwart young mountaineers entered the room with a quick "good evenin'"—the inevitable salutation of their class. "My sons, Andy and Shef," said the father proudly, and we gathered around the festive board.

THE MOUNTAIN NEIGHBORS DROP IN

There was the same supper which is given to every visitor in the Virginia mountains. Fried chicken, bacon, hot biscuits and coffee formed the meal. "Sometimes we're aout of butter and sometimes we haint," remarked Betsy as we sat down, and then she added pensively. "We're aout tonight." There wasn't much said at the table; everyone was too busy, besides which the presence of a stranger evidently awed the mountaineers.

After supper a prompt adjournment was made to the fireplace and the basket of apples came out again. Father, mother, Lize, the two tall sons and myself all clustered around the blazing logs, which occasionally fell asunder, throwing out sparks that quickly scattered the circle. The lamp had been lighted, but was a hollow mockery. In some mysterious manner the arrival of "a lady from New York" had been noised abroad, and the married sons and mountain neighbors began to drop in. The room was soon filled, and a dozen pairs of dark eyes surveyed me with a steady but embarrassing interest. I endeavored to rise to the occasion and be entertaining. They asked a few questions about New York and seemed intensely interested in my replies.

"Do you uns hev many haouses like this in New York?" asked Betsy.

When I replied that the New York houses were all built of stone or brick the men grinned and the entire party evidently believed I was joking.

As time wore on my hard ride of the day began to tell. "The Orator of the Mountains" observed my fatigue. "P'rap aour young sister would laik to go to baid," he suggested, kindly. As the room was full and there was evidently no upstairs, I declined. I said I was not sleepy. In reality I was abnormally wide awake, trying to figure how two narrow beds were going to comfortably accommodate six wide people, and how the hosts intended to distribute the said people in the said beds.

Time dragged its slow length along. The conversation had become general. Andy, one of the sons, had lost two cows in the mountains and was receiving the sympathy of his kinsmen. Something was said about the wildcats and bears which still roamed the forests of Powell's and Stone Mountain. The old minister was beyond question the ruling power of the circle. He was treated with great deference, but he evidently ruled by love, not fear, and one could not fail to notice his toleration and genuine Christian charity. He had none but good words to speak of all. A long silence fell, during which hosts and guests stared steadily at the flames. Then one by one the latter departed and the family was left alone.

NIGHT IN THE CABIN

"Thet's yon un's baid in this heah corneh," said Betsy, coming forward and turning down the cover. The tall sons rose and thoughtfully went forth into the still night. Mine host and hostess calmly began their preparations by the fire. I retired to the corner and followed suit.

Once in bed the wind came down from the mountains and played havoc with the cabin. It howled round the corners and whisked in through the cracks and chinks of the logs. The lamp had burned out and the firelight filled the room and danced on the bowed heads of Betsy and the Rev. Joseph as they undressed and talked to each other in low tones. A shadow flitted past my bed and Betsy climbed into her own. "Come on, Joe," she called, sleepily. From a murmured expostulation at a low chair near the fire I inferred that the minister was praying.

Then there was silence. The fire burned lower and the sounds from the mountains became more distinct. These were the calls of night birds, the soughing of the wind among the trees, a long, low cry of some animal and the tinkling of cattle bells. The door, like that of all mountain homes, had been left unlatched. The young mountaineers came in hastily, closed it without locking it and disposed themselves to sleep—somewhere—it didn't matter where. My eyes were closing——

When they opened it was daylight and one of the "boys" was making the fire.

"It ain't time to git up yit," he said, nodding pleasantly; "fire ain't burnin' sma't yit."

I followed his advice and went to sleep again. An hour later the noise of coffee grinding and the kettle singing outside roused me a second time.

The minister was combing his long gray hair by the fire.

WHAT HE'S WORKING FOR

"I wah thinkin' las' night," he remarked when I had made a hasty toilet and joined him, "o' somethin' you said. I 'low my life seems strange 'nuff to people from the city, but I hain't never hed no aim to change it. I hain't int'rested myself s' much in outside things, for thah's a right sma't o' things in these heah maountins to int'rest me. I've hed my tasks to do an' I've done 'em accordin' to my lights. I've hed protracted meetin's, 'n I've hed revivals, 'n I've brought souls to Christ, I 'low. I dunno why people talk abaout me; I dunno why they come so fah to heah me preach. I never yit wrote down a line o' whut I wah goin' to say. I choose my tex', think abaout it, divide it into heads, an' when I git before my people the ideas come jist like the little maountin stream thet bubbles up yonder. I know I feel whut I say, an' so do they. There hain't one o' them thet hain't cryin' an' sobbin' efore I git ended. An' that's whut I'm workin' fah an' thet's my rewa'd—t' feel thet I'm a liftin' these people frum sin, 'n thet whut I say is makin' 'em better men and wimmen.

"Sometimes I git wo'ked up right sma't myself. I rec'lec oncet thah wah a big revivah heah, 'n preachers cum from Lee 'n Scott 'n all raound to wo'k with hour sinnehs. They preached powerful thet night, 'n when they got ended they called for me to wind up with 'n exhortation. They knowed all abaout grammatics 'n could speak like books, 'n I felt a heap o' discomfort when they brung me up' befo' 'em all. Tha' wah mo'n a thousand folks raound, 'n I hadn't 'lowed to speak to 'em thet night 'n hadn't thunk o' whut to say.

"I begun right unsartin, I reckon, but befo' I hed talked long I fo'got abaout grammatics 'n only rec'lected thet heah wah a heap o' sinners to be saved, 'n thet I wah thah to talk to 'em. My voice wah weak when I started in, but I reckon it filled the hills befo' I quit.

"'Thah is them among you-uns, brethern,' says I, 'thet has nevah stopped long 'nuff in yo' busy lives to think abaout Christ—the Savioh who is always thinkin' abaout you. Yo' thot's an' yo' ha'ts air took up with yo' wo'k 'n yo' fahms 'n yo' fam'lies. You haint got time to think abaout rel'g'n 'n the plan o' salvation—leas' wise thet's whut you-uns say. 'N so praps you live along in sin, 'n the face o' yo' God is tuhned frum ye 'n yo' fam'ly is growin' up abaout ye 'n watchin' yo' ways. 'N bimeby th' little chillen raound yo' knee'll grone up big boys. 'N when ye labor with 'em to tuk frum thah evil ways—then, my brethern, them chillen'll say to you-uns, "You wa'nt a Christian, pap; you-uns wan't a chu'ch man; you-uns didn't harp on God 'n Heaven 'n Hell, 'n why should we uns try to be better than aour dad?" 'N then, my brethern, you'll see the folly ins yo' shif'lessness, yo' cablessness, yo' sinfulness. 'N when them boys o' yourn goes wrong, 'n thet wife o' yourn's under the flaowers that blossom in the maountins above 'n the little cabin's empty, 'n the chillin's all gone whah we call th' wo'ld, 'n among the sin 'n the toil 'n the sufferin' thah—whut ah you uns goin' to do then? Tuhn to yo' Savioh! Tuhn to th' Lord God thet made ye 'n thet you've scandalized all yo' shameful life! Yes, you'll tuhn then in yo' old age when yo' bes' days hev went, 'n yo' airthly frens hev left ye.

"'But oh, my brethern, why don't ye tuhn naow—this day— this night—this minute? Why don't ye throw off the shackles o' Satin 'n stand for'erd a sarvant o' Christ? Don't be afeerd to acknowledge him! Don't be afeerd to say ye hev sinned! Don't be afeerd to say befo' all the wo'ld "Th' Lord God is my Savioh! In th' Lord God I trust." Come naow while yo' chil'len kin see ye. Come naow while yo' wife is right a heah to shed teahs o' joy with yo's. Don't wait—don't put it off—don't say next yeah will do. Fo' the yeahs go by 'n the night cometh—'n praps you'll wait too long, my brethern 'n fin' nothin' befo' you but evah lastin' night.'

"I dunno whut else I said, but I got mo' 'n mo' wo'ked up, 'n the end o't wah thet everyone thah wah cryin' 'n shoutin', 'n some o' the wo'st men in the maountins come to th' mourners' bench. Thet wah a big revivah thet yeah."

As the old man spoke he seemed inspired. His form straightened, his eyes lit up and his voice rang out as if it might indeed "fill the hills." It was only for a few moments. Then age and sickness touched him once more upon the shoulder and the minister sank back into his chair by the fire and resumed his story in his soft, low tones.

"NEVER WAVERED"

"I don't know why they say I'm a good man, 'cos I'm not—I'm bad. I hev bad thoughts—I hev done bad things. But I hain't never injured a feller crecher, 'n I hain't never hed trouble with anyone, 'n' thah haint never bin an allegation brung agin me. Them little churches in the mountains here is whar I preached; often I hev preached out in the air, an' en the nat'ral tunnel, an' in the houses o' the mountain men. Whahevah I find myself and whahevah they ask it I hev preached. I've bin away from home fer weeks to oncet, preachin' an' prayin'. I've hed my times o' doubt, like all Christians: I hev 'em still. But I hain't never wanted to turn back, 'n' I hain't never wavered in my aims. I hain't travelled out o' these counties, 'cos my work's bin right a heah. I hain't no desire to travel out. I hain't interested in pollytics; I don't understand 'em. I hev done somethin' in the pollytics of Big Spring Gap, but I hain't goin' to do no more. Pollytics is a good thing to keep out o'. That's my conviction.

"NEVER HEARN O' MR. REED"

"No: I never hearn o' Mr. Reed. Who is he? I've baptized an' ordained some men that are known right sma't about heah. I 'low. Rev. Newton Griffiths, of Ohio, an' State Senator J. B. F. Mills, of Virginia, an' Joseph Warmpeler, o' Tennessee. My bes' sermons? I think one o' 'em wah 'Come Hither, I'll Show Thee the Bride—' the Lamb's wife—an' another. 'An' the Lord Shut Him In.' I hain't never borryed a sentence o' one o' my sermons, but some times I hev drempt one right through an' preached it the nex' day. I've read the book o' a man named Payne, 'lowin to preach agin religion, and ones by Andy Fuller, an' Buck, an' Clarke, an' Wesley, an' the Bible and Pollock's Pomes.[8] Thet's all."

"Draw up an' eat," said Betsy, and the old man's flow of eloquence was checked again. The breakfast was the same as the supper, with the addition of bacon. The young mountaineers had performed their ablutions in a small tin basin standing outside near the door—the same which I had used earlier in the day— and now came to the table with faces glowing and hair smoothly "spatted down." Shef, aged twenty-two, was getting ready for school. He is a bright young chap, and his father 'lows to "make an editor outen o' him" or a preacher, or a great man of some sort. Both the parents agree in this. Illiterate as they are, they mean that their children shall know as much as they can learn in this region. Each of the ten boys and girls can read and write, while the twenty-three grandchildren are following in their footsteps.

"I cain't read 'n' I cain't write," remarked Betsy, frankly, when the conversation turned on this. "I hain't never ben to school but two days in my life. But I can listen when other people read, an' I can hear whut they say," she added with a quiet satisfaction that was very pathetic. "An' ef I wan't so old I'd try to larn now. Hit ud be a right sma't o' company in the even'g when Joe's away. But my eyes are givin' aout—'n' I 'low hit's too late."

THE OLD MINISTER'S POETRY

After breakfast was over and the boys had gone, the old man opened his trunk and solemnly drew from its recesses a small leather-covered volume. In this book were his poetic effusions, for in his roamings over the mountains he had written seventeen poems, which he calls his Confessions of Faith. They are an outline of his religious views. He read a number of them to me when we went back to the fireplace, and from his manner of rounding the sentences and handling the book it could readily be seen that here was the darling of his heart.

The verses themselves were like the man—original, unconventional diamonds in the rough. A fair idea of them can be gained from this gem, which I jotted down from memory afterwards. I am sure, however, it is just as he read it:

> The road the Christian travels on
> Was built so high by Grace,
> The lion's whelp has never trod
> Nor vulture seed the place.

This might not meet the approval of Stedman or Aldrich,[9] but, after all, when we consider that the author's only idea of poetry was gained from "Pollock's Pomes," it should not be too severely criticized. There was some blank verse among the work which was very striking, but its intensely religious cast would make it out of place in a newspaper.

At 10 o'clock guide and horses appeared at the door and it was time to go. The entire family were in at the farewell scene. "I declah," said the old man. "I hate to see you'ns go. You'ns has bin a heap o' company, and my janders is almost gone. Drap us a line when ye get home, sayin' ye got thah all right." Then the impatient horses were off and a repetition of the slipping, sliding, wading and swimming came with the trip back across the mountains.

The first man I saw upon reaching the Gap was the old minister's life-long friend and admirer, Senator J. B. F. Mills, minister, politician and a power in the land.

WHAT SENATOR MILLS SAYS

"I consider Mr. Wells the greatest natural orator in the State of Virginia," he said. "His power over the class of people among whom he works is simply marvelous. I have seen whole congregations weeping or shouting, plunged in sorrow or carried out of themselves by his eloquence. He can sway them as he pleases. Within five minutes after he begins his sermons he has his congregation entirely under his control. He numbers among his friends some of the finest men in the State. I have known them to come miles to hear him, and to be as much affected by his words as the simple mountaineers themselves. I frankly confess that he can make me cry whenever he chooses, and I am not sentimentally inclined. If he had been an educated man there is nothing he might not have accomplished. As it is, he has buried himself in the mountains and toiled for no return.

"Of course the mountaineers idolize him; no other man can ever hold his place. His private character is absolutely above reproach. There isn't a person in the world who can breathe a word against him. He has simply worked and sacrificed himself for others, and, in a worldly sense, he stands today exactly where he stood when he began. He has his little home—nothing more."

The old orator of the mountains will not have even his little home much longer. The modern boom has struck the region. Coal and iron have been discovered in the mountains, and the camps of miners stand in what was a year ago an unbroken wilderness. The mountains that once echoed only to the howls of wolves and the halloos of mountaineers now throw back the shrieks of the engines as the South Atlantic and Ohio trains sweep daily through the gorges. At East Stone Gap, too, near the old minister's home, there is an abnormal activity. On the site of his birthplace, and less than a quarter of a mile from where he now lives, there is to be erected a magnificent new Baptist Academy. On the other side of him an immense hotel is to be built, while if the East Stone Gap Improvement Company carry out their plans he is in danger of being bounded on right and left by factories and boiler works.

PREPARING TO MOVE

The old minister is preparing to move. He doesn't like this abrupt ending of the good old days. He confided to me that he didn't see the use of it.

"Talk abaout civilizin' us," said he. "I kin tell you we wah a heap civiler befo' these things come in. Thah wan't the fightin' an' the shootin' an' the angry passions risin' that thah is naow. My health's broken down an' I can't last long, no how. I dunno what we uns 'll do, I'm sure. I aimed to stay right a heah an' end my days like they begun, but seems like 't can't be. Betsy, she 'lows she'd like to git a haouse off somewah, but I dunno 's I'd feel to home anywah but right a heah. I reckon we'll settle raound in Tennessee, an' I'll keep this old cabin an' come a heah when I feel like I must. Seems like the mountaineers are all agoin', 'n' I reckon we uns must foller."

Truly, the mountaineers are going. They have sold their little farms for much more than they ever hoped to get and those of them who are too old to take kindly to the ways of civilization here will strike further into the hills or into other States. But the breaking up of all the homes in the mountains will not occasion half the comment or regret that will follow the departure of Mr.

Wells. It is he whom the people love and upon whom they have depended to an extent that they only realize now when it is too late. He knows this, and it is the thought which will sustain and comfort him during his journey into the new region, which, wild and rugged as it is, he considers a "heap civiler" than this.

Source: "A Mountain Preacher," *New York World*, November 20, 1890.

FROM
"TRUE STORIES OF THE NEWS"

"JESSIE ADAMSON'S SUICIDE"

(1890)

"Stories of the News"

**Why a Girl of Nineteen
Killed Herself Yesterday in This City**

AN EXTRAORDINARY AND PATHETIC CASE

**She Had Tried in Vain to Obtain Clerical Work, and,
Failing, She Preferred Death to Starvation or Disgrace**

A young girl—she was but nineteen years of age—took her life yesterday morning in the miserable little room she rented at No. 124 East One Hundred and Thirteenth street, New York City, because she could not earn the bread she ate and because the man to whom she had plighted her troth was too poor to take her to him as his wife.[1] Her name was Jessie Adamson.

If you glance over the blotter of the One Hundred and Twenty-sixth street station-house you will see recorded there this statement:

"At 2:15 A. M. Jessie Adamson, nineteen years old, a salesgirl, committed suicide by taking bromide of potassium at Mrs.

King's boarding-house, 124 East One Hundred and Thirteenth street. Reported by Policeman McCusker."

This is the poor creature's epitaph. Here is something of her history and of the causes that led up to her tragic end in this Christian metropolis.

This girl, who swallowed poison yesterday, as she made her daily tour about the city in search of work saw the wealth of a great town spread everywhere before her eyes. But she had none of it. She saw her fellow-women rolling by listlessly upon the cushions of their carriages, while her feet were sore with tramping up and down the pavements, and the soles of her shoes were worn thin as tissue paper.

Had she been strong, she might have secured work in anyone of a thousand households. But she was too weak and delicate for that. Housewives would not look more than once at her pale face and slender form. She could not endure drudgery. She had done clerical work. For that she was fitted. She could do it again. But she could not find it to do. It was always "No; we are full," whenever she applied. And she applied with great persistency.

She was hungry and the meat she ate she could not pay for.

She was cold and she had not the wherewithal to clothe herself.

She had a lover, but he, too, was very poor.

She had a father, a mother, sisters, but they were far away and could not aid her.

She was a pauper, and so she died.

"If we had known, we might have stretched a hand to her, poor thing, in her distress," we say today. But today is too late. We bury her in the poor's God's acre, or perhaps the few old friends she left behind gather up her frail little body and hide it decently away.

We take care of the dead always.

Only nineteen years! She was born away off there, across the water, somewhere in Old England. The reporter first learns of her as a babe in London, with her seven brothers and sisters, at play, at school, asleep. She is still a child and, therefore, is happy.

Her father works at his trade of designing chandeliers, and it is to a pleasant home, a good wife and his laughing little ones that he comes back every evening when his day's work is over.

The little Jessie, with her sisters and brothers, after awhile goes out to school. She is quick and bright and active. She learns rapidly and she begins at her teacher's knees to form her letters—those letters she is to write with so firm and bold a hand fifteen years later, when on scraps of paper she bids farewell to the few people whom she leaves behind her.

She is ten years old, and the father brings her with the others to the New World. To Eldorado,[2] to the Fortunate Isles[3] they are setting sail. How many Old-World dreams has the New World shattered.

They had their own neat, cozy home and were doing well in London. But the little folk were growing up, and the fields were richer across the waters. And so it was that ten years ago the little blue-eyed, fair-haired Jessie landed in New York.

Her father selected a little workroom in Sixth avenue and put up his sign. He had brought over with him a snug bit of English money which he had laid up against a rainy day. Not a little of this it has cost him to transplant his family, lodge them in a new home and fit up his shop. But there was left still a cozy sum, and, moreover, had he not pitched his tent in a land flowing with milk and honey—in the Fortunate Isles?

But somehow his work at designing on brass and copper was not so successful as it had been in the old country. At any rate the money kept going out faster than it came in. The children were at school for a time, but one by one they had to be taken away from their books.

They were so many mouths to feed. And so one by one, as they grew old enough to assist in eking out the family fund, they got to work. Even then, however, it was a hand-to-hand struggle with the world. The contest is always an unequal one, and in this case the immigrants were worsted.

For seven years they fought the fight with their shoulders one against the other. Then they began to get discouraged. Seven years is a long time to wage battle with all the odds against you.

One day the sign was taken down from the shop. The shutters were closed and the place was deserted. The designer, who had grown gray and weary in the struggle, had picked up his pencil, his burin and his cardboard and packed them away.[4]

They had told him that there was more room to breathe in in Chicago and that he might do better there. Did he dream of the

Fortunate Isles again as he gathered his family together and told them of the journey?

The little Jessie, who had now grown into womanhood, they left behind. She had found work to do, and she would stay till things looked brighter. That was three years ago. It would have been better if the brave girl had not stayed.

She had an aunt already in the country, who was the wife of James Byron, employed by McBride, the printer, at No. 97 Cliff street. Her aunt would look after the girl. Her mother need have no fear on her account. So West her father and mother went, and Jessie remained here working away industriously, living with her kinswoman the while.

The three years passed; with "uneventful feet" she trod them. Her life was the quiet humdrum, everyday existence of all girls who spend their days in tending shop. She had to be on hand early in the morning, and at night she had to rest to be ready for the next day's labor. Sundays she had, but many a time she was too tired to enjoy her holiday. In such a life, rest is the pastime that weary eyes and hearts look forward to, and sleep the true recreation.

But she plodded along nobly. She earned only a few dollars a week, but she managed to feed and find for herself. There were days to come in which she would look back to her meager stipend as if it were the riches of Midas.[5] At any rate it furnished her with bread to eat.

Three years go by, and it is Summer. With the poor, the Winter is the time they dread, and the cold their fear. But with this poor child, misfortune was to crush her after she had passed safely through the dreary road, which all poor people tremble over as they enter it.

Summer had come and the August heat. It was not cold nor snow that our unfortunate had to struggle against at first. That battle would have to be waged in its good time.

First it was her aunt that fell down and sickened. So ill she got that they had to send her to a hospital. There she lies, bedridden, and in such a critical condition that they dare not tell her of the tragedy.

The home which had sheltered the hardworking little shop girl for almost thrice twelve months was broken up. She must look for shelter somewhere else. And that is how it was that Jessie Adamson went to the house in One Hundred and Thirteenth street, which she left yesterday forever.

Only a few days had she been there when she, in her turn, sickened and fell down by the wayside. She had got to be a bookkeeper in a great dry-goods establishment on Sixth avenue, and her ambitious little heart was as proud as a corporal at his promotion. She had worked so hard and so faithfully. And then in one hour to have the whole structure which her steadfastness had slowly reared totter and tumble to the ground!

She was sitting behind her desk one morning when she dropped in the harness. She had been writing. A dizzy feeling ran through her brain. It had been overworked. She was exhausted. She remembered passing her hand across her forehead and then nothing. She reeled and then sank in a swoon.

She did not die then. But it would have been better for the girl if the angel of death had gently laid her in his arms and borne her away forever. It would have saved so much heartbreak, so much anguish in the days that are still to come. Someone called a doctor and they took her home, carried her up the stairs to the top of the house and into the tiny, box-like room at the back of the place, where she had slept and dreamed, mayhap, like all young people, of the future and the golden chamber that someday was to be hers.

They laid her down on her cot and did all they could for her. But she was a very sick girl and it took nature some little time to bring her back to health. She was young and she got up again strong as before.

But, while she had lain tossing there upon her cot, the great busy world had been surging on outside as ever. She had been swept aside by the waves. Another girl had taken her place and there was no other place just then for her. Besides, she had lost the use of her right arm.

She had to begin all anew again—the battle for bread, the struggle for existence. She is no sooner on her feet, however, than she [has] taken up the quest—that tiresome, discouraging quest—for work.

She walked the streets all day searching for some cranny where she might clutch a hold. At night, foot-sore and very, very often heart-sore, she threw herself down on her bed to sleep. Perhaps her dreams were pleasant, and in them everything may have been light and joy and music. Let us hope so. But, then, again there was the rude awakening.

For over two months she went about on her hopeless errand. She was not strong enough for domestic service; she could not get the work that she could do. It was not that people were cold to her or cast her aside as they would a dog, but there was no room for her—that was all. And so she stood desperate and hopeless at last. Young as she was, she understood. The world had her at bay.

She had a lover. Down on the North River, at Pier No. 41, in the employ of the Delaware, Lackawanna and Western Railroad, there is a young man who looks after the freight that is deposited there. His name is R. D. Wilkins and he is the man who someday was to make Jessie Adamson his wife.

They had known each other for a long time and one day he had told her the old, old story.[6] Her last evening on earth the girl had spent with him at the house of their friend Mrs. Boldshaw, at No. 175 East One Hundred and Eleventh street. Under the moon they had gone out together. Shortly after 10 o'clock Jessie came into the house where she lived, alone. No one saw her again until she was in her death throe.

She must have gone out once more. She must have stolen out and bought the poison which she swallowed. Her sickness had taught her the uses of bromide of potassium, and that was the stuff she brought in with her.[7]

She had evidently come to her resolve after her meeting with her lover. He was earning so little, and she had nothing in the world but a few paltry debts. They looked so great to her, she who had held so little money in her life. Perhaps they amounted in all to $35. But each penny loomed up before her eyes like a doubloon. No, she had tried so long and so hopelessly for a chance to redeem herself. She could never do it, not if she worked for a half year of her holidays. And as for holidays, those she would never know again, unless she found employment. And that—where could she turn for it?

So she stepped out into the night and bought the poison that was to settle the problem once and forever.

Then she must have stolen up into her room again. There was

a pen and ink there, and she fished out from her few effects some scraps of paper. On one of these she wrote:

MRS. KING—Am indeed very sorry I cannot get the money I owe you, but it is an impossibility, so have decided to end all.

JESSIE.

My mother's address is No. 80 West Cortlandt st., Chicago, Ill.

On another slip she wrote:

DEAR AUNT: I must ask you to forgive me, but I could not help using the $20 you intrusted to my care. Indeed. I needed it.

Lovingly, your niece,

JESSIE.

The third was for her lover.

MY DEAR WILL: See that papa hears of my death and tell him how I love him. I trust you will forgive me. With fond love,

JESSIE.

Mammie's address is 80 West Cortlandt street, Chicago, Ill.

She sat there writing in the cold. There was a miserable little jet of gas which served for heat as well as light. She must have been very calm, for the notes she penned were written in a bold, clear hand and with a pen that never trembled once while she was holding it.

She had no time nor desire to indulge in any grief or sentiment. She was ready to die, and was going to meet death like a soldier. Her notes of farewell were as brief and to the point as army bulletins.

She hadn't a penny in the world, and she owed $15 for her bed and board. Twenty dollars, as the letter to her aunt confesses, which had been intrusted to her, she had spent.

Her lover? Yes; as she sat there shivering in the cold she must have heard again his whispers as he told that old, old story, the sweetest one in the whole world to hear. But its sweetness was soon drowned in the cries of despair with which her heart was wailing.

She was proud and high-spirited and independent. Between her dreams of a happy wedded life and their realization she saw loom up a gaunt, spare skeleton, and she knew it was Starvation. Possibly apathy and hopelessness and the long, long waiting had strained her mind a little.

The whole world was wrong, and she saw it in a distorted vision, as one sees objects through imperfect glass. And so she sat there pondering, wondering. And on one side of her stood always the gaunt, spare skeleton she knew was Starvation. On the other there was another just as gaunt and just as spare. And that was Death. Both were beckoning to her there in that chill little chamber and she must choose. She made the choice.

A lodger named Barnard, who occupied the room adjoining Jessie Adamson's, heard her groaning, as if in pain, about 1:30 yesterday morning. He waited a moment and then started to her succor. The door was not locked. He rushed into the room, and this is what he saw.

A girl with fair hair and a fresh English face was tossing upon a little iron cot—the kind they use in barracks. She was vomiting and moaning as if in great agony. At times she would stop, raise her head and press her hands against her throat and chest.

"You are very sick," he said to her.

"No," she answered, "it is nothing. I don't want any help."

He ran downstairs for Mrs. King, the landlady, and they came up again to the young girl's aid.

But in the mean time she had climbed out of her bed, picked up the basin she had been using, gone downstairs in her bare feet and her nightdress and emptied its contents in the bath-room. She did not wish them to know how she was destroying her life.

She was still moaning and in pain. Mrs. King guessed the truth at once.

"You have taken poison," she said.

"No, no," groaned the girl in answer.

They ran for a doctor.

But it was too late. When Dr. Van Fleet, who hurried from his house at No. 130 East One Hundred and Fifteenth street, reached her bedside she was dying. They listened to the death-rattle in her throat. She was approaching the land where there is neither hunger, nor cold, nor frost, nor any ill.

She was dead.

She was very fair to look upon yesterday morning when they had prepared her for the grave. She had blue eyes, but they were hidden underneath the lids. Her nose was small and delicate as if cut in a cameo. Her fair hair had been carefully brushed back against her pillow, and her hands were folded peacefully across her breast. The people in the house saw that everything that could be done was done, and then they came away and left her.

It was such a bare little place where she had lived. Beside the little cot there was a cheap chest of drawers of wood, stained brown, and a rude chair to match. Above the drawers hung a commonplace mirror, framed in plush. She had pasted up against the wall a couple of tawdry-colored prints of birds pecking at fruit.

Between the bed and the window a sheet had been stretched, which had served the young girl as her wardrobe. And what a meager lot of garments it hid from view—a worn serge skirt, a little hat trimmed with velvet and a sack. How mutely eloquent such things are at such a time, and what a pitiable story these poor old cast-off clothes suggested!

The floor was covered with a threadbare carpet, and a thin shade was at the window. And her own little effects? She had none. If she had any in the past she had disposed of them.

You must remember that she was very, very poor.

That is why she killed herself yesterday morning.

She had said to her lover several times that she wished that she was dead. He had paid no special attention to her outbursts. But he knew she was very unhappy.

Yet she tried very hard to be brave. Over at the home of the Boldshaws last Sunday evening she had laughed and jested and rocked their baby on her knees.

Was she acting a part, or did she go back to the darkness of her room after the brightness of her young friend's home—discouraged, disheartened by the contrast?

They were married and happy and had a roof-tree of their

own.[8] Her wedding day had been deferred so often. Would it ever really dawn?

But that mattered not now. Everything was over for her.

Think of it, ye dwellers in this great, rich city, especially those of you who have never known the bitterness of earning your own daily bread, or how salty it is when wet with tears. This young girl's heart was broken. This young girl's life was deliberately ended by herself yesterday morning.

And why?

Simply because no timely hand was stretched forth to help her; because she could find no respectable work that she, in her poor health, could do; because Debt and Starvation stared her in the face.

And so she killed herself.

Source: "Jessie Adamson's Suicide," *New York World*, November 25, 1890.

"THE HAPPIEST WOMAN
IN NEW YORK"

(1890)

Yesterday, for the First Time in Thirteen Years, Mrs. Dora Meyer Left Her Little Room at 506 East Seventeenth Street

FOR THE FIRST TIME SHE SAW THE "L" ROAD

She Was a Confirmed Invalid, but She Has Been Cured by Dr. Rixa and "The World's" Charity Fund, and a Carriage Ride Was Given Her Yesterday

Mrs. Dora Meyer was the happiest woman in New York yesterday.

Mrs. Dora Meyer is seventy-two years of age. She lives in a little room high up in the tenement-house at No. 506 East Seventeenth street. She is a widow. She is very poor. She has been very rich. She has few friends.

But yesterday for the first time in thirteen years she left the little room that had been a prison to her.

For the first time in all those years she went out upon the streets of New York.

For the first time she had a glimpse of the L roads and many other wonderful innovations in New York.[1]

Since 1877 she had sat a helpless invalid in that lonely room. She had a tiny glimpse of the sky from one of her little windows, and at a certain hour of the day a ray of sunshine crept in and played on the floor near the old woman's chair. When you consider that within a few weeks she has been practically cured and that yesterday, leaving the tenement house for the first time, she took a long drive about the city, drinking in the fresh air and basking in the sunshine, you can understand that it was a very important and a very happy day in Dora Meyer's life.

HOW DORA MEYER WAS FOUND

Her story is an interesting and pathetic one. But little more than a month ago, the woman reporter of THE WORLD found her during a mercy trip among the tenements.[2] It was necessary to climb three flights of narrow stairs and to make one's way blindly among numerous dark, winding halls. There was much in the house that was not clean, and many of the open doors passed by the writer showed glimpses of the grimy side of tenement life— the dirt, the poverty, the numerous neglected children and sick babies.

By accident the writer pushed open a door at the head of the third long flight of stairs, and, seeing that the room was occupied, stepped inside to ask directions. There was no filth here. Like all the others, the place was badly furnished, but it was different from them in being much cleaner.

The little black stove shone; so did the floor, part of which was covered with pieces of rag carpet. An old-fashioned Dutch table, a clock, a couple of chairs and numerous boxes completed the furniture.[3]

On a low couch between the table and the stove, where she could reach both conveniently, sat an old woman with one limb heavily bandaged and propped on a small box before her. She had the kindliest old face imaginable—just such a face as many of us carry in our hearts in memory of home and mother.

Every gray hair was in its place, the dark stuff dress was very neat, and through the glasses the brown eyes looked out with a peace and trustfulness undimmed by years of suffering and privation.[4] She was knitting busily.

THEY SAID HER CASE WAS HOPELESS

The reporter was accompanied by Dr. Alexander Rixa, the noted New York physician, and as the two stepped into the room his eye immediately fell on the bandaged limb. There was evidently work to be done here.

Would she permit him to examine it?

Oh, yes, but she had long since given up all hope.

And while the doctor gently removed the wrappings of the limb the old woman told her story.

She was seventy-two years of age, she said, a widow, childless and almost friendless. For thirteen years she had been confined to that one room with the disease which physicians call indolent ulcer.[5]

She had been told again and again that her case was hopeless and had almost come to pray for death. She had no money, but $5 a month was contributed to her by the Lutheran Church she had formerly attended. This paid the rent. Old clothes were occasionally sent her by charitable ladies, and her former employers on Sixth avenue furnished her with coal.

She lived on a sort of broth and black bread. She had not tasted meat for weeks, and had not even her beloved coffee, so dear to the German palate.

The night before, she said, she had been lying on her bed, unable to sleep with the pain, and she had prayed to God to send her some relief or permit her to go out once more and get one glimpse of the world before the end. A woman in the house cleaned up for her every week. She could stand sickness but not dirt. All this she told in German, thanking, in her quaint way, the strange lady and gentleman who took such interest in her case.

You don't want to hear about that limb, but it was a very serious case, and the physician looked grave as the last bandage was removed. To the writer's untrained eye it seemed hopeless indeed, so terribly was it eaten into by disease, but Dr. Rixa knew better. He examined it carefully, and then he spoke the first words of hope Dora Meyer had heard in many years.

"YOU SHALL WALK AGAIN,"
SAID THE DOCTOR

"We can cure that for you," he said. "All it needs is care and the right treatment. This it shall have, and it will be most well in a month. I promise you that you shall walk again." Dora Meyer could not understand at first, but when she did her joy was one of the most pathetic sights the writer has ever seen.

"And will it be so that I can go out? Can I leave this house once and breathe the fresh air again and see more of the sky than this little patch?" she gasped, all in one breath. The doctor said she could, and while he was sponging and rebandaging the limb the woman reporter promised her a long drive through the city and the Park just as soon as she was able to be out. It all seemed like a fairy tale to the old woman, and when she was given money from THE WORLD'S Charity Fund to buy nourishing food and supply her most urgent wants the tears of joy rolled down her cheeks. Then a call was made at the nearest drug-store, medicines were bought and sent her, with beef, wine and iron, and a deposit was left to supply future needs.

SHE HAD THE PROMISED RIDE YESTERDAY

Yesterday Dora Meyer had her ride, for Dr. Rixa's promise was fulfilled and the old woman is on the high road to recovery. The deep sores are healed, and clean, new flesh is forming.

The doctor called every day, detailed one of the hospital students to dress the limb when he could not, and did it all for no reward except Dora's thanks and the satisfaction of performing a remarkable cure.

THE WORLD'S Charity Fund supplied the medicines, and one of the rubber stockings used in such cases was obtained by the doctor from Nabra.

The old woman was accompanied on her drive by Dr. Rixa, whom she has learned to love as a son, and by the WORLD reporter. When they called for her at 3 o'clock yesterday she was like a child in her delight and her eagerness to be off.

She was carefully wrapped up and proudly performed the feat

of walking down three flights of stairs and into the carriage, with only a cane to assist her. Then the horses' heads were turned towards Third avenue and down to City Hall.

The old woman's eyes began to open wide as the sights and sounds of New York in 1890 were seen and heard. There were many changes in thirteen years, but her observant eyes seemed to miss none of them as the carriage rolled downtown.

ASTONISHED BY A HOUSE
IN THE CLOUDS

The Elevated Railroad[6] and the Pulitzer Building[7] struck her as the most wonderful. At the first glimpse of the glittering gilt dome of THE WORLD's home she cried out in astonishment, and her eyes grew bigger and bigger as the great structure came into view.

"Ach, Gott," she gasped.[8] "Sie bauen Hiuser bis in den Himmel! Wunderbar!" (They are building the houses into the clouds. It is wonderful). But then, in remembrance of what had been done for her, she added softly "Müssen lauter Ege d'rin sein" (they all are angels there!)—a compliment which assuredly no member of THE WORLD staff will be willing to take unto himself.

When the Elevated Railroad came into view that remarkable system by which people are whirled through the air completely dazed her.

"Ist mir ifeu, macht mir angst," she gasped. (It is so new it makes me feel afraid.)

At near intervals she murmured under her breath: "Gott ist gut" (God is good), and a moisture came into the brown eyes.

AS DELIGHTED AS A CHILD

It was a pathetic sight to see the happiness of this woman in being once more out in the world, among other people and like other people. Every face interested her, every building was eagerly surveyed.

"If all the rich men in the city would send me one penny's worth of bread I would never starve," she observed quaintly, after looking at some of the elegant carriages that passed.

We were in the midst of the afternoon procession now, and the scene became almost too lively for nerves unused to outdoor life. There was too much noise and confusion, too much bustle, too many [trams]. They made her nervous, although she tried not to show it, so the horses were driven to a side street and up to Central Park.

This was heavenly. She enjoyed every minute of it. Her eyes shone, the color came to her cheeks and she chatted like a child as the carriage bowled along the wide avenues and under the great trees.

"Here all the rich people drive—the fine ladies and gentlemen," she murmured, with genuine awe. She had never hoped to see Central Park again, and she looked at the grass, which is still green, with the expression of one who has been visually starved.

It was a very tired but happy little woman who was taken back to her home at 5 o'clock. She insisted upon walking up the three flights of stairs unaided, and laughed with delight when the neighbors in the tenement came out en masse to see her do it.

None of them had dreamed that she would ever walk again. She says she is content now, for the great desire of her life has been gratified. "Doch der Hebe Gott ist gut," she repeated; "er hat die Gebete einer armen Fran angehört." (The great God is good; he has heard the prayer of a poor old woman.)

Dora Meyer is too old to work. She has worked for sixty-odd years. But she has no money and few friends. The great dread of her life is that some time the rent money may not be forthcoming and she may be turned into the street.

If you want to complete the work which THE WORLD has begun in rendering this poor old woman the happiest woman in New York, why you can send a bill or a small check to THE WORLD (Metropolis Editor) for the Dora Meyer fund. A few hundred dollars would make her happy for life.

Source: "The Happiest Woman in New York," *New York World*, December 19, 1890.

"A STRANGE LITTLE EAST SIDE GIRL"

(1891)

Why Did Maggie Gilbert Throw Herself Out of Her Bedroom Window at 369 First Avenue?

She Is a Dreamer, a Nomad, a Fragile, Delicate Bit of Humanity, Whom Nobody In the Work-a-Day World of the East Side Pretends to Understand

Maggie Gilbert is a little dreamer, who lives away up in the top of a five-story tenement-house at No. 369 First avenue.

She is the same little girl who, on Tuesday evening, in a fit of despair or in a spirit of adventure—no one knows quite which—threw herself out of her bedroom window, down onto the roof of the adjoining house.

She is an odd mite of humanity, this little nine-year-old Maggie Gilbert. Gossips in the tenement say that Maggie's stepmother punished her Tuesday evening, and that she jumped out of the window in desperation. But there is very slight foundation for such a story. Maggie Gilbert is a little child, who moves about always as if walking in a dream. And the matter-of-fact people in an east-side tenement, who battle day by day against heavy odds for their bread and beer, can't understand her, that is all.

She is a pretty thing, as fragile as a flower. Why she did not break her body into bits when she leaped from the window is a marvel. It is quite a fall to the roof of the next house. They picked her up almost unconscious. Very soon after she was found she became fully so. Then the doctor gave her medicine and she fell into a quiet sleep. When she awoke yesterday morning she was a trifle weak but otherwise was as whole as if she had never taken the jump. At noon she was frolicking with the other children in the household.

A VERY PECULIAR LITTLE GIRL

Maggie is one of eight children. Tommy and Mamie are older than she, and Hannah came next after Maggie's birth. Then there are three chubby, flaxen little fellows, and last year the baby came. All but Maggie romp about and laugh and play and scream together just like other children in an east side tenement. But Maggie is different. She is an accident in their midst. They call her "queer."[1]

No one has ever been quite able to interpret her strange ways. She loves to wander out when the rest of the family, after a long day's work or play, are fast asleep, and watch the life of the east side as it moves and hurries and eddies along in the three broad avenues nearest the river.

Sometimes she romps with the other children. But oftener she leaves them to their play and saunters away to stroll up and down the streets alone. When she is in those moods she never talks much. And when her mother and father ask her what she is thinking about when she walks up and down the pavements all alone she never says. There is a side to this little east-side dreamer which she never shows to her brothers and sisters and which her father and mother can no more comprehend than they can Greek.

Tuesday afternoon the child played truant. She goes to the public school in East Twenty-third street, but for a long time it has been Maggie's habit to leave her lessons suddenly when the vagrant mood had hold of her and wander away at her own sweet will. Sometimes she does not go to the school at all.

A NOMAD OF THE EAST SIDE

At other times, when school is out, instead of returning home with her companions she disappears. Supper is spread, but Maggie's little chair is empty. Sometimes it is 8, sometimes 9, sometimes it is 10 o'clock before she returns. Sometimes, too, she does not return at all, and her father and mother have had on several occasions to search the streets for her till midnight.

When they have found her she returns willingly enough, but they can never get her to explain her conduct. She closes her tiny mouth in a quietly determined manner and is deaf and dumb to all entreaty. When she has so been found she has invariably been alone. She was hopping up and down the pavements, bathing herself in the glare of the gas lights and electric lamps, gazing into the shop windows, watching the passers-by; drinking in, like another "Petit Daniel," the glamour and music of a great city till she was drunk with it all.[2]

THE BOWERY A FAIRY LAND TO HER

You may smile at the music and the glamour of Third avenue and the thorough-fares lying between it and the East River. It is all paltry enough, to be sure. But you must remember that this little Maggie Gilbert had hardly ever been out of the east side, during the day, in her life. And at night she slept in a stifling inside room with three or four sisters lying beside her in the same bed.

What wonder that the Bowery by night was a sort of fairyland to her and by day the far-off squares and parks into which she stumbled became as dreamland?[3]

Whether she strolled further away at times during her nocturnal rambles no one except Maggie herself knows. She never says. She loves books and flowers and pictures and music. She, of course, has had little enough of all these things in her life, with seven brothers and sisters to demand their share of the week's earnings.

Perhaps she got far away enough some afternoon or evening to learn that all these beautiful things existed, if she could manage to walk long enough to find them.

At any rate her disappearances from home and school became more and more frequent. Her parents scolded her and tried to reason with her. Once her father whipped her. But nothing availed with the child. Tuesday afternoon she had played truant again. When Maggie's mother learned of it she scolded the girl and threatened to tell her father of her conduct. Maggie had eaten her supper, and at 9 o'clock, as was her custom, she left her mother, who was reading to the two older children, and went into the room where she slept.

The flat which the Gilberts occupy is on the top, on the south side of the tenement. It has the regular east-side tenement-house arrangement. There is a room facing the street and one facing the court. Between these there are two more rooms. In most houses these two middle rooms are windowless and dark. The room where Maggie slept, however, was a full story above the adjoining tenement and had a window in one corner looking towards the South.

It is such a little window. It is only about three feet high and a foot and a half wide. In fact, it isn't any bigger than the child who leaped out of it Tuesday evening. How she got out of it—for it only opened halfway—sprung, and made the leap down to the roof of No. 367, is as much a mystery as the little girl's whole life to her comrades. But do it, somehow, she did, and she cleared an alleyway at least four feet in width which lay between the houses.

Two of Maggie's sisters were asleep in the big bed in the small room when she climbed up to the window-sill. They didn't hear her pull up the sash, nor did they wake when she lay moaning on the tiles outside. The doors were open through into the room where Mrs. Gilbert sat reading, but the sound of her voice must have drowned the creaking of the window. No one in the back room heard that. But they heard the child moaning, and Mrs. Gilbert ran in to see what the trouble was. Two children were sound asleep on the pillows. Maggie, however, was not there, nor was she in the front room.

THEY FOUND HER ON THE ROOF

Mrs. Gilbert noticed the half-open window, and she looked out. She saw something white down on the roof outside.

She cried out: "Is that you, Maggie?"

"Yes'm," came back in a faint reply.

Mrs. Gilbert ran down the four flights of stairs and up into the next tenement. A tenant by the name of Armstrong had already heard the child groaning and had gone up to her assistance. He took up the fragile form in his arms and carried it downstairs. There Mrs. Gilbert met him.

The child was in her nightdress and her feet were bare. But she had put on her little cloak before she took the leap. When Armstrong found the child she was conscious, but she became insensible very soon after she was taken into the house.

An ambulance was sent for immediately, but Mrs. Gilbert would not allow the little girl to be taken to the hospital. The patrolman on beat picked Maggie up and bore her to the Gilberts' flat. There they laid the child on the best bed and Dr. Holden was sent for.

He examined Maggie's body and found, as if by a miracle, that no bones had been broken by the fall. A sedative was given the child and she soon was peacefully asleep.

SHE LIES ON THE BED LIKE A WAX DOLL

She was still asleep when a WORLD man called at the flat yesterday.[4] She looked as delicate as a leaf, and her two tiny arms were folded above her head. That little head was one mass of golden hair, which was cut short, and her deep-blue eyes, which were repeated in every one of her brothers and sisters, were hidden. She looked like a wax doll, put there by one of the other children, and in no wise suggested as she slept there—hardly breathing it seemed—the upheaval that her strange short existence on earth must have undergone.

Mrs. Gilbert was sitting by the child as she was sleeping.

"I don't know why Maggie did it," she was saying to THE WORLD reporter. "She is such a queer little body. No, no; it couldn't have been because I scolded her. I didn't scold her. I only told her that I would tell her father that she had run away again.

"And that was an old story to Maggie. She has given us so much trouble by her strange ways. We can't make her out. Her father once was for putting her out to Father Drumgoole's.[5] She couldn't run away there. But I said: 'Oh, wait a little longer. The child is a bit queer now, but she will outgrow it.' And I think she will."

"I never laid a hand on her, nor have I on any of my husband's children. He had six when I married him, the youngest only a year old. Maggie has given us more trouble than them all. But she is quiet enough generally. If she would only stay at home like the rest!"

DIFFERENT FROM ALL HER PLAYMATES

"She is always wanting to do something different from her playmates," Mrs. Gilbert went on. "She wants excitement and is always hankering after adventure. I think that is the reason she jumped out of the window. If she wanted to kill herself, why didn't she drop down in the alleyway instead of leaping over it? No, I think she meant to steal out again last night and roam the streets. Poor child, I don't know what she will do next."

The fact that Maggie had only a nightdress does in no way discountenance her mother's theory. For her father and mother have again and again hidden away her little shoes and stockings, but she would run out just the same in her bare feet. One of her vagrant moods was strong upon her Tuesday, and she began by playing truant in the afternoon. When she was sent to bed the mood still held her, and she intended to clear the alley, gain the next roof and steal down through the next house out into the avenue.

Two months ago Maggie's parents found that she had been going about among their friends and borrowing money. Once it was 25 cents she got in this way; once it was 50 cents. Another day she obtained $1. Then her father discovered what she had been doing and he whipped her. The child took her strapping without a word—without a murmur. But no endeavor could wring from her the motive for her wrongdoing.

It was discovered afterwards that the child had spent some of the money in candies; some of it in fancy colored prints; some of it went no one knows where.

And now the little golden-haired creature lies in her bed, saying nothing about her action, sleeping at times, and at times again playing with the babies. Thomas Gilbert is an honest, hard-working engineer. His wife is a stout, hearty, good natured woman, who spends her days mending, cooking, washing and tending eight children, six of which came to her as a wedding gift. The parents work hard by day and sleep sound by night. Seven of their children go to school, eat three meals a day till they have become as sturdy and fat a little race as it would be possible to find in the whole east side, and then at night, like their father and mother, go to bed tired out, glad to get there.

AN ODD BIT OF HUMANITY

But this odd little bit of humanity, who lies in the big bed in the front room there, she is different. Her brothers and sisters go to school; she dislikes the restraint and sighs to get away. They don't care much to go to the Church of the Epiphany every Sunday. But the little Maggie loves that, for she hears music there. When the others are asleep she is wide awake. When the boys and girls whom she knows are tumbling in rough sports she goes away by herself and dreams. What does she dream about?

They call her up in the tenement "odd" and "queer." No one seems to understand her there. Poor little Maggie Gilbert! There is no place for dreamers in a work-a-day world like the east side.

Source: "A Strange Little East Side Girl," *New York World*, February 12, 1891.

"PUT YOURSELF IN HIS PLACE"

(1891)

What Would You Do If, Like Poor Joe Clark, You Could Get No Work and Found Your Helpless Family Put Out Upon the Street on a Winter Morning?

One of the Many Chapters from Poverty's Big Book— The Misfortunes that Pursued a Family Despite All Efforts to Overcome Them— And All Joe Clark Asks Is Work

No. 506 East Seventeenth street is a great tenement-house that towers grimly above its neighbors. You step from the sidewalk into the narrow, dark hall, in which the sun never seems to shine, and from which flights of equally dark, narrow steps lead to the many floors above. There is hardly a glimpse of the sky obtainable from any of the windows, and such a thing as a blade of green grass is never seen. Poverty is everywhere. Hunger often raps at the doors and sometimes stalks boldly in and takes its place at the bare tables.

Glimpses into the different rooms show heavy-eyed women bending over washtubs or ironing-boards, nursing sick children or dividing a small loaf of bread among the little ones and waiting for the miracle to work.

In the two-room "suites" large families huddle together. To pay the rent is their highest ambition. Food, clothing, everything is sacrificed to that, and usually they manage to get together each month the few dollars that keep them from the streets.

But occasionally there is a "dispossession." Marshal and men invade the place and down the rickety steps bumps a trunk, a stove, an old sofa—the earthly effects of some family which is "behind the date."

The lares and penates are followed by a crying woman and some frightened children, who sit about on the sidewalk for a few hours and then disappear.[1] Where they go nobody knows, and apparently nobody cares.

A LONG STRUGGLE WITH POVERTY

But there was an eviction in this house yesterday which interested and affected even the inmates who are so used to scenes of misery. Mr. and Mrs. Joseph Clark and their four little children were turned into the streets, penniless and hopeless. The story of their long struggle and final defeat was familiar to most of their neighbors, and their children had made themselves loved in families where children are usually at a discount; so many sympathetic eyes watched them as they followed their few pieces of furniture into the world.

The Clarks are not the sort of people usually found in this class of tenement-houses. When they married, seven years ago, it is very unlikely that they expected to drift into one. Joe was a hard-working, steady young fellow, with a conviction that Lizzie was the best woman on earth and that he wasn't half good enough for her.

Lizzie felt very much the same way as to Joe's virtues and her own unworthiness. So they started in with a capital of youth, love, health and industry, and for a year everything went merrily. Joe worked twelve hours out of the twenty-four and thought himself an object for public envy. They had a few cozy rooms, which they furnished as well as they could, buying a chair one week, a few shelves the next, pictures the next, and making themselves a home.

When the baby came Joe was offered work in the Hoffman House and labored there for thirteen months.[2] Every week he brought home twelve silver dollars and handed them to Lizzie. They didn't represent much capital, but they looked as large as cartwheels to the little woman, and she invested them with a wisdom and economy which astonished her husband. They couldn't possibly have been happy under these circumstances, some cynics may think, but they thought they were, and Joe is wont to refer to those days with a suspicious quiver in his boyish voice.

A CHAPTER OF MISFORTUNES

By and bye the baby got sick, and there were days and nights of watching, hoping and dreading. There was a doctor's bill and a little coffin and a funeral. With the dead child, which was carried out to Calvary, there went much of the light and hope of the home. Joe lost his position, and things began to look darker.

They had to sell some of the furniture before he found work, but when he did he went into it with heart and soul to make up for lost time and to pay his debts. He worked steadily until last September. When the gas-fitting in the pencil factory on Fourteenth street was finished, Joe found himself again out of employment.

The little money saved was soon exhausted. They moved into the tenement-house at 506 East Seventeenth street and took up their abode in two back rooms on the fifth floor. There were three children by this time—Archie, a handsome, sturdy little chap of five, Fannie, three, and John, a precocious youngster of two.

There was rent to be paid, fuel to be bought, five mouths to be fed and no money to do it with. Joe walked the streets desperately from morning until night. Occasionally he got an "odd job," as he called it—four or five days' work in place of some sick man, or even a week or two. Then, just before Christmas, the baby came. He had found some odd plumbing and roofing to do at that season; so they pulled along. Lizzie had come down to washing but the baby's birth stopped that. Afterwards Joe sawed wood, ran errands, shoveled snow, did everything his hand found to do, and kept his family warm and housed.

In February, however, they fell behind in their account with the landlords, but Joe did some roofing on the house and that was accepted in lieu of rent. Then there came days when walking the streets and praying for work availed nothing.

The fuel gave out and the children were cold. Sometimes they were hungry, but they were the bravest little tots the writer has ever seen and they made no sign.

THEY ASKED FOR BREAD NO MORE

After a few times they noticed that their mother cried when they asked for bread, and that their young father dropped his head on his arms and could not talk to them or play with them. They never asked again unless the food was in sight and they knew it was there for them.

They have the faces and manners of a prince and princess— this five-year-old boy and his three-year-old sister. His tiny torn cap is lifted from his head whenever he enters a room, and his treatment of his sister is as gentle as Little Lord Fauntleroy's could have been.[3]

They probably cannot understand why they should feel hungry and why they may not have something to eat, but they ask no questions.

"God loves us, doesn't he?" asks Archie occasionally. And then softly to his sister, "When I'm big I'll buy bread and cakes for you."

The climax came yesterday noon. The Clarks owed $1 on last month's rent and for March up to date—some $5 or $6 in all. They received a notice of eviction last Friday, but appealed for and were granted one day of grace.

Marshal Lusk knew of the case and of the four children. He also knew that the baby was sick with croup.[4] Consequently he did not come until yesterday. But when he came he did his unpleasant duty. There was no harshness, no severity of manner, but the few bits of furniture which had not been pawned were carried downstairs and placed on the sidewalk, and the wife, the baby, with the three children who clung to her skirts, were turned out of doors together.

OUT UPON THE SIDEWALK

To the children it was rather a pleasant affair. There was lots of noise and bustle, which delighted them, and it was funny to see the little old stove taken to pieces and carried downstairs. They did not see the tears on their mother's cheeks, or understand why she held them so closely when she took them in her arms. Little Fannie took care of the baby. Her tiny arms hardly reached around the bundled infant, but she patted its back in a motherly way and chattered cheerfully about the "moving."

Mrs. Clark had a dime and the eye of Archie fell upon it.

"Shall I go an' buy quarter pound of sugar an' an ounce of tea?" he suggested, mildly.

The motion was seconded and carried, and young Archibald started off. There were a few hard rolls left and on these the family feasted.

Joe was the person most to be pitied. He stood nearby, with his teeth set and wearing the expression which settles on a man's face only once or twice in a lifetime. He spoke once and that was when Fannie came to him and laid her cheek against his knee. The hand he laid on her head trembled.

"We've seen some hard times," he said, "but this is the worst. I have seen it coming, and I've lain awake all night long, after hunting for work all day, and have pictured it to myself. It's been a sort of nightmare that has haunted me. Oh, if I could only find something to do!"

The last sentence was as sincere as any prayer that ever ascended. Later in the day he said to the writer:

WHO WILL GIVE HIM "A CHANCE?"

"I will do any work in the world that is honest. I will clean streets or break stones or work twenty hours a day, if necessary. Speak to someone about me. Give me a chance and I'll show that I deserve it. I am a plumber and gasfitter by trade, but I can do roofing or turn my hand to almost anything—and I'll work with all my heart."[5]

Then the doors were locked, and Joe and his family were out on the street with their helpless little children around them.

Joe Clark's face shows him to be an honest, straightforward, temperate young fellow. He is in bad odor with his landlords, Friedmann & Wentz, because he cannot pay his rent, but there is no one else to say a word against him.[6]

There must be work for such a man in a city like New York, and THE WORLD will gladly communicate with anyone who is willing to give him the chance he asks. There are many cases of eviction in this city weekly, but there are none more deserving of public sympathy and assistance than this. The Clarks ask only to be put in a way to help themselves.

Source: "Put Yourself in His Place," *New York World*, March 18, 1891.

"THE SILVER LINING OF THE CLOUD"

(1891)

Generous "World" Readers Come Promptly to the Relief of Poor Joe Clark and His Evicted Family

There's Plenty of Bread for the Children Now, They Have a Neat New Home and, Best of All, Joe Has Got Work—Acknowledgment of Kind Contributions and Offers of Work—The Happy Sequel to a Sad Story

High in the tenement-house at No. 434 East Sixteenth street there is a very happy little family. You wouldn't suppose that they are the same Clarks who were evicted from their home this week and whose pathetic story was told in Wednesday's WORLD, but they are.[1]

Only now there is happiness in place of misery, peace in place of anxiety, food for all in place of starvation and hearts so full of gratitude that tears come in place of words when they try to thank their unknown friends.

The great sympathetic heart of the New York public never responded more promptly to affliction than in the case of the Clarks. In less than twenty-four hours from the publication of their story dozens of sympathizers had written to THE WORLD, sending money, encouragement and offers of work.

A portion of the money was used at once, and with the assistance of THE WORLD woman, the family was located in its new home—two bright, sunny rooms in a much better neighborhood and house than the old. A supply of food was laid in, which seemed princely to the little family; clothes were redeemed from pawn, and Joe was able to make a "genteel appearance," as the ancient novelists say, when he called upon those who had offered him employment.

"BREAD ALL 'E TIME, NOW," SAYS JOHNNIE

The hope which has come into their lives has lent a cheerfulness and home comfort to their tiny rooms which even the shabby furniture cannot banish. The stove and the floor have been polished until they shine. The little kettle on the hearth sings merrily and two-year-old Johnnie expressed the sentiments of the family when he rubbed his cheek against the writer's and said, drowsily: "All so pity, and bwead (bread) all 'e time."

He soon fell asleep, with the same cheek pillowed on a bun which he was hardly hungry enough to eat, but with which he could not be compelled to part. Perhaps there was in his baby head some recollection of recent days when he had awakened hungry to find no bread, no fire and no hope awaiting him.

Although money was not asked, and although the boyish father had said again and again that all he wanted was a chance to help himself, $35 have been sent in for the family at present writing. Eighteen of this was used to pay the rent, buy provisions and fuel and redeem the clothing from pawn. The remainder will be expended for the benefit of the children, but, as Joe said feelingly: "Thank God I am placed in a way to help myself, and it rests with me now to care for my family. I appreciate all this more than I can tell. I am not good at speech-making, but I hope to show you what a fellow can do when he finds himself once more on his feet, with friendly hands extended to him."

JOE GETS WORK

For Joe has found work. Among the first communications to come in was the following:

NEW YORK, March 18, 1891.

To the Editor of The World:

Please send Joe Clark to No. 17 Delancey street, between the
Bowery and Christie street, and I will try to put him to work if he
understands roofing and plumbing.

H. WENDLING.

Joe read this with a kindling face. "That's what I want," he
said quickly. "That's the work I can do," and he started for No.
17 Delancey street like an arrow from the bow.

The writer was not surprised to see him return an hour later
flushed and out of breath, for he had run half the way back, but
triumphant. He is to begin work Monday morning with a steady
job, he says, a fine salary to start with and the promise of an increase if he gives satisfaction. And he is to have an employer who
treated him like a man and was so cordial and kindly in his reception that the susceptible young fellow came away ready to
work for him day and night if necessary.

THANKS TO ALL KIND FRIENDS

"I want you to thank all the others," he said, with a slight quiver
in the boyish voice, after he had stopped talking of Lizzie and the
babies and Mr. Wendling, and how he meant to work and what a
relief it was to feel that there was a future before the wife and
children.

"Thank them all for me. I did not know there was so much
kindness in the world. It is a great thing to feel that there are so
many men who would give a fellow a lift if they knew that he was
on his back."

Some of the letters received deserve a place here. It is a singular
fact that many of them are from people who have been in Joe's
position, and who know what it means to walk the streets looking for work while a starving wife and children wait at home.
Here is one:

To the Editor of The World:

Will you kindly give the inclosed $1 to Joe Clark, whose story is told in Wednesday's WORLD? I know what it is to be evicted with a young family.

H. A. D.

New York, March 18, 1891.

And here is another:

To the Editor of The World:

The $1 which I enclose is intended for honest Joe Clark, whose sad story was so graphically depicted in THE WORLD of Wednesday. Please say that it is from one who has known adversity and who trusts that many happy days are in store for the Clark family. Perhaps this chastening will prove to be Joe's salvation. Let us hope so.

GEORGE.

New York, March 18, 1891.

Here's a practical suggestion, which proves that the writer has "been there." The entire $6 was applied to the relief of the family:

To the Editor of The World:

Inclosed please find $5 to help Joe Clark while he is looking for work. Also $1 to advertise in your "Want" column for a place for him.

J.

New York, March 19, 1891.

The women are sympathetic, too.

To the Editor of The World:

Inclosed you will find $1 for Mrs. Joseph Clark from the mother
of a large family.

S. S.

Coney Island, March 19th, 1891.

Other contributions received were from "WORLD Readers,"
$1; L. E., $1; K. E. D., $1, and M. J. D., $2. None of the contributors sent names or addresses. Then there was $1 from G. F. H.,
Rochester; $1 from W., in Syracuse, and another dollar from
M. M. P., away down in Newport News.

On Wednesday morning a gentleman came to the office with
$18 cash, which he deposited for the Clark family. He said the
money had been collected in a large plumbing establishment,
where the workmen sympathized with a comrade in hard luck,
but he refused to leave the address and evidently did not care to
be thanked.

OTHER OFFERS OF WORK

Among the offers of work which came to Joe were the following:

To the Editor of The World:

If Joseph Clark, whose case you published in Wednesday's
WORLD, is still open for work send him to me tomorrow morning
with a line certifying who he is.

GEO. H. PLATT.

Gen. Foreman Harlem River Shops, N. Y., N. H.
and H. R. K. Co.

New York, March 19.

To the Editor of The World:

If Clark is as represented in your article, and a good plumber, I can give him work for at least eight months, and more than likely it will be permanent. Please let me know what has been done.

ARTHUR A. STRYKER,

William street.

East Orange, N. J., March 19.

J. B. Morrison, of Shelter Island Heights, N. Y., generously offered young Clark work, good wages and money in advance to pay rent for the coming month. Two New York ladies, who do not wish their names published, have sent offers of employment and Mr. Walter E. Scott, of No. 120 Broadway, was one of the first to extend a helping hand.

HE'S ALL RIGHT NOW

But Joe says gratefully that he can go along without further assistance now, and THE WORLD woman, who has watched him during his "trial by fire," agrees with him.

With the sincerest thanks to all, he has gladly braced his own shoulders to bear the care of his family, and with the energy and determination he will put into his work his success is assured.

The pictures of the family were sketched from life by THE WORLD artist, and are very truthful portraits of the Clarks and their really beautiful children.

Source: "The Silver Lining of the Cloud," *New York World*, March 21, 1891.

FROM
COVERAGE OF THE
LIZZIE BORDEN
MURDER TRIAL

"THE CASE OF
LIZZIE BORDEN"

(1893)

**Whichever Way You Look at It, It Is One Where
Superlatives Only May Be Used**

**THE YOUNG WOMAN IS EITHER A MONSTER OR
A BEING MOST CRUELLY WRONGED**

A Full Review of the Murder Mystery Which Everyone Is
Discussing—Theories as to How the Crime Was Committed
of Those Who Think Miss Borden Is the Murderess and of
Those Who Think She Isn't—Is There a Jack the Chopper?—
Resemblances to the Manchester Case

[SPECIAL TO THE WORLD]
NEW BEDFORD, June 3.—Lizzie D. Borden is a young woman
thirty-one years of age who has heretofore led a respected life,
who was identified with numerous religious movements, who, according to the testimony of her friends, was kind of heart and

thoughtful for the comfort and feelings of others.[1] Did this young woman split open her aged father's head with a hatchet as he lay sleeping on the sofa, and afterwards go back and batter his face and head with the same weapon that even the doctors who looked upon the hideous sight could hardly command their nerves? Did this same young woman, just before or just after this deed, strike down her stepmother and chop and hack her head and face until it was beaten almost out of human resemblance? Did she do at least one of these horrible deeds within twenty minutes' time, and was she at the end of that interval able to appear before neighbors she has summoned without a spot of blood on her clothing, without a sign of derangement or hasty adjustment of her dress, with the weapon concealed beyond discovery, and not even a scrap of direct evidence to connect her with the deed left undisposed of?

Did Lizzie D. Borden do all of this and do it in broad daylight, between 10:30 and 11 o'clock in the morning, and in a house close to the sidewalk of one of the most frequented streets of a town of 80,000 inhabitants, a house closely elbowed, and over-looked and surrounded by other houses with their windows and doors all open as in a hot midsummer morning?

THE TRIAL TO BEGIN TOMORROW

Twelve men, under the legal guidance of three Judges and the misguidance of six lawyers, are going to decide whether or no Lizzie Borden did all these things, and they begin their deliberations in this city at 9 o'clock on Monday morning next. If they find that Miss Borden did not do this with which she is charged she will go forth as a free woman, having endured, first, the horror of having her parents hideously butchered almost before her eyes; second, of having lain in jail for ten months, and third, of having a stigma for life upon her name—the stigma of having been suspected, arrested and indicted for by all odds the most fiendishly brutal double murder that the age and generation has known. If, on the other hand, the twelve men who are today un-known, find that there is a thread of circumstances sufficiently strong to warrant them in the belief that that of which she is charged is physically possible and that she herself did do it, then Miss Lizzie Borden will be hanged by the neck until she is dead—that is to say she will be so hanged barring legal technicalities or executive clemency.

After even this bold presentment of the case it is not necessary to say that the trial which begins here on Monday morning is going to be one of the most memorable in the criminal annals of New England. The finding of Miss Borden guilty would mean more than the branding of her as a murderess. It would mean that twelve men, after careful consideration of all that is said for and against her, believe her to be not only one of the most brutal monsters ever known, but that they believe her to be a woman in all respects the most astounding in point of self-command of which we have any record.

IF SHE BE GUILTY

The mere fact of a woman brought up in the atmosphere of wealth and what is called excellent social surroundings all her life, been respected, and who had interested herself zealously in religious and charitable work—the fact of such a woman in some access of frenzy committing a butchery that would have taxed the nerve of a Choctaw Indian squaw is perhaps conceivable.[2] But if you believe Lizzie Borden guilty you have to believe she did this horrible thing; that she turned her prim, orderly New England home into a shamble, and waded in the blood of her father and mother, as a butcher wades in the blood of slaughtered animals. You have to believe that she did all this not in any frenzy whatever, but with as much coolness and deliberation as she would rip a gown to pieces and plan the making of it over into some other form. You have to believe it possible, moreover, for this young woman not only to hack her father's head to pieces with an axe, every blow of which spattered her from head to foot with his blood, but that she did it, destroyed every vestige of blood-stained garments, made away with the weapons and presented herself spotless and tidy, showing no signs of violent exercise and with even her hair in unruffled adjustment, as she usually wore it. You have to believe that she accomplished this feat and had notified the neighbors and the police of the assault all within the space of twenty minutes at the outside.

In whatever way you look at the case of Lizzie Borden no half-way terms will describe it. It is one of the few instances where superlatives only can be used. She is either one of two things. Either she is the most brutally cold-blooded, as well as the most daring and self-poised murderess ever known, or she is the most foully wronged woman who ever suffered persecution under the name of the law. If she be guilty she is a psychological freak for the study of learned philosophers; if innocent she is an inexhaustible text from which to preach the barbarous villainies upon innocent people which our laws permit and commit.

THE STORY OF THE CRIME

The crime for which this young woman is to be tried was committed in Fall River on the morning of the 4th of August 1892. It was committed between 10:30 and 11:15 o'clock, and the house wherein it was committed was and still is known as No. 92 Second street. It is in the heart of town and within two minutes' walk of the City Hall. In this house for many years there lived four persons—Andrew J. Borden, Abbey D. Borden, Andrew's wife; Emma L. Borden and Lizzie D. Borden. The last two being the daughters of Andrew Borden by his first wife, who died over twenty years ago. On the 4th of August, when Andrew J. Borden and his wife were murdered, Emma Borden was not at home. She was away in New Bedford on a visit, and hence is entirely eliminated from all consideration in the discussion of the crime. She is the older of the two sisters and Mr. Borden had no other children living.

Andrew Borden was known as a hard-fisted, close-bargaining businessman, fond of money to the degree of being counted penurious.[3] He had no very warm friends and in his grasping, unrelenting way of doing business had made quite the number of enemies which such men usually raise. There were many men who had had their moments of hating him, although beyond certain unsatisfactory statements none of this had developed during the time immediately preceding the tragedy. In Fall River, Borden was counted one of the wealthy men of the place. His property was variously estimated at from $350,000 to $500,000. He owned a business block, still known as the Borden Block, farms, several houses, had manufacturing and bank stock and was the President of the Union Savings Bank.

THE BORDENS' MODE OF LIVING

Beyond the owning of things Borden's interest in life was moderate. All else was secondary to the mere satisfaction of feeling that he had things and the money to buy things with. Little of his money, however, went in the latter direction, unless the things he bought were permanent things, which always meant as much or more money than he put into them. While he practiced an economy in his household that was absurd for a man of wealth, he was not niggardly with his family.[4] They had enough to eat, the girls had good clothes, the house was comfortably furnished. Yielding to the pressure of the girls, the old man was even contemplating purchasing a house up on "the Hill," which is the swell part of Fall River. As for the girls, they both had money in the bank—about $2,500 each. Their father had given them a house and then bought it back from them, paying them separately. Their money in the bank represented the result of this transaction, with such additions as each might have made from time to time.

Leaving Emma out of the question, the general verdict on Lizzie among those who knew her is not unfavorable. She had been brought up under the hard, narrow lines of her father's character, and the making of money was the most solemn and imposing thing in life which her father had done ever since she could remember. While this had had its effect upon her habit of mind, she was yet capable of doing generous things and of taking an interest in the affairs of others, even to the extent of dipping into her purse. In the religious and charitable enterprises with which she liked to identify herself she quite maintained her share of the expense, and in case of deficiencies or extra expenditures it was very frequently she who bore the expense. She was considered a strong-minded, resolute girl, however, not winning or gentle of manner, and in features and physique rather heavy and coarse.

Such was the Lizzie Borden, of Fall River, before the circumstances came which have made some people believe she is an inhuman monster and caused others to think on her as a woman more cruelly wronged by legal persecution than any woman living.

LIZZIE'S RELATIONS TO HER STEPMOTHER

As to the exact state of affairs in the Borden household there is a conflict of evidence, but that Lizzie and her stepmother were not on cordial terms there is no question. Lizzie always addressed her and referred to her as Mrs. Borden, and in former years had hot words with her not infrequently. Between Lizzie and her father, on the other hand, there were many demonstrations of affection as would be expected of two such people. The house was a cold and cheerless one even under the most favorable circumstances, with the atmosphere of severe economy all-pervading and all things moving in narrow, sordid grooves. Borden and his wife lived happily enough, and between Lizzie and her father there were always kindly relations.

With these facts in mind respecting the Bordens and their household and counting in one Bridget Sullivan, a servant girl who worked for the family for nearly three years and whose testimony will be an important feature of the trial, let us come down to the morning of Aug. 4, the morning of the murders. There were in the house that morning four [five] persons—Borden and his wife, Lizzie Borden and the servant Bridget, and John V. Morse. John V. Morse is a brother to the late Mrs. Borden—brother-in-law, therefore, to Andrew Borden, and uncle to Lizzie.

Morse's home, until within two years prior to the murders, had been in Iowa. During the two years he had been at his old Massachusetts home making a visit. He was a frequent guest at the Borden house, and on the morning of the 4th of August was there in that capacity. He left the house early, however, and did not return until the murders had been discovered. He accounted fully and satisfactorily to the authorities for his movements during the interval, and has been left as completely out of all speculations concerning the crime as has Emma Borden herself, who was away on a visit to New Bedford. He will be a witness at the trial, but his testimony will bear solely upon the movements of the household during the early morning and before anything happened that was out of the usual routine.

JUST BEFORE THE MURDER

With Morse away we have the house stripped of everybody except those who were there, or, rather, those who are known to have been there at the time of the double crime. Of these four [five] persons thus left just two survive—Lizzie Borden and Bridget Sullivan.

Now barring out the testimony of Lizzie we have that of Bridget and of other persons showing the movements of Mr. and Mrs. Borden up to within twenty minutes, at least, of the death of Borden.

At about 10 o'clock Borden, according to his usual custom, went downtown. Morse having been gone from the house something like an hour. Borden went to the post-office and to the Union Savings Bank, of which he was the President, and there talked to the cashier. He stayed but a very few moments and then started for the house. At the time he got back Bridget Sullivan was washing windows. She testified that a few minutes before that she went and looked at the clock to see if it was time to begin getting dinner.[5] The Bordens had their dinner midday.

Bridget is able to say positively that at the time she looked at the clock it was 10:20. A few minutes after that Mr. Borden came to the front door; the front door was always kept locked because within a year the Borden house had been ransacked in broad daylight by burglars. When Bridget heard Mr. Borden at the door she went and let him in—that was about ten minutes after she had looked at the clock to see if it was time to get about getting dinner—in other words it was 10:30 when Borden got back to the house.

Bridget testified that he went into the dining room and sat down

and took a key and went upstairs by the back way; that he remained there but a moment, returned, placed the key on a shelf
and sat down in the sitting-room.

DID NOT SEE MRS. BORDEN

At the time Mr. Borden did this Bridget did not know in what
room Lizzie was. The next she saw of Lizzie was a few minutes
afterwards when Lizzie came through the sitting-room into the
dining room with an ironing-board in her hands. It was then
somewhere between 10:30 and 10:55, for about 10:55 o'clock
Bridget says she went upstairs to lie down.

During all this time, Bridget says, she does not know where
Mrs. Borden was. Lizzie had told her that Mrs. Borden had gone
out or was going out. Bridget had not seen her since between 9
and 10 o'clock in the morning, when she (Mrs. Borden) had told
her to wash the windows.

So leaving Lizzie ironing, or getting ready to iron, and Mr.
Borden, who had only been back from downtown fifteen or
twenty minutes, in the sitting-room, Bridget, at about 10:55
o'clock, went upstairs to lie down for a few moments. According
to her testimony, she had only been lying down for ten or fifteen
minutes when Lizzie called to her. Bridget knew by the excited
pitch of Lizzie's voice that something had happened. She sprang
from the bed and hurried downstairs. Lizzie was leaning with her
back against the back door and said that her father was "dead."
About this last expression there is controversy. It is disputed
whether Bridget testified positively that Lizzie said "dead" and
not "hurt." It is a fine point of memory for a terrified and ignorant girl to be exact upon, and that Bridget was both ignorant
and terrified there is no dispute.

HURRY FOR THE DOCTOR

But, at all events, Lizzie said her father was either dead or hurt,
and told Bridget to hurry and tell Dr. Bowen. Dr. Bowen lives diagonally across the narrow street and within hailing distance of

the Borden house. Dr. Bowen was out, and when Bridget returned with the message Lizzie told her to go for Mrs. Russell, who lived on Borden street.

When Bridget got back with Mrs. Russell Dr. Bowen and Mrs. Churchill were in the house. Mrs. Churchill told Bridget Mrs. Borden ought to be told, whereupon Lizzie said "I think I heard her come in."

Mrs. Churchill said Bridget had better go and look for her, and Bridget said she was afraid to go upstairs alone, and Mrs. Churchill offered to go up with her. They went upstairs and found Mrs. Borden's body lying on the floor of the bedroom between the bed and bureau. They went downstairs and Mrs. Churchill told Dr. Bowen that Mrs. Borden was murdered, too.

So, with the exception of what the accused herself tells, that is in substance all we know of the doings of the people who were in the Borden house at the time of the murder. At 10:55 when Bridget went upstairs to lie down Mr. Borden was in the sitting-room, alive and well. At from 11:10 to 11:15, that is to say from fifteen to twenty minutes later, he was lying dead with his head and face literally hacked to pieces.

Dr. Bowen, Mrs. Churchill and Mrs. Russell, as well as Bridget herself, all testify that there was nothing unusual about Lizzie's dress, that her hair was smooth and in order and that she gave no indications of having recently had violent exertion.

THE DRESS SHE WORE

Lizzie herself testified that she wore a blue dress, and the women who saw her during the forenoon and at the time of the murder was discovered bear her out in her testimony. She had on a blue dress when she was about the house during the forenoon. She wore a blue dress when the neighbors came in and found two rooms of the house turned into shambles and her father and mother lying dead in their blood, which had come from over twenty savage hacks with a hatchet or axe about the head and face and which had spattered and spurted over everything for many feet around their dead bodies. That the person who killed Mr. and Mrs. Borden was smeared and splashed with blood from head to foot when he had finished his awful job is beyond all manner of doubt. Yet, with the single exception of a point of blood the size of a pinhead far up on Lizzie's white underskirt, not a single drop was found on the clothing she wore twenty minutes before the murder was discovered and which she still wore when the neighbors came in in response to her summons when the crime was discovered.

Everything she wore, even to the soles of her shoes, was submitted to the minutest scientific examination by experts with the results that no blood or traces of blood were found. If in the search for evidence other garments that were blood-stained were found, the fact had not been made public and is held in abeyance by the prosecution for the production at the trial.[6] The impression, however, is that no such discovery was made, and that whatever evidence the prosecution has in reserve goes rather to the establishment of a monetary motive on the part of Lizzie for the commission of the crime than to anything directly connecting her with it.

MISS BORDEN'S STORY

One basis of the first suspicions against her was what were called her contradictory statements concerning her movements on the morning of the murders. These contradictions, however, so far as they have been made public, are for the most part trifling when account is taken of the necessarily agitated condition of the girl's mind at the time.

Her own story briefly is as follows: She said that her father complained of not feeling well, and that he lay down on the sofa, she adjusting the pillow for him; that her flat irons were not hot enough to iron with and that to put in the time while they were heating she went into the back yard. She stopped there for a few moments and picked up some pears which had fallen to the ground from the trees. Then she thought she would go into the barn for some sinkers[7] for her fish line, as she was going to Marion[8] the next day to fish. Her father told her there were sinkers in a little box upstairs in the barn and she went there to get them. She had not been in the barn before in three months. She went upstairs, threw open the door and stood there while she ate four pears. Then she looked for the sinkers and came into the house. When she got in she found her father murdered and summoned Bridget.

On her cross-examination she was confronted with the fact that she had once before said she went to the barn to get a piece of iron for her fish line and with the further fact that lying in the yard close to the barn door were pieces of lead with which she could have made sinkers. Then she was asked to explain how it was on that hot morning she went to the hottest place on the premises to stand and eat pears, a place from which, as she had testified, she could not see the yard or anybody who came into it or left it. To this Lizzie gave no other explanation than that she was confused by all the questioning.

THE TIME BETWEEN THE TWO MURDERS

The medical experts in Boston who examined the stomachs of the murdered man and woman testified that in their opinion Mrs. Borden was killed from an hour to an hour and a half before Mr. Borden. They based this belief upon the stages of digestion of the food in each of their stomachs and it has come to be the accepted opinion. If that is the case and Lizzie is the murderess, she must have butchered her mother about 10 o'clock, that is at about the time or before her father went downtown. This involves believing that with her mother lying slaughtered upstairs this unnatural monster of a girl went calmly about her ordinary household duties, that she chatted and laughed with Bridget— Bridget testified to that—and then took her chances on Bridget getting out of the way long enough for her to slip into the room and split open her father's head as it lay resting on the pillow, which she had smoothed for him to rest upon. It involves also, believing that after butchering her mother with Bridget about the house and apt to come upstairs at any moment, she was able to make way with her weapon and her blood-soaked garments of slaughter as quickly and deftly as she did after the murder of her father.

All this is, of course, simply beyond possibility of belief until it has been absolutely demonstrated to be true beyond a peradventure.[9] There are but two ways that can be conceived whereby this could be done, and even they are wild to the verge of grotesqueness, and involve a depth and genuine emotional depravity which it is almost fantastic to attribute to a girl of the character and environments of Lizzie Borden.

THEORIES AS TO HOW THE DEED WAS DONE

One of these is that she stripped herself when she did the deed almost, if not quite, to the state of nudity and the other is that she threw over herself some long enveloping rubber garment which thoroughly protected her clothing. As for the first theory, it belongs in the category of the Boisgobey school of French novels and the second involves an almost superhuman skill in hiding the blood-stained garment, to say nothing of the blood-curdling coolness of the girl in doing such a deed then dropping back without a ruffle in manner or even a flush on her cheek into the regular morning humdrum of work and the usual idle chatter with a servant girl who was on familiar terms with the household.[10]

There are indeed rumors of witnesses who will swear that they saw Lizzie up by the window under which the dead body of Mrs. Borden lay; that they were in the street and saw her distinctly stooping down over something, and that she had on a queer sort of a hooded waterproof. There are rumors of such witnesses as these, and if the prosecution has them actually in reserve their testimony will bear heavily against the accused, as well as add renewed sensation to this the most sensational, bewildering and utterly dumbfounding crime of the century.

But even supposing Lizzie did murder her parents, why did she hack and maim and batter them so like a devil incarnate? Each one of them had nearly if not quite a dozen blows on the head and the face, delivered with terrible force from the sharp and the blunt end of a hatchet or axe. Would not one or two at most of the dozen blows that split the heads to the brain have been sufficient to satisfy most murderers, especially if they were in a hurry?

Is it possible to think of a girl such as Lizzie Borden, who never did a deed of violence before, to anybody's knowledge, being suddenly transformed into such a monster of blood-thirsty savageness as to hack and chop mere senseless clods after the life was long gone out of them?

LIKE THE WORK OF A MADMAN

This whole affair of maiming is more like the work of a frenzied madman or of some person roused by hatred and thirst for revenge to the very ecstasy of madness, than that of a murder with a motive of mere pecuniary gain.

As a matter of fact not a cent of money or an article of value was stolen from the house at the time of the crime. Mr. Borden had a watch and a considerable sum of money on his person. Neither was touched. In Mrs. Borden's room not a thing was deranged or out of order. There had been no more struggle when she was killed than when Borden's head was split open as he lay sleeping on the sofa. Not a drawer was opened or any jewelry on Mrs. Borden's person removed. She was not asleep when she was stricken down and this with the absence of any signs whatever of a struggle, goes to show that she was either approached noiselessly from behind or that she was suddenly struck by someone of whom she had no reason to be afraid and against whom she was not on her guard.

And then what became of the weapon with which it was all done? The police and the doctors all agree that this weapon was an axe or a hatchet. What has become of it?

In the Borden cellar were found a number of axes and hatchets. All of them were clean; none of them had blood stains on either the wood or iron. One of them with peculiar spots on the handle was sent to Boston to an expert, who boiled the handle and reported that the stains were not blood stains. Another one with the handle broken off up close to the blade was found to have hair clinging to it. The hair proved to be the hair of some domestic animal and not of a human being. Lizzie Borden had written to a friend at Marion that she bought her a sharp new hatchet, but this it was afterwards shown was a joke in reference to some wood which the party of girls who were picnicking there had been unable to chop up. Lizzie was expecting to join this party the next day—the 5th of August. Indeed, it was only by a chance and by a change of prearranged plans that she was not with them on the day the murder occurred. It was in writing of this and of the wood that must be chopped that Lizzie spoke in a joking way.

SUSPICIONS AND RUMORS

So far as has been revealed by the evidence made public, the main ground of suspicion against Lizzie Borden is the negative one that nobody else could have committed the murders.

As soon as the detectives had convinced themselves of this they set about trying to find some motive for the deed. What success attended their efforts in this direction will be revealed at the trial. At various stages of the preliminary investigation, rumors of various kinds came to the surface. One of these was to the effect that Lizzie made a mysterious trip to Providence prior to the murder, and there consulted a lawyer with reference to her father's property in the event of his death. There were rumors, too, of dissensions in the Borden household over property matters, and that Lizzie had manifested jealousy of the influence which her stepmother exerted over her father in this respect. It was rumored, too, that Mr. Borden contemplated making a will whereby the bulk of his property would have gone to his wife, leaving the girls with but a limited proportion.

That Borden had been doing something to his will or contemplated doing something there is little doubt, for in his pocketbook after his death there was found a little scrap of paper on which were memoranda bearing upon the subject of a testamentary disposition of his property. It may be put down for a certainty that the prosecution will endeavor to establish this impending change in the will as the motive actuating Lizzie to the commission of the crime. What, if any, direct evidence they may have remains to be seen, but it will probably be found that they have none or next to none and that they rely upon circumstances alone to establish this New England bred girl is a murderess who rivals all other murderesses the world has ever known.

THE POISON THEORY

The usual weapon with the murderess is poison, and there will be an attempt to show that Lizzie attempted poison before she resorted to the axe.

The Borden family were sick some days before the butchery, and the sickness was traced, it was thought, to some milk into which somebody thought Lizzie had thrown something. Then a drug clerk was found who said that a woman who answered to Lizzie's description attempted to buy prussic acid of him just before the murder.[11] There was even a belief prevalent for a time that both Mr. and Mrs. Borden were killed by prussic acid before they were attacked with the axe. It was only lifeless bodies, according to this belief, whose heads the murderer chopped to pieces to divert suspicion from the real cause of death, which could otherwise more easily have been traced to the criminal.

Careful examination by the best chemical experts in Boston of the stomachs of the murdered man and woman failed to reveal any trace whatever of prussic acid. Lizzie herself positively denied that she bought or attempted to buy any prussic acid. If you believe it is probable for a young woman to do all the horrible things it was said at the beginning of this story the murderer must have done you will not be surprised if you learn that the same young woman was quite composed when she gave her own testimony at the preliminary inquiries and listened without agitation to the testimony of others, which she knew was throwing the drift of suspicion in her direction.

MISS BORDEN'S SELF-POSSESSION

A great deal was made of the fact that Lizzie Borden maintained her self-possession during the ordeal of questioning she underwent and that she was not seen to shed tears over the terrible tragedy. No particular comment was caused, however, by the fact that her sister Emma also was too stunned by the ghastly horror of the events which fell upon her to find vent for her emotions in the usual way of tears and hysterics. Indeed, as a matter of fact, there was nothing in Lizzie Borden's utterances or hearing from the time she revealed the tragedy until her arrest which is incompatible with belief of her innocence.

It will hardly be said that Supt. Byrnes is without experience in criminals, and he saw nothing in the contradictions of Lizzie's first stories to convince him that she even had guilty knowledge. Supt. Byrnes said that he had observed that a faultless repetition of the same tale was as often as evidence of guilt as of innocence, and that per contra he had observed that contradictions and variations from the first statements were very common where the persons making them were entirely innocent. The one showed a carefully rehearsed and prepared story, the other natural tricks and slips of memory of a person under great agitation trying to tell the truth. In the same way as regards Lizzie's alleged stoicism and her failure to put on mourning for her dead parents, it is not difficult to conceive a person precipitated without a moment's warning into the bloody horror into which she was precipitated, supposing her innocent, being dazed and stupefied beyond tears or the millinery of mourning. Would not a rush into mourning weeds, an hysterical demonstration of grief and a smooth, perfectly joined unvarying tale have [held] with many people quite as heavily against her as did her actual movements and language?

IS THERE A JACK THE CHOPPER?

But the question always has come up in the discussion of this astonishing case—if Lizzie Borden did not commit the murders then who did commit them? Who could have committed them? Until the Manchester girl was butchered with an axe and hacked and chopped about the head just as were the Bordens, and that too in broad daylight and with neighbors close at hand, it was thought to be utterly impossible that any outside person could have done the deed in the Borden house on the 4th of August last.[12] The Manchester girl lived in Fall River, too, or rather on the outskirts of Fall River. There is no suspicion that any member of the Manchester family composed her death. That she was murdered by someone who entered the house after everyone had gone away is admitted without question.

So it seems there is in Fall River some Jack the Chopper, who has the knack of hacking people to pieces with strikingly similar evidences of senseless brutality in each instance, and of slipping cleverly through the hands of the police just as did the Whitechapel murderer or the murderers in London.[13]

Up to the present writing the police in search of the Manchester murderer have only succeeded in capturing a bandana handkerchief, found a long distance away from the house where the crime was committed. People are now asking, if this murderer could do what he did in broad daylight and get away, why could not a murderer concealed in the Borden house have done the bloody work there and escaped?

HOW THE MURDERER
MIGHT HAVE WORKED

At the head of the stairs in the Borden house there is a closet in which he could have lain concealed. When Mrs. Borden came upstairs he might have approached her from behind, in the bedroom where she was found, and murdered her. Then he might have hid in his closet again until he thought there was another opportunity, sneaked downstairs and murdered Mr. Borden as he lay asleep on the sofa. Lizzie being, as she said, in the barn. After that he escaped to the street and goes away unnoticed with his weapon under his coat.

All of this of course does violence to a dozen probabilities, and enables the murderer to dodge what would seem to be almost inevitable chances of being caught at his work or seen coming away from it. But are there any more violated or the chances taken any greater in this case than they are on the theory that Lizzie Borden did the deed? Is it any more improbable that a murderer could have so acted and so escaped, than it is that Lizzie could have twice transformed herself with lightning change rapidity from blood-soaked butcher to spotless, primly clad young woman, free in the first instance from all signs of excitement or agitation and in the second only agitated as a girl naturally would be, who just discovered her father lying murdered at her feet.

In whatever way you look at this crime; in whatever way you can try to picture it and conceive how it might have been done, you have to make up your mind to accept things which are wildly improbable on the basis of any past experiences of human action. It is a mere choice of improbabilities at the best. Perhaps the coming trial may unravel it all and make what seems so complicated appear very natural and simple. That, of course, involves some very startling evidence being held in reserve by the prosecution.

PUBLIC OPINION DIVIDED

In a case of this kind it is natural to find public opinion divided into two hostile camps. If Lizzie Borden is innocent, the injury done her is so cruel that those who believe in her innocence are bitter in their denunciation of what they call her persecution and her persecutors. If, on the other hand, she is guilty, she is so inconceivable a wretch, so monstrous and frightfully dangerous a criminal, that those who believe in her guilt can have no patience with the sympathy that has been expressed for her.

It is safe to say that sentiment as to her guilt or innocence is about equally divided, with perhaps the more intelligent wing on the side of her innocence.

This last is evidenced by the number of well-known writers, particularly among women, who have come to her defense in print.

The near approach of the trial, and particularly the second and similar crime just perpetrated in Fall River, have again revived discussion of the case, which will increase as the trial develops, until it bids fair to become the most absorbing topic of conversation in New England.

And what of Lizzie Borden herself? This astonishing woman—either a martyr or a monster—how is she feeling the approach of the great and final ordeal she is to go through?

All who have had access to her in the Taunton Jail speak of her mild and self-poised demeanor, expressing herself as confident that her innocence, which she has never ceased to protest, will be made clear to all the world by the trial, which she welcomes for that reason.[14]

It will be one year on the 11th day of August next since she was arrested, although from the time of the murder she has practically been under arrest. In August she was taken to the Taunton Jail, where for a time confinement wore heavily upon her, and she could not sleep. This gradually wore off, but her health had suffered from the imprisonment. She never had a good complexion. Her face was inclined to the pasty sallowness incident to food such as people of the Borden type in New England are addicted to. The confinement has made her paler and has somewhat refined the rather coarse and heavy outline of her face and figure.

She will be taken to New Bedford, and either her sister Emma or some of her friends will sit by her during the trial.

It is a curious fact that while Lizzie Borden was never a very popular girl during the time of her prosperous, uneventful life in Fall River, she now probably has more and warmer friends there than she ever had before.

Source: "The Case of Lizzie Borden," *New York World*, June 4, 1893.

"LIZZIE'S DARK DAY"

(1893)

Strong Points for the State Brought Out
at the Borden Trial

ALICE RUSSELL DESCRIBES
THE BURNING OF THAT DRESS

New Mystery Furnished by a Ghastly Relic

Most Damaging of All the Commonwealth's Evidence Against
the Prisoner Brought Out—Alice Russell, Lizzie's Close Friend,
Takes Apparent Delight in Giving Evidence That May Convict
the Accused—Introduction of a Ragged, Blood-Soaked Handkerchief, Picked Up on the Borden Premises on the Day of the
Murder, the Sensational Feature of the Fourth Day of the Trial

[SPECIAL TO THE WORLD]

NEW BEDFORD, Mass. June 8.—This was the darkest day
for Lizzie Borden of any since the trial began. The full force of
the prosecution's attack was developed and the most damaging
of all their evidence against the prisoner brought out.

The one distinctly vulnerable point in Lizzie Borden's movements at the time of the murders and during the few days immediately following them was the burning of the light blue dress
with the dark navy blue diamond figure. It is upon this that the
Grand Jury indicted her, and it is this which will convict her if
she is convicted. Without that dress, the Commonwealth's case is
a mere tissue of speculation.

The Commonwealth established beyond a peradventure today,
in the opinion of all who heard the evidence, that Lizzie Borden
did on the Sunday morning following the crime, which occurred

on Thursday, burn such a dress in the kitchen stove and in the presence of two persons. The testimony of one of these persons was the feature of the forenoon's proceedings, and, indeed, of the entire trial up to that moment. Not only was the testimony itself the most startling of any heretofore produced, but the witness herself was a person of such singular individuality that she seemed typical of all the uncanny features of this amazing mystery as well as of the strange people and their strange and narrow lives who are the actors in it.

Miss Alice M. Russell is the name of the witness. For years she had lived next door to the Bordens, in a house now occupied by Dr. Kelly, and she was counted by Lizzie Borden among her closest friends. Yet today she took the witness-stand and not only testified to what will come nearer to putting a rope around her girlfriend's neck than anything yet brought out, but she did it with a vicious snap in her voice and a cruel compression of her thin, colorless lips, which suggested anything but sorrow for the fact that she was compelled to do so.

MISS RUSSELL'S STRIKING APPEARANCE

The personal appearance of Miss Russell is extraordinary. As she took the witness-stand today it seemed as though one of the strange women characters in which Wilkie Collins delights, and which flit like ominous spectres through deep shadows—through his mysteries—had walked out of the pages of one of the dead novelist's books into real life and real participation in a tragedy more awful and more wrapped in obscurity than any he ever evolved.[1]

Tall and slender and thin and sharp of feature, with a sallow complexion; yellowish gray hair, brushed tightly back to a coil like that worn by Lizzie Borden; a flat sailor-like hat, with a narrow rim; a face that is cold, matter-of-fact and non-sympathetic to a degree—such is the woman who testified today that Lizzie Borden on Sunday morning burned a dress which another witness who immediately preceded her had sworn that Lizzie wore on the morning of the murder.

Under the cross-questions of the counsel for the defense it was shown that the burning of the dress was in broad daylight in the presence of two witnesses and the house was surrounded and liable to be entered at any moment by police officers; that it was done openly, in other words, and without the slightest attempt at concealment and with a recklessness as to arousing suspicion which even drew comment from persons present, at the time she did it.

A RAGGED, BLOOD-SOAKED HANDKERCHIEF

The sensational feature of the day was the production of a ragged, blood-soaked, bandanna handkerchief which Deputy Sheriff Wixon, of Fall River, swore he had picked up by the side of Mrs. Borden's body as she lay dead on the floor where she had been stricken down by the assassin.

This is new evidence. What its full significance may be has not yet been developed. The Commonwealth was content with its production and identification. The counsel for the defense avoided all allusion to it in the cross-examination.

In the examination of Bridget Sullivan and Brother-in-Law Morse yesterday the District Attorney came back again and again to the question as to whether or no Mrs. Borden, while she was dusting in the dining room on the morning of the murder, wore anything on her head or had her hair tied up with anything, such as women frequently wear when they are dusting.

The Commonwealth by its witnesses distinctly established that Mrs. Borden did not wear anything on her head. The bandanna handkerchief was old and ragged and just such a one as a woman who was dusting would naturally select to wear over her hair.

CAN IT BE CONNECTED WITH LIZZIE?

The Commonwealth having established that Mrs. Borden had nothing of the kind on her head, at least when she was dusting downstairs, the question arises in what manner the handkerchief can be connected with Lizzie.

There have been rumors of witnesses who will swear that they saw a woman at the window under which Mrs. Borden's dead body lay; saw her there on the morning of the murder, at about the time it is thought Mrs. Borden was murdered; that this woman stooped over as though doing something with whatever was at her feet, and that on her head was something that resembled a hood.

The production of the handkerchief today has revived these rumors, as well as many other speculations as to its significance.

WOMEN STORM THE COURTHOUSE

Interest in the trial here in New Bedford has reached such a pitch that elaborate measures are necessary to keep it within bounds in the vicinity of the courtroom. Day by day the crowds seeking admission have steadily grown until the deputies and policemen who line the stone walk down from the Courthouse through the Courthouse yard to the sidewalk, have had to be increased in numbers. But even this was found insufficient to restrain the mad fury of the rush for the door when it is announced that so many as can be accommodated will be admitted.

There is no fence around the Courthouse yard. It is divided from the sidewalk by a low stone wall, the top of which is on a level with the lawn of the yard. The gateway is a mere break in this wall. This is the only access to the front entrance of the building, for along the top of the wall a rope had been strung to keep people from trampling over the lawn.

The pressure of the crowd around the gateway at critical hours is something fearful. The worst of it is that the crowd is almost entirely composed of women and young girls. Rough handling or shoving or even harsh language is out of the question with such as these.

THROUGH A DOOR IN A FENCE

To meet the emergency, it has been found necessary to erect a high board fence across this entranceway, about six feet wide, and in this fence to make a door. Through this the people will have to pass in orderly single file. Workmen are engaged on this job this evening and tomorrow the new arrangement will be in operation.

The persistent determination manifested by some of the women to gain admission to the trial is almost incredible. The Court-house, even when quite filled, will only seat 200 people. Not more than two thirds of this number are admitted, a circum-stance which is greatly credible to the good sense of the Chief Justice and to the firmness of the blue-and-gold-bespangled Sher-iff, who, with all his absurd pouter-pigeon strut and pomposity, is after all a very conscientious and capable officer. The trial has for this reason never lost its dignity nor the courtroom been made to assume the character of a mass-meeting.

When all who have a right to enter have been admitted then it is "first come, first served" for the public. The flood-gates are opened just long enough to admit a sufficient number to occupy the room without crowding and then they are remorselessly shut down.

It is in waiting for the chance to get in at this brief moment that the women have shown a patience and endurance almost beyond belief. After the gates have been closed in the morning those who were not fortunate enough to gain admission hover about the neighborhood all the morning, to be the first in line for the open-ing in the afternoon. They bring crullers and cookies and other New England food atrocities in their pockets, and actually camp out and lunch on the scene of the battle. They swarm all about the neighborhood and invade the verandas of adjacent houses until it has been necessary for the people owning them to have signs printed and posted up, warning them off.

CURIOSITY TO SEE MISS BORDEN

Next to the anxiety to get in the courtroom is the overmastering curiosity to catch even so much as a glance of Lizzie Borden. This afternoon, at the adjournment of the court, the street from the back entrance of the Courthouse, out of which she passes to her carriage, all the way down to the jail, three long blocks away, was literally lined on both sides of the way with wagons and carriages, many of them stylish turnouts.[2] In addition to this the sidewalks on both sides of the street were packed with people all the way down to the jail, standing as closely together as they comfortably could.

It looked like a country street down which a circus procession was expected to pass, and the extraordinary thing is that of all these people, both in the carriages and on the sidewalks, fully 80 per cent were women and little girls.

They saw nothing for all their pains. Miss Borden drives to and from the jail in a little old coupe drawn by one horse.[3] Since the crowds have grown so great the curtains of the coupe are so tightly closed that not a glimpse of her face or figure can be seen.

This evening the coupe was actually blocked and stopped in its passage by the great number of carriages, and, just for the tenth part of a second, Kirby, the deputy who has charge of the prisoner, pulled the curtains aside just long enough to peep out and see what was the matter and the glimpse of his grizzled face was all the spectators had to reward them for their patience.

LIZZIE'S VIVACITY DIMINISHED

The vivacity which Lizzie Borden showed yesterday under the influence of the bracing air and the cheering testimony in her behalf was somewhat diminished today. The weather continued cool, almost to the point of chilliness and the reefer jacket which she has heretofore held folded across her lap or kept lying on a chair by her side she has on today during all the morning session.[4]

Her face was pale, but without the sickly sallowness of the first two days of trial, and frequently she coughed hoarsely in a way which showed that the attack of grip which recently sent her to bed in the Taunton Jail with a sharp threat of pneumonia had not left her.[5] She took the same seat within the bar she occupied yesterday afternoon.[6] She sits close to her lawyers and immediately behind Mr. Adams.[7]

The object of this change is two-fold. First, it enables her readily to prompt her counsel, which she very frequently does, and, second, it gives the jury a good view of a young woman who, if not handsome, certainly does not look like she is capable of committing the hideous butchery with which she is charged.

ACCOUNTING FOR HER APATHY

There was in the demeanor of this either cruelly maligned or justly tortured young woman today another recitation of the stories of her stolid stoicism which went abroad at the time of the Fall River inquest and preliminary hearing and right here, in that connection, it should be said that by the very first witness called today the defense laid the foundation for an explanation, not only of any apparent apathy she may have exhibited during those early days of the investigation, but even for her contradiction and confusion of her utterances.

This witness was Dr. Bowen. He lives diagonally opposite the Borden house in Second street, Fall River, and it was he for whom Lizzie first sent when she discovered or saw fit to announce the murder of her father. Dr. Bowen testified that during the time she was giving her testimony at the coroner's inquest and at the preliminary hearing, Lizzie was under the influence of morphine, which he, Dr. Bowen, had administered to calm her nerves and enable her to sustain herself under the terrible strain.[8]

The doctor further testified that to a person not used to taking morphine its effect would be to cause confusion of memory and hallucinations.

SHE ALMOST FAINTS AGAIN

That this benumbed condition, if it existed then, does not exist now Lizzie Borden again showed by her appearance and movements during the testimony today. Much of this testimony was the most trying she has had to hear. Mrs. Churchill told with a greater intelligence and minuteness of detail all the events of that morning of the blood and slaughter than any witness who has testified before.

That any innocent woman, reared as Lizzie Borden had been

reared, could go over again in her mind the hideous scenes of that awful afternoon as Lizzie must have gone over then while Mrs. Churchill, in a clear, distinct voice was relating the events as they came under her observation and not betray any feeling whatever, is next to incredible.

That Lizzie Borden has an astounding command over her nerves she has maintained with sufficient emphasis; but she has also shown that there is a point where even her nerves give way under the strain. She fainted dead away when the axes, hatchets, the skulls and the photographs of the ghastly dead bodies were produced at the opening of the case for the Commonwealth. Again she visibly quailed during Mrs. Churchill's testimony, and when the sickening, blood-soaked handkerchief was produced she shrank and turned her head away from the sight of it.

She turned so pale, indeed, and for a moment had so collapsed and sinking an appearance that those who were watching her held their breath, expecting every moment that the fainting episode of the day before yesterday would be repeated.

INNOCENCE OR GUILT, WHICH?

All that Miss Borden has done or said is equally consistent with the theory of innocence or the theory of guilt. This is most strikingly illustrated in that worst of all things against her, the burning of the dress. A woman accused of a double murder of such a character that she must have been splattered and splashed with blood from head to foot when she did the deed burns up a dress which corresponds to one the witnesses describe as having been worn by her on the morning of the murder was known to have been committed.

That certainly is a portentous fact, pointing with dreadful emphasis to guilt, but, on the other hand, how would a guilty woman destroy an article which bore evidence that would hang her surely. She would never do it in broad daylight, in the presence of two witnesses, in a room with open windows and with a swarm of detectives prying about the place to discover precisely some such move on the part of a person whom they must necessarily have had under suspicion. Yet that is the way in which

Lizzie Borden destroyed the dress which the Commonwealth is making the pivotal point of its attack upon her.

When, on the following day, one of the witnesses to the destruction of the dress said: "Lizzie, I am afraid that the burning of that dress was the worst thing you could have done," Lizzie replied, "Oh, why did you let me do it? Why did you not stop me?"

THAT PERPLEXING EXCLAMATION

A guilty woman, relying upon the fidelity of a friend to screen her, might have made precisely such a remark as that, provided you can conceive of a guilty woman, then under suspicion, making a public bonfire of an article that she knew was damning evidence against her.

So, too, as an innocent woman so conscious of her innocence that she had no thought of being seriously accused of the crime, might have made precisely the same remark when a friend pointed out to her that she was under suspicion, and under grave suspicion, and when, for the first time, there came a realization of the awful significance of a purely thoughtless and harmless act.

Of course, in their closing appeals, the counsel for the contending sides will make the most of each one of these bewilderingly continuing circumstances, and the task of weighing and deciding the delicate probabilities will fall to the jury. It is a task which, as far as now has been revealed, will be one of the most difficult ever submitted to the judgment of twelve good and true men.

A GLANCE AT THE JURY

At the close of court yesterday afternoon Dr. Bowen had been called, but as it was then 4:50 the court adjourned and he did not appear. The rigid regularity with which the Chief Justice adjourns court at the appointed hour is only equaled by the promptness with which he and his two venerable associates appear on the bench at the time appointed for the evening.

At precisely 8 o'clock this morning the fussy little Sheriff uttered his usual portentous cry, "The Court," and in compliance with the good old custom of which, with so many of the dignified forms of more ceremonious days, still lingers in Massachusetts, everybody rose to his feet and remained standing until the three Judges had taken their seats.

The jury, as their faces became more and more familiar, does not impress one as being at all a massive body of men. Juror Finn fiddles with his mustache most of the time, and Juror Swift, who would somewhat resemble Judge Dewey were he but a little grayer of beard and hair, devotes a good deal of study to the new and particularly shiny patent leather shoes he wears. Juror Cole watches Lizzie Borden both openly and furtively a good deal of the time while important evidence is coming in.

The six jurors on the rear bench are noticeably bronzed, and their hair has the bleached appearance characteristic of men who are much exposed to the sun and wind. The six front jurors are either gray or near gray with the exception of Finn, who runs to baldness and sandyness.

Lizzie Borden came in and sat down as usual, as no women had yet appeared to bear her company in her ordeal. The trial upon her nerves began with the very first witness, Dr. Bowen. He was the first man on the premises after the murder and he described the gashes on Mrs. Borden's head with medical particularity.

Lizzie winced under even this preliminary to the still more sickening evidence to come, and her face assumed a set, pallid cast, which never left it throughout the day.

Dr. Bowen was the Borden family physician, and is ranked among Lizzie's friends. His story of his connection with affairs on the morning of the murder is as follows: "I started on my calls early on Aug. 4 and returned to the house between 11 and half-past. In consequence of what Mrs. Bowen said, I went to the Borden house and entered by the side door. There I met Mrs. Churchill.

"I said, 'Lizzie, what is the matter?' 'Father has been stabbed and killed,' she replied. I asked where he was and she said he was in the sitting-room. I went to the dining room and thence to the sitting-room. I saw the form of Mr. Borden on the sofa or lounge at the left of the sitting-room door.

"On inspection I found the face badly cut, probably with a

sharp instrument, and covered with blood. I glanced around the room, but nothing showed a disturbance of furniture. I went to the sitting-room followed by Lizzie. I asked if she had seen anybody. She said, 'No.' I asked where she was at the time. She said 'in the barn.' She said she was afraid her father had had some trouble with some man.

THAT NOTE FROM A SICK FRIEND

"Bridget took the key to Mrs. Borden's room to get a sheet, which she soon brought. Lizzie asked me to telegraph her sister, Emma, and I left the house. Before that I asked where Mrs. Borden was and was told she had received a note from a sick friend and had gone to visit her.

"On my return from the telegraph office I went to the kitchen and met Mrs. Churchill. She said 'I have found Mrs. Borden in the room upstairs.' I went up, and looking over the bed I saw the prostrate body of Mrs. Borden. I placed my hand on her head and found a wound there. She was dead. I never told anybody she died of fright."

LIZZIE'S DRESS ON THAT DAY

At the conclusion of this testimony, Mr. Moody, who was examining Dr. Bowen, approached the vital and delicate matter of the dress Lizzie wore on the morning and afternoon of the murder. The pink wrapper which is referred to in his testimony on this point came out in evidence later on. Miss Russell, when she gave her testimony, said that early in the afternoon Lizzie changed the gown she had worn in the morning for a wrapper, the general tone of which was pink.

Q. Did you notice the dress Miss Borden wore in the afternoon? A. I did, it was a pink wrapper.

Q. Can you describe the dress she had on in the morning? A. I cannot.

Q. Did you testify at the inquest that she had on a drab calico—an ordinary morning dress? A. I do not know what the color was. I can only say that it was some unattractive morning dress. I cannot describe a woman's dress.

Q. Would a faded blue appear a drab [color] to your eye?

Mr. Adams objected, and the question was withdrawn. Mr. Moody exhibited the blue calico dress.

Q. Is this the dress Miss Borden had on? A. I cannot answer.

Q. Does it appear to be like it? A. I cannot tell.

Q. Does it appear to be drab to you? (Objected to and withdrawn)

Q. What color do you call that dress? A. I should say it was a dark blue.

SOME POINTS FOR THE DEFENSE

This ended the direct examination, and the witness was turned over to the defense. It was Mr. Adams who conducted the cross-examination, this being the first time he had figured prominently during the trial.

After going over the story of the morning without any particular change or addition, with the exception of the statement that the wooden shutters of the room in which the body of Mrs. Borden was lying were partially closed, which may or may not be of importance, just as the further evidence for the state determines, Mr. Adams brought the witness around to Lizzie and her movements and so led him up to the morphine incident.

The point that the people were working over Lizzie in the kitchen, rubbing her hands and wetting her forehead, has an important bearing. In the testimony that followed Dr. Bowen's the defense came back to it and brought it into prominence. The subsequent witnesses were Mrs. Churchill and Miss Russell, and after both of them had testified to bending closely over Lizzie and ministering to her, they were asked the categorical question if, in this close contact with her, they had noticed any blood on her clothing and both replied positively in the negative.

Dr. Bowen continued his story of his relations to Lizzie that morning as follows:

"When I went downstairs the morning of the murder, after seeing Mrs. Borden's body, I saw Miss Lizzie in the kitchen and they were working over her, rubbing her head, fanning her, etc. I subsequently saw her in the room and gave her a bromo-caffeine to allay her nervous excitement and to quiet her.[9] I left a second dose and subsequently gave another administration during that day.

"I also prescribed for her for nervous distress on Friday, when I directed that she should take morphine, one-eighth of a grain, Friday night. I doubled the dose Saturday and continued on it Sunday, Monday and Tuesday. She had morphine all the time up to her arrest and for a few days after in the station. For several days before and up to the time of her testimony she took morphine constantly. I don't know if she was used to morphine. When morphine is taken in small doses for such purpose it will tend to confuse."

The morphine episode was an entirely new development and was evidently a great surprise to the counsel for the Commonwealth, as a little later on was the production of the bloody pocket-handkerchief to the counsel for the defense. Mr. Moody tried to break the force of it by a re-direct examination, confining himself, however, to the bromo-caffeine and leaving an opening for the jury to be muddled with reference to Lizzie's confused memory as to just when the bromo-caffeine and just when the morphine was taken.

BRIDGET SULLIVAN RECALLED

This closed Dr. Bowen's testimony, and then there was a little movement of surprise in the audience when the name of Bridget Sullivan was called. This is the first time since the beginning of the trial that a witness who has once left the stand has been re-called. It was done because the defense wished to recur once more the important matter of Lizzie's apparel on the morning of the murder, as well as to bring out the facts of the burglary in the Borden house which occurred in broad daylight about a year before the murder, and which showed that it was possible for depredators to get into the house while three or four people were up and about its different rooms and yet to make good their escape and never afterwards be heard from.[10] The burglary testimony, however, was excluded by the ruling of Chief Justice Mason, on the ground that it was too long prior to the murders to be connected with the case.

Gov. Robinson then returned to the subject of Lizzie's manner when she called Bridget downstairs and told her of the murder.[11]

Q. When you came downstairs did Lizzie seem to be agitated? A. She did. She was the most excited I had ever even seen her in my life.

Q. Was she crying? A. No.

Q. Sure? A. No, I know she wasn't.

Q. Didn't you testify at the inquest as follows: "Yes sir, she was crying." A. I don't think I did. I know she was not crying. If I did testify so, it was wrong.

This closed Bridget's testimony, and probably from this time forth this young woman who had been so long before the public will be heard from no more.

MRS. CHURCHILL'S ACCOUNT OF IT

Then Mrs. Adelaide B. Churchill took the stand and said she was forty-eight years old, though she did not look it. She is a plump, motherly looking woman, with a bright, kindly face and an enunciation of her English which shows her to be intelligent.

She told the part she bore in the events of that memorable 4th day of August as follows: "I live in the house next, north of the Borden house. I have known the family twenty years and was on social calling relations. On Aug. 4, I saw Mr. Borden about 9 o'clock standing by the steps. I don't know whether he went in or out. He was on the walk close by the steps on the side towards the barn, standing still.

"I went out about 11 to market. I made purchases and came directly back. I saw Bridget Sullivan going rapidly across the street from Dr. Bowen's. As I looked across at the Borden house I saw Lizzie standing at the screen door. I asked what was the matter. She said: 'Oh! do come over; someone has killed father.'

LIZZIE HAD BEEN IN THE BARN

"When I reached her door she was sitting outside the step and I took hold of her arm and said: 'Where were you?' She said: 'In the barn to get a piece of iron.' I asked where her mother was. She said she had had a note and gone away. She said Dr. Bowen was away and they must have a doctor. I went down Second street to send a man, and when I came back Dr. Bowen was there.

"Lizzie asked Dr. Bowen to send a telegram to Emma. When he was gone Lizzie said she wished someone would find her mother because she thought she heard her come in. Bridget and I went up the stairs part of the way, and when my head came above the level of the floor I saw Mrs. Borden on the floor. I came back. Don't remember whether Lizzie said anything about a noise which made her return from the barn.

"Lizzie had on a dress of light blue and white mixed groundwork with a dark navy diamond blue figure. I don't know how long she had it. I had seen it before."

Gov. Robinson, in his cross-examination, brought out the important point that no matter what dress Lizzie had on there were no blood spots on it.

MINISTRATION TO LIZZIE

Mrs. Churchill went on: "When I came back from going for a doctor Lizzie and I went into the kitchen. She was faint, and when Miss Russell came she fanned her and we gave her something to drink and bathed her head. I did not see any blood on her dress, hands, or face, nor was there any disarrangement of her hair or anything the matter with her shoes. There was nothing whatever unusual about her clothing."

An interesting point touched upon in the cross-examination of Mrs. Churchill was one that has not heretofore been brought out. Gov. Robinson asked her if, when Lizzie lay down on the lounge and when Mrs. Churchill was bathing her head, she saw anything which would lead her to believe that Lizzie had two dresses on. Mrs. Churchill answered positively in the negative.

MISS RUSSELL TAKES THE STAND

Miss Russell was the next witness called. Like nearly everybody else connected with the crime, she wore navy blue. Navy blue, in fact, seems to run through the entire story of the tragedy. Miss Russell wore it. Mrs. Churchill, who preceded her in the witness stand, wore it. The testimony of all the women witnesses is full of it. It appeared in a great rumpled heap in one of Lizzie's gowns on the District Attorney's table, and on a gown of navy blue hangs the vital part of the evidence by which the counsel for the Commonwealth hopes to put a rope around Lizzie Borden's neck.

During all the time Miss Russell was on the stand she never once looked in the direction of Lizzie, who kept her eyes steadily and intensely upon her face. Miss Russell gave her evidence as follows:

"Lizzie Borden visited me on Wednesday evening, Aug. 3. She came alone and stayed until 9 o'clock. Meantime we talked together. Something was said about going to Marion. She said she was going there for vacation and I said 'I'm glad you're going.' I had urged her to go and didn't know until then that she had decided to.

LIZZIE'S PROPHECY

"Lizzie then said: 'I feel that something is hanging over me, I can't tell what it is. It comes over me at different times, no matter where I may be. The other day at the table the girls were all laughing and talking and having a good time, and this feeling came over me and I couldn't join with them. One of them said to me: "Lizzie, why don't you laugh?" But I couldn't.'

"Lizzie said that Mr. and Mrs. Borden had been awfully sick the night before. 'We were all sick,' she said, 'all but Maggie (Bridget).[12] It was something we've eaten; I don't know what. We ate some baker's bread.'

"I asked her if it could be that, but she didn't know and then said she thought the milk was poisoned. I asked her how they got their milk and she said it came in cans. She said they were awfully sick. She heard her father and Mrs. Borden vomiting and stepped to their door and asked if she could help them. They said no. I think she said that Mrs. Borden thought she had been poisoned and was going over to Dr. Bowen's.

Q. Did she tell you anything else? A. I can't recall.

Q. Anything about trouble or tenants or anything of that sort? A. Oh, yes. She said "I feel afraid sometimes that father has got an enemy. He had had so much trouble lately with men who came to see him. One man came and I heard father tell him that he didn't care to lend his property for any such business. The man said he shouldn't think father would care, . . . and father showed him out of the house." Then she said that a man had been seen hanging around the house one night and that the barn had been broken into. "Well, you know that was somebody after pigeons?" I said, and then she told me that the house had been broken into in broad daylight, when Maggie and Emma were both there.

Q. Anything more? A. She said: "I feel as if I wanted to sleep with one eye open half the time for fear that somebody will burn the house down over me." She said this before she spoke of her fears of someone breaking in.

THE BURNING OF THAT DRESS

Miss Russell went on as follows: "Lizzie spoke to me of her father and said: 'I am sometimes afraid someone will do something to him. He is so discourteous to people.' Then she told me how he made her so ashamed of the way he treated Dr. Bowen, and Mrs. Borden had said she thought it too bad, also.

"I was in Mr. and Mrs. Borden's room while the officers were searching for the first time. They found the door locked and pulled forcibly open. Afterwards I noticed it fastened on Lizzie's side by a hook and screweye. This was pulled out. I saw her screwing it again later that day.

"I was at the Borden house most of that fatal day and remained there Thursday night. I did not suggest to Lizzie to change her dress or hear anyone else suggest it. I stayed at the house Thursday, Friday, Saturday and Sunday nights. I got breakfast Sunday morning. Afterwards I left the lower part of the house, and returned before noon.

"I saw Miss Lizzie at the stove with a skirt. Emma said: 'What are you going to do?' She answered, 'I am going to burn it up.' I did not speak. I went out and came in again. Lizzie had a small part of the same garment tearing it. I said, 'I would not be seen doing that, Lizzie.' She made no answer. She stepped back one or two steps.

OFFICERS WERE IN THE HOUSE, TOO

"I don't know as I saw the skirt at that time. Officers were then in the house. In consequence of this I saw Lizzie and Emma in the dining room and said to Lizzie: 'I am afraid it was the worst thing you could do to burn that dress.' She said, 'What made you let me do it?' A search was made for the note. Dr. Bowen asked if Lizzie knew anything about it. She hesitated, and said perhaps it was in the waste paper basket. The dress she burned was a light blue Bedford cord, with a small, dark figure.[13] She got it in the spring. I was there when she was having it made. I never saw it again until the Sunday morning after the murder. I cannot describe exactly the small, dark figure."

In the course of the cross-examination Miss Russell said: "Lizzie told me of her whereabouts when her father was killed. She said she was in the barn, and when she came in she saw her father. I asked her why she went to the barn and she said she went to get tin or iron to fix her screen. I think she asked somebody to find Mrs. Borden. While downstairs I started to loosen Lizzie's dress, thinking she was faint and she said: 'I'm not faint.' I cannot describe the dress she had on. When she went upstairs I went with her and was in her room before her change of dress. No one else was there.

"Saturday I went upstairs, and when I came back Lizzie was at the stove, with the dress skirt. I saw no blood on it. Emma was at the sink and turning, asked what she was going to do. Lizzie said it was covered with paint and she was going to burn it. I said, 'I wouldn't let anybody see me do that, Lizzie.' I went out and didn't see her burn it."

Policeman Allen was put on the stand, and testified to the discovery of the blood-stained handkerchief and to the fact that near the body of Mr. Borden, as it lay on a sofa in the sitting-room, was a table which had books on it. It was only two or three feet away, and had no bloodstains on it.

FINDING OF THE HATCHET

John Fleet, Assistant City Marshal of Fall River, was the last witness. The most important part of his testimony was as to the discovery of the small hatchet with the broken handle, with which the prosecution will attempt to show the crime was committed. The hatchet, he said, was in a box with other odds and ends. It had fine white ashes on the wood and the handle had been newly broken off.

Ex-Gov. Robinson had just begun a sharp cross-examination when the court adjourned for the day.

Source: "Lizzie's Dark Day," *New York World*, June 9, 1893.

"MISS BORDEN'S HOPE"

(1893)

Heavy Blow Dealt the Prosecution
Through Their Own Witnesses

Fleet and Mullaly Squarely Contradict Each Other

It Is Relative to Finding a Missing Hatchet Handle

Mullaly Swears that Fleet Found the Handle in a Box in the
Borden Cellar—Fleet Makes Oath that He Did Not Find the
Handle and that He Never Saw It—The District Attorney
Knew Nothing About the Finding of the Handle and Doesn't
Know Where It Is—The Defense Will Now Probably Try to
Show that the Prosecution Is Based on a Police Conspiracy and
that Lizzie Borden Is the Victim Thereof—Miss Borden Laughs

[SPECIAL TO THE WORLD]
NEW BEDFORD, June 9.—Not a single day of this astonishing Borden murder trial seems destined to pass without something entirely unexpected happening. Today, the fifth since the
trial began, a piece of evidence was brought out, under the mas-
terly cross-examination of Gov. Robinson, which, at one blow
knocked the underpinning entirely out from one of the most important parts of the structure which the counsel for the prosecution have with such labor been trying to rear. To explain clearly
exactly the significance of the prodigious treasure which Gov.
Robinson found in his microscopical [mousings] over the testimony of a witness, it is necessary to go back a little and explain a
pleat or two in the rope which the counsel for the Commonwealth are trying to weave around Lizzie Borden's slender neck.

In the opening of the case for the prosecution District Attorney Moody produced a hatchet with a blade three and one-half inches long, which the Commonwealth has admittedly adopted as the weapon with which the crime was committed. The gashes in the skulls of the victims, Mr. Moody said, were such as could have been made only by a weapon having a sharp edge that was exactly three and one-half inches in length.

Assistant Marshal Hillard was examined at length by the Commonwealth as to his discovery of this hatchet in the cellar of the Borden house. The two other hatchets and the two axes found in the same cellar, District Attorney Moody in so many words left out of consideration so far as the identity of the weapon with which the murders were committed is concerned.

THE SMALL HATCHET

The defense has set out to prove beyond a reasonable doubt that the heads of Mr. and Mrs. Borden were not split open with the small hatchet with a 3 ½-inch edge. Now the peculiarity of this hatchet is that it has no handle and, according to the testimony of the leading Commonwealth witness on this point, had none when it was found. This same witness, furthermore, testified that the handle had been broken off, and newly broken off, and that only the piece of it that fitted into the eye of the hatchet remained, and that that was still in its socket.

He swore distinctly that the broken-off handle was not in the box by the cellar chimney where the hatchet was found; that it was not anywhere near that box; that he had never seen it; that, in fact, it had never been found.

IMPORTANT POINT

The disappearance of this hatchet handle was one of the strong points in the prosecution. They had a theory, and testimony to support it, which brought this disappearance close home to Lizzie Borden and left a strong circumstantial probability that she herself had made away with it, and that she had done away with it, on the very morning of the murders and within a few minutes of the time the last one was committed.

The witness who was relied upon to furnish this testimony is Police Captain Felix Harrington. Capt. Harrington testified with minute details to Dr. Bowen taking off the stove lid in the Borden kitchen on the day of the murders, and shortly after they were committed, and to the things he, Harrington, saw in the stove on that occasion. The one thing he saw to which the counsel for the Commonwealth directed attention was a small cylinder wrapped in paper which lay where it had not burned. This cylinder was about 12 inches long and about 1 ½ inches thick.

It was the purpose of the Commonwealth, as outlined in Mr. Moody's opening, to establish that this cylinder was the missing handle of the hatchet which nobody had yet been able to find. It was the intention, in other words, to try and convince the jury that Lizzie Borden, after murdering her father and stepmother with the hatchet, had broken off the handle, thrown the blade into a box in the cellar in which were a lot of old hatchets and other tools, having first cleaned the blade and thrown a sprinkling of ashen dust over it, and that she had then taken the blood-stained handle, wrapped it in paper and thrust it into the kitchen stove to burn up.

With the testimony in support of this all in, Mullaly having sworn to the cylindrical object in the stove and Assistant Marshal Fleet having with great circumstantiality related the discovery of the handleless hatchet in the junk-box in the cellar, and with the point of the absolute disappearance of the hatchet handle established with great clearness, the counsel for the Commonwealth summoned to the witness-stand as a clincher to all this Michael Mullaly.

THE HANDLE FOUND

On cross-examination he distinctly swore that the handle to the hatchet was found; that he and the assistant marshal found it when they found the hatchet itself, and, as if that were not crushing enough, that they found it in the box with the head of the hatchet itself.

The witness had seen the marshal take the hatchet blade out of the box. There was a piece of the handle in the eye of the blade; it looked as though it had been freshly broken off. The hatchet was covered by ashen dust.

Even Gov. Robinson looked indifferent, as though he expected little when he asked:

"Nothing else was taken out of the box while you were there?"

"Nothing but the hatchet and the handle that had been broken from it," said the witness unconcernedly.

"Oh, just the handle of the hatchet; nothing but that?" remarked Gov. Robinson.

"That's all," replied the witness. "We tried it on the broken part and it fitted, but not exactly."

District Attorneys Knowlton and Moody looked startled, Mr. Adams and Mr. Jennings, of counsel, seemed fairly quivering from excitement.

Miss Borden leaned over and asked Mr. Adams, in an eager whisper: "What is it? Tell me about it!"

"Why," said Mr. Adams eagerly, "it is the hatchet handle. He has testified that they found the hatchet handle when they found the hatchet."

"And what does that mean?" asked the young woman. "Is it in my favor or is it against me?"

Nothing could more clearly show how far her mind was from what was going on than this question. Mr. Adams marveled at her obliviousness in not seeing what obviously was such a savage blow at the case the Commonwealth is trying so hard to make out. He explained to her what it all meant, and from that time on her eyes were bright with excitement as the dramatic episode proceeded to its climax.

"Oh" repeated Gov. Robinson, "you just found the handle to the hatchet; nothing but that. Where is that handle?" "I don't know!" replied the witness.

"Did you see it after that?" "No."

"How long was it?" "It was a little shorter than the handle of the one you hold in your hand," replied Mullaly calmly and still in blissful unconsciousness that he had revealed anything of importance.

The hatchet the witness referred to was one of the two that had been found in the cellar near the chopping block, and which it is assumed to have nothing entirely to do with the murders. Gov. Robinson asked: "Who took the handle out of the box?" "Mr. Fleet," answered Mullaly. "Mr. Fleet took it out and put it in again. I am quite certain about this. I don't know where the handle is now."

"Did you ever happen to mention this little circumstance to anybody?" asked the Governor, placidly. "No, sir, I don't think I ever did. I am sure I never did."

"Does the District Attorney know about it?" "I am sure I don't know," replied Mullaly.

NEWS TO THE COMMONWEALTH

Here Mr. Knowlton got to his feet and said: "We have not got the handle. I do not know anything about it. This is the first I ever heard of it. We are perfectly willing that an officer be appointed to go to Fall River and look for it."

"No," said Gov. Robinson; "we will not at the present go into that."

"I only speak in the interest of justice," said Mr. Knowlton.

"I don't want to seek justice in that particular way," dryly replied the Governor. "We will call Assistant Marshal Fleet. Witness, do not leave the room; remain where you are."

Assistant Marshal Fleet, who had been recalled, was down in the witness room below, and it was very desirable that nobody should have an opportunity to give him a hint of the fact that one of his subordinates had sworn directly the opposite to what he had sworn to but a few moments before.

A WITNESS IN A PICKLE

Fleet reached the witness stand entirely innocent of what was in store for him. At this juncture Mr. Moody made a last desperate effort to head off or at least modify the impending disaster. He claimed the witness as his own and denied the right of the defense to question him first. The Chief Justice denied the right.

"Mr. Fleet, will you please state what you found in the box by the chimney in the cellar?"

"There were some other tools besides the hatchet. I don't remember just what they were," replied the witness. Here the Governor picked up the hatchet and holding it out towards Fleet asks: "Was this what you found?" "Yes," said the witness, glancing at the hatchet.

"Who was with you when you found it?" "Mr. Mullaly."

"This small piece in the eye," said the Governor, holding the hatchet-blade up between the thumb and forefinger of his right hand, and touching the bit of wood with the index finger of the left, "this small piece in the eye has been driven out since then, has it not?" "Yes, sir."

"That was all there was in the box except the tools which you did not take out?" "Yes sir."

"You have no doubt of this?" "No, sir."

"You did not see any handle to the hatchet?" "No, sir."

"The handle to the hatchet was not in the box?" "No, sir."

"There was no handle to the hatchet in the box or anywhere near it?" "No, sir."

"You are quite sure about this?" "Yes, sir; I am quite sure of it."

"That is all."

The significance of this event in the trial, for it is an event, is not merely that it destroys a large section of the foundation on which the case for the Commonwealth rests. It goes even further than that. It not only makes two of the Commonwealth's most important witnesses contradict themselves, but it furnishes a formidable amount of ammunition for the defense in still another direction.

WAS IT A POLICE CONSPIRACY?

It is almost certain that the defense will ring all the changes on the theory that the case against Miss Borden is a police conspiracy; that, the Fall River police, utterly baffled, felt that they must arrest somebody, and if possible hang somebody, and that this unfortunate girl was the only one they could lay their hands upon. Unless the Commonwealth can in some way offset this crushing blow, it is interesting to imagine the dramatic force with which Gov. Robinson in his closing address for the prisoner will demand to know what has become of that missing hatchet handle. That he will leave little doubt in some, at least, of his hearers' minds that the police have made way with it because its disappearance was necessary to their case will hardly be questioned by those who know this remarkable lawyer's formidable power before a jury. This closed the one great central event of the day.

Beyond this the testimony that went before and came after was little more than a repetition of what had been told over and over again.

The pale-faced prisoner had to hear a more detailed description of the scene in the house on the morning of the butchery, and as of yesterday she had evidently tried to exert all her self-command to control her nerves. She grew paler, lowered her eyes and, as the ghastly details went on, raised a black gloved hand and held it to her face, half concealing it from view.

HE KNEW HOW SHE WAS DRESSED

There has been so much about navy blue and Bedford cord and calico and cambric[1] and basques,[2] which Gov. Robinson always calls "blouses," in this case that it has been quite bewildering to all save the women present. But Policeman Harrington showed himself to be a real master in all the most abysmal depths of millinery mysteries. When he was asked the old question as to what Lizzie Borden had on the afternoon of the day of the murder he reeled off a string of gores[3] and cut-biases[4] and demi-trains[5] and bell-skirts,[6] trimmed with an array of edgings and puffs and trills and whatnot, until the women in the courtroom looked at him in open-mouthed amazement, and poor Gov. Robinson, who several times evidently has been in a state bordering upon menial unbalance over the millinery intricacies of the testimony, fairly looked as though his brain were reeling.

"What," he asked faintly when the torment ceased, "was your occupation before you were a policeman? Were you a dress-maker?"

Even the grim judges on the bench looked at this as though a smile were within the remote possibilities of life, and the sad face of Lizzie Borden, which had been relaxing gradually as she looked at her lawyer in his wild-eyed bewilderment under the avalanche, now broke into a laugh, and with her handkerchief pressed to her face her shoulders shook for a moment with merriment.

Miss White is the official stenographer who took the testimony of Lizzie Borden at the Fall River inquest. The Commonwealth sought to introduce this testimony from the transcript of Miss White's stenographic notes. The defense objected on the ground that it amounted to compelling a defendant on trial for her life to testify against herself.

The question raised is, whether the testimony of a person who was forced to give evidence at a coroner's inquest can be introduced against that person after she or he has been indicted for the murder of the person or persons on whose death the coroner's inquest was held. Miss Borden was not only forced to testify at the inquest, but was refused the presence of a counsel unless she would plead to the charge of murdering her father and stepmother, on which charge she virtually was under arrest at the time.

The Commonwealth now endeavors to introduce the testimony she then gave while under the influence of morphine, as Dr. Bowen has sworn, and when with no counsel to protect her rights, she was badly brow-beaten, as the stenographers' report of the inquest shows.

It is in this testimony that occur the alleged contradictions and variations from this account of her movements which she gave in the terrible agitation immediately following the making public of the murders.

The Chief Justice at 3:30 this afternoon, when this point was raised, adjourned court until tomorrow.

Source: "Miss Borden's Hope," *New York World*, June 10, 1893.

"THIS IS THE REAL LIZZIE BORDEN"

(1893)

A Pen Picture and Character Study of the Most Interesting Woman of the Week

NOT THE STOLID, SPHINX-LIKE CREATURE THAT SHE HAS BEEN REPRESENTED

Fully Conscious of the Horror of her Position, but Bearing Herself with a Quiet Dignity Which All Observers Acknowledge—How She Looks, Dresses and Acts in the Courtroom—Her Tell-Tale Feet and Sturdy Little Fan Which Is Her Best Friend—Stories That Are Told of Her by the Women of Fall River and New Bedford—That Exciting Tale of Lizzie and the Cat—The Feminine Contingent at the Trial— The Prisoner's Daily Life and Her Plans for the Future in Case She Is Acquitted

There are two Lizzie Bordens.

One of them is the very real and very wretched woman who is now on trial for her life in the little courthouse at New Bedford, Mass. The other is a journalistic creation, skillfully built up by correspondents and persistently dangled before the eyes of the American people, until it has come to be regarded as a genuine personality. This last creature is a human sphinx, a thing without heart or soul; it is large and coarse and heavy; it committed a ghastly double murder in Fall River last August and it is now stolidly awaiting the result of a trial for that crime. It deserves no sympathy and receives none. This is the Lizzie Borden of the press.

As the Commonwealth of Massachusetts has already spent two weeks in an earnest but abortive effort to convict the accused woman of this crime, and as at this time her acquittal seems to be a foregone conclusion, it may be interesting to take a look at the real Lizzie Borden.[1] She will be shown here exactly as she appeared to the writer, who spent two days of the past week in a close study of her face, manner and character, sitting within touch of her while her trial was going on.

NOT AN AMAZON, AT LEAST

This New England woman, who is legally accused of the most brutal murders of the nineteenth century, is five feet three inches in height and weighs about 130 pounds. From the top of her head to the broad, sensible soles of her French kid boots she is a gentlewoman.[2] Even those who are most anxious to see her hanged (and they shall be referred to at length hereafter) admit that she is a "lady," and that her manner, under these very trying circumstances, is one not of indifference or bravado but of quiet dignity which is impressive.

Lizzie Borden has a very plain face. Her complexion is too colorless and pasty, her eyes are too light and china-like a blue. The eyebrows are long, heavy and triangularly arched. The forehead is low but broad, and it is pleasant to notice that the young woman still retains enough interest in life to curl her front hair. The bangs are evidently curled with a hot iron. If the heat of the morning session removes the pleasing effect, Miss Lizzie curls them again during the noon recess. The hair itself is of an indefinite shade of brown, and is worn in an old-fashioned French twist so popular ten or fifteen years ago.[3] Where this twist ends there is a really pretty curve at the nape of the neck, and the little tendrils of hair about it emphasized one of this woman's three attractive points. The other two are her hands and feet.

Returning to the hair, it will be noticed that it is kept beautifully clean and well brushed. Many women who consider themselves immaculately neat would find food for reflection in Miss Borden's hair, and, in fact, in her whole appearance. She is the best-dressed woman in the courtroom. She has an Irish nose, small and slightly tip-tilted; her ears are large and not quite close enough to the head.[4] Above them there are a few scolding locks, too short for the grasp of the curling iron.[5] Her chin and jaw are heavy, and if the Commonwealth of Massachusetts allows her time enough she will probably have another chin by and by; there is an indication of it now. But all these features pale into significance beside her mouth. It is by no means pretty, but there is strength in it and character, and just now there is infinite pathos.

LIZZIE BORDEN'S MOUTH

In shape it is like a crescent, with the ends pointing downward. At first glance the lips seem thin, but this is caused by the narrowness of their light and unhealthy pink border. When she speaks, her lower jaw drops in a peculiar way, and you can see that beyond that border the lips are colorless and heavy. The mouth looks best in repose. The nervous tension of the woman is shown by a frequent moistening of the lips with her tongue. The teeth are of medium size, and are well kept. The owner of them has called in the dentist when necessary, and he has done his duty. There are several conspicuous fillings in front, and two or three on the side, which would hardly be noticed without a close examination. The expression of Lizzie Borden's face is one of the saddest that can be imagined. It seems to hope for and ask for nothing. Somewhere about here is a cut of the mouth, which is photographic in its accuracy.[6] A careful study of it will repay the student of physiognomy.[7] In figure Miss Borden is short, but plump, with good-sized hips, and the rather heavy gait which usually accompanies such a build.

THOSE ELOQUENT FEET

Her feet are small, and exceedingly well shod. She holds in contempt such frivolities as patent leather and high heels; in place of these she wears soft, French kid, buttoned boots, with good sensible soles, broad toes, and low heels. These soles she trustfully presents to the spectators during a large portion of each day. She is evidently not used to being in front of a number of observant persons, for, as soon as she is seated, she hooks the heel of her right shoe over the lower rung of her chair and passes the instep of her left foot over the natural bridge thus formed. This shows those behind her that she wears black stockings and a white skirt with an embroidered flounce. It also indicates that she is ready for whatever may come. When the proceedings grow interesting, she changes the position of her feet for several others, each of which indicates exactly her mental attitude at the time it is made. When the prosecution is demonstrating with skulls and hatchets just how the murders were committed, the prisoner sits forward in her chair, and rests on the extreme tips of her toes. When Mr. Adams or ex-Gov. Robinson ties a witness up into a hard knot, she crosses her feet in a comfortable position and rests. Later on she returns to the first position. All this friction is rather hard on the buttons of the boots, but it will be noticed that the button which hangs on its head in a dejected manner during the morning session is proudly and firmly in its place in the afternoon. These movements of Miss Borden's eloquent feet have scraped almost all the paint from the rungs of the chair which she occupies.

THE BEST DRESSED WOMAN IN COURT

When she entered the courtroom, at five minutes of nine, last Monday morning, a profound sensation was created by the discovery that she wore a new dress. The descriptions of this, sent out during the week, have ranged from black calico to farmer's satin.[8] The material is really a black crepe with a narrow silk stripe.[9] The costume is made in the prevailing style, with puffed sleeves and haircloth lining in the skirt.[10] About the bottom of the skirt is a deep flounce of black lace, edged with a narrow black jet trimming. This same lace and jet appears on the waist— the former in a cape effect over the shoulders, the jet forming a V in the front and back of the bodice. There is no collar except that of the goods, and it is fastened in front by a small gold bar pin. The sleeves are puffed to the elbow, and tight-fitting from there to the wrist, where a cuff is formed of two bands of the jet about two and a half inches apart. The hat worn with this gown is a round black straw, turned up at the back, caught with a small rosette of blue-gray velvet ribbon, and faced with narrow velvet ribbon of the same shade. A small blue-gray pompon stands erect on the top and back of it is a black lace butterfly.[11]

These details may seem trivial, but they were of intense interest to the women of the courtroom, whose evident suffering when they could not get a good view was a very touching sight.

THOSE INEVITABLE BLACK GLOVES

Much has been said about the inevitable black gloves worn by Lizzie Borden, no matter how warm the day. It cannot be that they are meant to conceal the hand, for that, judging from its appearance in the glove, is small and very well shaped. After this long confinement it should be soft and white. There seems to be no good reason why the eager spectators should be deprived of the sight of it.

When she enters court the prisoner invariably carries a white handkerchief, a smelling bottle and a black fan. This fan deserves attention for, next to the Sheriff and Lizzie Borden herself, it is the most important thing in the room. To the lonely woman at the bar it takes the place of the sister and the friends who should be with her. It is a sturdy little fan or it could never stand the pulling, wrenching and twisting it receives from its owner, whose nervousness finds a partial vent in this way. In the years to come, if she is acquitted, Lizzie Borden may suddenly run across that fan in the depths of some forgotten trunk. If she ever does it cannot fail to bring these June days of 1893 back to her with infinitely greater vividness than any written record or spoken reminder could do. She will never be able to look upon it quite unmoved. The framework is of carved black wood and the material of black satin. On one side of this satin is painted a number of white daisies, faded now, where the owner's damp face has rested against them. The satin is creased here and there, and one or two large spots give mute testimony of last Monday's tears, the first tears the prisoner shed in public.

WHERE THE FAN COMES IN

But these do not indicate the fan's most important functions. When bloody handkerchiefs and ghastly photographs are waved in the air by the prosecuting attorneys, when the rattle of bones is mingled with the clash of hatchets, and when some expert learnedly discourses on the fifty-eight blood spots on some particular piece of furniture—in other words, when the situation would be unendurable to any woman, be she innocent or guilty, the fan is unfurled, the prisoner's eyes rest on its edges, its sides close around her face, and for a blessed half hour the courtroom is shut out. This is Lizzie Borden's favorite attitude, and no observant visitor can fail to understand just what it means.

Picture yourself in a small courtroom, longer than it is wide, packed to suffocation and receiving the hot air and blazing sunshine through four large open windows on the north and south sides. Up in front at the east end sit the Judges, three wise and venerable-looking men. To their left in two long, wooden benches, are the jurymen—typical New Englanders, every one of them. To the right of the Judges, directly opposite the jury, and occupying the two benches corresponding with theirs, sit two rows of New Bedford women, who form a sort of self-constituted jury. These women attend the trial every day, never missing a session. Almost everyone is firmly convinced of Lizzie Borden's guilt.

They have tried and condemned her, and it will probably be a sore disappointment to them to miss seeing her hanged. Their antagonistic influence can be distinctly felt. They sit and look at her with ghoulish eyes, and they have openly exulted with the prosecution on the rare occasions when a point has seemed to be scored. Immediately in front of the Judges and between these two juries is the bar. Here sit Miss Borden's lawyers—ex-Gov. Robinson, a typical New England lawyer of the old school; Mr. Adams, handsome, polished and self-possessed; Mr. Jennings, small, nervous and abnormally active when the examination of skulls and blood spots is in order.

These three men are massed together on the right, with the prisoner just behind them, where she can speak to one or all. On the left are her formidable antagonists, District Attorney Knowlton and his assistant, Mr. Moody. Mr. Knowlton is an exceedingly able man, but he is not beautiful. He looks like a bulldog with a beard, and Mr. Moody like a small and active terrier who sees a rat in the immediate neighborhood. Clustered around these two gentlemen are their friends and admirers, enthusiastic and in great numbers. There are no friends and admirers near Miss Borden. Surely no woman who has not been proved a criminal ever stood in so wretchedly lonely a position. Her sister, Emma, who would naturally be with her, is excluded from the courtroom because she is one of the witnesses. Other friends who might have come forward have been disposed of in the same effective fashion. Perhaps the Rev. Dr. Jubb should not be forgotten. The Rev. Dr. Jubb is the pastor of the Borden family. He has been a faithful attendant at the trial since its beginning, always sitting near the prisoner. But no one can watch Mr. Jubb's expansive smile or listen to his artless prattle without suspecting that he finds in this case a wonderfully interesting break in the monotony of a country clergyman's life. Mr. Jubb is not sacrificing himself.

NOW FOR THE WOMEN

Behind the prisoner is a wooden railing. Behind and around that railing are the newspaper correspondents. Back of them, filling every available inch of space and banked against the walls like an exhibit of poppies and dahlias at the flower show, sit the wives and mothers and maiden ladies of Fall River and New Bedford. These women form one of the most interesting exhibits in the case. Untrammeled by logic and unmoved by sympathy, they judge and gloat. They wear sailor hats and russet-leather shoes and brilliant red and pink and blue blouses. It is said in New Bedford that ex-Gov. Robinson calls every feminine garment a blouse, regardless of its appearance or use. The ex-Governor's mistake is entirely justifiable and natural. He has seen nothing else in the town. He gets a foreshortened view of those blouses, and that is all; if there are other garments worn he has to take them on trust.

The New England type of woman naturally predominates. It is an angular and bony type, whose hollow-chestedness cannot be concealed even by the brilliant blouse waists it affects. The eyes are cold, the features sharp, the hands and feet formed on a large and generous scale. It moves with a masculine stride and wears an air of determination which has overcome many a blue-coated and brass-buttoned official during the past two weeks. The patience of these New England women is shown by the fact that they congregate outside the courthouse two hours before the doors open, sustaining themselves during the interval with ginger snaps and more or less edifying conversation. In this crowd you can hear the most marvelous tales about the prisoner. There are new ones every day or two, and the bloodiest and the most ghastly is the best. The person who evolves them should come to New York and draw ten thousand dollars a year on the staff of a Chimney Corner Companion.[12]

THE STORY OF LIZZIE AND HER PET

The favorite story last Tuesday had to do with a cat—Miss Borden's cat. The animal was fond of Lizzie and Lizzie had betrayed some fondness for the animal. But one day, two or three years ago, the cat's attention became oppressive. It jumped into her lap while she was sewing and, being put down, it returned and then returned again. Lizzie Borden, so the story goes, laid her sewing aside with much deliberation, seized her pet by the nape of the neck, took it down cellar, selected a large, bright, shining axe and solemnly chopped off that cat's head. The blood spurted forth in brilliant streams. Lizzie gazed upon her work with satisfaction and dropped the headless body with the remark, "There, that beast won't bother me any more." Nobody would be authority for this story; everybody had heard it from somebody else. But it went the rounds all day long, and there was more blood with a sharper axe and more blows every time it was told. Towards evening the story had grown to such dimensions that the cat had been chopped to mincemeat, and Miss Borden was looking around for something larger.

THAT FUNEREAL COUPE

Re-enforced by several hundred additional women and children, the crowd of the morning congregates at the side-door of the Courthouse to see the prisoner enter her cab when leaving the courthouse at night. Much skill has been shown in making this vehicle as funereal-looking an object as could be found in a long search. It is a black cab, with heavy black curtains, which are always drawn over the windows. The horse is a black horse, and the lanterns at the sides have been enveloped in black cloth. A cadaverous-looking youth on the box adds the crowning touch to this cheerful picture. The cab is driven right up against the lowest of the four stone steps leading from the Courthouse door. Suddenly that door swings open. Preceded by the Sheriff and guarded by stalwart menials Miss Borden appears, takes two or three rapid steps, enters the cab, the deputy follows her, the door is slammed, the cadaverous youth whips the black horse and the black horse makes an earnest effort to trample under foot the surging women about. The women scatter in all directions, dropping their lunch baskets and ginger snaps and babies, but never for one instant removing their eyes from that little cab. They would rather be run over then miss seeing it whisk round the corner.

Here and there in this feminine contingent you may find a woman who remarks frankly that she "dunno" whether Lizzie Borden is guilty or innocent. She is a rare bird. A careful and exhaustive search may bring to light another woman who "dunno but hope she ain't guilty." That woman deserves pity, for she is an outcast and she is regarded with unmixed scorn by her stronger-minded neighbors.

THE FRIEND IN THE CASE

Miss Alice Russell, the former friend of Lizzie Borden, has figured so conspicuously in this case that a few words concerning her may not be out of place. She very obligingly appeared in New Bedford last Monday, and the writer was able to look at her with much interest and to form an opinion as to the character of this remarkable woman. The newspaper descriptions of Miss Russell have been much more accurate than those of the prisoner. In the years gone by the former was called "the belle of Fall River." She still retains a trace of her beauty, although her extreme angularity, nervousness and peculiar expression offset any favorable impression made by other features. She wears a blouse, of course, and a blue serge skirt with three rows of silk braid around the bottom. She scorns crinoline or haircloth, and this skirt flaps mournfully in the breeze. Over the blouse she wears a short jacket, which it would be an excellent idea for her to discard. It adds to her height and thinness. She grasps a small black bag with a firmness which indicates that it contains her return ticket to Fall River, and that she does not propose to lose it through any carelessness of her own. Her face is thin, her complexion and teeth good, her eyes deep-set and brilliant. She looks as if she were the victim of a New England conscience—the sort of conscience which insists upon its owner rising in the still watches of the night and walking the floor with it. Miss Russell probably walked the floor with hers for several nights. Then she testified about the burning of that dress, because she thought she ought to. She does not look as if she believed in Miss Borden's guilt, or would willingly and joyously offer testimony against her. She is not a strong-minded woman. If she were in Lizzie Borden's position she would probably utter a loud shriek and go mad.

THE "FALL RIVER SPHINX" A MYTH

It is time to touch upon the fact that Lizzie Borden herself is not the cool, stolid, sphinx-like woman which she has been represented to be. A close study of her will convince any intelligent person that she is a terrified woman, entirely conscious of the horror of her position, but bearing herself with the dignity which is her own, and with the sturdy spirit which she inherited from old Andrew Borden. The moistening of the lips, the twisting of the fan and feet, and, above all, last Monday's collapse in the courtroom proved this. If that decision of the Judges concerning her own forced testimony had been adverse, Lizzie Borden would not have cried. As it was, she did not cry for joy, as has been represented. She cried because she was touched by the fairness and justice of the decision. She has not had so much to do with fairness and justice that she can remain unmoved when they come her way. She will shed more tears during this trial, and the women who watched the last with such satisfaction and interest will see them. Lizzie Borden is on the verge of collapse. This is on the authority of one of the medical experts who testified last week. "That woman," said he, privately, to the writer, "is half dead now. She cannot hold out much longer." All the indications are that she will collapse during ex-Gov. Robinson's final plea in her behalf. It will be an eloquent plea, and it will put before the jury and the public for the first time the woman's real position in this case. She will be more than human if she can listen to it unmoved.

HER DAILY ROUTINE

The daily life of Lizzie Borden away from the courtroom is naturally a monotonous one. She rises at 6:30, bathes, dresses and breakfasts at 8. She is an omnivorous reader, and she spends every odd moment deep in some of the books with which her lawyers keep her supplied. She has read all of Scott, Thackeray, and Dickens since her imprisonment.[13] She prefers Dickens. Last Monday Gov. Robinson brought her three new summer novels, which she has been reading this week. At noon she has time for nothing but dinner and the necessary attention to bangs and shoe buttons. Immediately upon her return from the courtroom at 5 o'clock, she takes a second bath, eats "supper," as the New Bedford evening meal is called, and reads until bedtime. This with her is 10 o'clock. Whether she sleeps well no one knows. So utterly alone and apparently friendless is this woman that any inquiry as to her health is met by the Warden's vague statement that she "eats fairly well" or "hasn't eaten much today." From this one must reason. She herself never says whether she feels well or ill.

IN CASE SHE IS ACQUITTED

Lizzie Borden's plans for the future, always assuming that she is to be acquitted, are discussed with a great deal of interest, particularly by the men. It should have been stated before that the great majority of the men who have followed the trial are firm believers in her innocence. She cannot live in Fall River, for events have demonstrated that she has few friends there. To the end of her life many people will believe her guilty of this crime. Those who know say that she will go away and begin life anew in a strange country and under a new name. She will be a rich woman. Old Andrew Borden left almost $500,000 and no will. The money will be equally divided between his two daughters and it may be assumed that even after she has paid for the expenses of this trial which the Commonwealth of Massachusetts has deemed necessary, she will have enough to live upon. She and her sister, Emma, will probably take this money and go to Europe, where their chief object in life for the next few years should be to forget the circumstances under which it came to them.

Source: "This Is the Real Lizzie Borden," *New York World*, June 18, 1893.

"THE NEWSPAPER WOMAN'S STORY"

(1893)

When Max O'Rell first visited this country and turned the light of his kindly optimism on our people and institutions, he was good enough to approve of some of them.[1] It has been pleasant to notice that he found promise even in the American press, which does not usually appeal to European literary gentlemen who come to our shores in search of material. Max O'Rell paid special tribute to our reporters, and he was probably the first distinguished foreigner to look with wholly admiring eyes upon American newspaper women. He did not write of them at any length, but he lost no social opportunity of assuring them of his distinguished consideration, and of his belief in the possibilities within them. Even a verbal recognition of these possibilities, coming from such a source and at such a time, was highly gratifying to the newspaper women, whose ears were not attuned to such sweet sounds. Toleration, not commendation, was all they dared hope for, and it is very probable that Monsieur Blouet's delicate encouragement, long since forgotten by him perhaps, sustained many of them at a time when stimulating influences were badly needed.[2]

For then, as now, women in journalism were inexperienced enough to doubt themselves. They stood at the door of the sanctums, so to speak, but their invitations to enter were not urgent. Notwithstanding many claims to the contrary, they occupy practically the same position today. They are more numerous, and they are further in; but their tenure of office is distinctly open to discussion. If every woman were taken out of the field the newspapers would go to press at the usual hour. That the American editor ignores this fact and maintains his attitude of quiet resignation to the existing order of things, does great credit to his manliness and sense of justice. It behooves his woman assistant to bear carefully in mind the points which he is kind enough to refrain from mentioning. In many instances she does so, for if she is not an incurable amateur she is beginning to understand what is or should be expected of her. She knows that the newspaper woman of the future must lay the foundation of her own work by training up to it, and by familiarizing herself with all the details of the "business," as her male associates have done. Then, and not until then, will her position be assured.

In this respect several of the pioneers in the work set an example which too few of their successors have followed. First of them all was Jennie June, who thirty-seven years ago climbed the dingy steps that led to the editor and fame and "a new field for women." More than ten years later "Middy" Morgan took a desk in the *Times* office, and retained it for almost a quarter of a century. Later still, the *Sun* had Mrs. Beattie in its offices, Margaret Sullivan had risen in Chicago, Kate Field was writing editorials for the New York *Herald*, and half a dozen brilliant free-lances were sending their specials all over the country. These women understood their work thoroughly, and as a natural result they were head and shoulders above their fellow-writers at that time; two or three of them hold the same proud position still.[3] Their eventual successors have been rather slow in arriving, but perhaps they may be found in the group of young journalists who have come forward during the past eight or ten years, and who, as intimated above, are making a way not only for themselves but for those who will follow them. The manner in which they perform this work will settle the woman question, so far as journalism is concerned.

A small proportion of these younger women have already achieved the success which attends ability and hard work. We have acknowledged the comparative rarity of such achievement by loudly calling attention to it, and by publishing columns about the writers in our magazines and out-of-town newspapers, accompanying our tributes by alleged portraits which should go far towards reconciling to her lot the ambitious young woman whose stories are all returned. There are other considerations which should comfort the ambitious young woman, and they will be given here with much frankness and with the deductions to which they seem to lead. Back of this success of which she reads there are often disappointments to be met, humiliations to be borne, and obstacles to be overcome which only the heroines of the sketches can explain—and they, being sensible, will never do so. A number of these obstacles arise from the fact that the workers are women; for the successful journalist is rarely the one who confines herself to so-called "woman's work." There is less of that to be done on the daily newspapers than the average reader supposes, and what there is can be satisfactorily performed by any good man on the staff. So the really capable woman leaves her sex out of the question and writes fashions or police court proceedings with equal facility, but with this difference—that she is welcomed by the modistes, while to this day the police justices are unable to understand why she is in existence.[4] And a lack of appreciation, even from police court justices, is hard to bear. These facts are mentioned here because we have been giving the ideal journalistic life our exclusive attention in the cheerful stories we have sent abroad. There is a vast difference between what has been accomplished and what is claimed. It cannot be pointed out too soon for the benefit of the ambitious girls whose pathetic little letters are filling our editorial waste-baskets.

It has been loosely estimated that there are several thousand newspaper women in this country. In reality there are less than two hundred and fifty. There is a distinction between newspaper writing and writing for the newspapers, and the young lady who "does a little space-work" in the intervals of her social or business engagements was not considered in the compilation of these statistics.[5] The two hundred and fifty writers who have been considered are newspaper women in the best sense of the words. They hold staff positions on journals of good standing, or they have had experience which fits them for such positions; they have learned to recognize news when they hear it, and they know how to present it to the public in the most attractive form; they can judge of its comparative value and the amount of space it should be given in a newspaper; they can edit their own copy if necessary; they know something about a composing-room, and can distinguish between a form and a piece of type; they have learned why it is not a sheer waste of material to write on but one side of their paper; they know that a newspaper office is not a drawing-room, and that they cannot expect drawing-room manners in it; they have learned that the highest compliment an editor can pay his woman associate is to treat her as if she were a man, promptly reprimanding her for a blunder and giving her a word of praise for good work—if he happens to think of it. Last and most important point of all, these women earn their living with their pens. This is the crucial test. Luck, pluck, and influence may keep one afloat for a few months, but the editors of today are not knowingly buying bad copy. If one particular editor be disposed to overlook the charming Miss Blank's little errors of fact and grammar, the copy-readers, the associate editors, and the great power behind the throne will soon throw a search-light upon them which can have but one result. Miss Blank's work must stand on its merits. In no other profession does she have so many and such merciless critics.

All this, of course, applies to woman as a reporter, the field in which she is becoming most prominent, and in which man has, as usual, an advantage over her. Many men who cannot write are making good livings on the daily newspapers. Perhaps they are willing and able to work twenty hours out of the twenty-four— an excellent qualification; perhaps they have sources of information which others lack; perhaps they are "men of ideas," or "have the news instinct," which scents a story long before it lifts its head in the path of the average reporter. In any case they earn their salaries, and you will see them sitting at their desks as the seasons pass and as the official heads around them rise and fall. There are various reasons why a woman cannot take the place of such a man—as yet. She lacks the training, the instinct, the strength. Perhaps, too, she lacks the self-confidence, although that is the journalistic armor which, if she be wise, she will select first and wear on the outside. With self-confidence there are other qualifications which she must possess. That she should have a good education and some worldly experience goes without saying. She will also need tact, a cool head, clear judgment, the ability to think and act quickly, a good understanding of human nature, and above all an up-again-and-take-another spirit which no amount of discouragement can break. She will be tired and disappointed and heart-sick much oftener than even her intimate friends imagine; the good work of one day will be overshadowed by failure on the next, for her record begins anew each morning that she reports for duty, and on that day's work she must stand or fall back. It is the old story of the cat climbing out of the well. Her sex will hinder her one hundred times to once that it helps her; the air-castles she has spent months in erecting may be demolished by a word; her best work will be taken as a matter of course, and anything less than her best as a deliberately planned and personal injury. If at last a combination of these conditions leads the unfortunate woman to lie down, fold her hands over her tired heart, and conduct a funeral over her own remains, ten to one she will be called upon to write a page story; and of course it must be done at once. The true reporter will be able to resurrect that corpse and write that story.

Olive Schreiner emphasizes this point in her study "Was It Right—Was It Wrong?" The heroine, a hysterical young woman, succeeds in making herself and every other character in the tale profoundly wretched.[6] She is thinking of this "with her lips drawn in at the corners," when a messenger enters and announces that she has just ten minutes in which to finish an article on "The Policy of the Australian Colonies in Favor of Protection." "She finished the article," ends Miss Schreiner, admiringly, and the reader, while he sympathizes deeply with the editor who bought it, admires the author's insight into the exigencies of journalistic life.

The necessity of writing a page story in a few hours, when neither mind nor body was prepared for the strain, confronted the writer of this about two years ago, when Carlyle Harris, the medical student, was arrested for the murder of Helen Potts Harris, his wife.[7] The principals were students in New York City, Harris in the College of Physicians and Surgeons, his young wife in the Comstock Finishing School. They had been married secretly, and the secret had been kept for a year. Then circumstances forced the wife to tell her mother, who immediately demanded that a second ceremony be publicly performed. To this Harris at first objected, but finally yielded, and the date of the second ceremony was fixed. One week before this date the young wife died at school, after a few hours' illness, and with symptoms of morphine-poisoning. The newspapers published brief accounts of her sudden death, with the explanation that she had been taking medicine prescribed by Carlyle Harris, a medical student who occasionally visited her. The coroner's jury examined his prescriptions, which called for quinine capsules.[8] The student was exonerated, the girl was buried, and the matter was forgotten by all except a few friends and the mother, whose suspicions, formed at her daughter's coffin, strengthened daily. Six weeks after Helen's death Mrs. Potts came to New York and laid the case before the district attorney. It was suggested that Harris had substituted morphine for the quinine in the capsules. He was arrested—and a page story was in order. At six o'clock in the evening, after a hard day's work, the writer was ordered to prepare this story, and to have it finished by midnight. It was to be complete in every detail, beginning with the first meeting of the young couple and ending with the arrest of Harris that day. On the hypothesis that he was guilty, two columns were to be devoted to speculations as to what his motives could have been. The story was to be rushed into the composing-room as fast as written, and the proofs were to be handled by the managing editor himself. With these general directions, that gentleman went home to dinner, and the writer sat down beside a typewriter operator and began to dictate. Fortunately, she had the facts well in mind, and was interested in the case. She told the story as simply as possible, allowing her readers to shed their own tears, and at half-past twelve the managing editor laid down the last proof with the gracious assurance that it was "all right." The story filled seven and one-half columns in the *World*.

A very different assignment, and one which shows the necessity of strong nerves and good physique as reportorial equipments, was given the writer at another time. The Koch lymph cure was the one topic of interest to the people, and the newspapers teemed with it.[9] In the midst of the excitement one of the editors decided to have a realistic story on the death of a consumptive, as a background for the Koch claims. He therefore ordered the writer to go through the free hospitals, find a victim of consumption, sit down beside that victim's cot, observe every symptom and follow every change until death came, and to write a faithful story of what she had seen. It was not an exhilarating prospect, but she left the office at once, and finally, at six o'clock in the evening, found her case in the Charity Hospital on Blackwell's Island.[10] The physicians and nurses felt reasonably certain that "No. 13, in the phthisis ward, could hardly last until morning."[11]

Into the great unlighted ward the newspaper woman went. It was a very cold December night. By a fortunate chance No. 13's cot was near a window, through which the moonlight streamed. Screens had already been drawn, that the patient might not disturb her forty-seven fellow-inmates of the room, who were also in the last stages of the disease. As the reporter's eyes grew more accustomed to the gloom she could see the outlines of the long cots, and here and there, near her, a head was lifted from the pillow and hollow eyes stared at her curiously. The ruling passion was strong in death. It was seven o'clock when she began her watch in the midst of a silence broken only by the heavy breathing and inarticulate words of her subject and the hourly visits of the nurse, who made the rounds with a lantern. No. 13 died at half-past two in the morning. It had been a long vigil and one not easily forgotten, but the watcher remembers with satisfaction that she assumed the duties of attendant, so far as she was able, and perhaps made easier the end of a life which had evidently known very little human sympathy or tenderness. About one o'clock the dying woman suddenly clutched the reporter's hand, which had been on her pulse, and held it in a death-grip until the end. It could not have been removed without disturbing her, so it was left there, growing stiffer and damper, until it was finally released by the nurse from the dead hand which held it. It was numb to the elbow by that time, and horribly cold and wet.

When the body of No. 13 had been carried away, the reporter's ruling passion asserted itself. Fearing to lose the "atmosphere" of her story if she delayed writing it, she camped out in the corridor between the two phthisis wards and wrote it then and there, fortified by a good lunch which the nurses had kindly placed on her table. She finished the story at dawn, and rowed back across the river in the gray light of a winter morning, filling her lungs with pure air, and discovering, to her discomfort, that she had under-estimated the staying powers of the "atmosphere." It was with her still.

A much more cheerful incident in her experience will, it is hoped, meet the editorial direction that this paper be "personal and reminiscent." She had been sent by *The World* to the Virginia and Tennessee mountains to write special stories about some noted characters of that region. For three weeks she lived on horseback in the heart of these mountains, far out of reach of civilization. She dined exclusively on chicken and cornbread and performed her ablutions in the streams she forded or in the tin basins outside of cabin doors. She was accompanied only by a negro guide. In the daytime she visited the mines and the moon-shiners' camps. At night she slept in the cabins of the mountain-eers if she was near one, or out in the open air if she was not. She was in many of the districts where family feuds flourish, and she met, in the course of her travels, any number of mountain gentle-men who are living in enforced retirement and whose private graveyards are large and lonely. And yet not once in all this time did she receive a word or look which a brother could have re-sented had he been with her. The fact that she was a woman and alone was enough. She owned the mountains and she owned the mountaineers. She visited their cabins, played with their babies, rode with their sons, and gave their wives their first intimation that all dresses need not be made in two pieces. During this trip she spent a day and a night with the family of Rev. Joseph Wells, the "natural orator" of the Virginia mountains. The little one-roomed log cabin was almost one hundred years old, and the old minister had lived there as boy and man without the slightest de-sire for anything different. He had never seen a town or a rail-road, he had never heard a musical instrument played upon. But he had preached among the mountaineers for a quarter of a cen-tury, and, as he modestly confided to the writer, he had "brung a heap o' sinners tuh th' mourner's bench." Lying on the floor that night before the great fireplace, in which one immense log blazed, the old man told the simple story of his life, while the wild-cats screamed in the woods all round the cabin and the November wind whistled through the chinks between the logs. A page story of this had been ordered, so the newspaper woman jotted down in short-hand much of the mountaineer's recital, dialect and all. It was very nearly her undoing; for the speaker came behind her suddenly and glanced over her shoulder. He had laboriously taught himself to read and write a little, but when he saw the strange stenographic characters he was plainly alarmed, and disposed to regard both them and his guest as uncanny. She explained as well as she could, and he continued his story with many misgivings. Long after the family had gone to sleep (children, adults, and dogs all in the one room, according to the necessities of the case and the primitive customs of the locality), the guest, who lay awake listening to wind and forest sounds, heard the host and his wife discussing her in their corner. When the topic of the "strange writin'" came up again the voices fell to awed whispers, and it was evident that the old people were very much disturbed in their minds. She sent them the story when it appeared, and with the assistance of State Senator J. B. F. Mills, of Virginia, who was near Big Stone Gap at the time, the mountain preacher read it. She still cherishes the quaint little letter he wrote to her after the great undertaking was completed. It might have been written by a child, if one judged by the spelling and grammar, but the courtesy and hospitality of the mountaineer breathed in every line. He never mentioned the "strange writin'," but he gave her a most urgent invitation to "come an' live with me an' Betsy" if she ever tired of newspaper work in New York.

That time has not come. It is a peculiarity of the work that its slaves are willing slaves, who would not throw off their shackles if they could. Even the failures, and there are many of them, feel the fascination of the life and cling to it with pathetic determination long after hope has departed. It is for their sake and for the sake of those who may follow them that a glimpse of the dark side has been given here. It may help them; it certainly cannot hurt the fortunate ones on whom the sun of success is shining.

As for the writer, she gratefully acknowledges that she has been treated by the American editor, and by her men and women associates, much better than she deserves.

Source: "The Newspaper Woman's Story," *Lippincott's* (March 1893).

"WHAT IT MEANS TO BE A NEWSPAPER WOMAN"

(1899)

The young woman who wishes to do newspaper work, or, as she might prefer to put it, "enter journalism," should ask herself three questions. Having asked these she should reflect upon them for a long time. If, after a severe self-examination, she can answer them all affirmatively, it will be in order for her to consider the minor details connected with securing a position and holding it after she has secured it. The questions are:

Have I the brains for newspaper work, with the education and mental training which will enable me to attain success in a profession that is so exacting?

Have I the health to withstand the long hours, the nervous strain, the effects of irregular meals, and the frequent attacks of physical and mental exhaustion incidental to the life of the reporter?

Have I the character and dignity which will win the respect of my fellow-workers and hold that respect for all time; can I work among men on the footing of common interest and good-fellowship, with no tears, no flirting, no affairs, no question of sex? This is a question at least as important as the other two.

If the candidate can truthfully answer these questions in the affirmative she may call on an editor and ask him for a place. She should begin in a small city and on a small journal. New York, the Mecca of all newspaper men and women, is not for her. It holds out various inducements to trained writers and newsgatherers. It will give them fame if they deserve it, and money if they are willing to work for it, but it has no place for beginners. At least a year of preliminary work is absolutely necessary, and this can be best obtained in a small office where the various departments work together in harmony, and where the novice can soon gain an all-around knowledge which, later, will be invaluable.

BEST PLACE TO BEGIN NEWSPAPER WORK

If her native city has a newspaper or two she should make her journalistic debut there. Perhaps she knows the editor, or has friends who know him, or possibly she may have written some "pieces" for his paper at an early age. It will be necessary for her to see the editor and convince him that he should give her a trial "on space"—that is, add her to the staff of reporters on his paper, and pay her at space rates for whatever matter of hers he prints. At this point the question of money should be wholly a subordinate one. The privilege of sitting around in the office, of watching the daily routine and methods of experienced writers, of hearing the "shop talk" and absorbing the "atmosphere" is of the greatest value, and will be capital later. The editor who allows the novice reporter to do this is paying her well even if her space amounts to but two dollars a week.

Little by little the young reporter will begin to make herself really useful to her newspaper. She will write society items, club news, personal gossip and woman's columns. She will answer the letters of "Constant Reader," and other inquiries. She will take frequent assignments, and may occasionally help to read the "exchanges." At this point she may be given a desk, and the editorial department and the business office will consult as to the advisability of putting her on a salary. Her hours on a morning newspaper may be from about noon to midnight, subject to changes that meet the exigencies of a newspaper office. She must report to the city editor on her arrival, and await his convenience in the matter of assignments or other work.

Assume that she is finally given a salary of ten dollars a week. She will be expected to take all kinds of assignments, to bring in suggestions for "special stories," and to be available for almost any work that may be required of her. She will also branch out into semi-editorial work under such headings as "What a Woman

Thinks," "The Feminine World," etc. At this point it behooves her to be careful. She may be offered the editorship of a woman's department, and if she accepts it her opportunities for development will be much curtailed.

WHEN SHE GOES TO A GREAT CITY

If she clings to reporter's work, as she should do, she will begin to interview celebrities, get symposiums for the Sunday edition, "do" lectures, art exhibits, flower and cat shows, and take an occasional turn at book reviewing. Eventually her salary may be raised to twelve or fifteen dollars per week. The latter is about the maximum in the smaller cities of the East and West. When this point has been reached, and the ambitious woman reporter feels that she has learned all that the office and the city editor can teach her, she may turn her eyes toward New York or some other of our big cities.

Before packing her trunk it will be well for her to consider carefully the following facts: The advantages of newspaper work in the big cities are obvious; its disadvantages are perhaps not quite so universally realized. She will receive a larger salary in the big city, but the cost of living will be more than twice what it was in the place she is leaving. For instance, in Milwaukee, five dollars a week secured a large, warm, nicely furnished room, with board in a private family, while in a New York boarding-house eight dollars a week will pay for board and a cold tiny hall bedroom up several flights of stairs. For twelve dollars she can get a small but comfortable room on the second or third floor, probably overlooking some exceedingly unattractive back yard. If she pays this latter sum for her board (and the New York newspaper woman averages at least that), she must eat her luncheons downtown, which will cost about two dollars a week more. Her laundry bills will subtract an additional two dollars from her weekly income. She will also discover that she is obliged to eat her dinner downtown several nights each week at her own expense. This item, added to the expenditure for car fare, makes her actual living expenses about twenty dollars a week. I do not know a newspaper woman who has succeeded in living for less than this. If she begins, as she probably will do, on a salary of twenty-five dollars a week, there will be very little margin. She will spend her leisure hours during the first few months sadly comparing her actual outlay with the estimate she had so cheerfully made in her home city, and feeling that in some way she has been deluded and deceived.

BEGINNING HER CAREER IN METROPOLITAN JOURNALISM

If she has no friends nor influence in the big city to which she may go to follow her vocation—New York, for instance—and if her work has not been strong enough to attract special attention, the best thing she can do is to begin as a "free lance"—a term that is applied to the journalist who is attached to no particular paper and who sells her work at space rates wherever she can. The life of a "free lance" is interesting, but precarious. The reporter must have some money in reserve before she dare venture into so uncertain a field. The "free lance" may earn from five to fifty dollars a week. There usually will be a sickening uncertainty as to which of these amounts will be awaiting her. Her work is peculiarly discouraging, for the reason that much of it is lost by careless editors, much of it mellows indefinitely on the composing-room "galleys," and the remainder is often paid for at rates fixed, not by her, but by the various publications to which she contributes—and these pay as little as the law permits.[1] Nevertheless, she is pleasantly independent and usually well content with her lot. If she has a little money, and talent, patience, perseverance and "ideas," she will eventually succeed in gaining a foothold in some office. As a "free lance" she meets many editors and gains knowledge of the special needs of various newspapers, all of which is of value to her. If an editor eventually offers her a place he will either put her on space or give her a small salary in the beginning.

Once fairly placed, the real test of her ability and staying power begins. She will find her position radically different from the one she occupied in her native city. She will miss the courtesy and deference with which her former men associates treated her. It may annoy her to have her editor talk to her with his hat on his head and his feet on his desk; he is apt to do so. He is a busy man and his nerves are worn to shreds. He has no time nor inclination for drawing-room etiquette, and if he ever had instincts in that direction they have been ground out by experience with newspaper women who seemed unappreciative or disdainful of them. He will talk to the newcomer out of the side of his mouth, and make a careful inventory of her appearance and manner out of the corner of his eye. He will give her much more attention for a few days than she dreams she is receiving from him. If she is alert, intelligent, reliable and businesslike he will decide that she is "all right"—his highest praise—and he will treat her thereafter with an abrupt, matter-of-fact courtesy, and at times with a considerateness almost human. He will criticize her sharply when she needs it, and he will work her to death without compunction; but he will also give her an occasional word of praise, and, from start to finish, be thoroughly businesslike in his manner to her. This is the ideal type of editor. No newspaper woman could ask better fortune than to have him as a chief. The type is found in almost every office. However, there is another type one meets at long intervals—the man who, under cloak of his official position, brings a mawkish sentimentality into his intercourse with the women on the staff.[2] Fortunately, he is as rare as he is disagreeable, and it is not worthwhile to consider him.

MUST STAND OR FALL BY
EACH DAY'S WORK

When the young reporter is fairly settled in the field of metropolitan news-getting she may expect a year at least of interesting but exacting, disappointing, nerve-straining work, with very little financial return. She will report to the city editor every morning at eleven o'clock, and she will probably work until after midnight. She will frequently work days and nights on a story that may eventually be given but a "stick" of space (one hundred and sixty words) in the paper, or be even left out entirely. She will discover that her record begins anew with each day's work, and that she must stand or fall by that day's work, not by the successful achievements of last week. She will be forced to do many things that go against the grain, and her soul will be sickened and her heart made heavy by the sin and suffering she will see as she goes her rounds. She must be ready for duty day and night, at all seasons and in all conditions of weather. She must learn to write her stories wherever paper and pencil are available, no matter how great the uproar around her nor how short the time for the work. If she is an "all-around reporter"—as she should strive to be—she must take assignments such as are given to the men on the staff, and she must work them up in the same way. She must ask people questions they do not wish to answer; she must call on men and women who do not wish to receive a reporter. In her professional capacity she must often meet and be pleasant to persons whom she would not recognize in other conditions; she must expect to have "all sorts and conditions of men" try to use her as an advertising medium, and she must learn to disappoint them in the end. She must go to places she would not otherwise visit, see things she would far rather not see, and discuss matters professionally that she would much prefer to leave untouched.

THE NEWSPAPER WOMAN'S DAILY LIFE AND HEALTH

After a year of this work she will find that her space bills have averaged between twenty-five and thirty dollars a week, and that she has not saved a penny. She has, however, a capital of experience, she has the news instinct, she has learned to think and act quickly, and to write her stories without the "feminine touches" so dear to her heart during those peaceful days on her hometown press. She has also an interesting case of nervous dyspepsia, an occasional attack of insomnia, and a nervous system of whose existence she is becoming morbidly conscious.[3] If she is a wise young woman she will pause to reflect at this point, and she will begin her second year of work under modified conditions.

First of all, she will make a rule to eat her meals regularly, whatever the rush may be. She will devote some attention to the selection of these meals, and eat only nourishing, easily digested food. Moreover, she will sadly but firmly abandon the idea of any social life. When her work is done she will rest, dine quietly with a few kindred spirits, or go to a good play. She will insist on eight hours of sleep out of twenty-four. If she does not get this at night she will take it in the morning. And, finally, she will stop worrying. For about this time she begins to realize that the newspaper got on without her very well before she came to it, and that it might probably continue to exist if she were to leave it. She works just as hard as ever, but she regulates her life as much as such a life can be regulated. In fact, the reporter has got her "second wind," as a bright young writer puts it, and the outlook becomes more encouraging.

It cannot too frequently be asserted that the question of health is one of the most important the newspaper woman has to consider. With the possible exception of the trained nurse no other professional woman is subjected to so great a strain—and the nurse has intervals of leisure in which to recuperate. The woman reporter's opportunity for rest is, as a rule, limited to the two weeks' vacation given her each year by her generous employer. Through the remainder of the year she toils day and night, in heat and cold, in rain and sunshine. She is abroad in all kinds of weather, and she often is wholly unprepared for its sudden changes.[4] She travels over the length and breadth of the city in search of the material for her story, and, reaching the office absolutely exhausted and late at night, is commanded by her chief to "make the best thing she ever wrote" of it. All this is physically and nervously exhausting.

WOMAN JOURNALIST'S EARNINGS AND ADVANCEMENT

According to carefully compiled statistics the average newspaper woman breaks down at the end of five years of work. There is no reason why this should be so if she began that work with nerves and body in good condition, and tried to keep them so. Care, common-sense and system will enable her to go on indefinitely if she follows their very simple dictates.

In addition to her news work the reporter probably does "specials" for the Sunday edition. There is no reason why her income should not be thirty-five or forty dollars a week at the end of the second year. After she has worked in New York five years she should be earning at least fifty dollars a week. If she does she is prone to take an apartment in a hotel and spend most of it for living expenses.

As to the brighter side of the picture it may be said that the reporter is in constant touch with interesting phases of life. However hard her work may be, it is rarely monotonous. Each day brings her into contact with different persons and with varying conditions. She meets the brightest men and women of this and other countries and makes friends of many of them. She has an unrivaled opportunity for the study of men, women and human nature. She is using her brains and making a name for herself among her associates. She has opportunities to do much good in a quiet way. If she has ideals (and as a rule she has) it is no harder to live up to them in her profession than in others. Of the so-called "perquisites"[5] of the profession—passes[6] and gifts—the less said the better. The best type of newspaper woman never accepts these.

The lines of the woman editor lie in pleasanter places. She has a fixed salary and it is usually a liberal one. Her hours are less uncertain than those of the reporter, and she has more control over them. She writes hard and incessantly while she is in the office, and she has responsibilities from which the reporter is happily free, but she has, as a rule, more congenial duties, and her opportunities for advancement are better.

The woman editor "reads copy," makes suggestions, "builds heads," helps to "make up" the Sunday and special editions of the paper, reads and passes upon manuscripts, buys stories and pictures, takes charge of symposiums, and does a hundred other things that come before her in the course of the day.[7]

THE NEWSPAPER WOMAN OF THE FUTURE

Touching the sensational reporting formerly done by women, it may be said that such work has had its day. Women no longer go down in diving costumes, nor go up in balloons, nor fall in front of cable cars to test the practical working of the fenders. In justice to the women reporters who did work of that kind, it should be added that many of them—indeed, the majority of them—were good and modest girls, who accepted such assignments under protest, and only because the editor called on them for the work, and their living depended on their acquiescing. With the passing of the sensational specials should be chronicled the decline of the woman's columns and the woman's departments. They, also, have had their day.

To meet those and other changes, the newspaper woman of the twentieth century will be a new type, and much will be expected of her. She will be a well-educated, well-balanced, cool-headed and practical young person, with a body as carefully trained as her mind. She will know more about the English language than do most of her sisters of today, yet not a bit more than she will need to know. The newspaper woman of the future will have passed the experimental stage of her professional work. Concessions to her will be no longer be made, excuses for her no longer accepted. She will be out of the ranks of the amateurs and in line with the professionals. She must stand or fall by the same tests as are given to the man at the desk beside hers in the city room.

Source: "What It Means to be a Newspaper Woman," *Ladies' Home Journal* (January 1899).

THE CITY ROOM AND BEYOND: EARLY NEWSPAPER FICTIONS AND MAGAZINE STORIES

The rapid expansion of periodical culture at the turn of the twentieth century created an insatiable demand for short and serialized fiction, paving the way for Jordan's long career as a novelist and author of magazine stories. Jordan's turn to fiction was motivated in part by economic need. When her father suffered a significant financial setback during the Panic of 1893, she assisted her family by supplementing her salary as a reporter and editor at *The World* with the income she earned selling short stories to mass circulation magazines. Trained to meet newspaper deadlines, Jordan excelled at producing reliably proficient prose on a regular basis. She was adept, too, at plotting, ensuring that her stories built to the inevitable twist that readers had come to expect from popular magazine fiction in this period.

Just as Jordan's newspaper writing employed techniques such as scene development and symbolic detail that are often associated with fiction, her body of fiction is imprinted by her background as a journalist. Her first significant piece of magazine fiction, "Ruth Herrick's Assignment," which was published in *Cosmopolitan* in 1894, features a reporter-heroine, a figure who would become a staple of her work for at least two decades. Set partially in the newsroom of a fictional newspaper, the *Searchlight*, "Ruth Herrick's Assignment" was one of a number of stories that Jordan wrote in the city room of *The World* while waiting for reporters to turn in their copy for her to edit. Her surroundings influenced the content of her fiction and its realistic mode.

"Ruth Herrick's Assignment" became the opening story in Jordan's debut collection of short fiction, *Tales of the City Room*, which was published in 1898 by Scribner's. The book was recognized by reviewers as "the first emotional expression of the woman reporter in modern journalism."[1] As exemplified by the four selections collected here, the stories feature women reporters navigating overlapping worlds of work and romance. Some of these stories, such as "Ruth Herrick's Assignment," focus primarily on the protagonist's professional life. Other stories, like "A Point of Ethics," explore how working women created social and professional networks, forging bonds that transcend the workplace. And others, like "A Romance of the City Room" and "Miss Van Dyke's Best Story," pivot on the often irreconcilable tensions between the New Woman's career aspirations and cultural expectations of marriage and domesticity. In narrating this conflict, Jordan transforms the New Woman into a feminist heroine and sows early seeds of what would become the #MeToo movement well over a century later. Both "A Romance of the City Room" and "Miss Van Dyke's Best Story," for instance, open with male colleagues commenting on the physical appearance and desirability of Jordan's reporter-heroines.

The collection's women characters are united by a shared understanding of how patriarchal culture and gendered violence circumscribe their experiences. At the same time, as a series of thematically linked stories with multiple protagonists, *Tales of the City Room* allowed Jordan to explore different paths for women at the turn of the twentieth century. While some of her heroines find fulfillment in the success of their journalistic careers, others desire more conventional lives centered on heterosexual unions. These fictional stories provided models and guidance for real-life women, including those who aspired to enter the newspaper profession; they functioned as another means of conveying the advice that Jordan offered women in the nonfiction magazine pieces reprinted at the end of the previous section, "The Newspaper Woman's Story" and "What It Means to Be a Newspaper Woman."

The selections included here further demonstrate how the stories Jordan covered as a journalist inspired her fiction. In the short story "In the Case of Hannah Risser," for example, Jordan recycles material from "The Happiest Woman in New York," which was published as part of the newspaper series "True Stories of the News" and took as its subject an impoverished, disabled tenement-dweller named Dora Meyer. When Jordan initially published the fictional version in *Harper's Bazar*, her title character was named Hannah Risser. Republishing the story in the collection *Tales of Destiny*, however, Jordan changed the character's name to *Dora* Risser, transforming her into an amalgam of fact and fiction. The continuity between the fictional character and her real-life, journalistic counterpart suggests the writer's desire to lay bare—rather than disguise—links between her journalism and her fiction.

The male-dominated newspaper office, with its atmosphere of toxic masculinity, contrasts sharply with the homosocial space of the convent, the other setting that appears repeatedly in Jordan's early fiction. Published as magazine stories and collected in *Tales of the Cloister*, Jordan's convent fictions examine Catholic girlhood and the bonds that form between women—whether classmates or teacher and student—in single-sex environments. In these stories, as in the later May Iverson tales, the religious education provided by nuns lays the groundwork for Jordan's characters to develop as feminist heroines with creative and professional aspirations. While most of Jordan's working women are writers and journalists, the protagonist of "Between Darkness and Dawn" faces workplace prejudice as a woman physician. The story is part of a larger tradition of women's medical fictions emerging in the late nineteenth century that included novels such as *Dr. Zay* (1882) by Elizabeth Stuart Phelps, *A Country Doctor* (1884) by Sarah Orne Jewett, and *Helen Brent, M.D.* (1892) by Annie Nathan Meyer.

This section concludes with "Mrs. Warburton's Theories," which—like many of the pieces of magazine fiction in this edition—appeared in *Harper's Bazar* during the time Jordan served as its editor. In it, two unmarried professional women who live together befriend a prominent feminist intellectual, the eponymous Mrs. Warburton, a character likely based on the famous feminist activist Charlotte Perkins Gilman, whose work was published in *Harper's Bazar* under Jordan's editorship. Seemingly betraying the feminist principles she espouses in public, the widowed Mrs. Warburton makes a decision to remarry. "Mrs. Warburton's Theories" speaks to the ideological inconsistencies contained in the pages of women's magazines like *Harper's Bazar* and *Good Housekeeping*, which professed messages about marriage and consumerism that elevated domestic life as an ideal, while simultaneously encouraging women readers to pursue self-sufficient livelihoods and gender equality.

FROM
TALES OF THE CITY ROOM

"RUTH HERRICK'S ASSIGNMENT"

(1894, 1898)

Miss Ruth Herrick, of the New York *Searchlight*, had been summoned into the presence of the managing editor. It was without special alacrity that she obeyed the call. Even as she dropped her pen and rose from her desk in the city room, she seemed to hear the slow drawl of the great man's voice, uttering the words which so often greeted her appearance in his office:

"Ah, Miss Herrick, I have a big story for you—a very big story."

Usually she felt herself responding to this with a pleasant thrill of expectancy. There was keen satisfaction to her in the working up of a "big story"; she enjoyed the journeys and experiences it frequently included, and the strange characters among whom it often led her. Neither the experiences nor the characters were always wholly agreeable, but she never complained. Even the managing editor acknowledged this. He had been heard to remark, in an expansive moment, that Ruth Herrick was a very superior woman, with no nerves or nonsense about her. The gracious opinion was promptly repeated to the girl, and the memory of it had cheered her during several assignments in which nerves and a woman were equally out of place.

But tonight she almost rebelled. Strangely enough, she was not ready for the work before her. Her thoughts flew from the bent heads and hurrying pens around her to a dining room up town, even now alight and flower-trimmed for the little supper which had been planned to celebrate one of her greatest "beats." The *Searchlight* of that morning had contained her story; the chief and her fellow-reporters had complimented her; there were pleasant rumors that a more substantial evidence of appreciation would be forthcoming. All day she had idled, enjoying the relaxation from the strain of the past week, and looking forward to that dinner for various and personal reasons. The society editor, who had been invited, was just about to leave the office. She saw him wave the last page of his copy triumphantly in the air, as he reached for his hat with the other hand. He was to make the speech of the evening, and he had promised his hostess that he would explain to the non-professional guests what a "beat" really means to the newspaper and reporter that secure it. Earlier in the day he had submitted his definition to Miss Herrick for her approval.

"A big beat," he had read solemnly, "is an important exclusive story. If it appears in your newspaper, it is the greatest journalistic feat of the year, implying the possession of superior skill, brains, and journalistic enterprise by the members of your staff. If it appears in the other fellow's newspaper, it means that some idiot has accidentally stumbled across a piece of news which doesn't amount to much anyway, and which he has garbled painfully in the telling. Your newspaper gives 'the correct facts' the second day, and calls attention to the fake story published by your rival. Then you privately censure your city editor and reporters for letting the other newspaper 'throw them down.' Meantime, the other fellow, who published the story first, is patting himself and his reporters on the back, 'jollying' his city and managing editors, and crowing over his achievement on his editorial page. The reporter who brought in the story, or the 'tip,' gets some praise, and possibly a check. His position on the newspaper is secure—until he makes his next mistake. Tersely expressed, a beat is a story which only one newspaper gets, and which all the other newspapers wanted. A reporter with the right spirit will move heaven and earth to get it for the journal he represents."

"I've just prepared a graceful tribute to you," he called out as he caught her eye. "The chief says you're one of the most reliable members of the staff, can always be depended upon, and all that. They've been talking about you this afternoon in the editorial council."

Miss Herrick's face flushed a little as she returned his sunny smile. She was glad to have the compliment come to her in just this way. She was still blushing slightly as she entered the managing editor's office.

That gentleman sat at his desk, barricaded by waste-paper baskets and bundles of proofs. Small and grimy boys trailed in at intervals adding to the interesting collection before him, telegrams and cards and notes. An habitual furrow between his eyes was deepened—for the occasion, his visitor told herself in the bitterness of the moment—but the effect was softened by a really charming smile. It was said that the *Searchlight*'s presiding genius always wore that smile when he was giving a difficult assignment to one of his staff. It spoke of hope and confidence, and, incidentally, of the futility of excuse and objection. The young reporter had seen it before, and now found herself fixing a fascinated but hopeless gaze upon it. Her apprehensions were strengthened by the efforts of a young man with weak eyes and a corrugated brow, who sat in one corner diligently playing on a typewriter. He stopped long enough to recognize the young woman, and to run through a brief but expressive pantomime descriptive of the work before her. This habit had endeared him to the members of the reportorial staff.

The managing editor cleared a chair by an energetic sweep of one arm and, still smiling, looked keenly at the girl through his half-closed lids. Then he asked abruptly: "How much do you know about the Brandow case?"

Ruth Herrick's heart leaped suddenly. Was he going to give her that famous case after all? She had hinted last week that she wanted it, but he had sent Marlowe instead. Marlowe, she had noticed, had made an ignominious failure of it. She smiled inwardly as she recalled the column of vague conjecture and suggestions sent in the day before by that unhappy young man.

"I know that Helen Brandow is accused of having poisoned her husband," she replied quietly, "and that the evidence against her is purely circumstantial. I am familiar with all the theories that have been advanced, including those in the *Searchlight* this morning."

The young man at the typewriter looked up quickly at this, but the managing editor's face was impassive.

"She has refused to see reporters or friends," continued the girl. "So far as can be learned, she has not spoken a word since her arrest. Her trial will begin Monday, and she is awaiting it in the prison at Fairview. She is young and handsome, and her family is one of the best in the state. Public sympathy is wholly with her, and everybody says that she will be acquitted."

The managing editor's smile reappeared.

"Good," he said briskly. "I want you to take the first train to Fairview and interview that woman tomorrow morning."

"I'm almost positive she won't talk," murmured Miss Herrick doubtfully, but even as she spoke the last spark of rebellion died out, and she was planning ways and means.

"It is your business to make her talk," was the encouraging response. "Interview her and write the best story you ever wrote in your life. Everyone else has failed. If you are ambitious, here is your chance to distinguish yourself. I will have a boy at the station with letters which may help you. Good-night."

Eighteen hours later she sat in the Fairview prison. It was easy enough to get there. The warden unbent marvelously under the influence of a strong personal letter and Miss Herrick's face. The girl felt quite like a distinguished guest as the stern old fellow spoke of stories of hers which he had read, and newspaper cuts of her which he had seen, "which," he added kindly, "don't look much like you."[1] Then he was led to speak of Mrs. Brandow, to whom he and his wife had become much attached during the long months of her imprisonment. She had been restless and sleepless of late, and hadn't eaten much. He mentioned this last circumstance with a feeling he had not shown before. Evidently the sufferings of one who could not eat came keenly home to him. When his wife entered the room, it was with the keys in her hand,

and the gratifying announcement that Mrs. Brandow would receive the caller for a few moments. For this Miss Herrick mentally thanked the prisoner's lawyer, whose faith in the ability of his client to rebuff reporters had been artlessly displayed during her call on him two hours before.

When the newspaper woman passed through the door of the cell, her eyes, unaccustomed to the semi-gloom, saw but dimly the outline of a slender, black-robed figure, sitting at a small, plain table. The cell was larger than those in city prisons, and some effort had been made to render it habitable. There was a thick rug before the small iron bed, virginal in its white coverings. A heavy cashmere shawl opposite it concealed the white-washed walls. The hand which put it there had sought to cover all trace of stone and iron by friendly draperies, but Mrs. Brandow would not have it so. A small dressing-table held a number of silver-backed toilet articles, looking strangely out of place amid their grim surroundings. The light in the cell came through a small window and the barred door leading from the corridor, which was clean and damp, and glaringly white. The reporter hesitated an instant, and then went quickly forward.

The face which turned toward her was not the kind of face she had expected to see. Newspaper men had been gushing in their descriptions of the famous prisoner, possibly because their imaginations were stimulated by the fact that many of them had never seen her. Helen Brandow was not really beautiful; Miss Herrick was quick to recognize that as the other woman advanced to meet her. She made a hasty mental note of the healthily pale complexion, the dark, wavy hair, with its severely plain parting in the center, the heavy eyebrows, the too firmly closed lips, and the royal carriage of head and body. But it was the prisoner's eyes at which she looked longest, and into which she found herself looking again and again during the interview that followed. They were brown, a tawny brown with yellow lights, but wholly expressionless. They looked into Ruth Herrick's now, coldly and with no reflection of the half-smile which rested on the prisoner's lips, as she motioned toward the chair she had just left, and seated herself on the bed. "I feel like an intruder, as I always do when I am making these unsolicited visits," said the reporter. "I wish I could tell you how I appreciate your kindness in receiving me at all." She was leaning back a little in her chair, and her strong, young face and fair hair were in relief against the rich background of the drapery on the wall. In one quick glance her gray eyes had taken in every detail of the prisoner's surroundings. She looked at the prisoner again, with something very frank and womanly in the look.

"I was not moved by a purely philanthropic spirit," responded Mrs. Brandow.

She contemplated her visitor with something akin to interest, but there was a suggestion of irony in her contralto voice. "Mr. Van Dyke assures me that you will not misrepresent me if I have anything to say," she continued; "but I have nothing to say. I asked you in to tell you so, and to thank you for the roses, and for your note, both of which pleased me. The letters of introduction you bring convince me that I am safe in doing this, and that you will not go away and picture me as tearing my hair and deluging my pillow with tears. You will observe that my hair is in good order, and that the pillow is quite dry."

"I cannot fancy you less than composed under any circumstances," said the visitor, who found her own composure returning to her, accompanied by a strong sense of surprise and interest in the personality of the woman before her. This was not the Helen Brandow of the press, but an infinitely more interesting character, who should be given to the public, through the *Searchlight*, in a pen-picture to be long remembered. Miss Herrick's spirits mounted high at the thought.

"I am glad you like the roses," she added. "I did not send them to win a welcome, but because a nice old woman in the village gave them to me as I was coming here this morning. She was working among them, and the sight was so pretty I couldn't help stopping. It made me think of my own home, down South. The roses are the common, or garden variety, you see, but they have the delicious, spicy fragrance which seems to belong only to the roses in old-fashioned gardens. The owner of these succumbed to my youthful charms, and I brought away her best. I felt guilty, but not guilty enough to refuse them. It eased my conscience to leave them here for you."

Mrs. Brandow regarded her with a faint smile. "It had not occurred to me that the old women in this village spend their time in the peaceful pursuit of rose-growing," she remarked. "When I have been escorted back and forth they have been suspended over picket-fences watching me go by. I never saw any roses, or any redeeming traits in the inhabitants."

"Perhaps you were too preoccupied to notice them. Aren't you becoming a little morbid under this trouble?"

The newspaper woman was acutely conscious of her daring as she spoke, but the woman before her was plainly not to be approached by ordinary methods. She showed this still more clearly in her reply.

"Perhaps. I have had no desire for self-analysis of late. I used to tear myself up by the roots to watch my own growth, but the process was not pleasant. I am now trying to confine my attention to the things outside of me. It is less interesting; occasionally it wearies me. And I always abuse people and institutions when I am weary."

If there was a personal application in this, Miss Herrick passed it by with the smiling calmness of the trained reporter. "You are quite right," she said cheerfully. "But it would be infinitely more interesting to talk about you than about anything else. I should think you would be forced to turn your eyes inward occasionally, as a refreshing change from the things which weary you."

"The inner view is no longer pleasant."

Mrs. Brandow's smile, as she spoke, was not particularly pleasant, either. The reporter's thoughts flew suddenly to a certain Mary Bird, who had lost her reason under peculiarly depressing circumstances, which Miss Herrick had been unfortunate enough to witness. Mary had smiled on the newspaper woman once or twice, and the latter, although not imaginative, remembered the smiles too vividly for her own comfort. When the prisoner spoke again, however, the resemblance, if there had been one, vanished.

"I have often felt that I should go mad in this place," she said, suddenly, and with a complete change of tone. There was almost an apology in her voice and manner. "But I am quite sane," she added, "and it is a pleasure to me to have you here, and to talk to you. I had not realized, until you came, how much I needed something to break in upon this hideous routine, and change the current of my thoughts. For one year my mind has fed upon itself. I have spoken at the rarest intervals, and then only to the warden and his wife. Now I suddenly find myself struggling with a desire to become garrulous, to pour out my soul to you, as it were. I could almost 'tell you the story of my life.' All this would be an admirable illustration of the limitations of a woman's capacity for silence—but it isn't amusing. It shows me that I am not quite myself; I am nervous, and not wholly under my own control."

"I wish you would talk to me," said the reporter, earnestly. "Use me as a safety-valve. Tell me the story of your life, as you say. It would interest me, and might help you. Or try to imagine that I am an old friend, who wants to know of your life here."

"If you were, I think you would be pained by the recital. And, besides, if you were, you would not be here. Even my wildest fancies never take the form of yearnings for old friends; their society would be too depressing, under the circumstances. No, I am glad you are a stranger, with a certain magnetism about you which interests me, and fills me with a silly desire to know what you think of me, and whether you fear me, or believe in me."

"I am sure I could not bear trouble with more philosophy than that you show," said the girl, evasively. She felt a strange reluctance to analyze her own impressions, but she watched the development of the other's peculiar mood with an odd mingling of womanly sympathy and professional interest.

"I am not as philosophic as I may seem. I have given myself up to the horror of this place, until, as I said, it has almost unnerved me. If I were myself, I would not be sitting here, talking almost confidentially to you—a stranger. Why should the presence and sympathy of another human being affect me, after what I have suffered and endured?"

"You have never been a happy woman?"

The reporter looked thoughtfully at the rose she held in her hand as she spoke, and pulled off its petals, one by one.

"For five years I have been the most miserable woman on earth."

The expression of the prisoner's face had changed. The smile was gone; the brown eyes looked at the falling petals in the other's lap, with the dreaminess of retrospection in their glance.

"Five years ago I married," she went on, almost to herself. "Since then I have known the depths of human misery and degradation. Within a week of my marriage I knew exactly what I had done—I had tied myself for life to the most consummate scoundrel in existence. He spent his time devising ways of persecuting and humiliating me, and his efforts were eminently successful. He made me what I am."

"You should have separated from him."

"Yes, but that was impossible. My mother, who is dependent on me, and whom I love as I never loved anyone else, lived with us. He was sending my little sister to school. It pleased him to make a parade of what he was doing for my people. And his mother begged me to bear with him, to give him another chance, as he would go headlong to destruction if cast off entirely. I did bear with him—I gave him every chance, and he—he—"

The woman's voice broke. The listener had felt her face flush as the other's words came to her, and now, on a sudden impulse, she took the prisoner's hand. The white fingers closed suddenly upon her own with such force that the stone in a ring she wore sank into the flesh. But the act was involuntary, for the hand was dropped again with no indication on Mrs. Brandow's face that it had been offered and accepted.

"He was like an insane man," continued the prisoner, her low voice gathering strength and force as she went on. "He brought persons to the house whom no respectable house should shelter. He forced me to receive them and humiliated me before them. I bear today the marks of his violence. I rose in the morning wondering what new and devilish torture awaited me, and I lay quaking in my bed at night knowing that I would soon hear him kicking at my door. I think I was hardly myself during that time, but I endured while it was I alone who had to suffer. But one night he raised his hand to my old mother, when she was trying to protect me from his brutality, and struck her down. That night I killed him."

For an instant Ruth Herrick's heart stopped beating, but she sat motionless, watching the woman opposite her. There was no change in her calm face. Mrs. Brandow raised her eyes to it for a moment and dropped them again.

"I killed him," she repeated dully. "I have said it over to myself a good many times during the awful days and nights I have spent in this place. I have even said it aloud to hear how it would sound, but it didn't relieve me as it does now. And you—you look as if I were talking about an insect. I felt that way at first. It didn't seem to me that he was a human being, and I killed him as I would have killed a poisonous thing that attacked me. I gave him poison which I had had for years and which was said to leave no trace. I had intended to take it myself if the worst came to the worst; I had never dreamed of giving it to him. But I did. It was all done in a minute and then—my God!" she broke out suddenly. "Can you realize what my life has been since? Can you imagine the horrors of my nights here, filled with thoughts of him moldering in his grave, and put there by me? When I have fancied my reason leaving me I have almost hoped it would go. But I am sane yet, that I may realize what and where I am, and suffer as I had never dreamed a human creature could suffer and live. Can't you say something? Or have I gone mad at last, and am I sitting here gibbering to the walls? Is it so common a thing for you to have murderesses—?"

"Does your mother know?" asked the reporter, quietly. They were the first words she had spoken, and she realized fully their possible effect.

The other woman's form relaxed. She fell on her knees, with her head buried in the white covering of the little iron bed. The first tears she had shed gushed from her eyes. Her figure rocked as she sobbed and moaned.

"No, no!" she said brokenly. "She believes in me—she does not suspect."

The newspaper woman dropped her elbows on the table before her, buried her chin in her hands, and thought it over. How it had all come about, she could hardly realize. She glanced again at the crouching figure on the floor, and wondered vaguely why it had been given to her to watch the awful travail of this woman's soul. Something of the story the public understood. It had furnished the motive for the crime. It was whispered that the death of Jack Brandow had much improved that part of the country where he had lived and moved. He had goaded this woman to madness. The revolt, the temptation, and the opportunity had presented themselves simultaneously, and she had fallen as stronger women might have fallen, Miss Herrick thought, had they been so tempted. And then had come the awakening, the desolation, the despair.

Ruth Herrick was usually a cool, unemotional young person, but she was profoundly moved now. Many thoughts crowded into her mind. She recalled what she had read of Helen Brandow's past life—the good she had done as a girl at school, her adoration of her mother, the hundreds of noble men and women who were her friends, and whose faith in her innocence was so steadfast. They were moving heaven and earth to save her now, and when their success had seemed assured, she had ruined all by this hour's talk which was just ended. Ruth Herrick almost groaned as the situation unrolled itself before her. It was something she had to face. She knew now that she had suspected almost from the first what the climax might be, and had resolutely put the thought from her. And now she had the "biggest beat" of the year. Already she could see the commotion in the managing editor's office when the news came in. He would be startled out of his usual calm. He had spoken of her chance to distinguish herself, but even he had asked but an interview. In his wildest imaginings he had not dreamed of a confession. She knew that. But she had it. If anything but the life of a human being had been at stake, how proudly and gladly she would have gone to him, and how hard she would have tried to write the best story of her life, as he had ordered. But—this other woman at her feet. Something within the reporter asserted itself as counsel for her and spoke and would not down. Ruth Herrick's voice seemed to her to come from a long distance when she at last spoke.

"Do you realize what all this means to you? Had you forgotten that you were talking to a reporter?"

The woman on the floor sat up and raised her face to the speaker's. It was deathly pale, but calm, and the mouth was firm. "I know," she half whispered. "I forgot. But it is just as well. I could not have endured it any longer. It was a great relief, and I am ready for—the end."

"But if you had not spoken you would probably have been acquitted. Do you know that?"

"It doesn't matter," repeated the other, wearily. "If I had not told you, I should probably have told the warden. My nerves were at the highest tension, and you were present when they snapped. That's all. I am quite willing to bear the consequences of what I have done."

For a moment there was silence in the cell. The reporter looked through the barred door, out into the whitewashed corridor where a narrow shaft of sunlight fell. To her excited imagination there was something prophetic in the sight. Far down at the end of the hall, a scrub-woman hummed a street air as she worked. The whole life of Helen Brandow, if, indeed, she were allowed to live at all, would be passed in some such place as this if the *Searchlight* published that story. If it did not—Ruth Herrick set her teeth, and stared unseeingly at the opposite wall. If it did not, it would be because she withheld the news, to which, by every claim of loyalty, her newspaper was entitled. She withhold it!— she, "one of the most reliable members of the staff!" Was it not only last night the chief had said so? Something hot and wet filled her eyes. She, the practical; she, the loyal;—she was going to allow her paper to be "thrown down" on the biggest story of the year! For, above it all, a little refrain sang in her ears, and it was, "One-more-chance—one-more-chance—one-more-chance." The scrub-woman seemed to be singing it, too, and it kept time with the clang of an anvil in a shop nearby. Ruth Herrick dashed the tears from her eyes, and swallowed a lump that rose in her throat. When she spoke again there was no trace in voice or manner of the mental struggle through which she had passed.

"I am going to forget this interview," she said. "I am going to let you have the chance which a fair trial will give you. You could not talk to a jury as you have talked to me, but it will not be necessary. You will probably be acquitted. Everybody says so, and a great many people believe in you. And then you will begin life again. No one shall know that I have talked to you, and you must promise me that you will talk to no one else. Do not see another reporter."

She smiled ironically at this stipulation of her own. "He might be more loyal than I," she thought.

"I will do just as you say," said the other woman. She did not understand the sacrifice, but she knew what the decision meant to her. She dipped a towel in water and bathed her face and eyes. Then she took the newspaper woman's hands in her own and kissed them almost shyly.

"Thank you," she said. "Thank you very much."

The key turned noisily in the lock, and the reporter passed out.

She went back to whisper one more warning. "Do not let them put you on the stand."

She heard the door clang, and the key turn, as she walked toward the warden's office.

"That's good," she murmured in grim self-abasement. "In another moment I should probably have been helping her through the window."

"So Mrs. Brandow has been acquitted," said the managing editor of the *Searchlight* to an assistant, as the news came in two weeks later. "And the whole country is shedding tears of joy over her, and they're having bonfires tonight up in Fairview. I believe she's guilty; but a pretty woman who can hold her tongue will escape the consequences of almost any crime. Strange how Miss Herrick failed on that case; she felt it, too. Has been working day and night ever since, and all that sort of thing. But, after all, you can't depend on a woman in this business."

The managing editor was more nearly right than he knew.

Source: "Ruth Herrick's Assignment," *Cosmopolitan* (July 1894). Reprinted in *Tales of the City Room* (Scribner's, 1898).

"A POINT OF ETHICS"

(1898)

"As I understand it," said Virginia Imboden, reflectively, "the question resolves itself into this: To what extent can a woman of irreproachable character assist a woman of no character without being injured in the eyes of others?"

Frances Neville changed her position restlessly, and lifted a hand in protest against such an unqualified statement.

"You have put the case much too strongly," she objected, "if you are speaking of Miss Bertram."

There was a slight irritability in her tone. Miss Herrick, who was at the piano, carelessly playing Chopin, caught it, and whirled round on the stool to face the group of friends who were scattered about her apartment in various attitudes of restfulness. Virginia Imboden lay on the rug before the grate, her fair head vividly outlined by the dancing flames. Frances Neville was stretched on the broad divan near her, and in the depths of a great easy chair Mrs. Ogilvie, whose somber gown recalled her recent bereavement, had been dreamily listening to the music, which swept her thoughts back to the old days when she and John were so happy together.

To her, as to Ruth Herrick, the words just spoken were a discord in the harmony of a social evening after the strain of the week. Miss Herrick rose and turned on the electric light, whose radiance, under silk shades, threw a softened light over the apartment. Her guests, startled by the unexpected illumination, blinked protestingly at her as they changed their positions to more conventional ones, while she drew the shades to screen the rooms, with their picturesque group, from the gaze of inquisitive neighbors. Outside, the wind whimpered through the courts of the big hotel, and the cheerless rain of November beat against the window-panes. Mrs. Ogilvie lent ear to it for a moment, and turned with a little shiver from the mental contemplation of the obtrusive grave on the hillside to the homely picture of the fire-light blazing on the hearth.

"If you girls are going to discuss that subject," laughed Miss Herrick, apologetically, "you will need all the light there is. Ruminating in the dark, to Polish music, is apt to make one's point of view a little morbid."

She dropped into a "cosey hollow" near the fire and clasped her hands behind her head in her favorite attitude of rest and reflection.

"Now that we have the honor of your attention you shall decide the question for us," said Miss Imboden, with conviction. "It must be taken up and disposed of. It's something we have to settle, and we cannot shirk the issue any longer."

Ruth Herrick smiled down at the earnest face upturned to her.

"You make it highly impressive, Virginia," she said gently— "almost too impressive, I think; for, after all, the issue, as you call it, is a very simple one. It has to do with a bright and charming young woman who has come among us, of whom we know little, but of whom we have grown very fond. Isn't that all?"

"How trying you are!" murmured her friend, protestingly. She drew her dark brows together in a frown, then went on quickly.

"That isn't all. It isn't even the beginning. Here is the situation, impartially put. A woman (young, and clever, and charming, I grant you) comes to us from nowhere. Her life, so far as we are concerned, apparently began the day we met her. None of us has heard a word from her of home, or parents, or friends. None of us knows where she came from, or what or who she is. Before we realized what this might imply we became fond of her, as you say. Insensibly she grew into our affections and our lives. We asked her no questions and she volunteered no information. After this condition has been existing for several months we discover that she is a marked woman in our profession—that she is credited with a past—that her reserve, reticence, and gayety are making her talked about—and that we are coming in for some share of the—the—well, feeling that exists about her. Now, if this is so, are we held to her by our friendly interest? If we *knew* she was all

right it would be different, because then we could speak about
her with the force and courage that we should have. But we don't
know, and that's the trouble."

Miss Herrick became serious.

"I didn't know it was so bad as that," she said quietly. She
looked at the others with a question in her glance. Even Mrs.
Ogilvie lowered her head in reflective consideration of Miss Imboden's statement.

"I had not realized," continued the hostess, gravely, "that it
had gone so far. The problem has seemed to me a very simple
one—no problem at all. Whatever the girl has been, she is now
all that she should be, so far as we know. We know how hard she
works, how plainly she lives, how lonely she is except for our affection and our companionship. If she has done wrong and is trying to make amends, this is no time for us to push her back.
Surely, as her friends, we should give her all the help we can. I
don't wish to dictate or to suggest to anyone of you what her
course should be, but to me we seem very smug and virtuous as
we sit here criticizing this girl from our own self-assured little
pedestals. How do we know what environment and temptations
she may have had? How do we know what we should have done
if we had been in her place? I shall certainly continue to love her
and to tell her so. And if the uplifting influence of my society will
help her," ended the girl more lightly, "she shall have all that I
have time to give her."

She crossed to the piano and drifted into the rhythmic melody
of the Twelfth Nocturne, while Mrs. Ogilvie leaned her cheek
against the unresponsive wood of the instrument and listened.
From her comfortable rest on the big divan Miss Neville took up
the discussion.

"You were always something of a prig, Virginia," she said,
with vivacious bluntness.[1] "But you're fairly distinguishing yourself tonight. You're not talking to Park Row.[2] You're talking to
Miss Bertram's friends."

Miss Imboden flushed a little.

"I don't forget that I'm speaking to my own friends, too," she
said with dignity. "If you have any idea that I would say these
things to anybody else, banish it."

She raised her voice a little, above the seductive swing of the music.

"Surely you don't misunderstand me—all of you," she urged. "I don't want to seem 'smug' and self-satisfied, as Ruth puts it. No one is fonder of Miss Bertram than I. But I'm alone here in New York, and I have nothing in the world except my health, my very ordinary journalistic ability, and my reputation as a 'hard-working and respectable lady,' to quote my appreciative janitor. Can I afford to jeopardize the most precious of these by being the acknowledged friend of a woman whose reputation is, as a matter of fact, the subject of unpleasant talk? My mother sits in our little home out West reading the newspaper clippings about my work and pasting them in a scrapbook. Every word she reads or hears about me is precious gold to her. Can I run the risk of having my name and hers carelessly linked in newspaper gossip with another name that is mentioned with sneers? This isn't mere fancy. It has been done already—and in connection with you, Ruth," she broke in suddenly, wheeling about and facing her incredulous hostess. "Herforth said to me today, 'I saw Miss Herrick at the theatre the other night with Miss Bertram. They're not friends, are they?' and his accent of surprise said more than he meant to, I assure you. Mr. Davidson has spoken to Miss Neville about it—very nicely and guardedly, of course, but what he said amounted to a warning, and half a dozen of our women friends have labored with us individually and collectively along the same lines. You must all admit that. I'm willing to help Miss Bertram in any way I can. I'll advise her about her stories, I'll divide my assignments with her, as we're both on space, but as for 'the precious boon of companionship,' that's another story![3] Does my companionship do her good enough to compensate for the harm hers does me? And what is true in my case is true in yours. There is the situation in a nutshell. I don't like to say these things. I almost hate myself while I'm saying them, for they seem such worldly counsel. I know how much finer Ruth's point of view is. But we must remember where we are. Truth is speaking to you, my friends, though Truth realizes that it may not prevail in a gathering which is decidedly not in sympathy with the speaker."

She ended with a stage sigh, and the others laughed, glad of any relief in a topic that had been depressing to all.

"Doesn't it seem to you," said Mrs. Ogilvie, in her quiet way, "that before we decide this question the person most concerned should be heard from? Surely there is some way of learning the truth and of defending her—or of getting her to defend herself. The person we should hear from next is—"

"Miss Bertram," said Miss Herrick's maid, at the door. With a quick and expressive glance at the group, the hostess went to meet the new arrival.

"If that had happened in a play," murmured Miss Imboden, "we should have thought it a very forced situation. And yet here she is, at just the right moment, to speak for herself. Query, will she speak?"

The young woman who was entering the room with Miss Herrick came forward with the assured air of one who joins a circle of tried friends. She greeted the others with the brilliant smile and charm of manner to which they had all succumbed early in their acquaintance with her, and sank contentedly into a low seat near the fire. Her cheeks were flushed by her encounter with the boisterous wind outside, and a few drops of rain sparkled on her dark hair. Looking at her a little consciously, the group became aware of a change in her manner—a brightness, a sparkle, an apparent freedom from care which they had not observed before. Miss Herrick was the first to comment upon it.

"You seem very happy," she said, resting her hand affectionately on her friend's shoulder. "I hope something nice has happened to you."

Alice Bertram caught the caressing hand in her own, and held it against her cheek with such an ecstatic little laugh that the others smiled in sympathy.

"I am happy," she said emphatically, "and something *very* nice has happened. I have won a big wager, I have proved the truth of my most cherished theory, and tonight I'm at liberty to tell you girls all about it—you dear girls who have been so good to me. I shall never forget that. Do you suppose I haven't realized how fine it has been of you to take me as I am, without a question even in your manner—to take me into your big hearts so thoroughly and so warmly? Every day and every night I've thought of the goodness of it and the beauty of it. I've known how strange my reserve must have seemed to you. Anyone but you would have tried to break through it, and would have asked me about the past I seemed so anxious to conceal."

She looked at them fondly, her eyes resting longest on Miss Herrick, who smiled back at her in warm responsiveness. Virginia Imboden had colored a little, but was looking at the new arrival with a reflection of the other woman's joy in her clear eyes. Miss Neville and Mrs. Ogilvie were eloquently silent. Alice Bertram's glance swept round the circle and rested reflectingly on a ring on Miss Herrick's hand, which she had kept in her own. She twisted this about rather nervously as she continued.

"You must have wondered who I am. I know you have realized that I am not what I seemed to be. The part I played was so new to me that I'm afraid I didn't do it very well. I'm going to ask you to let me tell you the whole story tonight. I warn you, though, that it's very egotistical, and I shall talk about myself the whole time! I came to tell it to Ruth and to ask her to pass it on. It is part of my good fortune to find you all together, for I'm going away tomorrow, and shall not return. I'm so glad my last night in New York will be spent with you."

She stopped for a moment.

"Going away!" they echoed, in dismal chorus. Mrs. Ogilvie crossed the room and dropped onto the ottoman at Miss Bertram's feet, her eyes full of tears.

"We shall be so sorry to lose you," she said softly.

"I know—I'm sure you will," the girl told her, looking down into the wet eyes with a responsive dimness in her own. "But we're not parting forever. I'm going out of newspaper work for all time. But I hope to see you girls very often, in the years to come."

She laughed a little nervously.

"I hardly know how to start my story," she said. "I feel as if I ought to say 'I was always a strange child,' as the romantic heroines of fiction usually begin. I was not an especially strange child, but my father was and is a strange man. You all know of him."

She mentioned the name of a man famous throughout the country as one of the West's great mining kings. His eccentricities of character were as conspicuous and as much discussed as his vast wealth. The newspaper women recalled the printed stories of his princely home, his beautiful wife, his munificent gifts to various public enterprises, and, above all, his odd theories and experiments. Despite his wealth, he had socialistic leanings, and was idolized by his miners, they knew. And this was his daughter—this quietly attired young woman who had worked side by side with them for six months in the relentless grind of journalism.

"When I left college," continued that young person with a businesslike air, "my father naturally assumed that I would develop into the modern product that he most despised—the society girl. My brothers, of course, he took in hand as soon as they were graduated. He gave them a rigorous business training, and they had to work their way from the bottom as faithfully as if they hadn't a cent. They were bright boys, and father was very proud of the way they got on. He used to talk about it a good deal, and then look at me and sigh. It was trying, especially as I had some of his spirit in me, I suppose, so I resolved to give him a little surprise. Am I boring you to death?"

She looked deprecatingly at the interested faces around her, and, reassured by their expressions and emphatic denials, went on.

"One day my father was particularly vigorous in his denunciation of idle women. I felt, foolishly, that his remarks were directed at me. He was really very fond of me, but I think he classed me with my pet kitten in the matter of intelligence, notwithstanding my university diploma. I let him talk until he had finished, and then I told him calmly that I was quite as competent to support myself as my brothers were, and that I could, if necessary, earn as much money in a year as they had earned during their first year of work.

"My father laughed good naturedly at this," added Miss Bertram, smiling again at the recollection. "He scoffed at the whole idea as utterly absurd. It piqued me, and on the impulse of the moment I made a wager with him.

"On my twenty-first birthday he had invested a very large sum of money for me. I was to have the yearly income to spend. I offered to wager the entire sum (everything I had in the world, you see) that I could go to a strange city, take a new name, and earn my own living for six months. I was not to take a penny with me, except the money to pay for my ticket to New York, and I was not to borrow a cent from anybody. I was to pay for my own clothes, food, and lodgings for six months. If I failed, every cent I had in the world would go back to my father, and I was to live for five years on what he chose to give me. If I succeeded, he was to double the gift he made me on my twenty-first birthday, and he was to consent to my going abroad at the end of the experiment for a post-graduate course in German universities."

She stopped for breath, while her hearers closed about her with enthusiastic comments and questions.

"I have succeeded," she told them, with shining eyes. "The six months ended last night, and I sent my father a telegram. I also sent him a telegraphic copy of the amounts of my weekly earnings, which the *Searchlight*'s auditor gave me when I asked for it. I have not been a brilliant journalistic success, but I have supported myself in comparative comfort. Working on space, I have averaged twenty dollars a week for six months. My brothers did not earn more than fifteen when they began to 'make their living.'

"I told the city editor last night that I was going to resign, and he asked me to reconsider the matter, and said he'd put me on a weekly salary of twenty-five dollars if I would stay. Of course he hasn't the faintest idea who I am. I got him to write out the offer, and tonight I'm going to mail it to my father—just for glory and to down him more thoroughly. Before I left my room tonight I got a telegram from him. Here it is. Isn't he a dear?"

She unrolled the slip of yellow paper and gave it to Miss Herrick, who passed it round to the others. The girls read it eagerly.

"Our loving congratulations. Your mother and I are prouder than ever of our girl. Come home at once and show your brothers how to make a success of life."

"Isn't he fine?" repeated his daughter with conviction. "I'm going home tomorrow. I have saved enough to take me there in a new gown and with a general effect of affluence. I shall have the best accommodations all the way. It will take the very last cent I have saved, but that doesn't matter. I've won my wager and I'm content!"

She tossed the telegram into the air and caught it again with a gay laugh.

"I have no regrets over the end of my newspaper life," she

added soberly, "except that I shall miss you girls—dreadfully. I've grown very fond of you." She hurried on as if not daring to dwell on this too long. "I'm going abroad almost immediately, to be gone two years; so I shall not see you for that time, unless you run over there. My family will come next summer, as usual, and we shall travel about—I don't quite know where. Of course the work was hard and often unpleasant, but now that it's over, I don't mind that."

She folded the telegram and her face clouded at a sudden recollection.

"I don't know whether you have heard this," she said, "but it has come to me within the last day or two that a few busy-bodies have been saying unpleasant things about me. They're the type who won't admit that they don't know everything. They know nothing about me, so they made up some interesting and exciting yarns and told them freely. I believe they have made me out a sort of adventuress."

Her lips curled as she spoke. Evidently she had no idea of the nature of the "interesting and exciting yarns" she mentioned. "I'm glad I didn't know about it sooner," she ended lightly. "It might have worried me. I hate to have my affairs talked over by strangers."

She rose as she spoke, but let them sweep her back into her chair amid a whirl of protestations, for another hour of excited questions, ejaculations, and plans for the future. Then they let her go, promising to see her off for the West the next day.

Left alone, her friends dropped meekly into chairs and surveyed each other, Miss Imboden with some embarrassment, Miss Herrick a little triumphantly, the others smiling in serene acceptance of the situation.

Miss Imboden spoke first, as befitted the young person who had discoursed so fluently on the same subject earlier in the evening.

"It's all delightful," she said, "and I'm heartily glad. I hope you won't set me down as a double-dyed young prig who goes about tearing her friends up by the roots in her anxiety to discover whether they are good enough for her. Do you think I should have told Alice that I have not been as—as loyal to her as she thought me?" she asked anxiously.

Miss Herrick responded promptly.

"Not for the world," said she. "This is an easy problem. I saw the deadly purpose in your eye toward the end of the evening and stopped it with an awful glare. That was emphatically the time for one of your 'brilliant flashes of silence.'"

She helped Miss Imboden into her coat and tucked in her sleeves with sisterly care.

"A certain amount of precaution is an excellent thing, little girl," she said seriously. "Theoretically you were all right. Practically you were wrong, as you now know, in this case. The rest of us felt that, because we're older and more experienced than you. Perhaps we read human nature a little better."

A sudden thought struck her, and notwithstanding Miss Imboden's flushed cheeks she added, teasingly:—

"After all, the great question of the evening is still unsettled: To what extent can a good woman help an erring sister without being injured in the eyes of others? Think it over, Virginia dear, and let us know!"

Miss Imboden has not solved her problem yet.

Source: *Tales of the City Room* (Scribner's, 1898).

"A ROMANCE OF
THE CITY ROOM"

(1898)

Miss Bancroft raised her eyes from her work and turned them absently upon the small messenger who had stopped at her desk. They were beautiful eyes—"like no other eyes in the world," one infatuated young reporter had solemnly affirmed; but tonight they were tired and rather sad. Miss Bancroft had had a trying day. She had pursued an elusive news "story" the length and breadth of the city until late at night before finding it. She had been thrown into contact with a great many disagreeable persons. Moreover, she had had the depressing experience of seeing the individual who knew most about the story walk cheerfully away with a man reporter, ostensibly to have a drink, but in reality, she was sure, to give that youth exclusive information for a rival newspaper.

As she wrote her story tonight in the city room of the *Searchlight*, she reflected gloomily that the *Globe* would probably come out the next morning with a "beat" on the same subject which would bring her before the city editor for explanations that she could not give and for a possible reprimand that she was in no mood to accept. She took from the boy the package and note he offered her, both of which, she noticed, bore her full name plainly printed on the typewriter. As there was no time to examine them she placed them carelessly on one side of her desk, among a mass of accumulated mail, and returned to her work philosophically determined to make the most of the material she had secured.

Her pen flew steadily over the paper for an hour, and sheet after sheet was added to the pile of "copy" at her right hand,

wherein her story was told in the clear, concise fashion for which
she was noted. When the last word had been written she glanced
at the clock over the night city editor's desk. It was after twelve.
There was no sound in the room but the clatter of typewriters,
the scratching of the swift pens of her associates, and the shuf-
fling feet of office boys who filed in and out with messages and
copy. In the pitiless glare of the electric light the faces round her
looked worn and haggard. She sent her story to the night city editor's desk, and leaning back in her chair in the moment of relaxation after a mental strain, sympathized with herself and her
fellow-workers with the intensity of overtired nerves. Was it all
worthwhile? she asked herself wearily, as she had asked many
times before. She thought of the home down South, which she
had left so hopefully three years ago to seek her fortune. As she
closed her eyes she could see every feature of the old house nes-
tled so cozily in its setting of blossoming shrubs. Again she heard
the sighing of the night wind among the pines and the sleepy call
of birds to one another. She could almost smell the perfume of
the roses that climbed over the verandas and looked in at the
windows of her own little room. In fancy she saw that room, its
walls covered with the pictures she loved, the dwarf bookcase
filled with her favorite books, the desk at which she had written
her first ambitious "literary" efforts, the small white bed where
she had slept such deep, untroubled sleep in those peaceful days
that seemed a thousand years ago.[1] Perhaps her mother slept
there tonight, dreaming of her "little girl" all alone in far-away
New York. A great wave of homesickness swept over the newspaper woman as she came back with a shock to the present.

At his official desk, the night city editor was scowling over
some telegrams which had been placed before him. Herforth, the
star reporter, had finished a page "special" and was executing a
small and quiet jig beside his chair by way of "restoring his circulation," as he put it. Several others were collecting and paging the
scattered leaves of their copy, preparatory to handing it in, while
a number of less fortunate reporters worked on hurriedly with an
occasional anxious glance at the clock. Over the whole room
hung the tense atmosphere of a newspaper office late at night. In
the nervous depression of the moment Miss Bancroft forgot the
brighter side of her work, of which she was keenly appreciative in

her normal frame of mind. Her dark head drooped wearily, and her gloom deepened, as she mechanically arranged her papers and began to search vaguely for the key of her desk. She had forgotten the messenger's package and note, both of which stared up at her with mute reproach as her eyes fell thoughtlessly upon them.

She lifted the package from its resting-place and untied the string with listless fingers. As she tore off the wrapping-paper and raised the lid of the long box, she uttered a little exclamation of delight which made Randall, at the next desk, look up from his work with a sympathetic smile. Carefully tucked away under waxed paper, and resting on a bed of moss and ferns, were exquisite red roses, whose breath seemed like a greeting from the southern land to which her homesick soul had but now turned. The reporter buried her face in their dewy fragrance, while her eyes for a moment grew dim. It was very sweet to realize that someone had been thinking of her and planning this pleasure for her tonight of all nights. She looked for the card which should have accompanied the flowers, but found none either among the roses or in the box. The latter she now observed lacked the usual imprint of the florist. There was absolutely nothing on it to show whence or from whom it had come. The note was still unopened, and to this she turned. A thick sheet of creamy paper, typewritten on both sides, fell from the envelope as she cut the edges. It bore neither date nor signature, but the printed words stood out boldly on the white page, and these were clear enough. Miss Bancroft crossed her feet comfortably, leaned back in her chair, and began to read.

"DEAR MISS BANCROFT—You do not know me, and I beg that you will make no effort to discover who I am. Excellent reasons forbid my coming to you and telling you what you are to me. There is a barrier between us which nothing can remove, and I can only look from behind it for such glimpses of your face as I may get. To you I can be only a shadow. To me you have been and are the inspiration that has helped me to go steadily on in the way marked out for me. Perhaps it may please you a little to know this, and to realize that there is a human being near you whom your mere existence has made happy. Sometimes I know that you are tired, for I can see behind the brave, unflinching spirit you show to the world. At such times I long to say something to comfort you—but I may not. Will it interest you to know that you have a devoted and unselfish friend to whom you are more than all the world? If it will, remember this. Please accept the roses as a small reminder of the southern land we both love."

Miss Bancroft experienced a revival of interest in life. She read the letter again, seeking vainly for some clew which might lead to discovery of the writer.[2] Her thoughts swept quickly around the circle of her friends and associates on the *Searchlight*. Assuredly one of these was the man. One by one she called them up in mental review, dismissing some quickly, others more doubtfully, but all finally. She glanced again at the bowed heads of the men around her. It was impossible to picture any of them as the author of the letter she held in her hand. Several of them had loved her and had told her so, with the engaging frankness of their kind. Many of the others were happily married or engaged, or in love with "sweet girls" whose photographs they had exhibited to her with pride. A few were too cold or too ambitious, she thought, to care for anyone. The barrier of which her unknown friend wrote was a tangible one. It concealed him well.

Miss Bancroft took the note and flowers home with her that night and fell asleep with the fragrance of the roses filling her rooms. It greeted her again as she awoke refreshed and ready to take up the work of the day in her usual blithe spirit. The morning sun, pouring through her open windows, fell lovingly on the great roses which someone had lavished on her. She speculated over them pleasantly as she dressed, but after she reached the office its rush and swirl banished them and the sender from her mind.

She had almost forgotten both when the second letter came exactly a week later. The long box and the creamy envelope lay side by side on her desk as she entered the *Searchlight*'s city room late Friday night, and she broke into a gay smile even over these prosaic things. It made Randall, sitting next to her, speculate long and moodily as to the giver. There was no uncertainty about her facts on this occasion, and she plunged into her story with a vigor and evident zest which made the muscles in the lips of the night city editor relax perceptibly as he observed her. When he glanced at her again two hours later she had finished her story and was lifting a mass of dewy red roses from the long box, whereupon the night city editor looked wise and thought he understood the situation, but did not in the least.

The second letter, written on the typewriter like the first, was a little longer than its predecessor. Miss Bancroft read and reread it slowly.

"DEAR MISS BANCROFT—Your acceptance of the flowers made me very happy. It is infinitely sweet to me to have even so slight a bond between us as the presence of my roses in your home. Will you let them speak for me as I may not speak for myself? They will ask for nothing; they will only tell you that in the big and selfish world in which we live there is a man who loves you, who is watching over you, who is doing all that a shadow can do to guard you and smooth the path for the dear feet that should not be making life's journey all alone. The knowledge of this cannot hurt you. There is nothing disrespectful in the honest love of a man, even though that man is unknown. I know there are many others who love you, too. I do not know whether there is anyone who has won your heart. I do not seek to know. I believe I love you well enough, unselfishly enough, to rejoice when some happy man, who is worthy of you, marries you and takes you away from us. Every womanly woman is happiest in the home of a loving wife, and you are all womanliness. Good-night. Take the roses home with you, and let them speak of rest, and peace, and happy dreams."

There was a puzzled look in Miss Bancroft's brown eyes as she laid the letter down. She speculated over it on her way home that night, and the next day, to her dismay, she discovered that the mystery was making her self-conscious. She found herself looking with suspicious eyes at her good friends on the *Searchlight*. The frank and warm *camaraderie* of her associates, which had been so pleasant a feature of her journalistic life, seemed to her now, in some spots, the cloak of a deeper affection. She tried to analyze the feeling back of the courtesies that were shown her, and the invariable good fellowship with which she was treated.

She was, however, too well poised to permit this condition to last. As successive Fridays came, always bringing their red roses and their odd concomitant, a typewritten letter which breathed the most delicate tenderness, her interest in the unknown sender grew deeper and softer.[3] All unconsciously, perhaps, her hidden correspondent was laying bare his soul to the woman he loved. It was a noble and upright soul, she recognized. The whole world might have read the simple, manly letters in which week after week he poured out his heart to her. Nor were they wholly sentimental letters. The Shadow was consistent in his resolve to ask for nothing while giving all. When she had learned to acquiesce in his incognito and ceased marveling at his complete knowledge of her and her life, she discovered, as the months went by, that the strong personality behind these weekly letters had become one of the most powerful influences in her career. The Shadow's point of view was unique. His letters were sometimes long, sometimes short, always interesting. He touched lightly on many subjects, and she was the gainer. He commented on the style of her stories. He criticized her English, and gave her a list of books for reference and study. He praised her work freely, where there was ground for praise, and criticized sharply and discriminatingly where censure was demanded. He suggested and advised as only a loyal friend could, and beneath it all was an undercurrent of deep, unselfish tenderness that touched her heart. The sweet unspoiled nature of the woman responded to this as the flowers he brought her responded to her care of them. Unconsciously, as time passed, she grew to lean on him, to watch for his letters, to rely on his judgment, to act in important matters as she believed that he would have her act. The atmosphere of his sturdy devotion was as real and as sweet to her as the perfume of his roses.

"Don't be too pathetic in your pathetic tales," he wrote her once. "Let your readers shed their own tears"; and the memory of the terse comment was a fixed one, which strengthened her work materially.

"You are looking pale," he said another time. "Take a few days off and go to Avondale. It is only two hours from New York, but it's plunged in the profoundest slumber. It's the ideal spot for tired brains and nerves. All around it are hills, which shut out the big bustling world. In it are quaint old-fashioned houses, and men and women not less old-fashioned and equally quaint. Over the peaceful little river that flows through the town are rustic bridges, where you can sit and dream, or fish if you care to (you'll never catch anything), and look at the willows waving in the summer breeze and the cows standing knee-deep in the clover-fields. The air is full of the perfume of old-fashioned flowers that grow in every garden. You will find bowls of them in your room at night, and the room itself will smell of lavender. Go there, take Lubbock's 'Pleasures of Life' with you, —and forget for forty-eight hours that there is a newspaper in the world."[4]

The letter came to her one hot Friday night in August. The next morning she took the train for Avondale, where she spent two ideally restful days. She found the little town exactly as he had pictured it, and as she strolled along its quiet streets she wondered how the Shadow had come to know it, and when he had been there last. For a moment, the idea lingered with her that, perhaps, after all, they were to meet. It had been more than a year since the first box of roses had come to her as the one bright episode of a depressing day. But if he had ever been in Avondale, he had apparently come and gone as mysteriously as he seemed to do everything else. She made no secret of her own identity or work, but the "quaint men and women" who eyed her with such artless curiosity gratified her with no reminiscences, and had evidently never before seen a representative of a great modern newspaper. Helen Bancroft went cheerily back to her work and her role as the inspiration of a shadow, and if the thought occurred to her that the role was a trifle unsatisfactory because of the steadfast obscurity of that shadow, she stifled it as one would check disloyal thought of a friend. The conviction had already come to her woman's soul that what he desired was best. She seemed to herself to be living in two worlds—one, the rushing, practical planet on which she worked by day; the other, a peaceful, happy sphere wherein he dwelt, and whither his letters sometimes transported her.

For more than two years the letters and the red roses came with unbroken regularity. When at last a certain Friday evening arrived and they did not, Miss Bancroft stared at the top of her unvisited desk as if some perplexing phenomenon had taken place. She would have been scarcely less surprised at the failure of a physical law than by this lack of fidelity—she could not call it forgetfulness or indifference—on the part of the Shadow. The face of the world seemed changed to her as she went home that night, and the sudden realization of what this meant made her heart contract. Perhaps he was only testing her—proving to her at last what a factor in her life he had come to be. But she rejected this thought at once; she did not know his name or face, but she knew the man too well to think self-love could thus claim him, even for a moment. Perhaps all was not well with him. There had been a persistent minor note in his recent letters, bravely as he had tried to stifle it. Last week's roses, almost withered now, looked sadly up at her as she entered her apartment. She had kept the flowers, of late, until the next box came to replace them. Tonight, as she watered the grateful roses, her imagination saw in their droop and languor the mute symbol of the passing from her life of something of whose full sweetness she was just beginning to be conscious.

The days went on, and brought no sign from the Shadow. They all seemed alike to the young reporter, who kept her sad reflections in her own heart and gave no outward sign. She felt her friend drifting from her, perhaps through a misapprehension which she had no power to correct. It was as much beyond her to reach or affect him as if he lived in truth in another world which he had shared with her, but from which she was now shut out. She missed his flowers, she missed his letters; above all, she missed the sense of companionship and protecting tenderness which had enveloped her so mysteriously and so long.

She was recalling these things one cold night in February when she wearily entered her apartment. On the hearth, in her cozy study, a bright fire burned cheerily. The attentive maid had drawn up to it her favorite easy chair and had placed her slippers near the warm glow. She sank into the chair with a sigh of satisfaction, brushing the snow from her jacket, and recklessly exposing the soles of her little boots to the heat as she settled her feet on the fender. The sudden blaze that had greeted her had died down, and the room was almost in shadow. As her eyes wandered listlessly over her books and pictures they fell on something oddly familiar. Was that great vase on the table, which had held the Shadow's offering for so long, again full of fresh red roses? Miss Bancroft rubbed her eyes and looked more closely. Had she fallen asleep and was she dreaming of the roses that had filled it so constantly until three months ago? The perfume of the flowers seemed very real. They *were* there—"the beautiful darlings!" she whispered, as she went to them and laid her face against them. To her excited fancy they seemed to laugh up at her. "Here we are again," they said. "It's all right—everything is unchanged"; and the whole world was brighter for the assurance. She lit the gas hastily and rang the bell. There had been no letter with the flowers, the little maid told her. They had come without a card about four that afternoon, and she had taken them out of the box and put them in water as she knew Mademoiselle would have wished. The box? But yes, here it is—a large and ornate affair, with the name of a famous florist on its cover in gold letters. This unusual feature surprised and temporarily disturbed Miss Bancroft. Never before had the Shadow sent her such a clew. Surely, if she wished, it would be comparatively easy to trace him now. She dismissed the idea from her mind for the present. He was still her friend, and all was well with him. He had sent her the roses to tell her so. That was enough.

She dressed for dinner in high spirits, putting on her best gown in honor of this spiritual caller, and singing a favorite song which was in harmony with her mood. The little maid smiled to hear again the blithe notes that had been silent of late.

> "For the spring, the spring is coming,
>   'Tis good-by to ice and snow,
>   Yes, I know it, for the swallows
>   Have come back to tell me so,"

sang the soft contralto voice.[5] Spring had already come in her heart—for the roses told her so.

Herforth called on her after dinner, formally arrayed in his evening clothes, and with a startling chrysanthemum in his buttonhole. His first words lowered Miss Bancroft's spirits.

"Got the roses, I see," he said, nodding toward the blooming jacqueminots in the vase on the table.[6]

"Did—did you send them?" faltered the girl. She was conscious of a sinking sensation, as if something were falling away from her.

"Only in a way," said Herforth at once. "I acted as an agent." He had dropped into an easy chair, and as he spoke he regarded her rather curiously with his sleepy blue eyes.

"Do you remember Hatfeld?" he went on. "Awfully good-looking chap, with light hair and dark eyes. Reserved, but I found him one of the most charming fellows I ever met when I came to know him. Nobody on the paper knew him well except me. Wasn't at the office much except at night, and then did his work in a little room off the night editor's sanctum. I liked him and dined with him a lot, and he used to let me talk about you most of the time. Well, he was consumptive, poor fellow.[7] Didn't tell me anything about it until three months ago, when he went to Algiers for his health.[8] The night before he sailed we dined together, and went afterwards to my room to smoke. Am I boring you with all this."

"Go on, please," said Miss Bancroft, in a low tone.

She was standing at the window looking out at the snow, which was falling heavily. The sudden question evidently startled her, for she shivered slightly as she turned toward the young man and then glanced away again.

"We talked a good deal," continued Herforth, animatedly, "and I tried to brace him up as well as I could. Prophesied that he'd come back in six months perfectly well—and all that sort of thing. It had no effect on him, but he was awfully cool and plucky about his condition. He told me that his father and mother had both died of consumption, and that the doctors had given him no hope. He said that was why he had never married. He would not make the woman he loved wretched and hand down a legacy of physical ill to his children. And then he said something that will interest you."

Herforth had been speaking rather lightly, but if she had noticed it Miss Bancroft would have known that beneath the careless tone lay a warm sympathy for his friend. She did not notice it. She was not thinking of Herforth just then. His few words had brought before her very vividly the farewell scene he was describing. She saw the two men together, and while the face of one was hidden from her she could see in his attitude the despair against which he had so bravely fought. She left the window and sat down in a low chair, her face a little in the shadow. Herforth went on slowly and more seriously.

"Just before we parted, Hatfeld turned to me and said: 'I'm going to have them cable you when it's all over, old man—not that I want to depress you, but because I want you to do something for me. Don't ask me why or anything about it. But when you receive that cablegram, I want you to send a box of red roses to Miss Bancroft.'"

Herforth paused a moment and poked the fire with creditable considerateness. His voice had become a trifle unsteady. Though he could not have analyzed it, for he knew they had never met, there was something in Miss Bancroft's manner as she listened which moved him strangely. She looked at him and opened her lips, but closed them again without speaking. The expression in her beautiful eyes made Herforth turn his own away.

"I got the cablegram this morning," he said softly.

Source: *Tales of the City Room* (Scribner's, 1898).

"MISS VAN DYKE'S
BEST STORY"

(1898)

When Miss Van Dyke joined the staff of the *Evening Globe*, the men of that small but ably conducted sheet bestowed on her a due amount of critical observation. After cursory but thorough consideration of her appearance and manner, they decided that she "was all right," as Matthews, the political editor, elegantly put it. That important point being settled, they proceeded to waste a great deal of their time at her desk, telling her about their wives or sweethearts and their personal affairs. This retarded her work and annoyed the managing editor; but it gave her a sweet sense of good-fellowship with her associates, and made her very happy. As she was fully twenty-three, she gave the younger reporters much motherly advice, which they immediately forgot, and assumed the role of sister to several of the older ones. On the very rare occasions when she worked late at the office, one of her fellow-workers escorted her home, or, if this was impossible, the city editor sent a messenger boy with her. She was a small woman, with appealing blue eyes and the usual journalistic assortment of nerves. They felt it was quite out of the question for her to be on the streets at night alone—in which opinion Miss Van Dyke concurred.

She did not say much about herself, having discovered at an early period of her newspaper experience that the interest her good comrades felt in the conversation lagged as soon as they ceased to do the talking. Nevertheless, on several occasions she had managed to inject into the train of reminiscences a few of her own, and one of these had made the rounds of the office and was generally regarded as very touching.

"When I left the convent," said Miss Van Dyke, in telling the story to her ardent champion, Matthews, "the nuns knew that I had decided to go into journalism. One of them, Sister Clare, was very fond of me, as I was of her. The day I was graduated, she took me into the convent garden for a little farewell advice. It was all very good, and I was very much touched—especially by her last words. I shall never forget them. As she kissed me good-by, she held me in her arms an instant, and said: 'Farewell, little one. May angels ever guide your pen!'

"I think of it so often," added Miss Van Dyke, looking up into the young man's face with childlike eyes dimmed by the recollection. "And when I have a story that is at all unpleasant to handle, I keep that advice in mind. It has prevented me from making a great many mistakes, I'm sure. One couldn't write improper or slangy things with those sweet words in mind."

The picture appealed to the office taste. It was pleasant to think of little Miss Van Dyke (they always punctiliously gave her the title) "turning out her copy in the shadow of an angel's wing," as the sporting editor remarked. That youth was so deeply affected by the charm of the incident that he once referred to it with almost lachrymose feeling, after a very late supper, and actually came to blows with someone who laughed at him. He got a black eye for his pains. Miss Van Dyke saw the bruise the next morning when he came to the office. There was, in fact, little that her sharply observing blue eyes did not see, but she never heard the story of its origin. She continued to turn out innocuous copy, and to suggest, by request, appropriate birthday and Christmas presents for the wives of her friends. She also listened earnestly to the recital of long conversations that had taken place between reporters and the young women with whom they were in love. Miss Van Dyke interpreted to the reporters what the young women might have meant by certain remarks, and as her sweet good nature unconsciously made these interpretations bear a somewhat flattering air, her popularity grew apace. Even the office boys heeded her mild requests, and the managing editor went the length of remarking that she was a hardworking, level-headed little woman.

A few days after this momentous dictum, the managing editor accepted a suggestion from his chief to retire from the management of the *Evening Globe*. His successor came into the office unhampered by any knowledge of the members of the staff. He gave out an oracular utterance to the effect that he was after "hot stuff" for the paper, and consequently the reporters, wishing to retain their official heads, bestirred themselves to give him what he wanted.

He was a young man of intense and feverish activity, and the repose of Miss Van Dyke's manner did not appeal to him. So, too, her correct and colorless little stories, perhaps because constructed in the cool shadow of the angel's wings, struck him as having no "go!" Being a young man of frank nature, he did not take the trouble to conceal his impression, and Miss Van Dyke awoke to the painful consciousness that she was disapproved of by the new editor.

She was thinking of this as she stood at a window in the editorial rooms about half-past six o'clock on the afternoon of election day. There rose to her ears, from "Newspaper Row," the din of tin horns, fervently tooted by enthusiastic Tammanyites, who saw the approaching end of the so-called "reform administration."[1] Even at this early hour it was admitted that Tammany had carried Greater New York by a sweeping plurality. The frantic shouts of loyal adherents of the Wigwam came to her from City Hall Park, where the crowd was watching the bulletins in front of the great newspaper offices for the returns.[2] The *Evening Globe* was still on duty, its members toiling in the city room with tense nerves and haggard faces. From the basement came the thunder of the presses as they ground out the extras containing the latest news.

Miss Van Dyke knew that with the single exception of herself every woman on the paper was hard at work. The reflection was not a pleasant one. She brooded over it as her sorrowful eyes looked at the surging throng below her. While she gazed abstractedly at it a great roar came from the packed mass of humanity across the street. Another district had sent in returns for Tammany. The ringing cheer swept through the crowds in Park Row and across City Hall Park, to be taken up by other throats and sent in waves of sound up Broadway.

"Well, well, well,
Reform has gone to Hell,"

rang in her ears from the hoarsely shrieking throats of thousands
of excited men. Miss Van Dyke turned from the window with a
shocked expression.

Matthews brushed past her, his hat on the back of his head, his
tie under his ear, his expression eloquent of disgust. He had not a
word or glance for her—he who was usually her most loyal and
devoted slave, and who had assured her that he should always
continue to be at least this, as she would make him nothing more.

"A landslide for Tammany, isn't it?" called one of the artists as
Matthews passed his easel. "Everything will be wide-open after
this! Good times coming in the Tenderloin again. Eh, old man?"

"Coming," repeated Matthews, with contemptuous scorn.
"They've come. It's broken loose already. The Tenderloin has
been celebrating for two hours past. By this time it's a blaze of
the old-time glory."[3]

He strode on, into the managing editor's office. With a sudden
impulse Miss Van Dyke followed him. An inspiration had seized
her, and she acted upon it without giving herself time for a second thought.

Her timid rap on the editor's door was unheard. She pushed it
open and entered the "kennel," as the box of a room was irrever-
ently styled by the staff. The tired-looking young man sat at his
desk, which was littered with papers, telegrams, and long columns of "returns." He was talking quickly to Matthews when
she entered, and both men looked in surprise at the small black
figure before them.

"I beg your pardon," hesitated the girl. "I am sorry to interrupt you, but I have a suggestion for a special which I thought
you might like to have me work up."

The managing editor's lips twitched rather impatiently, but he
answered her with the businesslike courtesy he showed to all the
women who worked for him.

"Thank you, Miss Van Dyke," he said, "but we're very busy
now. If you don't mind waiting until morning I can give your suggestion more careful consideration."

"I'm afraid it's something that won't wait," the girl persisted.

She flushed a little. "I want you," she added, "to let me do the Tenderloin tonight—to describe its celebration of Tammany's victory from a woman's point of view."

Matthews uttered a startled ejaculation, but neither Miss Van Dyke nor the editor heard it. The latter had turned quickly, a sudden interest in his cool gray eyes.

"That's good," he said promptly. "Do it by all means. New thing—fresh point of view. Write the best story you ever wrote in your life. You've got a splendid chance to turn in a good piece of work."

He thought a moment, and added more slowly: "Of course you must have someone with you. I'll send Henderson along, and you can go from place to place in a carriage. Or perhaps Matthews would like to go," he added, turning to that young man with a sudden twinkle in his eyes, which showed that he had not been so oblivious to the social conditions of the office as he had seemed.

At this opening Matthews broke out in vigorous expostulation.

"She can't go," he said excitedly. "It's madness. I don't know what you're thinking of. It's not Miss Van Dyke's kind of a story at all. Why don't you send Miss Masters if you want a Tenderloin special?" he demanded, forgetting the deference due his superior officer in his agitation.

The editor considered his objections gravely.

"That's true, Miss Van Dyke," he said, turning to her with a sudden lapse of interest. "It isn't your kind of a story, you know. Are you quite sure you realize what you're attempting?"

"I should like to take the assignment," the newspaper woman returned nervously but firmly. "I think I can give you what you want. At least, I'll do my best."

"Well, all right then," said the young man, briskly. He tapped his bell, and told the office boy who responded to get Henderson and a carriage. When Henderson entered, almost at once, he gave him some concise directions in a low tone. Then he turned again to Miss Van Dyke.

"I think a couple of hours uptown will be enough," he said kindly. "It won't be a pleasant experience for you. Then come back to the office and write the story while it is fresh. Turn it into me when you've finished it and go home for a good rest. Of course we won't expect you down tomorrow, as we'll have your copy all ready for the first edition in the morning. I've told Henderson to take you to a few places only, but they're typical, and you'll get the atmosphere. Are you going, Matthews?"

With words much too emphatic that youth declared that he was not, and reiterated his reasons, to which the managing editor lent but an indifferent ear. He had turned to his desk and was deep in the election returns again, so that he did not even hear Miss Van Dyke's timid "good-night" as she left his office. He had, in fact, forgotten her and her assignment within five minutes after her departure. This was not the case with the now miserable Matthews.

When Miss Van Dyke returned to the office at two o'clock in the morning she found that young man awaiting her with anguish on his brow. He had confided to all his associates on the *Evening Globe* the tragedy of the night, to which they listened without much comment. Ordinarily, it would have excited a great deal, but the work on election night was too pressing to permit of idle talk. He turned upon the tired reporter, as she entered, a face on which reproach and scorn were strongly blended. She lifted her hand, and the motion of the delicate fingers silenced the words that rushed to his lips.

"If you say one word to me," she asserted, "I shall cry." There was a treacherous break in her voice, though she had tried to make the words light. "I'm worn out," she continued, "and I have my story to write before I can go home. I know everything you want to say. It will be a waste of time to go over it. I want to be left in peace to do my work."

He opened his lips to speak, despite her protest.

"If you have any friendliness at all for me," she begged, "go away and leave me alone." And with a lowering brow he went.

Miss Van Dyke wrote her story, putting into it the best work of which she was capable. The wild scenes of the night were like a horrible dream in their effect on the quiet little woman who had gone to them still full of memories of convent gardens, and dimly lighted chapels where black-robed nuns prayed silently. She described them vividly and strongly, setting them down as she had seen them, not wholly understanding what she wrote, but giving to the public a story whose realism haunted many a man and woman who read it the next day. It was the report of innocence on vice, made with the fidelity with which a little child tells of some horror that it does not comprehend, and for that very reason describes the more effectively. Miss Van Dyke finished her story as dawn was breaking. Then she went alone through the gray streets, past dimly burning lamps, to the elevated train which carried her to a station near her uptown boarding-house. There had been no arrangement made by the office for her safe conduct on this occasion. It had been taken for granted that a young woman who had done an election night special, describing the gayest scenes in gay New York, could afterwards make her way home alone.

She did not come to the office at all the next day. It was well that she did not, for the larger part of the day was given to the discussion and mental digestion of "Little Van Dyke's story." For the first time the members of the staff did not trouble themselves to say "Miss" Van Dyke, which they had been so careful to do before. The quiet little woman and her story were the talk of the office, and the comments upon both made Matthews set his teeth. Henderson epitomized the general feeling by his one remark at the end of a spirited debate as to how much she understood of what she had written.

"Anyhow," he said, with somewhat feeling sarcasm, "the angel was certainly off duty, temporarily"; and during the yell of laughter that followed, Matthews was conscious of a lust for Henderson's blood that alarmed him by its intensity. Later in the day, he overheard further remarks suggesting the general view of Miss Van Dyke's story.

"It's a corker," said the managing editor, with generous enthusiasm.[4] "One of the best things of the kind I ever read. I might have known she had it in her. That quiet, shrinking type of woman always has."

"What a stunning bluff she put up on us!" laughed another man. "She took us all in—every one of us—with her convent manner and her nursery eyes. I thought she was fresh from vernal fields, but I guess she knows a few things." Matthews, listening to it all, wondered if he were becoming the victim of homicidal mania, since there seemed no other explanation for his feverish longing for the gore of these friends of his.

"Let's make her feel at home when she drops in," suggested the bright young woman who did sensational stories for the *Evening Globe*. She wore blonde hair and much red paint, and she had always resented keenly the deep respect shown by the staff to Miss Van Dyke.[5] The Tenderloin story was one she would have been glad to write if she had thought of it. Not having done so, she was pleased by the sentiment concerning Miss Van Dyke which that young person's story had called forth so freely.

"This will do it," she added jocosely, as she produced a large placard and nailed it above Miss Van Dyke's desk. It bore what the bright young woman called a sentiment appropriate to the occasion. "Welcome to Little Van Dyke," it read, in large black letters—"the Tenderfoot of the Tenderloin."[6] When the brilliant originator of this heard the laughter that greeted its appearance, she realized that success had crowned her sisterly efforts.

"Little Van Dyke" arrived at the office at eight o'clock the next morning, and marveled at the silence that fell over the city room as she came in. The heads that usually rose to greet her remained bent over their desks. Her friends—and she had many—were bitterly chagrined by the step she had so innocently taken. Her enemies—and she had a few—exulted openly over it. Nevertheless, everybody waited for someone else to utter one of the pleasantries all knew were coming. The force of habit was strong, and despite themselves the staff shrank from speaking to this convent girl as they would have spoken to Miss Masters. As she approached her desk, Miss Van Dyke saw the placard hung on the wall. On her table were bottles, glasses, cigarette stumps, and other reminders of her recent experience. They watched her look at these, and then brush them aside, her pale cheeks flushing as she caught the implication. They noticed her slight figure straighten as she read the lurid sentiment on the wall. Then she tore it down and dropped it into her waste-paper basket, brushing the debris from her desk into the same receptacle as she took her seat. Several of the men who liked her, and who had thought that a little experience of the kind she was having might do her good, now felt that the matter had gone far enough, and rose to speak to her. They were interrupted by conversational pleasantries bearing on the case from some of the younger men scattered about the room.

One of these, a youth to whom Miss Van Dyke had always objected, and whom she had rather pointedly avoided, sauntered up
to her now with a lounging familiarity that made the blood of her
champions boil.

"Why didn't you take me with you last night?" he asked in an
easy, off-hand way. "I should have enjoyed it first rate, and you
could have shown me a new phase of life."

The others followed his lead, not from cruelty, but because the
situation appealed to their peculiar sense of humor.

"Well, we've got almost as much of it as if we had gone,"
said one, comfortingly. "Miss Van Dyke's story conducted us all
through the gilded haunts of the Tenderloin. She exhausted the
subject, I tell you," the speaker laughed.

One of the girl's friends swore softly at this and she heard him.
He would not have sworn in her presence last week, she thought.
He seized his hat and left the room precipitately, missing the ex-
planation which she now made to the assembled company.

"I can't understand your attitude this morning," she said with
a dignified warmth. "I went on that assignment because it seemed
to me a chance for good work. The managing editor liked the
suggestion and told me to carry it out. I wrote a faithful report of
what I saw, and that is all there is to it."

They listened quietly, with the mental reservations of those
who knew more about the subject than the speaker did. Wheeler,
one of her friends, came to her a little later.

"I could have told you, little girl," he said very gently, "what a
serious blunder you were making. If I had been here I would most
certainly have warned you that night. But I knew nothing about
it until I came yesterday morning and found the office teeming
with the story. It was a horrible mistake for you to make. It's an
assignment no woman should have taken, and no good woman
would have dreamed of attempting it—if she had realized what
she was doing," he added hastily, as the girl paled under the
words. "I'm afraid it will take you months to live it down."

Absurd as the words sounded, Miss Van Dyke found them very
true. As the weeks passed she tried to slip back into her quiet little niche on the paper, but they would not have it so. Even the
managing editor unconsciously added his share to her weight of

woe. He had highly approved her Tenderloin story, and now, from day to day, he gave her others along similar lines.

"Give us something as good as that Tenderloin special, Miss Van Dyke," he would say, in open self-gratulation that she had emerged from beneath the angel's wing. At each repetition of the words the girl's heart grew heavier.

She wrote the stories with photographic accuracy, and they were satisfactory, although no other ever contained the brilliant work of that fatal night. She never became reconciled to the fact that the men now treated her as one of themselves, with a good-natured *camaraderie*, in which, however, the deference of the old days was wholly lacking. She knew that they called her "Little Van Dyke" and that "The Tenderfoot of the Tenderloin" still clung to her as a sobriquet.[7] Also that there was no further reference to the angel that guided her pen. The managing editor's approval and the off-hand kindliness of her associates did not repay her for this lack, which she felt in every fiber of her sensitive nature.

Even the devoted Matthews was changed. He was as respectful, as deferential, as in the old days—even more so, as if he wished to make up, by his personal efforts, for the change in the office atmosphere. But he was irritable and moody and wholly unhappy, and each new assignment given to the "Little Tenderfoot" wrung his manly soul. Very early in their acquaintance he had laid his heart and hand at her feet, and she had declined both with gentle firmness and womanly appreciation of the honor he had offered her. He had never mentioned the matter again, but she had felt, until that eventful night, that he remained unchanged.

She was thinking it all over one afternoon, as he came to her desk in the city room.

"How much longer are you going to endure this?" he asked brusquely. "Do you realize that you're taking rank on the paper with Miss Masters, who smokes and drinks, and is regarded as 'a good fellow' by the boys? Don't you see that your assignments are getting more and more objectionable all the time? Why don't you chuck it all?"

Miss Van Dyke turned her head wearily. "How can I?" she asked dismally. "I've got to make a living somehow. The way the men treat me is bad enough, but there's another thing that's worse. I'm in the position of the author of 'The Deceased Wife's Sister.'[8] Everything I write is compared with that wretched Tenderloin story and found wanting. 'Give us another as good as that,' the editors say, and when I turn in the copy they look it over and grumble, 'Well, this is pretty good, but it isn't a patch on your election night special.' It's just as Mr. Wheeler said the next day. I shall never live it down, and yet I'm chained here, and there's no chance of my getting away."

The tears filled her eyes as she spoke. She openly wiped them away, glad that no one saw them but this loyal friend, who had been so faithful.

Matthews seized his opportunity, clever man that he was.

"Let me give you an assignment," he said earnestly. He leaned over her desk and took from her little hand the pen with which she had been drawing erratic designs on her desk blotter as she spoke.

"Drop this," he said urgently, his dark face flushed with earnestness. "Drop it for all time and come to me. Let me take care of you forever. Surely there is nothing finer in being a self-supporting woman than in marrying a poor human being like me and making him happy."

Miss Van Dyke looked into his dark eyes, her own falling beneath their expression of love and longing. In a sudden mental illumination she realized why it had been so hard for her to bear her little trials of the past two months under their critical but loving gaze. He had been so fine through it all. He had suffered for her and with her, and it had been unnecessary pain—for she knew now that she had loved him all along.

His stalwart form was between her and the desks near hers. It would be a human bulwark between her and the world, as long as it had life and strength, she knew. The career on which she had entered so happily seemed to have passed beyond her control. Others were shaping it—to her undoing. After all, a woman's place is in a home! She put her hand on the brown ones lying near her, which promptly caught and held it fast. A careful inspection out of the corner of his eye showed Matthews that Henderson was watching the little scene with polite interest. He had to content himself with a very tender pressure of the hand he held in his own.

"I—I think I'll take the assignment," Miss Van Dyke whispered shyly.

For the first time since Tammany's return to power, the cloud lifted from the brow of Matthews.

Source: *Tales of the City Room* (Scribner's, 1898).

FROM
TALES OF
THE CLOISTER

"BETWEEN DARKNESS
& DAWN"

(1901)

The graduation exercises were in progress. Elizabeth Van Nest heard the opening notes of the overture to "Die Zauberflöte" as she walked down the long corridor toward Commencement Hall.[1] Many of her friends and classmates were members of the convent orchestra, and they had practiced the music of the graduation programme until even Mozart's melodies beat drearily against the ear. Elizabeth had laughed with them over the seemingly endless repetitions, but now the music took on a sudden and unexpected charm. Her eyes filled with tears, and the hand that held her essay trembled a little. The heavy perfume of the flowers banked against the stage floated out to her. In half an hour she would be standing there delivering the valedictory.

She wondered vaguely if she could do it—if, with this sickening sense of loneliness and loss strong in her, she could say to that waiting audience the farewell words that had come so easily to her tongue during the rehearsals of the past week. She must do it, and do it well. It was the closing act of her school life, and she ought to leave as pleasant a memory behind her as she took away.

In her heart she knew she would. She usually did things well—
this calm, self-contained pupil of whom the nuns expected so
much. Then, too, she reflected, Sister Estelle would be in the
wings with her, and Sister Estelle would help her if she faltered.
Dear Sister Estelle, who had never failed her from the day she had
been brought to the convent, a little child, and was given to the
sweet-faced nun as a special charge.

Today they were to part, she and this woman who had been
the strongest element in her life for twelve years—guide, philosopher, teacher, sister, mother, all in one. After today she could call
at the convent at proper intervals and talk to Sister Estelle—
perhaps through the wire grating in the little reception-room.
Her heart contracted at the thought. She had never before rebelled against a rule of the great institution, but this seemed very
hard. The proper intervals would be far between, she reflected
with some bitterness. She was to go to Chicago the next day to
begin the study of medicine. She had chosen her profession, and
Sister Estelle had approved the choice, which was enough. The
thinly veiled disapprobation of her guardian and other friends
counted for little against that.

She had reached the entrance to Commencement Hall, but she
passed it, and, after a preliminary tap, entered a room a few
doors beyond. It was empty except for a Sister, in her severe black
garb, standing at the window overlooking the convent garden.
The nun did not turn. She slipped her arm around the girdled
waist, and laid her cheek against the stiff white linen that covered
her friend's bosom. The little act meant much, for caresses were
rare between these two, who understood each other so well without them.

The young girl looked up into the nun's eyes and wondered
whether it was fancy or if the lids were a trifle reddened. She
dared not think so, for that might mean the loss of her own self-
control. Sister Estelle did not approve of tears even when shed in
such circumstances as these and by the pupil of her heart.

"How can I get up there and read to them," Elizabeth asked,
"with our parting before me? You will help me, I know; tell me
that I must do it, and that I shall do it well."

The nun smiled serenely. "Assuredly you will do it well, my
dear," she said, almost lightly. "We cannot have you fail at this of

all times. You will do justice to yourself and to us." She hesitated a little. "I will be near you," she added, simply.

The repetition of the familiar assurance that had run like a golden thread throughout the years silenced them both. By a common impulse they turned unseeing eyes upon the smiling garden below, while memories rose before them.

"I will be near you," Sister Estelle had said to the frightened little girl when darkness fell on her first night in convent walls. "I will be near you," she had repeated at the crisis in the long illness several years later. Elizabeth recalled now those nights of delirium in which the silent black-robed figure had remained at her bedside to do battle, the child thought, with the phantoms and goblins that filled the room. The gentle sister had indeed been with her in all the marked episodes of her schoolgirl life; she was with her now in this last scene. They turned and read the same thought in each other's eyes. The nun took her pupil in her arms and held her there.

"No, dear child, it is not for the last time," she said, with quiet confidence. "I have been with you until now—I shall be with you in thought and spirit and heart in the years to come. There is nothing I can do for you in the big world outside, but I can think of you and pray for you here every day. In the times you need me you must come to me. They will be many at first, for the world will have unpleasant surprises for you, and you will turn to me, I know—my little one, my little girl."

She kissed the wet cheek upturned to her, and drew her pupil gently toward the door. A ripple of applause rolled toward them from the hall. The orchestra had just finished. They walked quickly down a side corridor which led to the stage wings. The fresh young voices of the convent quartette were raised in the song that preceded the valedictory. Elizabeth Van Nest smoothed her gloves, shook out her white plumage, and looked up into her friend's face with the smile and assurance of her childhood days.

"I will do my very bestest best," she said, tenderly. "Could I do anything else, with you looking on?"

Miss Van Nest's fellow-students at the medical college did her the honor to speculate about her with much interest. She was head and shoulders above them in her work; that they all felt and most of them admitted. It would have been difficult to do otherwise, with the faculty treating her as a genius given into their developing care. Miss Van Nest had chosen surgery as her life-work, and Dr. Lincoln, the famous consulting surgeon of the clinic attached to the college, made no secret of the fact that he regarded her as a phenomenon. He invariably selected her as one of his assistants in operations, and made curt, illuminative comments to her as the work progressed. He had even been heard to warn her not to study too hard—a caution rarely given by the great doctor, who held the days all too short for the things to be done in them. Notwithstanding this warning, she continued to work eighteen hours of the twenty-four. There were no distractions, for she had few acquaintances and no intimates. Several times a year she left the city for a few days, and it became known in some mysterious way that she spent them in a distant convent with a former teacher to whom she was devoted, and who continued to exercise great influence over her. It was whispered that she had been led to adopt surgery as a profession by the advice of this cloister friend. Dr. Lincoln sniffed openly when the surmise came to his ears.

"She will be a surgeon because she was born one," he said. "She has the brain, nerves, and hands for it." He loaded her with work, which she cheerfully accepted, and boasted to his colleagues about her, predicting that she would do great things.

She was graduated with honors which would have turned the head of one not so well poised. She did hospital work in Chicago for two years, and then went abroad for four more of supplementary training among the horrors of hospitals in great European cities. When she returned to her own country and established herself in New York, her fame had preceded her. Dr. Elizabeth Van Nest promptly took a place in the front rank of her profession, and enhanced the reputation already acquired by a series of brilliant operations. One of these was performed in Chicago, and while the newspapers were still full of the marvel of it, for the case was an unusual one and the patient a woman of national fame, the surgeon slipped away, leaving no address except in the patient's home.

"The convent again, I suppose," Dr. Lincoln reflected, dryly. "Hasn't she got over that habit yet? It's twelve years since she was graduated." Then his stern eyes softened. "If it's a weakness," he added, "it's her only one, and I wish she had more. She ought to have some strong human interest in her life." For Dr. Lincoln was fond as well as proud of his brilliant pupil.

Dr. Van Nest's heart felt no such need as she rang the convent bell on the afternoon of her arrival in the city of her girlhood. She looked up lovingly at the cold gray walls, and a film came over the eyes usually keen and steady rather than soft. The familiar little portress of years ago opened the door, and her shy exclamation of recognition and delight was music in the doctor's ears.

"I had no time to write to Reverend Mother," she explained as she entered the little reception-room. "I came West unexpectedly, and did not know until last night that I would be able to leave Chicago today. But surely she will permit me to see Sister Estelle without delay. Please tell her that I am here, Sister, and that I am—heart-hungry."

The portress hesitated. "I am sure you may see her, Miss Van Nest—Doctor Van Nest, I mean. You see we know all about you, even here, and we rejoice in your success. But you must be prepared for some change in Sister Estelle. She—she has not been well."

Dr. Van Nest grew a little indignant. "Why was I not informed?" she asked, quickly. The portress looked at her with a smile which deprecated the unconsciously assumed professional manner.

"It was Sister Estelle's own request that you should not know," she said, softly. "You were abroad, and she feared your anxiety, if you knew her condition, might interfere with your work. She believed there was no cause for anxiety. She knew you would come to see her as soon after your return to America as you could."

Dr. Van Nest became again the child of the convent. "Let me see her," she begged. "Let me see her at once—not behind the grating, but here, or in the garden, by ourselves. Please ask Reverend Mother."

The little portress departed, leaving the impatient visitor alone. Dr. Van Nest looked around her with a reminiscent smile. It was years since she had been in this particular wing of the great building, but nothing was changed. The same high polish shone on the waxed floor; the same chairs stood at precisely the same angles in the same corners; the same religious pictures hung on the walls;

the same wax flowers stood on the same small table. There was the desk which the child Elizabeth Van Nest used to approach, shaking in her little shoes, to be reprimanded for some childish mistake by the nun who sat there. Here at last there was a change. The nun was there no more. Dr. Van Nest recalled a line in one of Sister Estelle's letters, sent her in Paris,

"Our dear Sister Raymond has found her reward."

It seemed a long time that she waited. When at last a step came along the hall, she rose and went forward in her impatience. It was the portress, alone, but she anticipated the words on the other's lips.

"I am to take you to the west parlor," she said. "Sister Estelle is not well enough to come to you here. She will see you there alone."

Dr. Van Nest followed her guide without a word. She kept close beside her as they walked through the halls, but the nooks and corridors where she had played as a child had now no memories for her. The gentle portress prattled on artlessly, but the visitor did not hear her words. Her mind was concentrated on the dread of what was to come. She paced the west parlor in a fever of foreboding. Then came a light step, slow and hesitating, but unmistakably the step she awaited, and Sister Estelle stood in the doorway, supported by the arm of Sister Rodriguez, the convent infirmarian. The doctor went forward without a word, took the slender, emaciated figure in her strong arms, and carried it to a reclining-chair. It was a pathetically light burden, though Sister Rodriguez looked with deep respect at the superbly formed woman who bore it, and who had won so enviable a position in the big world that the knowledge of it had penetrated even to the convent pharmacy. She went away and left them together, speechless, the visitor's dark head buried in Sister Estelle's lap.

"Oh, why—why did you not tell me?" she cried at last. The hand that lay on her lap trembled slightly.

"Why should I, dear?" the nun asked. "You could have done nothing—even you could have done nothing for me." There was a caress as well as a compliment in the words. "Weak lungs are not in your line of work. And I was so proud of you, so anxious for you to be the successful woman you are. It is a great gift you have, my dear child—this ability to relieve and save. I could not distract you in your work, as you would have been distracted if you had known. And now I am happy, for I have been permitted to remain until you came, and to see you again."

Dr. Van Nest kissed the thin hands without speaking. Rebellion was in her heart—rebellion against her own helplessness in the face of this disaster. The hollow voice, the bright spots in the cheeks, the brilliant eyes that shone like polished agate under the band of linen across the brow—all these things testified eloquently that Sister Estelle's "reward" was soon to come.

"Can you stay here with me until I go?" the nun asked, almost diffidently. "They have told me"—she hesitated—"that it will be but a short time. Reverend Mother has kindly given her permission for you to stay if your duties will permit."

"I will not leave you for a moment," said the other woman. She added, with an uncontrollable sob: "What shall I do, what can I do, without you? All my work has been for you—to please you. Your letters and your love have made me what I am. In every crisis of my life you have been with me; I could not have met them without you. I have come to you always, and you have never failed me. How can I live on alone?"

The sick woman looked at her with wet eyes. "Listen to me, my little girl," she said. "This may not be so great a separation as you think. The memory of me will always be with you, and you know whether I shall forget you when I am with God. You know how I would have you act. And if you have sometime a peculiar, pressing need of me, perhaps I may be permitted to come to you. Our Lord may grant us this. Why not? When He gave you to me for all these years as the child of my heart." She bent forward and kissed the bowed head in her lap. "Remember," she said, softly. "I promise. If you need me, and if it is permitted me, I will come to you."

Dr. Van Nest, aged thirty-eight, stood at the window of her New York office and looked out at the falling snow. It was Christmas day, but the season had little holiday significance for the famous surgeon. She had worked as usual, driving in her carriage from hospital to private house, and carrying from place to place with her the constant thought of a white face and a pair of pained, appealing eyes.

When she entered her house late in the evening, the smiling maid had pointed to a varied assortment of packages, which had not yet been opened. Large boxes, with the names of prominent florists on their covers, breathed sweetly of the love of friends. Telegrams and notes were piled high on her desk. She unwrapped several of the packages, and her lips set a little grimly over the cards that accompanied them.

"From your grateful patient," she read. "With the deepest appreciation of all your kindness," ran another. "To the dear doctor to whom I owe my merry Christmas," was the inscription of a third. She dropped them with a sigh, looked out of the window, and then with her characteristic walk began pacing up and down the long room, her hands clasped behind her, and her forehead puckered with thought and anxiety.

"The doctor's worried over some case," the maid reported to the cook. "I can always tell when she's anxious."

Dr. Van Nest's footsteps on the polished floor echoed rather inharmoniously in the large room. On the hearth a bright fire sparkled, but its cheery invitation did not lure her from her restless tramp. Before her there were always the same pale face and dark eyes pathetically full of love and trust. The doctor uttered a sigh that was almost a groan as she at last sank into a chair before the grate and looked into the glowing coals. They formed at once into the outlines of the haunting face.

"I am going to lose that case," she thought, forebodingly. "And I'm going to have a nervous collapse, too," she continued, with grim conviction. "I never felt like this before. I have no confidence in myself. I am as nervous as an hysterical schoolgirl. And how she trusts me!"

She sat brooding dully for a moment.

"I can't feel as I want to about her case. Is there something I don't foresee?" she went on, putting the situation before herself with rigid truthfulness. "Lincoln agrees with me. So does Dr. Vandeveer. Still, I cannot help feeling there's something under it all that none of us grasps. There is this sense of some unapprehended element in the case which always comes up whenever I think of it. And I—am to operate on her tomorrow. She trusts me as if I were infallible!"

She threw back her head with an air of rebellious hopelessness.

Before her came the picture of the patient as she had looked during the preliminary examination of the day before. She had come out of the ether repeating a portion of the Apostles' Creed.[2]

"I believe in God, the Father Almighty," she had murmured; then, suddenly, "And I believe in Dr. Van Nest, too; oh, I do believe in her. I believe in Elizabeth."

The consulting surgeons had smiled irresistibly; the little incident revealed so fully the discussion that must have been waged in the patient's home. Her friends had urged a man surgeon for the operation. But Dr. Van Nest had been conscious of an unfamiliar lump in her throat. For the first time in her professional experience she was not feeling sure of herself. She wondered whether the patient had felt it, and whether these lynx-eyed male colleagues had any suspicion of it. Her strong, white hands were as steady and as deft as ever, but she felt her heart sink. Was she to fail now, for the first time, and on this friend of her heart—this friend who had come, it seemed to her, to fill the place of Sister Estelle, dead these eight years? The sufferer would permit no one but her to operate. This life, so dear to her and to others, lay in her hands—and for the first time in her experience she shrank from the responsibility. She felt suddenly cold, and held her hand to the blaze. It shook visibly. Dr. Van Nest sprang to her feet with an exclamation of anger.

"Fool that I am," she said. "I am letting myself go to pieces. I shall be in fine condition for tomorrow's work." Her eyes filled with sudden, rare tears. "She is the only being I love," she breathed, "and I am going to lose her. First, Sister Estelle. And now she must go—and under my hands at that."

Her thoughts flew to the grave in the convent cemetery out West, marked by a simple pine board darkened by the storms of many seasons. A childlike longing for the familiar touch and voice, so dear in the years gone by, overwhelmed her. She felt like the panic-stricken little girl of thirty years ago—the child who had been calmed and cheered by a white hand and a soft reassuring voice.

"'I will be near you, dear,'" repeated the doctor, sadly. "If she could be near me now, she would pull me out of this condition I'm allowing myself to get into. Oh, for a moment with her here and now!"

She looked up almost expectantly, as if she had uttered the words of an incantation. The little clock ticked steadily on the mantel, the fire crackled on the hearth, and the wind of December sang its elfish song at the windows. That was all.

She resolutely pulled herself together and rang the bell. Night had fallen, and lights were flashing from the windows of the neighboring houses.

"Bring me something to eat, and then I am going to bed," she said, when the maid appeared. "I must have a good night's sleep—if I can."

She seemed to have slept for a very short time, when she awoke with every sense alert. It was yet night, but through the large windows hygienically open at the top she could see the pearl-gray shadows that preceded dawn. On the hearth the fire burned low, but each object in the room was distinct in the dim light. The clock ticked cheerily. She could not quite distinguish its face across the room, but as she strained her eyes in the effort it struck five.

It was not usual for her to wake at this hour, but she experienced no surprise or annoyance. Instead, she was conscious of a vague but trustful responsiveness. She let her eyes roam slowly around the room, and smiled to herself. Fear and unrest had left her; she felt composed, wholly at peace. She threw back the covering and sat up. As she did so a soft hand touched her own. It was years since she had felt it, but she recognized it at once, and without the slightest shock or fear her mind adapted itself to the experience. She turned quickly and saw Sister Estelle standing at the side of the bed. She was a little in shadow, but her tall figure in the somber habit of her order was clearly defined, and under the white band across her brow her dark eyes shone luminously. The smile with which she met the doctor's eyes was the old sweet smile of long ago—loving, reassuring, and touched now with a peaceful gratitude which her first words explained.

"You are glad to see me," she said, quietly—"and you are not afraid."

The doctor put the hand to her lips and held it there. It was firm and cool, and there was the same velvety texture which the schoolgirl of twenty years ago had secretly admired. She echoed the other's words.

"Afraid, Sister?" she said. "Of you? Never in the world. My heart is too full of love and gratitude."

She bent nearer to the other as she spoke, but as she did so the nun's figure drew slightly away. The movement did not hurt her. She understood, and there could be no thought of disappointment in the presence of that steadfast, loving smile. She sank back on the pillow with a sigh of perfect content and happiness.

"You have come," she murmured. "You said you would, and I have looked for you all these years since you left me."

"You did not need me before. You thought you did at times," added the nun, "but you did not. Could you think that I would fail when the hour came? You need me now, and I am here."

"Tell me of yourself," begged the doctor.

The Sister shook her head. "That I am here, through God's mercy, tells you that all is well with me. I have come to tell you what you need to know—things that will help you," she said. "You have reached a crisis in your career. Tomorrow will be the turning-point. If you had failed in the case of your friend, you would have turned morbid and introspective; would have lost confidence in yourself. You will not fail. I have come to tell you so. The case is as you have diagnosed it, with the one additional element which you have dimly felt throughout, but could not place. You had a similar case in Paris—Madame Bertrand's. You made notes of it at the time. They are in the lowest, left-hand drawer of your desk, hidden under old newspapers and clippings. They will give you the key to the situation."

Dr. Van Nest drew a long breath. "I have it now," she cried. "This is almost the same case. They are so rare; it is odd that I should have two of them in my experience, but not as strange as that the recollection of the other should not have come to my tormented mind. I remember the other one perfectly."

The scientific interest of the discovery obscured for a moment the full realization of the strange experience through which she was passing. Sister Estelle resumed:

"The operation will be a success," she said. "Your friend will regain her health. So sleep, dear child, and wake calm and strong for the work you have to do."

Dr. Van Nest threw out imploring hands. "Do not leave me yet," she begged. "How shall I know in the morning that it was not all a dream? How can I tell then that you truly came to me as you promised, and that it was not a phantasy of the night?"

Sister Estelle smiled. "Tomorrow you will find your notebook. That will supply what you need. But that you may know the sweetness of our Lord in letting me come as I promised, you shall have an unmistakable sign that I was here. Peace be with you."

The clock chimed the quarter, and Dr. Van Nest looked wide-eyed at the place where the nun had been. The coals in the grate had turned to ashes. The gray of the eastern sky was quickening into light. Through the open windows came sounds of the awakening city, the blowing of distant whistles, the rumble of wheels borne in on the cold, bracing air of the day that was just born. Some were already at their work. Dr. Van Nest closed her eyes, sank back among her pillows, and fell asleep to prepare herself for hers as she had been told.

It was late when she awoke, and she had to dress and breakfast rapidly to keep several morning appointments. She was almost herself—quick, alert, clear-eyed. She pushed resolutely into her mental background the memory of the night's experience. This was the close of the nineteenth century, and she was a *fin de siècle* product.[3] Visions could hardly be taken more seriously than to gather from them such comfort as they might yield. She smiled and sighed at the same time as she entered her library at two that afternoon. She had to go to her friend's house at three to perform the operation, but in the interval she would look in the old desk that held the accumulated notes of years and see what her notebook said. Her hand trembled a little as she unlocked the lowest left-hand drawer.

Far back in the corner, dust-covered and hidden under some French journals, was the forgotten notebook. But this was broad daylight, and the life of the great city was going on outside of her library windows. It had merely been a logical trick of memory, she reflected, that had brought the thought of the book to her while she slept, and had connected it with Sister Estelle.

She sat down and plunged into its record. Yes. Here was the case of Madame Bertrand. She read with close attention, absorbed in the purely scientific interest of the subject. Suddenly she gave a little gasp of satisfaction, and made two or three notes. Her dream, if a perplexing psychical freak, had proved a profitable aid, and it was sweet to have dreamed of Sister Estelle as coming to her in her need.

A wave of perfume—sweet, heavy, full of memories, was borne in upon her sense. She looked up wonderingly and inhaled it deeply. The air was perfumed richly with mignonette.[4] There was none in the room, none on the desk, none in the old notebook she was reading. No mignonette was near her that cold December day.

She went to the window and leaned forth. The perfume failed her utterly. It did not come from without. From somewhere in her room it rose in such a whiff as she had not known for years. There had been a great bed of it in the convent garden; it was Sister Estelle's favorite flower.

Sister Estelle's favorite flower!

Dr. Van Nest's heart gave a great leap. The perfume was still with her and around her. Her nostrils and lungs were full of it— as full as they had been the day Sister Estelle had been laid away in a grave which the doctor's own hands had lined with the simple flower the dead nun loved.

For one moment she was rigidly motionless, her mind working, not feverishly, but with intense activity. It had been no dream! Sister Estelle had really come to her in the hour of her trying need, as she had promised. Here was the sign which was to convince her how peculiar a privilege she had been accorded in that personal visit of her old convent guardian. It brought a certainty as great as Dr. Van Nest had ever known in her life.

She rose to her feet and stood erect, her eyes shining, a beaming confidence written on her face. She looked at her watch. Quarter of three! With swift despatch she threw on her coat, drew on her gloves, and put on her hat. Then, with a quick, long breath, she grasped firmly her surgeon's case, walked briskly to the door and flung it open. It closed after her with a sharp click.

Source: "Between Darkness & Dawn," *Harper's Bazar* (March 1901). Reprinted in *Tales of the Cloister* (Harper & Brothers, 1901).

"IN THE CASE OF
HANNAH RISSER"

(1902)

"If you wish a story of human interest," said Miss Underhill, distinctly, "I think this one would do. It is unique, and has fine possibilities of pathos. It might almost evolve into a 'teary tale.'"

She leaned her elbow on the city editor's desk as she spoke, and regarded that awe-inspiring young man with a serene eye. She was not easily impressed, and she wholly declined to look upon him with the reverential wonder which the other members of his staff affected. It happened, therefore, that the city editor had days of but lukewarm enthusiasm over Miss Underhill's work, and this was one of them.

"Don't see much in it," he said, tersely. "Old woman, old attic, old story. We've done it too often."

Miss Underhill smiled in the slightly superior manner that invariably got on the city editor's nerves.

"Oh, but this is so different," she said. "This old woman—my discovery—has spent twenty-nine years in one tenement-room on Forsyth Street.[1] During those years she has never left that room. She is a cripple, and she sits in a chair by the window, and all day long, with her hands folded in her lap, she looks down on the festering street and thinks.[2] She is absolutely alone. If the neighbors remember to bring her something to eat during the day, she has it. If they forget, she doesn't. Usually, one of the tenement women comes in at night and puts her to bed. Sometimes they forget that, and then she dozes in her big chair until morning. A little Jewish society pays her rent and has paid it for many years, but no one else except the tenement women does anything for her.[3]

She has become to them and to their successors during these years a kind of legacy, passed from one to the other. She goes with the rooms and the occupants must look out for her."

The city editor looked bored.

"Can't see it yet," he announced, brusquely. "Can't see more than a few paragraphs at the most."

Miss Underhill passed over the interruption with her usual blithe unconcern.

"What I want to do," she continued, cheerfully, "is to take the old woman for a drive. I want to get her out of that tenement-room—for the first time in twenty-nine years, remember—and show her the world. I want her to see the Park and the trees and the sky, and the river and the boats on it, and the elevated trains and the tall new buildings; and I want to write a story telling what she thinks of New York after her Rip Van Winkle sleep."[4]

The city editor's lips relaxed in an unwilling smile.

"That'll do," he said, briskly. "Go ahead."

Miss Underhill went ahead with characteristic energy. She had, also characteristically, made all her arrangements before she consulted the city editor, in serene assurance that the story would "go," as she put it to herself. She even remembered to mention to the old woman her share in the programme. A small detail like that Miss Underhill sometimes forgot.

"I'm going to take you for a drive," she said, cordially. "I want you to get a breath of fresh air and to have a good time. Then I'll make a story of it."

Old Mrs. Risser looked worried. It was a vast undertaking to her—this drive, and not to be lightly assumed. She listened without enthusiasm to Miss Underhill's rapidly outlined plans of nurses to carry her down the stairs, quiet horses, rubber-tired wheels, and kindred comforts. Neither did the beauties of nature, held up to her imagination, inspire her with interest. Once only her faded old eyes showed a gleam of satisfaction, and this was when Miss Underhill dwelt on the commotion the proposed drive was already creating in the tenement.

"They'll all be at the windows to see you off," she announced, and Mrs. Risser listened with a satisfied quiver of her loose old lips and unconsciously drew herself up in her chair.

The next day Miss Underhill drove down Forsyth Street with a comfortable sense of satisfaction in her breast. She was getting a good story and she was at the same time doing a kindly act—a combination not so frequent as it should be in her journalistic career. She had borrowed the brougham of a wealthy friend for the occasion, and the splendid horses picked their way through the filthy street with a suggestion of outraged daintiness in their knee action.[5] The coachman held his head unusually high. He did not approve of these slum excursions. Miss Underhill smiled serenely at the dirty waifs of humanity drifting behind and running beside the carriage. The odors arising from neglected ash-barrels and decaying refuse offended her nostrils, but did not affect her high spirits. She ran lightly up the three flights of tenement stairs leading to Mrs. Risser's room and tapped gayly on the door. The noise of moans and lamentations from within broke upon her ear, mingled with another rhythmic sound. She hesitated a moment and walked in.

In her accustomed chair sat Hannah Risser, stiff in the unusual freshness of a new gingham waist. Her hands and face offered mute but eloquent testimony to the efforts of a trained nurse who had scoured them enthusiastically and was now energetically at work brushing into smoothness the old woman's gray hair. Big tears fell unchecked on the smooth expanse of gingham over the victim's breast, and great sobs shook her thin figure. At intervals a moan burst from her, mingling dolefully with the cheerful voices of two Salvation Army girls who stood beside her singing a hymn with great vigor. The nurse looked harassed but undaunted. Her eye brightened a little as Miss Underhill entered. "She's ready," she said, tersely.

Perhaps it was the curt professional tone, or possibly a sense of entire helplessness in the hands of others, that made Mrs. Risser break into another anguished wail. The Salvation Army lassies, ignoring both this interruption and that of Miss Underhill's appearance, fell on their knees and offered up a short prayer. Then one of them volunteered a kindly explanation to the reporter, who stood still, reverent but puzzled.

"She thinks you and the nurse are going to take her to some home for old ladies," she said, "where she cannot see the tenement people or have her own home. She wishes to stay here. She likes her home."

Miss Underhill smiled her thanks and crossed to the weeping old woman. Sitting down before her, she took one of her subject's unwilling hands in hers.

"Now, Mrs. Risser," she said, "I want you to enjoy this drive, so I'm going to say a few words to you before we start. I give you my word of honor that this is to be only a drive and that I will bring you back here safely in three hours at the most. You shall return and stay here, and your life will go on as usual. I am glad you like it. I do not intend to interfere in it. But I want to give you one good time. Are you satisfied?"

Mrs. Risser looked doubtful.

"You sure bring me back—sure?" she asked.

"I surely will," the girl answered.

"Tell her so, too," she said, turning to the Salvation lassies. They bent over the old woman and whispered to her quickly for a few moments. Miss Underhill caught the words "kind lady," "nice time," and "fresh air" in occasional staccato tones. Hannah Risser wiped her eyes, sniffed drearily, and announced her willingness to go. The men Miss Underhill had engaged to assist the nurse in the difficult work of getting her patient downstairs entered and the descent began.

The task was a formidable one, but an unexpected factor made it less painful than Miss Underhill had dared to expect. That factor was the simple vanity that blossomed suddenly in Hannah Risser's heart. On every landing was an impressed group of tenement women, gazing at the scene with wide-eyed awe; and their interest in the episode of which she was the central figure soothed the old woman to serene unconcern as to her own danger or discomfort. She smiled patronizingly upon her friends and nodded innumerable farewells, which they returned with the stiffness of unwonted ceremony. Miss Underhill's glowing face shone radiantly from the group as she directed and advised in her practical, assertive manner. Once on the street, it was a simple matter to lift the woman into the low carriage and settle her comfortably among the soft pillows. As she yielded to their invitation, Miss Underhill was pained to observe the dark cloud returning to her brow.

The horses leaped forward joyfully, spurning the uncongenial soil with their proud hoofs. The early afternoon sun blazed hotly

on the baking street and was thrown back in waves of heat from
the grimy tenement walls. Ragged and dirty children followed
her triumphal progress with shrieks of friendly interest, but all
this escaped Hannah Risser. She had turned her head and was
looking up at the dirty windows of her own little room, and as
she looked the tears welled forth again and splashed drearily on
the light wrap her new friends had thrown over her old shoulders. Miss Underhill observed them, but wisely said nothing,
trusting to the charm of the new impressions and experiences
awaiting her companion in the next three hours.

The misery and squalor of the tenements dropped behind them
as the carriage rolled into wider, cleaner streets. Miss Underhill
drew a long breath as it reached lower Broadway, where the air,
though heat-smitten from the asphalt walks, was at least free
from disease-breeding odors. She chatted cheerfully to the unresponsive figure at her side, pointing out the tall new buildings,
the black line of the elevated road in the distance, and the dark
shadow of moving trains; but for these things Hannah Risser had
no heart. She cowered in a corner of the carriage, casting furtive,
frightened glances out of her tear-dimmed eyes and clutching the
side of her seat with a feverish grip. Sometimes she whimpered a
little under her breath.

All this, Miss Underhill reflected calmly, was but natural. The
great city had grown up around the old woman as she slept, and
not even the sound of its heart-throbs found its way through the
four thick walls that sheltered her. How could she be other, at
first, than nervous and a little frightened? Once out of the business center, away from the noise and the roar of traffic, and
among quiet streets with beautiful homes, she would begin to
look about. And when the soft green avenues of the Park unrolled
before her, and the gorgeous panorama of the Hudson and the
Palisades met her view, the old woman would awaken and rejoice, and on the horrible walls of her beloved room would hang
for all time the pictures of memory she brought home from this
drive. Miss Underhill, pre-eminently matter-of-fact though she
was, felt a lump in her throat as this occurred to her. It was a
unique privilege to open such a vista to a starved human soul and
mind.

The sharp click of the horses' hoofs as they struck the asphalt paving changed to a soft rhythmic beat as they turned into the Park at the Fifty-ninth Street entrance. A wave of coolness and freshness rolled to meet them as they entered, and, to Miss Underhill's suddenly excited fancy, the great old trees seemed to bend and whisper a welcome to her protégée as the carriage rolled under their spreading branches. The newspaper woman's voice was a little hushed as she pointed out to the old woman the cool, green vistas opening at every side as they passed on. The ripple of water was heard in the distance, mingled with the laughter of little children. Through the trees they got glimpses of the lake and the swan-boats and their happy freight. Tame squirrels sat by the road-side and chattered at them fearlessly. Over the Park brooded the silence and green restfulness of an August afternoon whose intense heat made humanity take its outing lethargically.

Old Hannah Risser gulped down a heavy sob and lifted her voice in the first remark of the afternoon.

"I got a geranium," she said, "in my winda." She was looking with a patronizing eye on a bed of that flaunting flower.

Miss Underhill, encouraged by this tentative advance, showed a polite interest.

"Yes," the old woman rambled on. "It's awful pretty. It's got red flowers. Miss Callahan she waters it for me most efery day. I hope it ain't dying now."

She wept afresh at this sad thought, and Miss Underhill hurriedly called her attention to a group of children playing happily on the Carousel.

"We got nice, little children in our house," said old Hannah, still harping on the joys of home. "Little Josie Eckmeyer iss only four yearss old, but she comess to me efery night to kiss me when she goes to bedt."

Her tears burst forth again, and the occupants of passing carriages looked with curious interest at the artless abandon of her grief. When the newspaper woman spoke it was a little more incisively than she intended.

"You must be very uncomfortable in that place," she said. "How can you bear the noise and the smells and the awful heat of it?"

Her companion looked frightened and ill-used.

"It's a very quiet place, our house," she said, quickly. "We don't never haf such noices like they haf across the street. Of course the womans and the mans has little troubles, but that iss not my business. Mr. Rooney he threw Mrs. Rooney out a winda last week. She was hurt awful. She showed me the black marks on her back, and she had a arm broken. All the mans and womans has their troubles," repeated Mrs. Risser, philosophically.

"But they come in and they talk to me in my little room," she continued, eagerly. "They tell me about all the other neighbors, and they ask me what they must gif the childrens when they are sick, and they bring me little things what they cook. They don't often forget me—not often; they never left me without anything for more than two days. 'Most always they come in four or five times efery day. Sometimes," here the old woman's voice quivered in reminiscent ecstasy—"sometimes one of the womans brings me a glass of beer."

For some reason she began again at this point to weep with great bitterness. Miss Underhill moved impatiently in her seat. This would be indeed "a teary tale," she reflected, if she put into it half the tears old Hannah Risser had already shed. Somehow, this "special" for The Searchlight was not developing quite in accordance with her wishes. She turned to the cowering figure at her side.

"Well," she said, briskly, "you're going back to all those joys very soon. But just this moment you are having an experience you will probably never have again. Try to get the benefit of it. Breathe deep and take some fresh air into your lungs. Look about you, and see the grass and the trees and the blue sky overhead. When have you seen the sky before?"

Old Hannah drew herself up, with a little suggestion of hurt pride in the gesture.

"In my little room, my little room"—she repeated the words, dwelling upon them lovingly—"by the winda where my chair iss. There I can see a big piece of sky, 'most as big as a little carpet. It is blue, and sometimes white clouds go by on it. And sometimes I see black clouds there, and at night I see the stars."

The reporter sat silent, baffled. This old woman, who could find comfort in clouds and stars against a background of sky "almost as big as a little carpet," sat unmoved by her side, looking with eyes that saw not on the new world opened before her. The carriage turned out of the Park and began the journey up River-side Drive. The coachman let the lines relax in his hands and the horses fell into a slow, gentle trot. Here they were at home. Their nostrils expanded as they sniffed the cool breeze rising from the Hudson. Below lay the river, warm in the sunlight, but rippled by a light wind. On its blue bosom were innumerable craft—yachts, rowboats, and the stately river steamers whose passengers could be seen leaning idly over the deck rails. All this color gleamed against the rich background of the magnificent Palisades looming protectingly behind. Mrs. Risser gazed upon it with a listless eye.

"I got a cat at home, too," she said, suddenly. "She catches mice. She caught one under my bedt yesterday. She catches all wot she wants. We don't haf to give her nothing to eat."

Miss Underhill preserved an eloquent silence. She saw her story fading to a dim outline of what it should have been. She thought she saw, too, the cynical smile on the lips of her arch-enemy, the city editor. The voice at her side babbled on.

"Sometimes it's real cool in my room," it said. "The buildings iss so high the sun can't get in, and I ain't on that side, anyhow. And Mrs. Eckmeyer she brings me a pitcher of water in the morning and sometimes I wet a towel and put it on my head. It's cool."

Miss Underhill continued silent. A satisfactory paragraph for the "story" had just occurred to her. She rehearsed it mentally:

"She looked out over the expanse of water and tears filled her dim old eyes, those eyes which for thirty years had gazed upon nothing but the grimy walls of the opposite tenement and a tiny patch of blue sky which the great building could not quite shut off.

"'When I was a girl,' she said, softly, 'my husband and I used to sit on the river-bank and watch the boats go by. That was long ago—but this makes it seem yesterday.' Her lips quivered a little."

Miss Underhill was conscious of a sudden interruption. The real Hannah, not the Hannah of her "story," was sobbing again at her side.

"Where are we going?" she whimpered. "We have went so far. Are we in another city? I don't feel well. I think I catch cold. I got some good medicine in my house wot the Salvation girls give me. It always makes me well. It cures anything wot I got."

Miss Underhill addressed the coachman.

"Drive back," she said, curtly. Then she turned to old Hannah with her charming smile. She had recovered her good-humor when the reflection occurred to her that her story could tell what Hannah Risser *should* have felt during that drive. No one would be the wiser, and Hannah herself, once back in her tenement-room, would no doubt corroborate any recital in which she had played a touching and admirable role.

"We're going home now," said the reporter, cheerfully. "We will be there in three-quarters of an hour."

Mrs. Risser looked doubtful, and her suspicions were intensi-fied by the fact that the coachman returned by a different route, kindly desiring to give the old woman all possible variety. He, too, was more cheerful. The drive was almost over and Miss Underhill's prospective tip pleasantly in the foreground of his thoughts. He suddenly remembered with a twinge of conscience that she was invariably very generous on these occasions. Mrs. Risser seized the side of the carriage with a firmer grip, sat as near the edge of the seat as she dared, looked at the unfamiliar route with scared eyes, and contributed another copious flow of tears to the collection of stains on the borrowed shawl. Beside her the reporter, whose mind was now at rest, mentally outlined telling bits of her "story":

"The carriage turned into the evil-smelling tenement street, from whose refuse-covered cobble-stones the heat seemed to rise in a perceptible haze. Old Hannah Risser gave one last long backward look at the world she was leaving—the beautiful world that lay so near to and yet so hideously far from that little tenement-room. Then her gaze rested on the crowded streets, the half-naked chil-dren playing in the gutters, the swarming life of the tenement. A change passed over her face; her features twisted for a moment, but with a mighty effort she forced them into calm. This was her life: she must return to it, for He who put her there had some good purpose in it. She seized the reporter's hand and kissed it.

"'Good-by,' she said: 'Thank you, and God bless you. You have shown me today a glimpse of what I hope awaits me after I take my next—and last—long drive.'"

"That will do pretty well for an ending," reflected Miss Underhill, comfortably, "when I've polished it up a bit. Of course I must make her an educated woman who has seen better days."

A movement beside her aroused her from her pleasant reverie. The carriage had reached the tenement region, and was rolling swiftly through its swarming streets. It was growing late and the push-cart men and peddlers were coming home after their day's work. Some Chinese laundrymen had left their ironing-boards for a breath of air and were sitting on the curb exchanging repartee in pigeon-English with a little group of hoodlums.[6] A few feet away, a street organ was grinding out an ancient waltz, and several ragged little girls were dancing to the music. A long gasp of delight fell on Miss Underhill's ear. It came from the lips of Hannah Risser, who was sitting up gazing around her with shining eyes. She craned her neck around to look at the tenements that fell behind them. The carriage turned a corner sharply and entered another street, a shade filthier, more crowded, more evil-smelling than the last. Two drunken men lurched uncertainly along the sidewalk. Hannah Risser sent her glance wide-eyed down the street until it lit and rested on a scrubby tenement in one of whose windows bloomed a red geranium. She clutched Miss Underhill's arm with quivering fingers and uttered a shrill cry. Her face was transfigured. The listless, sick little old woman had become an ecstatic creature, hysterical with joy.

"*Ach Gott!*" she shrieked, "*Ach Gott!*—there's my little home. I'm back again, I'm back." She closed her eyes and struggled for breath. "*Ach Gott!*" she gasped. "*Gott sei dank!*"[7]

The nurse and the bearers were waiting, and they carried the happy old woman up the dirty stairs. Her exclamations of delight and her beaming face left no doubt in their minds as to the success of Miss Underhill's experiment. That young lady herself lingered for a confidential last word when the others had departed. She had given the friendly Mrs. Eckmeyer money for the purchase of an evening meal, and the little room was full of the smell of frying meat. Miss Underhill held out her hand, which old Hannah Risser did not hasten to kiss. She put her own into it, limply.

"Come now," said the girl, "say you've had a good time."

The old woman hesitated. A shiver passed over her as memory

brought up for an instant the terrors of the day. Then her nostrils caught and drew in the mingled odor of frying eggs, bacon, and hot coffee. After all, it was over and she was home. Why bear malice? She grinned good-naturedly.

"Ach, yes," she said, handsomely. "I hat a goot time. Sure!"

It was a very "teary tale" Miss Underhill turned into the city editor. New York wept over it the following morning. So many letters poured into *The Searchlight* office offering the old woman homes of all degrees of luxury that Miss Underhill was forced to write a brief supplementary article explaining that Hannah Risser was "permanently and happily provided for" through *The Searchlight*'s efforts.

To the writer of this simple narrative she told the plain, unvarnished facts, and generously added the moral lesson the episode had taught her.

"I think of it," she said, "when I go to all these sociological meetings and hear people worrying about relieving the condition of the poor. I sympathize heartily with that work. But I have learned this lesson very well: that there are times when what the poor want more than they want anything else on earth is simply—to be let alone!"

Source: "In the Case of Hannah Risser," *Harper's Bazar* (August 1902).

"MRS. WARBURTON'S
THEORIES"

(1908)

It was at one of Henrietta Twombly's receptions that Jessica and
I were privileged, for the first time, to gaze upon the intellectual
countenance of Mrs. Warburton and to listen to the words of
wisdom that fell suavely from her lips. That we experienced more
pleasure in the indulgence of the second privilege than in that of
the first was due to the existence in us both of an almost abnormal love of beauty and to the presence in Mrs. Warburton's face
of several features that at first sight painfully repelled us. Her
eyes, to begin with, protruded to a degree which gave her an expression of chronic surprise; that they were softly brown, and at
times of a really extraordinary brilliance, were but meager aids
to reason for checking our recoil. We objected, also, to her
mouth, which had a trick, highly unpleasant to Jessica, of smiling
on one side only, thus suggesting a half-mouthed heartiness more
than half depressing. In time, I admit, the incongruity of this
phenomenon fascinated me, but Jessica's prejudice against Mrs.
Warburton's smile remained violent and unreasoning. She shunned
the contemplation of it to a degree bordering on rudeness, and
passed the early part of the evening lurking behind portières and
potted palms that they might blot it from her view.[1] Thus, though
frequently within sound of the soothing ripple of Mrs. Warburton's contralto voice, Jessica missed many of the choicest gems of
thought with which that eminent person favored us. Pursuing my
individual researches, however, I was enabled not only to hear
these, but to discover that the lady, though still further handicapped
by an insignificant and characterless nose, had as compensations

an admirable complexion, beautiful teeth, a superb carriage, and a really surprising amount of magnetism, to which both men and women promptly and happily succumbed. So great was this last, indeed, that she was soon surrounded by her fellow guests, who, after reluctantly yielding themselves to our beaming hostess for the introduction, remained chatting easily with the lioness of the evening for a few moments, and then, with expressions of artless surprise and relief, attached themselves permanently to her circle. Accustomed as I was to similar assemblages where the guest of honor stands in a corner supported by the hostess and one or two intrepid friends, while the remaining guests remain aloof, feverishly seeking within themselves sentiments worthy the ears of a celebrity, I was naturally much impressed by the phenomenon before me. I approached, I joined the circle, and I listened.

Mrs. Warburton was holding forth, as was expected of her and in response to the rather too obvious leads of the hostess; but doing it so artistically, so subtly, with such a charm of individual appeal to this or that one of her listeners, that they proved the accuracy of her shots like targets which ring when the bull's-eye is struck. One or two even had the temerity to disagree with her, and this apparently delighted her so much that her brown eyes seemed to pop out of her head with excitement and interest as she laughingly met the issues they raised. I saw Jessica's blond head shining among the draperies of a window not far away, and under cover of the focused interest I imperatively motioned her to approach. She came with reluctant feet, and eyes, as it were, turned inward.

"You're missing everything," I explained to her in a reproachful aside. "She's holding them all. George Everett has left his gum shoes in the hall and settled at her feet for the evening, and Professor Olivier, who, to my certain knowledge, has played solitaire in a corner at each of the last five receptions he has attended, is glued to her side.[2] She appears to be fascinating them."

Jessica's delicate brows arched higher.

"Fascinating them—with that *smile*?" she murmured, disdainfully.

"With it—or notwithstanding it," I retorted. "I don't pretend to have analyzed the thing at this early stage. It's a condition I'm mentioning—not a theory. Look at her now."

Jessica looked, and looked intently. Almost in the instant Mrs. Warburton caught her eye.

"Miss Belden agrees with me on this point, at least," she exclaimed, gayly, nodding toward my friend. "She said the same thing before I thought of it, in her second book. It interested me then, but did not quite convince me. Afterwards I discovered its truth."

Neither Jessica nor I had the faintest idea what especial point she meant, absorbed as we had been in our own exchange of confidences, but Jessica swayed forward, as I subsequently explained to her, like a fascinated bird under the eye of the calculating serpent.

"Unquestionably we are right," she smiled, "if we agree. Who dares dispute us?"

She was still on the outside of the circle as she spoke. Mrs. Warburton made two quick steps forward from the center, and with a touch, surprisingly cordial, intimate yet dignified, drew her within.

"Professor Olivier dares," she explained, "and you shall help me down him. I must make the most of our agreement this time, for I know very well that you will never agree with me again. You are so conservative, and I—they tell me—am so extreme!"

There was a chorus of courteous protest in which the voice of Professor Alphonse Olivier rose loud and clear. He had in my hearing, but a fortnight ago, denounced Mrs. Warburton's latest magazine article as the vaporings of an hysterical woman, lacking literary style, logic, and fact, and of actually immoral tendency, but he seemed to have reversed this severe judgment now as he stood beaming upon her with his near-sighted gray eyes.

A prolonged sigh at my left ear drew my attention from this pleasing picture of masculine subjection. Turning, I recognized Griffing, a clever young artist, dragged by an intellectual mother to this and similar gatherings where he made no secret of his gloom and isolation. He openly approved of me, however, finding my conversation, he gratefully explained, wholly free from "theories and ideas, don't you know." Sympathetically I withdrew with Griffing to a distant corner, where we sat down side by side. I, too, was a little tired of theories and ideas.

"What does she write about, anyhow?" demanded Griffing,

gazing drearily at his shoes. "You know I never read women's things, but I've got a general idea that hers are worse than the average. Wants to revolutionize society, doesn't she, and elect women Presidents, and put babies out to farm, or something like that?"

I hastened to turn the sunshine of an optimistic mind on this cold gray cloudiness.

"Not a bit. Your course in art has not taught you to draw conclusions," I explained with brisk severity. "All she wants is entire equality for women and men. Men don't give their lives to domestic service and the care of children; and she thinks women should not, unless they consider it their special vocation. Certain women who like children should be trained to care for them all, she says, leaving their mothers, not thus determined to the task, free to enter the arts and professions if they choose. She thinks, too, that women should not wait to be wooed. They should go a-wooing, if they care to. According to her theory, for example, no shrinking maidenly modesty should prevent me from asking you here and now to—"[3]

But with a gulp of alarm young Griffing had fled, leaving a train of stuttered excuses in his wake. Subsequently I caught sight of him lurking in the shadows of the outer hall, from which safe shelter he made frantic signals to his mother, conveying his filial readiness to escort her home. To such of these as she saw that strong-minded lady made no response. Once during her ponderous passage through the rooms she stopped for a few words with me, and in the course of these I caught over her shoulder a glimpse of her son's white, stricken face turned on us from afar. I knew he imagined I was asking her for his hand, and the reflection led me to prolong the interview to a degree which evidently caused Mrs. Griffing much surprise and gratification. I learned, incidentally, several interesting facts about Mrs. Warburton. She was a widow, and childless—a condition in which even the loyal soul of Mrs. Griffing seemed vaguely to see a providential hand.

"Her husband didn't live long," explained Mrs. Griffing, simply. "My son thinks she killed him with her ideas, but, of course, it wasn't anything *she* did—it was pneumonia."

She drifted away after this handsome vindication of her friend;

and with a sudden realization that the night was advanced I again sought Jessica. I found her wearing the expression of alertness her face takes on only when she is intensely interested.

"She's really worthwhile," she conceded, dropping on a convenient divan, tucking a small cushion comfortably behind her back, and pulling me down beside her with the obvious intention of talking it all over, then and there.

"She's wrong about everything, of course; I never knew a woman whose conception of the universe was so consistently upside down. But she's diabolically clever about it, and she has persuaded herself that she's sincere. I really believe she thinks she's right. For the rest, we must cultivate her. Thank Heaven, we've both reached the stage where we don't care what people's opinions are, if only they don't bore us. Whatever Grace Warburton may do, she'll never do that. I've asked her to come to dinner Tuesday night."

"Has she the privilege of bringing her smile along?" I asked without enthusiasm. I am never as enthusiastic as Jessica over the prospect of guests—possibly because I do the marketing and because Jessica's criticism of my efforts is often painful to my sensitive nature.

Jessica surveyed me disapprovingly. "I think I can say one or two things that will remove it if she has it with her," she remarked with conviction. "I let everything go tonight because this was really no place to argue." She launched into an animated monologue on Mrs. Warburton's fallacies, during which I succeeded in enjoying a brief but restful nap. I had not yet felt the force of the lady's personal appeal to the degree Jessica had.

Mrs. Warburton arrived promptly at eight the following Tuesday evening, in a gown whose attractions brought a light into our world-weary eyes. It was one of her good points, hitherto unchronicled, that she dressed superbly and with sympathetic understanding of her own type. We had invited only one other guest, Jessica remaining firm in her faith that the occasion warranted a presentation of her views as well as of those of Mrs. Warburton. The fourth member of our little party was a newspaper editor, rather yellow as to his journalism, but of great personal charm, and with a brain whose strength even Jessica humbly acknowledged.[4] As for me, I openly sat at his feet and quoted his opinions as often as she permitted me.

The evening opened auspiciously. Ushered into my bedroom to take off her wraps, Mrs. Warburton commented at once and rapturously upon the rising-sun quilt made by my great-great-grandmother—a proper appreciation of which is indispensable in guests in our home. She also said fitting things about our Delft and brasses, and realized the antiquity of the Japanese prints on our dining room walls.[5] Moreover, she hung in rapture over Hedwig's mayonnaise, and mentioned casually that "The Walkürie" was her favorite opera.[6] I melted to a degree which imperiled the firmness of the frozen punch, while even the editor, frankly prejudiced against her as "a menace to the community," turned on her a momentary kindly gleam. We had reached the salad before Jessica lured her toward her hobby, which Mrs. Warburton needed no urging to mount. She leaped into the saddle with a bound. Once there, if I may be pardoned an abrupt departure from metaphor, she rested her elbows on the table, buried her chin in her hands, and turned on us the effulgence of her brown eyes.

"You're such an inspiration to me, you two women," she began, with a long-drawn breath. "You would repudiate my convictions with your last breath, both of you, yet you are living them—a great many of them, at least—every moment of your inspiring lives."

I opened my mouth, but Jessica spoke first. She usually does.

"Dear lady," she said, suavely, "what you call our 'inspiring lives' is really a difficult and painful scramble for the accumulation of an income large enough to live on in this expensive city. There is nothing inspiring about it."

"But your professions—your splendid work—your books, your lectures, your influence over the tender minds of your pupils"— began Mrs. Warburton.

"We loathe 'em all," explained Jessica, with great calmness. "If there's anything we loathe more than our professions, it's those innocent young minds you mention, and if anything could be worse than the young minds, it's the possessors of them—the pupils—"

I hurriedly interrupted. Jessica was well under way. If she were permitted to continue she would say much more than she meant and then fiercely insist upon its truth, as was her impulsive way.

"You mean," I said, gently, "that we are free to live our lives as we choose, and that, aside from our professions, we have no heavy cares or responsibilities."

"Yes, yes. And you have this charming home, and are *so* happy in it," gushed Mrs. Warburton.

"Of course we're happy," remarked Jessica, ungratefully, "if happiness is gained by a certain amount of material comfort. We are happy as a cat is happy, stretched before the fire. But the nearest thing to an emotion Helen ever experiences is when she grieves for days over the breaking of a Belleek cup;[7] and as for me, the only one I ever have is when she does something more than usually maddening and I am able to relieve the mental congestion of months by telling her in one glorious *quart d'heure* what I really think of her.[8] Do you call that happiness?"

"She never used to talk like that," I explained, sadly. "It's the effect of age creeping on apace. I noticed it first twenty-six years ago last April—a tendency to crabbedness and waspishness."

But Mrs. Warburton was pursuing her own thoughts. She brushed aside my feeble interruption and leaned toward Jessica, her brown eyes aflame.

"Don't tell me," she cried, with tragic emphasis, "that you think you'd be better off if you were nursing a dozen squalling babies all at once. Don't say that."

The editor devoted himself hurriedly to his ice. For an instant even Jessica was dashed, but only for an instant.

"No-o," she said, consideringly, "I won't say that. I should not want a dozen at a time, and I certainly should object to twelve squalling at once. But eliminating myself from the question, I can only say I firmly believe the woman who brings children into the world, supplies a home for them, trains them properly, and makes her husband happy, is worth fifty independent spinsters and 'their influence over young minds.'"

The editor applauded, for these sentiments were much to his liking. Mrs. Warburton rose impulsively from the table and walked around the dining room, beating her hands together.

"Oh, blind, blind!" she murmured, almost chokingly. "You're

all blind, and the blindest are those who should see most clearly. That's the biggest stumbling-block in my path—that I can't make the unmarried women, the professional women, the working women, realize their glorious freedom and opportunities. Wives and mothers see it fast enough; they often tell me they feel their burdens; they'd follow me if they could—lots of them. But you free and childless women—each of you, every last one of you, has hidden in her a sentiment—a tradition—whatever it is, that makes her hanker for the ball and chain."

She sank down again in her place as she spoke, her eyes dim. In none of us at that moment was there the slightest doubt of her absolute sincerity in her grotesque point of view.

"What—er—is your exact idea of the ball and chain, Mrs. Warburton?" asked the editor, with interest. "Do they represent to you matrimony and maternity?"

Mrs. Warburton straightened herself.

"Not necessarily matrimony and maternity in themselves," she told him, composedly, "but the abuses to which they lead—the shifting of all the domestic burdens onto the woman's shoulders. My creed is very simple; I have set it forth many times: A woman and man should marry if they love each other, and they should have children if they both desire them, and they should continue faithful to each other. But—the partnership should be an absolutely equal one. The woman should be as free from the responsibility for the home and children as the father. She should be as free as he is to do her work out in the world, have her interests and her friends, live her individual life. The home-making and the child-training should be done by women hired for the purpose and who have chosen these as their especial fields. No intellectual woman should be degraded by waiting on a man."

The editor looked pained.

"But if she loves him," he objected, feebly.

Mrs. Warburton's voice took on its platform note.

"Ah, there you are again," she cried, "with the truly masculine theory. If she loves him she must wait on him. The proof of women's love, in men's eyes, is servitude."

Jessica's glance met mine, and we rose and led the way into the drawing-room.

"Only the other day," murmured Mrs. Warburton, softly, as

she walked beside me, "I saw an exquisite woman, fitted for the highest duties, sewing buttons on one of her husband's garments. I cannot tell you how inexpressibly the sight pained me."

"Bet it would have pained him a lot if she hadn't sewed 'em on," muttered the editor, sulkily. It was obvious that the conversation was getting on his nerves. Seeing this, Jessica tactfully led him to a little alcove, whence the smoke of his cigar soon curled forth. Mrs. Warburton, sinking into a great-chair before the open fire, surveyed it with a sternly disapproving eye.

"Oh, how can you?" she sighed. "How can you let him smoke in these exquisite rooms—so fresh, so virginal—"

"Dear Mrs. Warburton," I pleaded, "we'll never, never think alike on any of these things. But we like you very much, and surely we can be friends and still hold our own opinions, can we not?"

Mrs. Warburton pressed my hand and sighed again.

"Oh yes," she said, "of course we can, and we will. But I'm disappointed. I wanted you both under my banner." Then, with the tact that usually distinguished her, she turned the conversation to Jessica's latest educational textbook, and the discussion of woman and her ball and chain was over for that evening.

Our acquaintance with Mrs. Warburton, thus auspiciously begun, ripened by slow degrees into a really pleasant friendship. We saw much of her as the months passed, and even as the intimacy grew so grew our admiration for this gallant leader of a cause already lost. She had many qualities none too common in this disappointing world. She was frank, she was loyal, she was honest, and she revealed occasionally the artless simplicity of a little child. Moreover, she was also busy, and she had the worker's respect for the time of other workers. She lectured, wrote, lent her presence to such assemblages as she felt might help her mission, and yet found leisure to drop in upon us with delightful informality and enjoyment equally delightful because so obvious. Once we attended a reception in her apartment far uptown, but we never repeated the experience. With a charity far broader than our own, Mrs. Warburton threw open her home to extremists of every type, who, in turn, were attracted to her by her radical views. On this occasion I fell into the hands of a woman anarchist whose yearning for the blood of somebody, anybody, was as strong as it was ungrammatically expressed. She was short-haired and un-manicured, and altogether objectionable, but she held me fast in a corner for almost an hour. I subsequently learned that during this period Jessica was favored with the views of a languorous youth whose immediate conviction that she was his affinity was unshaken by the presence of a wife and a little brood at home. We both drew a long breath as we emerged into the outer air.

"Ugh!" groaned Jessica, "how can she, with her daintiness, en-dure them? For she is as dainty mentally as she is physically, though she doesn't know it. How can she tolerate these creatures in her home? Really, we'll have to drop her if she keeps it up."

We did not drop her. We merely dropped her receptions, and, under plea of excessive work, urged her to come to us when she could, and forgive our failure to return the visits. This she did with the utmost good nature. She seemed to have a genuine liking for us, and her frequent fierce arguments with Jessica were evi-dently highly stimulating to them both. Our housekeeping was also of interest to her, and the steadfast glitter of our metal be-longings filled her with awe.

"How do you keep them so?" she once asked, curiously. "Surely you don't debase yourselves by cleaning them?"

We hurriedly mentioned our incomparable waitress.

Mrs. Warburton's face shone again.

"Ah, surely," she said, graciously, "you hire it done by an intel-lectual inferior. That is right. That is what I do. Only," she added with unconscious pathos, "mine doesn't clean things after I've hired her."

It was plain that she did not. Our visit to Mrs. Warburton's home had taught us that.

Toward spring she came to us less frequently, and finally did not come at all. In June we had a hurried note from her, explain-ing that she was leaving town for the summer, regretting that time would not permit a farewell call, and referring vaguely to a reunion in the autumn when she returned to the city. Jessica and I looked at each other.

"She's offended," announced Jessica, positively, "but at what, in Heaven's name? Have you done anything, Helen?"

I hastily disavowed the tacit charge.

"You, perhaps, with your blunt speeches—" I suggested.

Jessica smiled in her most superior fashion.

"My blunt speeches!" she repeated. "Grace Warburton has said more brutal things to me in one evening than you and I could think of in a month if we put our minds to it. That was one of her charms," she added, reflectively.

I sighed, for this was true. No amount of plain speaking would hurt Mrs. Warburton, and I recalled now that our last evening together had been unusually harmonious.

"Have we begun to bore her, do you think?" I hazarded. Jessica turned upon me an expression made up, in equal parts, of human exasperation and Christian forbearance.

"How could we bore her?" she demanded, tersely. "She has read our textbooks and she thinks we're literary." To this retort a reverential silence seemed the only fitting tribute, and I gave it.

We discussed Mrs. Warburton's letter further for a few moments; even, casually, for a few weeks. Then, leaving town ourselves, our mental picture of her faded into a dim background, in the darkest recesses of which lurked mysteriously a ball and chain.

It was not until the following November that Mrs. Warburton emerged from the obscurity in which, so to speak, she had been enveloped. We were back in the city, and our editor friend casually mentioned, during a call one afternoon, that the distinguished apostle of sex equality had married. We gasped in unison.

"Whom? When?" we demanded.

Our guest confessed that the details had escaped him.

"It was done pretty quietly, I fancy," he hazarded. "It would have to be, wouldn't it, in the circumstances? Wouldn't she be guyed a lot, and all that, for going back on her colors?"[9]

We pointed out that matrimony did not necessarily include the change of Mrs. Warburton's convictions.

"Probably her husband is in sympathy with them, and will conduct himself accordingly," Jessica explained. "But it's odd she didn't tell us. I'd like to see her again."

The wish evidently lingered in the mind of our editor, for a fortnight later he presented us with Mrs. Warburton's new address, which he had secured from her publishers.

"I forgot to ask her present name," he admitted, cheerfully, "but here's where she lives, and they'll know there, of course, who she is."

Jessica and I hesitated a week more over the little slip of paper.

"I suppose we really ought to keep away," I murmured at last. "And yet—With anyone but Mrs. Warburton this silence would naturally suggest a willingness to be deprived of the delights of our society. But with her it may mean a dozen other things— poverty, a fear that we will misunderstand her, or some such reason. On the whole, I think we ought to look her up."

We did, the next day, choosing the late afternoon for our call. It was not difficult to find—East Sixty-fourth Street, which proved to be an extremely unpretentious apartment-house with rows of fire-escapes zigzagging dizzily down its front. The janitor, who opened the door and promptly wiped his hand on the side of his trousers after doing so, knew where Mrs. Warburton lived.

"Up three flights, first door t' the left," were his terse directions. We followed them. A knock at the door brought forth presently the sound of uncertain footsteps on the other side.

"But one moment," said a familiar voice. "Ah, *mon Dieu*, zose darknesses!"[10] The door opened, and the subdued light of the hallway fell on the round pink face of Professor Alphonse Olivier. It flushed deeper for a moment, then beamed upon us. Both his hands came forth in eager greeting. Excitedly, delightedly, with many gesticulations and much speech, he ushered us in.

"My vife she prepare ze suppaire," he then explained, happily. "Zen she come to us, *oui*? If I tell hair zat you are here, some-zing burn, *certainement*.[11] Ze fairst days all burned—eferyzing. But I teach hair, and she improve—*mon Dieu*, 'ow zat voman improve! It was ze miracle, *vraiment*."[12]

We sought to leave, explaining that we would come again, but he would not hear of this. He led us into a tiny "parlor," in which, among other things, we recognized the dim brass of the samovar in Mrs. Warburton's former home. Some effort had been made to brighten it up. There were several brazen flushes on its cheek.

"We 'ave no *fille*," explained our host, with artless candor.[13] "My vife she do all—eferyzing. She cook, she wash, she scrub. It iss her wish. I teach hair. We 'ave not much of ze American dollaire *maintenant*.[14] Later zey come, *oui*."[15]

He continued to beam upon us, his slippered feet resting comfortably on a hassock before him, his shabby smoking-jacket unbuttoned for greater comfort.[16] The pipe he had put down at our entrance lay on the floor, smelling horribly. From the kitchen, at the end of the hall, came the clatter of dishes, the brisk opening and closing of stove-doors, the sound of swift footsteps moving to and fro. An odor of boiling onions was wafted to our nostrils, together with the unmistakable scent of something burning. Our host's jaw dropped as this last was borne in.

"It burn—somezing," he murmured; "it always burn—somezing. But she improve, *oui, oui*, she improve."

Mrs. Warburton—no, Madame Olivier henceforth—came to the door at this moment, and, beholding us, stood there for a transfixed second. She was enveloped in a huge calico apron; a cap was on her head, and she vaguely held a kitchen towel in her hands. Suddenly dropping it, she came forward, turning first to one and then to the other of us her radiant brown eyes and her queer crooked smile.

"You dears!" she cried in her deepest 'cello tones. "You dears! Oh, the joy of seeing you again! I was going to write you this very week." She kissed us rapturously. Then, as the scent of the burning food followed and caught up with her, she gasped: "And won't someone tell me quickly what to do with little sausages to get the fat cooked out of them?"

The abrupt transition was so like, yet so unlike, Mrs. Warburton, that Jessica and I, after an heroic effort at self-control, succumbed to helpless laughter. In this, after an instant of puzzled reflection, our hostess light-heartedly joined. "It was funny," she gasped at length, wiping her eyes. "I don't blame you. I know it was funny." In chorus we started a fresh outburst.

Our host in the meantime had rushed to the rescue of the sausages. On his return he stood silent and serious, his gray eyes upon us, a puzzled frown upon his brow.

"W'at it iss zat iss so funny?" he asked. Then, as we three remained still helpless and beyond speech, a light broke over his pink face.

"Oh, la, la! I see," he cried. "It iss zat my vife cook an' vork aftair zoze writings an' zoze lectures she 'as gave. Zat it iss, *oui*."

He beamed on us so delightedly over this discovery that we again became reduced to helplessness, but his wife succeeded in nodding a confirmation of his surmise. The Frenchman shrugged his slender shoulders.

"Humph!" he said, "w'at zey are, zoze writings an' zoze lectures?" He paused for a reply, but none came. We leaned exhausted against the wall. Professor Olivier held his hand before us, and lightly fillicked an imaginary something between his thumb and second finger.[17] Then he blew upon it delicately, to convey to us a sense of its disappearance into thin air.

"Zey was not wort' zat," he concluded, oracularly. "Zey was only ze foolish—w'at you call it?—ze foolish notions of voman. My vife, she 'as learn bettaire." He dropped his hand on her shoulder as he spoke, and she quietly laid her cheek against it. There was deep meaning in the look they exchanged.

"I 'ave teach hair," ended the husband, gently.

Source: "Mrs. Warburton's Theories," *Harper's Bazar* (March 1908).

III

THE NEW WOMAN COMES OF AGE: MAY IVERSON AND THE SEEDS OF #METOO

First introduced in the short story "As Told By May Iverson," which was published in *Harper's Bazar* and *Tales of the Cloister*, the fictional character of May Iverson was closely associated with her creator. Mining her own experiences as an intellectually precocious convent girl, a newspaperwoman, and a magazine editor, Jordan wrote three books devoted to May's adventures: *May Iverson—Her Book* (1904), *May Iverson Tackles Life* (1912), and *May Iverson's Career* (1914). Like J. K. Rowling's Harry Potter novels and other popular young adult series, Jordan's May Iverson stories chart her protagonist's coming of age, from a student debating suffrage and collaborating with classmates on her school newspaper to a professional woman establishing a career in the male-dominated field of journalism.

"The Voice of Truth" and "What Dreams May Come," the first two stories included here, feature May as a student at St. Catharine's and an aspiring writer. They also introduce her close friends, who similarly envision futures as career-oriented New

Women, while contemplating the pull of motherhood and traditional femininity. In the next two stories, "Woman Suffrage at St. Catharine's" and "I Introduce Beauty Culture," May and her classmates continue to debate women's rights and gender roles as they enter adolescence. Written for a popular audience, these stories engage issues—such as voting rights and beauty standards—taken seriously by feminists then and now; they do so with a light-hearted, often comic touch.

Originally serialized in *Good Housekeeping*, *May Iverson's Career* finds Jordan's protagonist leaving behind the comfortable world of the convent, with its nurturing and supportive maternal figures, for a career as a journalist in New York, confronted head-on with a patriarchal culture that sought to disempower women at every turn. Once again, Jordan draws from her own life, taking recourse to fiction as a means of addressing taboo topics and exposing the realities of gendered abuse and discrimination in the workplace. In "My First Assignment," May confronts—and triumphs over—the condescension and doubt of male colleagues when her editor dispatches her to spend a night in a haunted house (an episode that Jordan later revisits in her autobiography, *Three Rousing Cheers*). In "The Cry of the Pack," Jordan returns to the topic of sexual harassment in the workplace, which she began to explore in *Tales of the City Room*. This time, Jordan explicitly addresses the psychological effects of sexual violence, even as the story concedes that not all men are predatory "wolves"—a precursor of the defensive "not all men" memes that arose in response to #MeToo.

Like the stories from *Tales of the City Room*, those in *May Iverson's Career* offer a behind-the-scenes glimpse into the newspaper industry at the turn of the twentieth century, emphasizing women's experiences and exploring bonds formed between women journalists and the women who were the subjects of their reportage. As its title suggests, "The Case of Helen Brandow" refers back to Jordan's reporting on the Borden trial in "The Case of Lizzie Borden," as well as the controversy generated by Jordan's first foray into fiction, "Ruth Herrick's Assignment," in which the accused woman was also named Helen Brandow. The Borden verdict remains up in the air to this day, and Jordan asserted her own belief in Borden's innocence in her autobiography. Yet, in staging fictional encounters between women reporters and alleged killers, Jordan makes her women suspects guilty of the crime—at the same time that she incriminates their murdered husbands as perpetrators of domestic violence.

The final selection included here, "The Revolt of Tildy Mears," finds May in a new role that correlates to Jordan's own professional advancement: the reporter-heroine is now an assistant editor at a woman's magazine, working on a profile of a prominent suffrage leader. While Mrs. Warburton of "Mrs. Warburton's Theories" bore resemblances to Charlotte Perkins Gilman, Jordan's fictional suffrage activist, Dr. Anna Harland, is unquestionably based on Rev. Dr. Anna Howard Shaw, as the character's name suggests. "The Revolt of Tildy Mears" can thus be read fruitfully in conjunction with the final section of this edition, which includes excerpts from *The Story of a Pioneer*, Shaw's autobiography written collaboratively with Jordan. Transcending the divide between fiction and fact, Jordan's May Iverson stories offer readers an imaginative space in which to navigate the inevitable contradictions between feminist ideals and women's lived experiences.

FROM
MAY IVERSON—
HER BOOK

"THE VOICE OF TRUTH"

(1904)

One day during rhetoric class Sister Irmingarde wrote a sentence
on the board and said she wished us girls to think about it. It was
this: "The lives of great failures are not written."

She asked us what we thought it meant, so we discussed it earnestly and, I trust I need not add, intelligently; for, as I have often
explained to the gentle readers, we girls at St. Catharine's are students of singularly mature minds and rare intuition.[1] But all the
time the others were talking I was thinking how interesting it
would be to write the story of a great failure; and then suddenly I
remembered that I could, because I knew one. Well indeed, alas!
can I write of a great failure, for I was it; and as most of the other
chapters are cheerful and end well, perhaps the gentle reader will
not mind a sad one for a change. It is not going to be easy to tell
this, for great failures are terrible things, and the people who
make them usually feel dreadful and are embittered for life; and
sometimes they die of broken hearts, like Horace Greeley.[2] No
wonder they don't write about them. But I will do it because I am
a Literary Artist, and because truth is mighty and must prevail,
and because, after all, I am only fourteen, and no one but Juliet
ever knew everything at that tender age.[3] So I will pluck my quill

out of my breast, as it were, the way the mother pelican does, and I will write this dark chronicle of a brilliant young life and how it clouded up all of a sudden.[4]

The great failure was my paper. I had set my heart on it and my young ambitions—and one has a great many young ambitions when one is fourteen. All my friends knew I was the editor, so they subscribed, and I planned to send a copy to papa every week, with my name at the top of the editorial page. The name of the paper was *The Voice of Truth,* and its motto was *Uncompromising Fearlessness.* The girls made it "the official organ of the students of St. Catharine's Academy," and Mabel Muriel Murphy's father told Mabel Muriel he would be our financial adviser.[5] He did that because Mabel Muriel was the business manager. It was very convenient for her, too, because when we were getting it ready, and spending lots more money than we took in, Mabel Muriel always telegraphed to her father and he sent money right away; and then Mabel Muriel's books showed a large profit. You can see what a good business manager she was and how clever we were to think of a financial adviser and have one.

Mabel Blossom was the circulation manager, and she was fine, too. She made all the girls subscribe, because she told them if they didn't nothing about them would come out in *The Voice of Truth*; and then she started a Roll of Honor and a Roll of Ignominy, and had proofs of them printed and sent them around. In the Roll of Honor she printed every week the names of all our friends who subscribed—the fathers and mothers and sisters and brothers outside of St. Catharine's, you know; and in the Roll of Ignominy she printed the names of our friends who ought to subscribe and didn't.[6] It was, indeed, interesting to see how they hurried to get out of the Roll of Ignominy, and into the Roll of Honor. Mabel hardly ever had to print their names in the Roll of Ignominy more than once. Mabel Muriel Murphy's father laughed about that. He said it was "forcing" circulation; but it wasn't. It was just an effort to uplift our dear friends and do them good. We knew *The Voice of Truth* would uplift them, and inspire them to better, nobler lives, as soon as they began to read it.

Maudie Joyce was the managing editor, and I was the editor-in-chief, so of course I took charge of the editorial page, which papa has always said is the backbone of a paper and by it the journal stands or falls. Papa says, too, that no journal can live unless it instructs the masses. So I made up my mind that *The Voice of Truth* should have a backbone and instruct the masses, and be a kind of beacon light in the stormy sea of life, the way a lighthouse is, you know.

The first thing I did was to study all the great New York newspapers, so I could copy the best things in each one in my paper. I gave most of one Saturday to it, and Maudie Joyce helped. After we had read them all for hours and hours I decided I liked the *Sun*'s editorial page best because it was so bright and funny, and, besides, I knew I could write editorials just like it. And we agreed we'd have "all the news that was fit to print," like the *Times*; and we would be dignified and scholarly and quarrel with all the other newspapers, like the *Evening Post*; and we would have beats, like the *Herald*, and the weather in Paris, because that would be so exciting. And I thought how surprised and proud papa would be when he turned in disappointment from his morning *Tribune* and found the news he wanted every Saturday in his *Voice of Truth*. Then we decided we would attack the rich, like the *World* and *Journal* do. Mabel Muriel Murphy's father was the only very, very rich man we knew, so of course we had to attack him, and we did, too, fearlessly and openly, and he didn't seem to like it when we told him. But Mabel Muriel explained to him how it was part of the policy of the paper, and that he had to be our financial adviser and the Soulless Corporation with its Heel on the Neck of the Poor besides. So he was, and we gave it to him good and hard in the editorials I wrote.

Then we wrote to all the great papers, asking them to exchange with us, and we wrote to the President and members of the cabinet, telling them to give us all the news beats before they gave them to the other papers. That was Maudie Joyce's idea, and it was fine, too, though they didn't do it, for some reason. I suppose they thought perhaps we didn't "wield enough political influence." Little do they wot that my father is a general in the army. I was glad to remember that, for I thought perhaps he would come up for promotion some day, and then there would be trouble about it, and *The Voice of Truth* would have lots of beats and lay bare the innermost recesses of everybody's heart.

After we finished our letters to the President and his advisers (we asked them to advise us before they did him, but they didn't do that, either)—well, after that we wrote to all the girls we knew in different cities, who used to be at St. Catharine's, and we asked them to be special correspondents and send us everything that happened. We said they must be truthful and fearless and not mind whether people liked what they wrote. The *news* came first, and their duty to us was paramount. Maudie said that. I don't know what it means, and I haven't time to find out, but it sounds well. I hope it doesn't mean anything wrong. We told the girls we would pay them what all the New York newspapers pay their correspondents, and we would give them "double rates for beats." "Beats," you know, are stories no other paper gets. Mr. Murphy suggested that, and he told all the editors in his city about our paper and how his daughter was running it. I had to correct this sad error publicly in the first issue of *The Voice of Truth*, for of course Mabel Muriel wasn't running it. I was. Mr. Murphy did not like it when I said I must write a correction, and he was quite slow about sending checks for a week or two, so that Mabel Muriel had to talk to him very earnestly, and even hint that perhaps we wouldn't let him be financial adviser any more. That brought him round in a hurry. We knew it would.

Of course all this time the paper was just "in the air," as real writers say. We hadn't begun to write for it or print it, but we thought about it and talked about it a great deal, and every letter we opened seemed to be full of money for subscriptions. We charged four dollars a year, because that is what most weekly magazines cost, and we knew *The Voice of Truth* would be better than the magazines. It would have all the news and "high-class literary features" besides. I was sure of those, because I intended to write them myself.

After we got this far we asked permission to go to the nearest town for the day, and the Sisters let us go, with one of the graduates to look after us. So, of course, we had to tell *her* our secret, and she was very nice about it and quite interested, especially after she saw the big roll of money Mabel Muriel Murphy had to spend. Some of it was her own, and some her father had given her, and the rest was "annual subscriptions payable in advance," the way they all are, you know. We went right to the best printer intown—the four of us, Mabel Blossom, Mabel Muriel Murphy,

Maudie Joyce, and I, with the graduate hovering modestly in the background (she didn't put on any airs over us or call us children that day, I can tell you!), and we told the printer what we wanted. He didn't seem much impressed at first, and he began to tell us how cheaply we could get up a little "four-page folder." He seemed to think we had only a few pennies to spend. But by-and-by Mabel Muriel Murphy took her big roll of money out of her pocket, and carelessly let two or three twenty-dollar bills fall on the floor, and picked them up again absently, as if it didn't matter; and I wish you could have seen that printer sit up and take notice, the way babies do when you dangle watches in front of them. His eyes were just as big and round as theirs, too.

He began to bring out nice sheets of creamy, thick paper for samples, and he showed us different kinds of type. We told him we would use very, very large type when we had "beats" and very small type the rest of the time, because we wanted to crowd a great deal of news into our paper. We asked him to get an artist to make a nice picture for the top of the first page, with an angel blowing a trumpet on one side and a pole for wireless telegraphy at the other side, and Truth flying through the air and hitting the pole. We didn't know just exactly how to show Truth, but finally Mabel Blossom said we'd better make it a balloon thing coming out of the trumpet and on its way to the wireless pole, so we did. By that time the printer was very kind, and willing and eager and anxious to please, and he called two other men into help, and they all seemed as interested as we were. One of them said he knew Mabel Muriel Murphy's father, and he told the printer he could sell Mabel Muriel the shop on credit if she wanted it, but Mabel Muriel didn't. She engaged him, though, to do all the work, and he said all we had to do was to bring in the "copy" and he would attend to the rest. Then we decided on the size and the paper and the number of pages. The printer thought we ought not to have more than eight to begin with, and he pointed out that it would be a serious mistake to give people more than their money's worth. We saw that, too, right away. Then he showed us the big machine, like an enormous typewriter, that would "set" all our "copy"; and first I thought I'd better come down and learn to set it myself to avoid errors, but the printer did not agree with me. He said that editors rarely did that now "in the large centers," and finally I saw that it would probably take a good deal of time, so I gave it up. Thus do we live and learn.

We were with the printer hours before everything was settled, and the graduate was quite nervous about getting back to St. Catharine's so late, but our consciences were at peace, for we knew we had done well. All we had to do after that was to write the paper and telegraph to our correspondents to rush their news, the way real editors do. While we were intown we sent telegrams to all of them to send their beats for next week's paper, and in a day or two they began to come in.

Then things got exciting. Maudie almost lost her head, for she was the managing editor and had to see to lots of things, and Mabel Muriel couldn't help her much because she was persuading people to advertise. She was clever about it, too. She got lots of the girls to advertise for things the other girls had borrowed from them and had not returned. The advertisements were like this:

> If Kittie James will kindly return the chafing-dish she borrowed from Adeline Thurston two weeks ago, she will be more lady-like.

Adeline only had to pay twenty-five cents for that, and she got her chafing-dish back the first morning *The Voice of Truth* came out, so we saw that it did pay to advertise, though Kittie didn't speak to Adeline for days and days afterwards. Mabel Muriel got the merchants to advertise, too, and she had a new idea about them that worked beautifully. Right below their advertisement of anything she printed the name of some girl who had tried the thing and knew it was good. This way, you know:

JAMES J. WEBSTER

HABERDASHER   286 FRONT STREET

EASTER HATS A SPECIALTY

Maudie Joyce Got Hers There!

Mr. Webster liked that very much when Mabel Muriel showed him the proofs, and he wanted us to print a picture of Maudie in the hat, but she wouldn't let us. We were fearless with the advertisers, too, though, and told the truth about them. One man's advertisement was printed like this, and he was so angry when he saw the proof that he took it right out and wanted his money back. It said:

WILLIAM SMITHERS, FLORIST
Cut Flowers and Potted Plants
Watch Him. They Are Not Always Fresh
Mabel Blossom Got Stale Ones
There Last Week.

So you see they were often unreasonable and hard to please; but we expected these slight annoyances in the beginning, so we were not surprised. However, I am ahead again. It is so hard to remember that when the time comes to tell anything you must wait till another time, the way Henry James does.[7] The paper wasn't really out yet. I've just absently told you some of the things we did before it came out. And in the meantime our work on it was a great secret from the Sisters, for we knew if we told them they would want to help us and see all the articles, and we wanted the credit ourselves.

As I said before, the copy from our correspondents in the "large centers" began to come in, and it was fine. Jennie Farrelly lives in New York, so she wrote a beautiful piece about what "Parsifal" meant, and how long the kiss was.[8] She timed it with her watch; and it was a beat, for no other paper had that. We sent Jennie "double rates." Mamie Chester lives in Chicago, and she knew a girl who was in the Iroquois Theatre fire last winter, so Mamie interviewed her (she wasn't dead) and wrote a thrilling description.[9] That was a beat, too, because that particular girl had never talked to reporters before. Our Philadelphia correspondent wrote a lovely piece about Ethel Barrymore[10] at home, and we were all so interested; for we saw her in "Cousin Kate,"[11] and she was just sweet, besides illustrating the tragic truth that girls who don't marry are terribly lonesome when they get to be old. But the very best news of all came from Nettie Upson, in Springfield, Massachusetts. Nettie's mother has a Japanese butler, and he told Nettie all about the war with Russia, and how much braver the Japanese are, and how sometime Japan and America will clasp hands across the sea like brothers and go down the ages together and fight all the other nations of the earth and civilize them. It was beautiful, and Nettie wrote it all so

thrillingly that Maudie Joyce cried when she read it. I guess there
are not many correspondents who can make their managing editors shed scalding tears over their papers.

But the gentle reader must not suppose that I was idle while my
dear friends and colleagues were thus active. No. I was at work—
on the editorial page—and I wrote every word of it myself, after
a careful study of the *Sun*'s style. First, of course, I said things
about President Roosevelt, pretending to pat him on the back,
but really showing how he had failed this nation in its darkest
hours of need.[12] (I like him myself, and so does papa, but of
course I had to be fearless.) Next I wrote a funny little poem and
said a man in Schenectady did it, and after that I made up some
queer names people might have, and I printed them.[13] Then I
wrote the Paris weather, like the *Herald* does, and I told about
the Soulless Corporation with its Heel on the Neck of the Poor,
the way the *Journal* does, and I explained that it was Mr. Murphy. I told how he ground down his employees on starving wages,
while his daughter lived in luxury and had more pocket-money
than any other girl at St. Catharine's.

That inspired me—you know how it is when you get started—
so I wrote another editorial, and said that *The Voice of Truth*
would constantly and fearlessly expose wrong wherever it was,
and that it would hold up the faults of the girls at St. Catharine's
for their good. I said how rare are the friends who will tell one
the truth about one's self, and they don't last long, anyhow; and I
said *The Voice of Truth* would be such a friend to the students
and would turn its X-rays on the evil in all their hearts. Then I
went onto tell the girls what was the matter with them. Even my
dear friends should not be spared, I said, so I began with Maudie
Joyce, and advised her not to be queenly so much or have so
many airs, and I said Mabel Muriel Murphy was improving but
still had much to learn, and that Mabel Blossom was lazy.

Mabel came in while I was writing this, so I read it to her, and
she was not pleased the least little bit. But after I reasoned with
her she saw it had to be, so she said I could print it if I would let
her write an editorial about *me*. At first I didn't want her to.
There were enough, I thought, and it didn't seem modest for the
editor-in-chief to be on the page that way. But Mabel talked and

THE NEW WOMAN COMES OF AGE

talked, so finally I gave in and she went off to write it. I wish you could have seen it when she brought it back. What I had said was kind and friendly and loving, but what Mabel Blossom said about me—her dear friend—was dreadful. She said that I had "started out to be a pretty good sort" (Mabel has not a polished literary style), but that literature had been "too much" for me. And she said I was conceited and had no sense of humor, and that I took myself too seriously, and that Maudie Joyce and Mabel Muriel thought so, too. She said other things, too, that I will not repeat. I had to put them in the paper, because I promised to; but I don't have to put them here, and I won't.

My young heart sank as I read my friend's editorial, but what could I do? So I put it in the page, under the heading Mabel wrote, "*Is There Hope for May Iverson?*" and right above it was my name as editor-in-chief. Was that right or fair? I pause for a reply, as real writers say.

When I wrote the editorial about Mabel Blossom's faults I had forgotten some of them, but now I remembered more; so I wrote them right in for the child's good, and when I showed it to her she couldn't say a word, for they were all true, and right well did Mabel Blossom know it. That filled up most of what was left of the editorial page, so I just dropped in a few more thoughts, and then I sent the copy to the printer, which I had to do, of course, before it could be published in the paper. After that I rested—and I needed to.

The Voice of Truth came out the next Saturday. Across the top of the front page was our picture of the angel and the trumpet and the wireless pole, but the artist had forgotten the balloon thing, which was Truth. However, I guess it looked better his way. It was very pretty. In the first column was the article on "Parsifal," and next to that was "Ethel Barrymore at Home," and beside that was the "Iroquois Fire." Then you had to turn the page, and you came right to my editorials. They looked beautiful. The printer had used big type with lots of white between to fill the page, and the eager eye of the reader could fall on the alluring titles. "Greeting—and Our Aims" was one. "His Workmen Cry for Bread"—that was about Mr. Murphy. "Ignoble Faults in Lovely Natures" was about the girls, you know. "Showing

His Teeth" was the one about the President, and then there were the poems and the weather and the rest. And of course the one about me, which I trust I need not mention again.

The next page had Mabel's Roll of Honor and Roll of Ignominy, because she said they were very important and must come near the front of the paper. After that we had advertisements and "Academy Notes"—a whole page of those—and "Advice to the Faculty," by Mabel Blossom. She wrote the headlines herself, and the second one was "An Eloquent Plea for Less Studies and More Fun, by a Brilliant but Overworked Student." And she says I am conceited!

Well, I haven't time to tell about all the rest. There was a love-story by Maudie Joyce, a beautiful one where they don't see each other for sixty years and then are reunited, and die smiling in each other's arms. I cried quarts over it! Adeline Thurston had a poem, of course; and we printed one of Kittie James's compositions to encourage her in her studies. Besides, we needed something to fill the page. And that was about all, I think, but we explained that we would have more next week when the President and cabinet officers began to send us beats.

One of the girls put a copy on Sister Irmingarde's desk, to surprise her—and I think it did. For while we were all reading the paper together and talking it over, and before we had time to mail any copies to subscribers, I saw something black coming along the hall, and first I thought it was a cloud, and then I saw it was Sister Irmingarde. So did the others. We all looked at each other, and somehow in that very moment I began to feel queer, and to wonder whether the paper was so good, after all, and to think perhaps we had made some mistakes. The girls did, too. They told me so afterwards. When Sister Irmingarde reached us we all stood up, of course, and we saw that she had *The Voice of Truth* in her hand and that her face was very white. She tapped the cover of the paper with her finger, and when she spoke her voice sounded queer.

"Have any copies of this gone out of the building?" she asked.

We said, "No, not yet," and her face changed right away, and she wiped her forehead as if she felt warm, though it was a cold day. Then she looked at us again in an odd way, and when she spoke she seemed to be speaking to herself, not to us.

"You haven't the remotest conception, evidently, of what you've done," she said, very slowly. "So I suppose we must try to remember that, after all, you are mere babies!"

We did not know what she meant by those enigmatic words, and she never told us. But it was, indeed, easy to see she didn't like *The Voice of Truth*. She made us promise to destroy every copy and never to do anything of the kind again without consulting her. And she seemed to think we were so terribly young! That worried us most of all. Perhaps we are babies and don't know it.

But one thing is sure. No baby could pay the bills that printer sent Mabel Muriel. Mabel Muriel couldn't, either. They made her hair stand right straight up. But she telegraphed to our financial adviser, and he came to St. Catharine's and advised us to pay the bills; and then he did pay them. So you see he was quite useful, and maybe it uplifted him, too. For I am 'most sure that during one morning, at least, while he was examining all our bills and writing out checks to pay them, he was too busy to be a Soulless Corporation with its Heel on the Neck of the Poor!

Source: *May Iverson—Her Book* (Harper & Brothers, 1904).

"WHAT DREAMS
MAY COME"

(1904)

Sometimes when the day is over and darkness has fallen, and the big, bright star we always look for is shining above the cross on the convent chapel, Maudie Joyce and Mabel Blossom and I sit close together in the window-seat of my room and have long, serious talks. We cannot see each other's faces very well, so if Mabel laughs we do not know it; but I think she does not, very much. Even her frivolous nature seems to be sobered then, and uplifted, too, as well indeed it may be, by the beautiful thoughts Maudie and I express. Often Mabel herself talks, quietly and with strange insight and intelligence for one so young—but has she not associated with Maudie and me for three years? Thus we reveal our innermost hearts to each other, and mention things our young lips might hesitate to utter in the garish light of day, as real writers say, and tell what we are going to do in the world when we are older and go out into it and begin to Live—really live, you know, and not just stand around and absorb knowledge the way we do now. And right here I will express an important thought while I think of it. It is this:

Everybody seems to remember that people can eat too much and drink too much and sleep too much, but, alas! none of our thoughtless elders realizes that the schoolgirl's mind should not be crammed too much, and that something dreadful will occur if it is. So they keep on putting things into our brains and adding more and more until no one could tell what might happen to us if we had not learned long since to hurry and forget a great deal. That saves our minds and leaves us room for thoughts that we really have to think—and, of course, a very important thing to think about is the big world that lies outside these convent walls.

We have the strangest ideas sometimes about that. The Sisters seem to dread it for us, and they often speak of it as if it were a terrible beast that couched at the entrance, ready to spring upon us when we came out. But we cannot think of it that way. Maudie asked Mabel one evening what she thought the world was like, and she said she thought of it as a kind of a big party she was invited to, where she would meet a great many people, and like them a lot, and dance with some of them, and hear music all the time. Maudie said she thought it was more like a vast picture-gallery, where there would be a great many things to look at; or a play, as Shakespeare says, where she could have a seat away down in front.[1] But I said at once that I didn't want it that way—to sit on chairs and look at things, I mean; and that if it was a play I wanted to be in it, right on the stage, doing things myself in my humble fashion. Then Mabel giggled and I hastily changed the subject, for I was not quite sure what she was laughing at; but I meant it just the same.

When we get very, very serious indeed we talk about Careers, for Careers are indeed interesting, exciting things, and most women seem to be having them. We have all decided that we will be very great and noted and sit on the topmost pinnacle of fame, and give our autographs to people. I will be literary, of course, and write wonderful novels with human heart-beats in every line, and the masses will weep over them. Then all the girls at St. Catharine's, the ones who are not sitting on the pinnacle of fame themselves, will boast of how they used to know me, and tell anecdotes of my youth, and write letters reminding me of themselves and asking for copies of my books with their names in them. All the magazines and newspapers will have illustrated articles every week called, "May Iverson at Home," and the pictures will show me writing more great books at my desk, or holding one in my hand and gazing into the future with the inspired eyes of genius. Perhaps some of them will show me clasping my brow with my hand and thinking thoughts. Sarah Underhill Worthington[2] is always doing that in her photographs, and Charles Dudley Warner[3] and others I have seen. My face will have lines all over it, proving that I have Lived and drunk deep draughts from the very dregs of Life; but it will be kind, too, and I will be kind inside as well, especially to young authors, and read all their early manuscripts, and try to keep them from bruising their tender feet on the rocky pathway I have trod.

I will probably live all by myself in a great old house by the sea, for I know that when I begin to do real writing I shall be strange and tragic and broody, like all other gifted ones, and have to live alone the way the True Artist must. But mamma and papa and Grace and little Georgie can come to see me sometimes, between books, and I will greet them with a sweet, sad smile, and wander with them by the ocean's edge, and say things they will hurry home to write down. Besides, of course, my home will be a Mecca for other great souls who will seek me from afar.

You can see it will be a lonely, yea, a tragic life, and probably it will not last long. I used to think, last year, when I was younger, that I would die when I was sixteen. But now I begin to think I may live to be 'most thirty, and thus have plenty of time to accomplish all my fondest dreams and pass away before I am tired of them.

Mabel Blossom says she is going to be a famous doctor, the most distinguished woman physician in America, because that is what she would like best. We know she has talent, for she gives medicine to all the minims when they are sick, and once she nearly killed little Jennie Osborne; but that was a youthful error, and, as Mabel truly says, practice alone makes perfect.[4]

When Mabel is a doctor she will be such a good one that her very name will be an inspiration, and women all over the country will utter it in trembling tones. When men doctors have given up all hope for the patient, someone will say, "Send for Dr. Blossom," and Mabel will enter in a black, tailor-made gown, and her presence will be a benediction or something in the room. The patient will sit right up and be interested, and Mabel will save her life while the men doctors look on in awe and great respect. They will say, "Thank you, doctor; you have taught us much," while the patient's family kiss Mabel's strong, skillful hands. All the medical journals will have articles by Mabel, and newspapers will talk about her and tell of her wonderful cures; and of course she will get very rich, for her prices will be enormous. But she will never charge the poor anything at all, and her beautiful home will ever be a refuge for those who are ill and need their money for something else. Maudie and I are both enthusiastic over Mabel's career, and we are letting her try all her medicines on us, so she can begin immediately without waiting till she graduates. Mabel says it may interrupt our careers but it will help hers, and if anything happens to us she will mention our names as "martyrs to science" in her first medical article. Sometimes Mabel is slightly selfish, alas, in her absorption in her science, for only last month she begged Maudie to break a leg or arm so Mabel could set it. Maudie wouldn't do it, because commencement is 'most here, and she has an essay to read, but Mabel never remembered that, the thoughtless child.

Maudie says she is not quite sure what she will do, so she is keeping her mind open, but she thinks perhaps she would like to be a great actress, like Madame Duse[5] or Sarah Bernhardt,[6] and elevate the stage. At night she will have multitudes at her feet, swayed by her lightest word or gesture, and all day long when she is not acting she will have classes of chorus girls and young actresses, and talk to them about high ideals and find good managers for them.

You see how anxious we all are to help others. I hope the gentle reader has observed this, for it is the thing we are taught in the convent, and it will go out into the world with us and last as long as we live, as it always does in convent girls. It is called "the Community spirit" in the cloister—and it means that every Sister thinks more of others than of herself, and that each is working for all the rest and will make any sacrifice for them. It means, too, that while each Sister is humble and lowly and doesn't think much about herself, she must do her very best and develop herself spiritually to the highest degree, because she is one unit in a great body—the Community—and the Community as a whole must be as perfect as any human body can be. It is a very, very beautiful thing, and we girls admire it so much that we are resolved to carry that spirit into the world, and help others and be our best selves, not for reward, but to "raise the standard." Sometimes Mabel and Maudie and I talk for hours about how important it is to be good and honorable and fine, even if it keeps us too busy to be successful. We have promised each other that we will never lose our "high standard of personal honor," as Sister Irmingarde calls it, because if we did we would have to blush for each other, and that would be indeed terrible.

We are always going to keep together, of course, and help each other a great deal in every way. I have promised Mabel to read all my novels aloud to her patients in the hospitals, and Maudie says she will have her chorus girls come and sing for them. Mabel says that in return she will have her patients tell us their sensations, so I can write them in my books and Maudie can act them when she does Camille or any other play where the heroine dies. We have agreed to meet every year and spend a week together, and tell each other what we have learned in the meantime, so we can keep even, you know.

One of the subjects we like best to talk about is the friendships we are going to have—the men and women we will "select from the whole world to come into the individual circles of our lives," as Maudie says. She has her list all ready. Eleanora Duse is at the head of it, and Sarah Bernhardt is next, and then come Margaret Sangster[7] and Dr. Henry Van Dyke[8] and Ethel Barrymore.[9] She likes Mrs. Sangster and Dr. Van Dyke because they write so beautifully about girls, but she thinks it would be kind of restful afterwards to talk to Ethel Barrymore. *My* list has Mr. Henry James and Mr. William Dean Howells[10] at the very top, and Marconi[11] and President Roosevelt and A. Henry Savage Landor,[12] because Mr. Landor has delved so deep in life and felt so many things. Besides, he says he has never had a dull minute, and that is just the kind of a life I expect to have, so we shall have much in common. There are no women on my list, as I fear, alas, I may not have time for them. But if I had, I think I would like to spend my few moments of leisure with Sister Irmingarde.

Mabel Blossom has Mark Twain at the head of her list, because he says such funny things and can cheer her up so much after the strain of the day.[13] Next she has Dr. Grace Peckham Murray,[14] because she knows so much and is so nice; and she said she guessed she would have Margaret Deland,[15] too. But the minute she mentioned Margaret Deland I remembered that I would probably have more time than I realized at first, so I put Margaret on my list right off, and I pointed out to Mabel that as she was literary, too, I had a greater right to her than any doctor had. Mabel did not like it very much, but she is a reasonable child and knows logic when she hears it, so she said she would take Mrs. Humphry Ward instead.[16] Then she added Harry Lehr[17] because he is so entertaining and laughs so much, and Marianna Wheeler[18] because she knows all about babies. Mabel said that as a doctor she would need to know a great deal about babies, and no doubt Miss Wheeler would tell her lots and lots, and let her visit the Babies' Hospital whenever she wanted to.

It is, indeed, a beautiful thought that out in the wide world these friends are waiting for us, knowing naught of our existence nor of the close ties the future holds for them. We often wonder how our meetings will come about and whether they will learn to love us right away or whether it will take some time. Mabel and Maudie do not seem to be worried about that a bit, but I sometimes feel a chilling doubt. Maudie even knows just how her meeting with Duse and Bernhardt will happen. She will have finished the last great act of her play some night, she says, and suddenly she will become conscious of two stately figures in her dressing-room. One will be Duse and the other Bernhardt, and they will be there hand-in-hand, to tell her that at last, after years, they meet for the first time, and together, America's great actress. They will mean Maudie. Then their eyes will fill with tears and they will be unable to say more, but Maudie will understand, and that will be the beginning of a life-long friendship. It is beautiful to hear Maudie talk. She gets so excited that her voice trembles, and one evening she cried when she was telling what Bernhardt would say to her. Mabel Blossom giggled, which was not nice under the circumstances, and Maudie got very angry indeed and went off to bed and would not talk about Careers for a whole week. Instead, she made Welsh-rabbits in her room every night, and invited me and Kittie James and Mabel Muriel, and didn't ask Mabel Blossom, so Mabel's lot was a sad and lonely one.[19] You can believe she was serious enough the next time we discussed Careers!

That was only last night, and Kittie James was there, too, so she began to tell what *she* wanted to do. Kittie is very young, not fourteen, so her mind is not very mature, and of course she has not studied life's grim horrors the way Maudie and I have. Kittie said she used to think she would like to be a nurse, and minister to the sick, and be the angel at the bedside and soothe the savage breast, and then lay a flower above the patient's still heart when he was gone. Mabel Blossom got up then and left in a great hurry. She said she had to study, and we all felt more confidential, some-how, when she was gone. Kittie went onto say that she had been thinking lately, though, of other ways of living, especially since her sister Josephine's baby came, and she said she had almost de-cided to give up her life to her little nephew and care for him while George and Josephine went to parties. She said he was just as cunning, and was beginning to walk and to say words, and George had taught him to say "Kittie," and he did, in the cutest way. And she told us all about him and how he looked, and how many teeth he had, and how he played with a feather for hours and hours, and it was very interesting. Mabel came back then and got as absorbed as we were. Then I told about Georgie, my little nephew. He, of course, is much more interesting than Kit-tie's nephew, because he is four years old and has a very active mind. I told the girls all the bright things he had said, and they got more and more serious, and pretty soon we all stopped talk-ing and sat very still.

After awhile I began to think, and somehow, all of a sudden, I felt dreadfully lonesome. First I thought about home and papa and mamma and Grace and brother Jack and little Georgie, and I could see him playing on the rug before the fire with his tight curls standing straight up from his head the way they do. Grace always lets him have a frolic in his nightgown before he goes to bed, and he looks so cute and dimpled and cuddly, and there is the sweetest expression about his knees! I could see him plainly as I sat there, and see Grace at the piano and papa reading the evening paper and mamma rumpling my brother Jack's hair as she sat in a corner with him. They have a way of getting off by themselves sometimes for little talks. A great big lump came in my throat and I wanted dreadfully to see them. Then I remem-bered that after I left school I could live with them always and not be parted. I was thinking how nice that would be and feeling better, when suddenly, just as if someone had made a picture of it, that old house by the sea came before my eyes—the one, you know, where I am to live when I become distinguished and queer and have to be by myself and write novels. It looked so cold and lonely that I shivered and got close to Maudie. I could hear the waves beat upon the rocks, and see the gulls hovering over the water, and hear my own footsteps echo as I strode in fancy down my desolate marble halls. Big tears rolled down my cheeks, but it was so dark no one saw them, and I remembered that if I was to be alone all my life I might just as well get used to it now and begin to bear my troubles without telling the girls. It didn't cheer me a bit to think of all the books I was going to write or the friends I was going to have, for I remembered that probably they would all be interested in their own husbands and wives in the selfish way people have. I felt worse than ever when I thought of that, and I don't know what I would have done if I had not remembered Maudie's old plan and mine, that I was to marry a brave young officer, and she was to marry a strong and noble man who would break her will, and we were to live next door to each other so that all our children could play together. That seemed more grateful and comforting, somehow, than the lonely house by the desolate sea, so I wiped my eyes and began to imagine just how the house would look and how I would "shine at social assemblages," as the papers say about mamma. I remembered how nice it would be to draw great artists and authors around me in my own home, especially if I had Algernon and the children there first (Maudie and I decided mine was to be Algernon and hers Philip).

I was just thinking how cute the baby would look in little blue pajamas like Georgie's, and planning how well I'd bring him up, avoiding the mistakes dear mamma made with me, when Maudie spoke up so suddenly she made me jump, and asked if I had forgotten how we were to live side by side. Before I had a chance to answer she said her mother had told her it was a serious thing to decide on a career too soon, and had advised her very earnestly not to do it, but to wait till her mind was even more mature. Maudie said that was why she was not quite sure she was going to be an actress. She said it seemed wiser to keep her mind open and in an unprejudiced condition so she could consider any other offers that came along.

Mabel Blossom giggled then, but Maudie didn't seem to mind. She added very calmly that the world needed home-makers and good mothers just as much as it needed geniuses, and she admitted that sometimes, especially in the twilight hour, her thoughts turned with a strange persistence to domestic topics. She said that all the time I was talking about my home by the sea she was trying to think whether she'd put curtains like Mabel Muriel Murphy's into her future home or Indian draperies like those Kittie James's sister Josephine had. And she said right out that she had lain awake hours one night wondering whether she could afford to dress the baby in white all the time or whether she would have to put little gingham "creepers" on him in the mornings.[20] Then she began to talk again about how Philip was going to look, and his crisp, black curls, and how his eyes would alternately flash fire and melt with tenderness, but we did not pay much attention, for we had heard all that before. Besides, I was thinking of Algernon, lying wounded in some distant battle-field under Southern skies, and of how I would fly across the world to his side and nurse him back to health. For I have now decided that I won't have him killed by the enemy the way he was at first. That plan was made when my mind was crude and immature.

All of a sudden Mabel Blossom drew a long sigh, and then another, and when I asked her why she did it she said it was because partings were such terrible things and hard for the parent heart to bear. Maudie looked at her rather suspiciously, but I asked what parting she meant, and Mabel said she had long since decided that her youngest daughter was to be a nun, and she was just beginning to realize how hard it would be to see her take the black veil![21] Then she giggled, of course, Dear, dear Mabel—we must make allowance for her youthful frivolities, but they try even our stanch hearts at times.

She broke the spell, as she 'most always does, so we laughed, too, but not as much as Mabel did, and got up and put our arms around each other and stood that way for a moment looking out at the big, bright star we love. Our star, we call it, and we have promised to think of each other when we look up at it in future years. It will remind us of the "Community spirit," too—"too low he aims who aims beneath the stars," you know—and of something else very beautiful and sacred. I think we all thought of that something else as we gazed at it, so far, so pure, so friendly in its good-night glance at four little school-girls. I wish I could write just what we felt in that uplifting moment, full of so many emotions, but we have time, as Sister Irmingarde says, for only one more thought. This is it, and the frivolous reader may skip it if she wants to. It seemed to me as we turned away that we can never fail, or have doubts, or fall below our standard, if only we look up at that star very often and remember all it suggests.

Source: *May Iverson—Her Book* (Harper & Brothers, 1904).

FROM
MAY IVERSON
TACKLES LIFE

"WOMAN SUFFRAGE AT ST. CATHARINE'S"

(1912)

I may as well admit at once that Maudie Joyce was the first girl at St. Catharine's to feel any real interest in Woman Suffrage. Usually I am the one in our school set who thinks of new things, and does them; so the other girls have got in the habit of waiting for me, and not trying to think themselves, in their crude, immature way. But Maudie thought of suffrage all alone, though perhaps Kittie James helped to put the idea into her head.

You see, Kittie started an anti-suffrage club, almost as soon as we got back to school in September, and she made herself the president of it at the very first meeting. Before the meeting was over, Maudie Joyce asked Kittie what the club was for, and Kittie didn't know; and Maudie asked what the members were going to do, and Kittie didn't know that, either. Kittie said she just wanted to have a club because they had one in Chicago, and her sister, Mrs. George Morgan, belonged to it. She said the nicest feature of the Chicago club was that nobody in it did anything, and they joined because they didn't have to do anything. It was a beautiful club, Kittie said, and so restful.

Maudie walked off to a corner after these words fell from the lips of our young friend, and I followed her. I suppose we looked aloof and lonely and disapproving. Anyway, when the rest of the girls had watched us awhile, most of them came over to the corner, too, and the end of it all was that Kittie only got three members for her new club. Mabel Muriel Murphy joined because Sister Edna, the nun she likes best, approves of gentle, womanly girls. Kittie told Mabel the gentlest and most womanly thing a girl could possibly do was to join her anti-suffrage club. Kittie said the real aim of her club was to keep women in their homes, where they belonged, when they weren't at her club; and she said Mabel Muriel Murphy wouldn't have to have a single new idea all the time she belonged. Mabel said afterward it was true, too; she didn't have any.

But the whole thing seemed silly to Maudie and me. We are very intelligent girls, if we are only sixteen, and we have lots of mature ideas and emotions. If we join a club at all, we want to do something in it, even if it is only to eat. There weren't going to be any "spreads" in Kittie's club, she said at first, because she has a delicate stomach, and the convent infirmarians, who look after her, think she mustn't eat between meals. They don't let her eat much at meals, either, so Kittie is against girls overeating. It *is* an awful thing to behold, when you are held down yourself.

However, Kittie went right on with her club, though, of course, she felt dreadfully disappointed when Maudie and I didn't join. Well, indeed, did she know what that meant, and how impossible real success was without us. So she "strengthened her party," as papa says great statesmen do, by giving offices to her friends. She made Mabel Muriel Murphy treasurer, because Mabel Muriel's father is rich and loves to pay bills; and she made Adeline Thurston secretary, because Adeline likes to write poems, and Kittie said writing reports of her club would be even more interesting than poetry. When Maudie asked how there could be any reports if there wasn't anything done, Kittie said the club would write up the things that were not done. Then she looked past the sides of our faces and changed the subject by making Hattie Gregory vice-president.

We left the meeting after that, and went to my room and ate

pickles and talked about how sharper than a serpent's tooth an ungrateful child is.[1] Kittie was 'most like our own child, for she is more than a year younger than we are, and not intellectual; and Mabel Blossom and Maudie Joyce and I have really directed her education since she came to St. Catharine's, three years ago.

While we were talking, Maudie said she wondered what Mabel Blossom would think of all this. Mabel hadn't come back to school yet, but she was coming in a few days. Before I could answer, Maudie spoke again, in the quick way she has when she thinks of something. It's just as if someone had touched a button in her brain, and often Maudie jumps when it happens. She jumped this time, and so did I, for I wasn't expecting her to, and the doctor says I am a nervous girl, singularly high-strung. Besides, of course, I have the artistic temperament, and you know what that does to folks. So I jumped, and then got cross over it, the way any literary artist would, who likes to be "well poised and dignified," as Sister Edna says. Maudie Joyce didn't even apologize. She just sat staring in front of her for a minute, as if she saw something that wasn't there. Then she said, very slowly:

"May Iverson, let's be suffragettes!"

I jumped again, because the idea surprised me so much, and I said:

"But we aren't suffragettes, so how can we be?"

Maudie looked at me with a patient expression, like the one Sister Irmingarde wears sometimes in the classroom. I analyzed it once, for literary practice, to help me to observe life and put down all I see: it had astonishment in it, and pained regret, and resignation, and a kind of holy calm, struggling up through hopelessness. After I analyzed it, I wrote it all out and showed the paper to Sister Irmingarde, and asked her if I was right. She looked very much surprised at first, but finally she said she thought I had every ingredient right but one, and she would let me guess at that. Then she smiled her lovely smile, and changed the subject by asking me why my marks weren't higher in algebra. Of course all this hasn't anything to do with suffrage, or anti-suffrage, either. I just put it in to show how acute I am, so the gentle reader won't be surprised when I read people's hearts the way I'll have to before I get through with this chapter.

We will now return to Maudie. For a long time she was silent, and thought gathered deeply on her beautiful, high-bred face. At last she said, very solemnly:

"We are, too, suffragettes. We've been suffragettes right along, May Iverson. Only we haven't known it."

I gasped then, and began to say I couldn't be anything like that without knowing it, for my first lesson in life had been to know myself, and I learned it when I was twelve. But Maudie went right on, rudely interrupting me. She said she hadn't known her own heart till she went to Kittie's meeting and heard Kittie talk. She said all the time she was there she kept feeling more and more uncomfortable and stirred up inside, but she didn't know why. She even thought it might be indigestion. She said it was only this minute that it burst upon her gloriously that from the very beginning of Kittie's meeting she had been a suffragette, unconsciously working for the cause, and trying to get independence of thought for women. She added that when she heard Kittie James express her silly little ideas, they made her so annoyed that she 'most wanted to slap Kittie. Then she woke up and knew she was a real suffragette, because that's the way they feel in England. She read all about it in the newspapers, and a friend of her mother had seen Mrs. Pankhurst in Chicago.[2]

By this time Maudie was very much excited, so when I didn't answer right off she said she was ready to die for the cause, and if I didn't feel that way, too, and join the suffrage club she was going to get up, she'd never speak to me again as long as she lived.

Of course that's no way to talk to the daughter of a general in the army, who is a literary artist besides, and I pointed this out to Maudie in tones that were cold and firm. I said she couldn't force me to anything by threats, but that she must appeal to my reason and convince me that suffrage was a good thing for women. And I added, frankly, that I didn't think she could do it now, anyway, because she had annoyed me very much by the way she began. I was 'most sure already I wasn't a suffragette and didn't ever want to be one.

Maudie changed her methods then, right off. She has associated with Mabel and me so long that she has a good deal of sense. She begged my pardon very politely, and she fixed me in a big, comfy chair, and gave me a glass of ginger ale and a cookie, and started into appeal to my reason.

She said, with her first words, that she was glad to have *my* reason to appeal to, and not the other girls', and she asked me to imagine how I'd feel if I ever had to appeal to Kittie James's reason. When I clapped at that, like a real audience—for anyone who knew Kittie could see what a powerful point it was—Maudie asked me if I was willing to follow the banner of Kittie James "in a struggle which was of vital import to the human race." (She got that out of a newspaper. We have to read one every day, for our Current Events class.)

I stood right up, and said I didn't want to follow Kittie's banner, or anybody's but my own. I said I just wanted to spend my life elevating the masses, by writing pure literature for them, and I didn't see why men couldn't go on voting, and doing heavy work like that, while we women uplifted them. I felt just full of thoughts, but Maudie made me sit down before I could say any more. She said I had promised to let her appeal to my reason, and she wished I would do it and not interrupt. That was a rebuke, and it annoyed me very much. I sat down right away; but it was quite a long time before I could get my intellect calm enough for Maudie to appeal to it. I kept thinking, instead, of crushing things I might have said before I sat down, and it was dreadfully hard not to get up again and say them then. They would have been a help to Maudie, too.

But Maudie was going right along with her speech all the time, and getting more excited every minute. I don't believe she really cared much about suffrage when she began, but by the time she finished she was ready to give up her work at St. Catharine's, and her dream of being a great actress, and go right out and be a suffragette, and get arrested and sent to prison. She had read about the English women in prison, and how they were fed through tubes, and she called them martyrs in a deathless cause, and said she was going to have Adeline Thurston write a poem about them.[3] I spoke up again, then, and reminded her that Adeline was an anti-suffragist now, and would only write poems against suffrage. Maudie groaned and said: "This issue will split the convent. It will be like West Point at the outbreak of the Civil War, when the cadets had to take sides for the North or the South."

And she looked at me with her eyes blazing, and said, "May Iverson, at such a crisis will you be on the fence, thinking about life and trying to write stories, or will you be out on the great battlefield, fighting shoulder to shoulder with your dear ones!"

I tell you that made me sit up. When there's any fighting to do, no Iverson turns his back upon the foe. I saw at once that it was time to take sides, and that it was going to be terribly exciting. Kittie James was already in the enemy's camp, with three of our friends, and here was Maudie getting up an opposition party. I had to decide quickly, and I did it. The audience was convinced on the spot, and it got up and kissed Maudie and told her so. My, but she was glad! She just hugged me, though usually she's a very undemonstrative girl. Then she said: "Now we've *got* to get Mabel Blossom on our side. The three of us can sweep the girls off their feet; but if Mabel goes over to Kittie, you and I will have a battle to hold our own." And she added, gloomily: "We can never tell how Mabel Blossom will act about anything."

I knew that was so, and I promised Maudie I would appeal to Mabel's reason, and try to make her join us the very minute she got back, before the other girls saw her. I said I'd meet Mabel at the station, and ask her which she preferred to associate with on an intellectual level—Kittie James or us. I thought that might fetch Mabel; she is so proud of her intellect. Maudie said it was worth trying, but she shook her head and said it would be just like Mabel to join the other side, so she could develop their intellects. Then her face brightened and she jumped; so I saw that she had another idea. She did, too. She said I might tell Mabel she could get a feeding-tube, and use it on Maudie if she wanted to. Maudie said she had wondered how a person felt when she was fed through a tube, and now she was going to get one right off and find out. She said she knew Mabel would be simply delighted to try such an experiment. Mabel was going to be a doctor, so she'd have to know about it sometime, and it might as well be now.

I wasn't very enthusiastic at first. It seemed to me like what Sister Irmingarde calls "an irrelevant detail." But I knew Mabel Blossom would join any society in the world for the sake of trying a medical experiment on someone, so I told Maudie the tube was surely the quickest way of getting to Mabel. Wasn't that bright? Maudie laughed hard; she doesn't always. We put Mabel's name on our list without waiting. So now we had three members—a president (Maudie, of course); a vice-president (Mabel); and a secretary (me). Just then Janet Trelawney knocked at the door and came in, and as soon as we mentioned our club she joined it without waiting for any details, because she liked us better than she liked Kittie. We were glad she didn't insist on having an office, because there weren't any left; but we gave her a glass of ginger ale and a cookie to celebrate on. There was really something to celebrate, for, you see, we had four members, the same as Kittie had, and her club was a whole hour older than ours.

You'd better believe the next twenty-four hours were fevered ones. Whenever we saw a girl alone anywhere we appealed to her reason and got her to join St. Catharine's suffragettes. Janet Trelawney caught one girl in a bathtub, and wouldn't leave her till she promised to join; and Maudie Joyce gave her best coral chain to a new girl, to convince her reason. It did, too, though she had half promised Kittie to join the antis.[4] All I did was to appeal to the girls' reasons and read my stories to them; and they were so proud of being seen seated beneath the trees with a real author that they joined, "not single spies, but in battalions," as Shakespeare says.[5] I got nine one Saturday, so you can see how a love for good literature is fostered in our convent school. Betweentimes we made banners with "VOTES FOR WOMEN" on them. Mabel Blossom was with us by this time. She joined just as soon as we mentioned feeding Maudie through the tube. Before that her mind seemed to be "clouded with a doubt," like King Arthur's.[6]

Perhaps you think Kittie James was idle all this time. She was not. The very moment Kittie heard about our club she began to work like mad to make hers bigger. She was unreasonable about it, too, and instead of seeing that we had a right to our own sacred convictions, Kittie thought we got up our club to kill hers. She hardly spoke to us on the campus at first, but pretty soon she saw how silly this was, especially as it made her miss lots of fun that had nothing to do with suffrage clubs. So she began to drop into my room again in the evening, the way she always had, but she wore such an impatient and busy look that it got on Maudie's nerves.

I am very broad-minded and just, so I can't help admitting that Kittie's club was really a success, after all. Her sister, Mrs. George Morgan, sent her lots of advice about it, and told Kittie everything the Chicago club did; and her brother-in-law, George Morgan, was tremendously interested and made heaps of suggestions. Kittie took them, too, and made her club socially exclusive, and had parties, and things to eat, even if she couldn't eat them herself. Mabel Muriel pointed out to Kittie, very politely, that this was no reason why other girls shouldn't eat, and Kittie saw it that way at last, though Mabel Muriel said to see Kittie stand around and look at the food as it disappeared was enough to ruin one's appetite. Of course our clubs were making life very gay; for when we had a tea, the antis gave a reception, and when they had a musicale, we had an authors' reading and I read a story. It all took up so much time that Sister Irmingarde got nervous and began to make pointed remarks about study; but Maudie told her we were merely girding on our armor for the vital struggle on life's grim battle-field. After that Sister Irmingarde didn't seem to be able to say anything for a few minutes, though we could see she was impressed.

Then, all of a sudden, the way dramatic things happen in books, the crisis came. Kittie James challenged Maudie to a suffrage debate! She said we could have it in the study-hall, and both clubs could come, and some of the other students and Sisters. She said we could have a jury to decide which side won, and give a silver cup to the winner. She said the jury was George Morgan's idea, and the cup was hers—but I knew that before she told us. Imagine Kittie James thinking of a jury! She told me afterward, with her own lips, that she thought we should have to borrow one from a courtroom in Chicago, and she asked George to manage it, because he is a lawyer. George didn't. He said some of the Sisters would do. So we asked Sister Edna and Sister Irmingarde and Sister Estelle, and they all accepted. Then we ordered programmes, and flowers, and lemons and sandwiches, and other important things, and for days and days we were so busy we didn't stop to decide who was going to debate. When we asked Kittie she said very coolly that she was going to do it for her side, but if Maudie didn't feel up to doing it herself, she could ask someone else to represent our club. Kittie said she thought the president ought to do it, so she was going to do her duty; but she didn't want her decision to influence Maudie in any way.

I wish you could have seen Maudie's face, and Mabel's, when Kittie said that. I suppose mine looked funny, too, but of course I couldn't see mine. When Maudie could speak, she said she would represent her club, and that, as Kittie was very young and inexperienced, and ought to have every advantage, she could begin or finish—Maudie didn't care which. Kittie said she would end the debate, and she bowed to us all and went away, leaving the loudest silence behind her that I ever heard.

The gentle reader cannot understand how strange it was, because the gentle reader doesn't know Kittie James. But we girls did, and to think of Kittie making a speech, and trying to express thoughts! I just simply haven't got far enough in my literary art to describe our emotions. I don't believe even Shakespeare could do it, or Henry James. Why, the first days Kittie was at St. Catharine's, she came to my room one night and woke me up to ask me why it was that she always felt so much sleepier in the morning than when she went to bed at night. She said sometimes she couldn't sleep at night, but she could always sleep after the bell rang at six in the morning. She said she had been wondering about it, and couldn't understand. Another time she interrupted Maudie, when she was writing an essay one night, to ask her why folks felt homesick when they were away from home. She stayed and talked about it a long time. She said her stomach felt as if she were dropping from the top floor of a high building in a dreadfully fast elevator, and she wanted to know why that was. Finally, Maudie and I told Kittie not to waste her time trying to think, but to come right to us when anything puzzled her. And she always did, until now. Now she was being a leader of thought and patronizing Maudie Joyce!

Maudie had been working on some new banners with "VOTES FOR WOMEN" on them, for we were planning to have an open-air demonstration on the campus the next day. But Maudie put the banners down the very minute Kittie left, and went off to write her debate. I knew by the look in her eye that her proud spirit was stirred to its depths, and I felt sorry for Kittie. Kittie wasn't a bit sorry for herself, though. Mabel Blossom was so much interested in the challenge that she followed Maudie to her room, and told her she needn't eat through the tube until the day after the debate, though we had already fixed the tube day, before we knew about the debate. You'd better believe Maudie was glad to postpone it. The tube was going to be heroic, but not intellectual, of course.

Every day from then to the day we had the debate, Kittie James went around the halls looking important and murmuring to herself. She'd get off on the banks of the river that runs through the convent grounds, and put pebbles in her mouth and practice oratory, like a man I read about somewhere.[7] Finally she swallowed a pebble by accident and had to stop, so we had some peace. It was time, too, for I was getting dreadfully tired of hearing, "I say to you, students of St. Catharine's Academy," coming from all the nicest nooks on the grounds. I think Maudie would have had to go to the infirmary in a day or two more, she was getting so overwrought.

We were all pretty edgy by this time. If you have delicate nerves in your fingers, you know how perfectly awful you feel when you try to pare a peach. That's about the way every suffragette at St. Catharine's felt when an "anti" came round where she was. As for our lessons, Sister Irmingarde told me with her own lips that if I didn't do better during the coming month she would be reluctantly forced to change her mind about my ability as a student. You'd better believe that stirred me up! I dropped everything at St. Catharine's except study and suffrage. When the other girls had "spreads" in their rooms, Mabel Muriel Murphy and I were studying in our rooms with wet towels on our heads; for Sister Edna had reproached Mabel Muriel, too. But when there was suffrage or anti-suffrage going on, we were both at our posts, like the boy on the burning deck.[8] For by this time it was a vital, burning issue, as the newspaper said, and was disrupting the girls, just as Maudie had thought it would.

The evening of the debate came at last. We had it in the assembly-hall right after supper, and Sister Irmingarde and Sister Edna and Sister Estelle were the jury, as they had promised to be. The anti girls were all on the left side, and we suffragettes sat on the right; and on the platform there was a speakers' rostrum, with a glass of water on it. When I saw those three nuns lined up in their chairs, and some other Sisters in the audience, I felt sorry for Kittie and Maudie. Sisters, especially the Sisters who teach us, make a very critical audience, and we girls had often indeed observed that they had a strange, cramping effect on our style—the kind one's family has. Both Maudie and Kittie looked nervous, I thought, and dreadfully serious. Kittie wore her newest dress—one her sister had sent her the week before—and Maudie had on a new embroidered blouse. They were pale but firm.

Maudie began, and, dear me! wasn't I proud of her! Maudie has one fault, and I have pointed it out to her freely, like a true literary artist to whom art comes before all. She uses too many big words, and is what Mabel Blossom calls "highfalutin" in her style. (Mabel has pointed this fault out, too.) But she began to debate in the simplest, most natural way, so that the Minims could have understood her if they had been there. She said afterward that she did this because she wanted the antis to grasp her meaning.

Maudie said that the time came to every girl when she had to look into the depths of her own heart, and make up her mind what her life was going to be. Then, when she decided, all she had to do was to go ahead and make it that. You see how simple that was. The antis began to look bored right off, but I gave Maudie a smile of loving encouragement. She said there were only two things a girl could do—she could be an ivy and cling to things, or else she could be a strong support and let things cling to her. Then Maudie drew a long breath and said the very best thing any girl could have clinging to her was Principles. She waited for that to sink in, and we suffragettes applauded. Maudie went onto talk about Duty and Responsibility and the Community Spirit of Helpfulness.

Then she started in, in earnest. She said it was natural for the slothful and indolent to shirk work. She said we saw it done every day by some of those around us at St. Catharine's. It was easier to let the world go by, Maudie said, than to help to make it move; but, if everybody shirked, what would become of progress, and who would pass on the torch from hand to hand? She said butterflies were very pretty to look at, but there was no place for them in a beehive. They did not help the soul to climb. Kittie

James stood right up when Maudie said that, and tried to speak, but Adeline Thurston pulled her down. Maudie said the way to live one's life was not in slothful pleasures, eating "spreads," and neglecting one's studies, but to join hands in a ring of helpfulness that would reach round the world. She said it made her feel 'most sick sometimes to see opportunities for universal brotherhood and the community spirit lost by girls who had the priceless advantages of living at St. Catharine's and seeing the example of others who took life seriously; and she said love should be our guiding principle, and that every girl should devote half an hour to the reading of the best books every day. Then she told about the man who rapped on the door of his beloved, and was asked, "Who is there?" and he said, "It is I." But the door didn't open; and he rapped again, and was asked who he was, and he said, "It is I," and still the door didn't open. The third time he said, "It is Thou," and the door opened right off.[9] Maudie said that was what we must all do—rap at the door and *be* what's behind it. Then, all of a sudden, she sat down, and we girls clapped like mad. The antis looked at one another and smiled in a tired way.

When Kittie James got up, I thought she looked puzzled. She seemed to be thinking over Maudie's speech, and there was so much in it that I guess she didn't know just where to begin. But at last she said the previous speaker had told a pretty story, but that it reminded her of another one about two doors—one with a lady behind it, and the other with a tiger, and the man rapping at them didn't know which was which; and she said that was the way with a good many doors in life, and it was a mistake to be the thing inside until you were sure it wasn't a tiger.[10] All the girls laughed at that, and so did the three Sisters on the jury. Sister Irmingarde looked quite proud of Kittie. Then Kittie James asked what would become of the wounded if the world was made up entirely of people fighting all the time, and she asked how anybody could expect to read half an hour a day when we had so many other things to do. She said it was very pretty to talk about hands joining in a big circle all around the world, but sometimes those hands might be neglecting other things they had to do; and she said when it came to "spreads" and indolence, she thought they were pretty evenly divided among our dear companions. She took up everything Maudie had said and answered it, and then, all of a sudden, she sat down, too, and we girls looked at one another and had a kind of queer feeling—as if we were at a picnic, you know, and there weren't any pickles or hard-boiled eggs. Sister Edna is always talking about "an effect of incompleteness," when the girls dress too quickly and forget a tie or something. Someway, we got that kind of an effect right there.

In the meantime the jury were talking together, and everybody sat very still. At last, in about five minutes, Sister Irmingarde stood up. She said she had been asked by the other members of the jury to give its findings, and she said that at first it had not seemed easy. So much, she said, had been expressed, and so many different ideas introduced. However, she added, she and the jury had been given to understand before the debate that it was for and against suffrage. And all of a sudden I understood exactly what had happened.

Both Maudie and Kittie James had been so interested in suffrage, they hadn't said a word about it. They had just stood on the platform, throwing out different lines of thought, the way conjurers throw out long colored ribbons over an audience, and they expected that poor jury to gather up all those threads and make a ball of them, because they couldn't do it themselves. Isn't this a clever way of describing what they did? Whenever thoughts like this befall me, my chest swells, and I realize how my Art is growing inside of me all the time. When I wrote my first book, I couldn't have done this. I should merely have said, briefly and plainly, that both Maudie and Kittie James, when they rose to debate, *forgot all about their subject*!

However, Sister Irmingarde was explaining this now, and she added that the fact was really "something of a relief to the jury," as the Sisters had feared the suffrage issue at St. Catharine's might divert our attention from our studies. We had now, she said, "effectually dispelled that fear." Then, with her wonderful smile, she concluded:

"Under the conditions, we, the jury, are not prepared to pass upon the suffrage question or the issue of the debate. But we are glad to testify that the debate has afforded us an hour of genuine enjoyment."

Wouldn't that make you proud? It made us all so happy that the suffragettes and the antis left the room with their arms around one another's necks; and Kittie James and Maudie Joyce got up a "spread" in Maudie's room that was the biggest we have had this year.

But that night, after the Great Silence fell, and all the lights were out, and I lay awake wishing I hadn't eaten that last rarebit, I began to wonder if Sister Irmingarde and the jury *really* had been complimenting us. This reflection had not occurred to the other girls—but my intuition is deeper than that of their young and heedless minds.

The next morning Maudie came into my room while I was dressing. She looked pale and wan, so I wasn't surprised when she sat down in a chair and hid her face in her hands.

"May Iverson," she said at last, "why didn't you tell me last night that I had made a fool of myself?"

I hesitated. Then I spoke the truth, straight from a friend's loyal heart.

"I didn't know it myself," I said, "till after I was in bed. Then, of course, I had to wait."

"Do you think all the other girls know it, too," she asked me, "by this time?"

I nodded and reminded her that Kittie James had been a—had forgotten, too. Maudie sat for quite awhile without a word. Ne'er before had I known Maudie Joyce to be too sad for speech. Finally she got up.

"This ends the clubs, and settles suffrage and anti-suffrage at St. Catharine's," she said, with a slow and terrible grimness. "Can't you just hear all the Sisters and the girls laughing at the mere mention of them?"

I could. I surely could. I just put my arms around Maudie and held her tight. While we stood there we heard some girls coming down the hall. Their feet were clattering on the polished floor, the way horses' hoofs sound in army plays. There must have been five or six of them. When they got outside of my door they laughed—dreadful, curdling laughs. Maudie turned paler.

"They know I'm here. They saw me come in. It has begun," said Maudie Joyce, setting her teeth.

"Any girl," she added, in trembling tones—"any girl that even mentions the word suffrage or anti-suffrage to me is my mortal enemy for life. But you may write a story about it, May Iverson, for I know how you love to dissect the quivering human heart."

Then she sat down and told me all her terrible sufferings, and how she wanted to die; and I knew that my dear, dear friend felt better.

Source: *May Iverson Tackles Life* (Harper & Brothers, 1912).

"I INTRODUCE BEAUTY CULTURE"

(1912)

The idea came to me in the classroom one day while Kittie James was reciting, and, like most of my ideas, it came very suddenly. One moment my mind was a perfect blank. The next it was working so hard I thought Janet Trelawney, who sat behind me, would hear it buzz.

My mind usually is a blank when Kittie James is reciting. Poor Kittie is not a bright student, alas! and of course I always know a great deal more about the lesson than she can possibly tell Sister Irmingarde. So I let my intellect rest. That day Kittie was talking about the ancient Greeks and their manners and customs. She seemed to think they were some kind of weird prehistoric animals, like the megatheriums and pterodactyls we read about in our geology. Even that impression was an intellectual improvement for Kittie though, for only last week she told me with her own lips that she didn't believe there ever had been any ancient Greeks, anyway. She said she was perfectly sure the men who wrote school-books put in the ancient Greeks to fill up—when their imaginations got tired after inventing so much about the earth being a round ball, and the stars being billions of miles away, and things like that. She said she knew full well those things were not true either, though she rarely said so because most people believe everything they read and there is no sense in arguing with them. She said the only person she ever opened her heart to about her lessons was George Morgan.

George is her brother-in-law because he married her sister Josephine. Kittie and I adore him and he is simply heavenly about sending us boxes. Kittie said George laughed at first when she told him she didn't believe the things in her school-books; but when she asked him if he thought the long flash of a falling star was really the light from a burning world that had been destroyed millions of years ago he looked serious. Kittie said she couldn't light a match in her room at night without having Sister Irmingarde see it that very instant from *her* room 'way off in another wing of the convent. So Kittie added that no one could convince her the light of that burning world was only reaching us now, because it had taken millions of years to make the weary journey. Kittie told me George admitted that astronomers had yet several things to learn, and that he didn't take much stock in them, either; and he added that personally he had few prejudices and would as soon listen to Kittie's theories as theirs.

This pleased Kittie very much, so she told him all her theories right off. They had a delightful and intellectual conversation, but it doesn't belong in this place, so I will not repeat it here. None of what I have said really belongs, but it doesn't have to. It is only put in for atmosphere, anyway, and to get the gentle reader even more interested in Kittie. There is one thing I must add, though, while I think of it. George told Kittie that very night that my fiction and her science were making life one glad, sweet song for him. Those were indeed his words, and they bring me right back to my fiction now, like the weary bird to its nest. But for fear the reader's mind may be a little confused by passing so swiftly from Kittie to the ancient Greeks and burning worlds and then back to Kittie I will repeat my opening remarks:

My mind was a perfect blank and Kittie was reciting about the ancient Greeks.

Suddenly a word caught my attention. It was *Beauty*. Kittie said the Greeks loved beauty so much that they were willing to give their whole lives to the pursuit of it. That is exactly the way I feel a great deal of the time, so I began to think about the Greeks and beauty and how important beauty is and how it refreshes the eye and the soul, too. No matter how tired I am, for instance, I always feel rested when I look at Sister Irmingarde. There is something in her eyes and in her face—but I will not begin to tell about that now, for if I did I should never get back to Kittie and the ancient Greeks. However, I looked at Sister Irmingarde for a few minutes and felt rested and refreshed, as usual. Then I looked at my dear companions, putting the ancient Greeks up behind them as a kind of a background—like an imaginary frieze, you know—and the shock was so great I almost groaned aloud. It was as if I had been living blind among horrors and had suddenly been given sight.

I began with Kittie. Kittie has never been beautiful, though she has a lovely nature and a sweet expression. Several years ago, before she got so fat, she used to look really soulful at times. But no fat person can possibly look soulful, as I have oft pointed out to Kittie. As I looked at her now I saw clearly that she had almost obscured her soul, as it were, by chocolate cake and pickles and marmalade and fudge, for next to her dear mother Kittie loves rich food. Elsewhere, as real writers say, I have told how I "reduced" Kittie and took off twenty pounds of her flesh in three weeks. But by this time Kittie, alas! had gained them back again.

Much as I loved Kittie, I averted my eyes from her and looked at Maudie Joyce. Maudie is usually rather nice to look at. But now she was studying hard, with her left hand thrust through her hair, and her hair all rumpled, and her knees crossed (in spite of all the nuns have said about *that*), and her teeth chewing her lower lip the way they do when she is nervous. So I had to stop looking at her, for beauty was not in her, as the poet says.

Then, like the Greeks of old, I went on a quest for beauty. Of course I sat in my seat just the same. It was only my eyes that moved—but they roamed from face to face in that great classroom and with every roam my heart grew heavier. I have already told my gentle readers how keen my insight is. They will not be surprised to learn, therefore, that as I looked from face to face I knew just why each one was not beautiful; and, what was much more important, I knew what to do to improve it.

Kittie James was fat, as I have said, and her complexion was pasty because she ate too much. Adeline Thurston was round-shouldered from writing poetry. Mabel Blossom had chewed the inside of her face and pulled at her lips and ears till it was hard to imagine how they would look if she ever let them alone. Maudie did the same thing, though she had a queenly carriage. Mabel Muriel Murphy, though neat and tidy, looked as if she hadn't any emotions. She was just placid and peaceful, like a cow contented with her cud. (That is more alliteration. Please read it aloud and see how nice it sounds.) Janet Trelawney was too thin. She had no graceful curves. And so it went. Every girl I looked at had something the matter with her. Even my own appearance had faults, though I forgot about these till Maudie Joyce and Mabel Blossom and the other girls pointed them out to me in the evening. But of this more anon, as real writers say.

I hope the gentle reader knows me well enough by this time to realize that, after I had grasped all this, I did not remain idle. Nay, I called a meeting of the girls in our special set that very night. I asked them to come to my room so we could talk as long as we pleased without being interrupted.

They were not very enthusiastic when they came. You see, I had to make them understand right off how vital the matter was, and to do that I had to tell them immediately what was the matter with their looks. I did it. I said it was necessary, of course, to be perfectly frank, no matter how much frankness hurt the victim. I said I was like a surgeon, causing pain for the patient's good. Then I told the girls the worst things about themselves, and said I'd tell them more when we met and how to remedy these sad defects.

They were not a bit grateful. When they came in the evening, they all talked at once and wasted a great deal of time telling me what was the matter with my looks, instead of getting right to work on themselves, the way I wanted them to do. But I finally comforted them by saying that I knew I looked worse than anyone else. I didn't think I did, really, away down in what Mr. James calls my "abysmal self"; but they did; and they all gave so many reasons for thinking it that I simply couldn't fix my mind on the ancient Greeks for almost an hour.

At last they let me talk awhile, and I told them what a wonderful power beauty was, and that there wasn't any of it at St. Catharine's so far, but how we might get some if we tried. Mabel Blossom spoke right up and said she thought so, too, and that she had an idea. Usually, I am a little afraid of Mabel's ideas. They are not practical. But she seemed very much in earnest, so I invited her to express it.

Mabel got up very solemnly and said everything I had said was true, and that there was much to be done, and we must all put our shoulders to the wheel. But she said if every girl worked by herself nothing would be accomplished. Each girl would put cold cream on her face for a few nights and then forget about it. But, Mabel said, if the whole school worked on *one* girl the results ought to be glorious. Everybody cheered that and they all talked at once, but Mabel Blossom lifted her lily hand and checked them, for she had more to say. As I looked at her I had a strange sinking sensation—for full well I knew now what this would be. I was right, too, as I most always am. It is wonderful how I can tell what the girls are going to do even before they do it. This is partly, of course, because I know the girls so well; but most of my strange insight is due to the artist's knowledge of the poor, weak, Human Heart.

While I was thinking these thoughts Mabel went right on talking. She said that as I was the girl who thought of the plan I ought to be the subject of the experiment. She said that was only fair to me—to let me be the first girl to get the good of my own idea. Besides, she said, I had confessed that I needed it most. I tried to speak and tell her I didn't want to be so selfish; but she raised her voice and made a motion that I should be the girl, and Maudie Joyce seconded it, and in another minute it was carried unanimously. Perhaps the gentle reader thinks he can imagine my emotions, but he can't, so I will describe them myself.

It is a strange and unsettling feeling to have a beautiful idea and tell it to one's dear companions, and then have them take it and change it so one hardly knows it oneself. I didn't exactly want to go on with the plan, and yet I couldn't stand the thought of dropping it and having the girls laugh at me. I had wanted to improve the looks of the whole school. Now the whole school wanted to improve *my* looks. I had wanted them to put their shoulders to the wheel. Now they wanted me to be the wheel! Still, as Mabel Blossom pointed out, the principle was the same, and it was the principle that was important. Mabel said that after the school had made me perfect they would have a model to go by and could make themselves perfect, too, avoiding the mistakes they would naturally make at first with me. She said sometimes whole features were changed by beauty-work, and of course errors were apt to creep in; but she was sure the girls would do the best they could. She said she thought the way to begin was for me to stand out in the center of the room and let the girls study me, and discuss my physical faults and how to correct them. She put that motion and Janet Trelawney seconded it, and it was carried unanimously like the first—and all the girls seemed perfectly delighted.

Was that fair? I would pause for a reply, but it is not worthwhile. Full well do I know what the reply could be.

Finally they let me speak. I said I thought it would be better to rest now, after doing so much, and begin our new work the next night. But Mabel said no, and the other girls agreed with her. She said the time to begin was at once, while they were full of eagerness and enthusiasm, and would I please hurry and get into the middle of the room. She dragged a footstool forward and made me stand on it, and all the girls stood around and studied me and looked more and more depressed; and ever and anon they shook their heads and sighed. Mabel reminded them of what I had suggested about being perfectly frank and using the surgeon's knife; and she told the girls not to mind my feelings, because everything they said, even if it seemed harsh and cruel, would be for my good.

For a while no one spoke. They all seemed too discouraged. But finally Adeline Thurston said that of course my feet were too big, but she didn't see that anything could be done about them. Mabel said, very crossly, that she didn't see what could be done, either, and that there was no sense in starting with the simply impossible things. She said it would be better to begin by telling me that the green dress I was wearing made my skin the color of a lemon, and she thought I ought to know it.

Maudie Joyce said it was the way I wore my hair that had always worried her more than anything else about me. She didn't think it went with the shape of my head. But when all the girls agreed to that, too, and Mabel pressed her to suggest something better, Maudie said she couldn't think of anything that would make my head a good shape and that she guessed the hair was like the feet—too hard to take up at first. Then there was a long silence and they all looked more discouraged than ever. I made up my mind that very minute never to have another idea if I could possibly help it.

Finally Kittie James said, timidly, that there was a curve in my chin that might make it look double when I was older, so all the girls made suggestions about this and agreed that I must give my chin fifty up-strokes with the backs of my hands every night and every morning. They passed that unanimously, too; and Mabel Muriel Murphy said my mouth was beginning to droop at the corners, and she thought fifty upward strokes night and morning might remedy that in a few years. She said she had seen her mother do it.

The girls were getting enthusiastic again. Maudie said one of my teeth was crooked, but she knew a dentist in Chicago who would straighten it while there was yet time if I would wear a wedge for three months.[1] Mabel Muriel asked if anything could be done about my ears, and they decided nothing could without risking my hearing, but they advised me to wear my hair over them. Adeline Thurston said she had always thought it was a pity my hands were so large, but she supposed it was because I played the piano so much; and Kittie James asked if it wouldn't help my eyebrows to have about half the hair taken out of them. Mabel Blossom said my eyes were all right, and it was lucky they were, with so much wrong in other places. But she added that they had a near-sighted look and I might form the habit of squinting if I wasn't careful. She said she knew one girl with eyes like mine who squinted so much no one could bear to look at her.

Kittie James said she wouldn't listen to anything about my eyes because she simply loved them. I looked gratefully at Kittie, but before the look really got over to her Kittie said she was afraid I would have to work hard before my carriage would be erect and graceful; and Maudie said specialists were doing wonders for noses now; and Janet Trelawney, who hadn't spoken before, but who looked more discouraged over me than 'most anyone else, said that she thought it would help my general effect a lot if I didn't talk so fast. Kittie James spoke up again and said I was neat, *anyway*, and they all agreed that I was and seemed glad to be able to say something pleasant at last. Then they sat and looked at me awhile and sighed and seemed more depressed than ever.

At last Adeline Thurston began to talk about my literary faults, but you'd better believe I stopped that and pointed out with icy dignity that my looks and not my art were what they were there to criticize. Mabel Blossom agreed with me; and she reminded the girls that if they began to talk about my literary faults, too, they'd never get through.

That started them off again, and they got pencils and paper and took notes which I need not repeat here and made out a list of daily rules for me to follow. There were hundreds of rules when they got through, and the list looked miles long. I tore it up as soon as I was alone, but I remember some of the things I was to do. Here they are:

> Walk five miles a day with a book on your head.
>
> Push the corners of your mouth up every night and fasten them up with court-plaster.
>
> Pull half your eyebrows out with pincers.
>
> Sleep with a rubber band under your chin. Rub your chin every morning with a lump of ice as large as a hen's egg. Keep rubbing till the ice is melted.
>
> Wear a Greek fillet around your hair and keep your head erect with a velvet strap from the fillet to the back of your collar.[2]
>
> Consult your companions before you buy a new dress, to be sure they can stand it.

There seemed millions of other things, but I was too hurt to pay much attention to them. I saw, however, that if I did even a quarter of them every day I wouldn't have time to do anything else.

After they finished writing the things for me to do they were pretty tired and quiet for awhile. I had a chance to say a few words myself and I said them. I said I was very much interested in all they had told me, but that it seemed a dreadful thing for me to be getting all the attention when others needed so much. I urged them again to go into the thing together. I pointed out how much more fun it would be to take the exercises at the same time, and do all the queer things together and then talk them over, than for one person to do it alone. Besides, I reminded them it would be very unpleasant for me, after I was perfect, to have to look at them the way they were now. Before I had finished talking half the girls came over to my side, and the end of it was that they all began to tell one another of serious faults they had observed in one another.

Then things got exciting. They forgot all about me, and I was glad they did for a few minutes. I sat back and looked on. I didn't say much more about how the girls looked. I had already told them most of the worst things; but different girls kept calling to me every minute to ask if something someone else said was really true—and of course I usually had to agree, because it 'most always was true.

At last, out of all the confusion, we evolved a plan of work. We decided to keep the beauty culture right in our own class and to help each other all we could for one week. A list of recommendations was to be given to every single girl to suit her case, and she was to work as hard as she possibly could to correct the imperfection her dear companions couldn't stand. We saw from my list how impossible it would be to do everything, so each girl was to work on one or two vital things.

For example, Kittie James had to walk five miles a day with a rubber undervest on and not eat a thing except at the convent-table. Mabel Blossom had to do all her studying with her hands tied so she couldn't pull her features about. Adeline Thurston said she thought it would be simply fascinating at the end of the week to see how Mabel's features really looked. Adeline had to have a board between her shoulders all her free hours and practice walking two hours a day. Jennie Hartwell, whose hips were simply enormous, had to roll on her mattress one hundred times every morning and one hundred times every night. Mabel Muriel Murphy had to drink four quarts of hot water every day to improve her complexion, and read Byron and Keats and Tennyson in the hope that they would stir up her emotions and give her an intelligent expression.[3] That was *my* idea. Mabel Muriel didn't like it very much, but she had to do it just the same. I started her on Keats.

> "St. Agnes Eve—ah, bitter chill it was.
> The owl with all his feathers was a' cold."

I thought that poem would make Mabel Muriel cry if anything could, but it didn't. The only things that interested her were the "candied apple, quince, and plum" the heroine and hero ate. She read the description of the supper to Kittie James:

> "With jellies soother than the creamy curd,
>   And lucent syrups, tinct with cinnamon,
>   Manna and dates, in argosy transferr'd
>   From Fez; and spiced dainties, everyone,
>   From Silken Samarcand to cedar'd Lebanon."[4]

Those two girls were simply fascinated by that menu. They gave a convent spread two weeks later as near like it as they could. Mabel Muriel's rich father sent the things from Chicago. Most of us were sick after the supper—but this is not the place to describe the banquet nor our sufferings, terrible though they were. It is very strange, but every time I write a chapter in my book I think of half a dozen things before I get through that would have been better to write about. This seems incredible, but it is indeed true.

Of course everything we did in our beauty treatment had to be done very quietly so as not to attract the attention of the nuns and worry them by making them imagine something was going on they didn't know about. For it is a sad fact that, no matter how many beautiful ideas we girls have at St. Catharine's, and how hard it is to carry them out, we have to keep up our regular school routine just the same. We try all our experiments in recreation-hours, and I suppose we wouldn't have much chance even then except that we have the beautiful system of self-government, which makes us responsible only to God and our consciences for what we do. As our consciences are always clear and our objects high, and we are really stepping heavenward the whole time, nobody fusses much unless we make serious mistakes. We don't very often; but several serious things happened during the beauty culture. The worst was that Jennie Hartwell fell out of bed while she was rolling a hundred times on her mattress to reduce her hips and broke her wrist. She didn't tell why it happened, however, which was indeed noble of her. Then Kittie James caught cold and 'most got pneumonia from walking in her rubber undervest and getting overheated and sitting in a draught afterward; and I got so tired walking five miles every day, with books on my head instead of in my hand, where they should be, that I couldn't sleep nights and almost had nervous prostration.

But the worst thing of all happened without any of us noticing it at the time except Sister Irmingarde. Of course she noticed it. Sister Irmingarde really notices everything we do even when her eyes and her thoughts seem to be on higher things. All I was thinking of these days was how to do everything I had to do in class and on my beauty list. It took every minute of my spare time, and as things seemed to be the same with the other girls no one saw much of anyone else. Besides, no one wanted to. I got so I didn't even care to meet one of the class on the grounds, for as soon as I did she stood me up against a tree or something and looked me over to see if I was making progress. And while she did it she repeated all my imperfections till I got dreadfully tired hearing about them.

All the girls were bad enough, but the girls of my special set were the worst. You see, they loved me most, so of course they could say the hardest things. When they did that I told them all over again about their faults, and by the time we separated every-one was angry. I got so I hid when I saw any of them coming, and a good many other girls seemed to feel the way I did about it. So instead of seeing groups scattered over the convent grounds, as in the dear old days of last month, everywhere I looked I saw one girl alone. Sometimes she was taking calisthenic exercises. Some-times she was practicing a stately walk, with her chin up and her shoulders back. Sometimes she was giving herself facial massage. Sometimes she was inhaling and exhaling five hundred deep breaths, as Janet Trelawney had to do every night and morning. Sometimes I would see Mabel Muriel Murphy under the willow with a mirror in her hand practicing "assuming an intelligent ex-pression." Mabel Muriel had to do that every day. But whoever the girl was, and whatever she was doing, she was *alone*. The only time the girls of our class got together was during recitation-hours or in the study-hall.

At such times Sister Irmingarde studied us with her quiet, watchful, thoughtful look, which grew a little more serious as the days went on. Once or twice when I glanced at her I noticed that she had caught a bit of her lower lip between her teeth, which was a way she had when she was puzzled and was thinking something out. At last she sent for me and asked me why I was alone so much of late. I told her frankly that it was because I was the victim of painful physical blemishes which distressed my dear friends, so I was keeping by myself till I got over them. Then she sent for Mabel Blossom and asked the same question, and Mabel said she had twisted her features so much that she was ashamed to let her classmates see them. After that she sent for Mabel Muriel Murphy and Maudie Joyce and Kittie James.

Mabel Muriel told Sister Irmingarde she had decided never again to associate with her dear classmates till she had acquired a bright, intelligent expression; but she said she didn't mind being alone because she didn't care as much for the girls as she used to. Maudie said the conversation of the other girls had become so personal lately that it had made her nervous and she didn't enjoy talking anymore. Kittie James told Sister Irmingarde she never looked in a mirror anymore without seeing herself as others saw her, and Kittie cried and said she would die if she couldn't get thin and beautiful like the ancient Greeks. After that the whole story came out, and Sister Irmingarde discovered that every single girl in our set had got the idea that all the other girls hated to look at her. As this is a most unpleasant feeling it was making some of them sick and all of them nervous.

When Sister Irmingarde ordered our entire class to report to her in the study-hall at eight o'clock that night we suspected what was going to happen—and it happened.

First she gave us a general talk about beauty and told how it was in the eye of the beholder. She discussed what she called its "relative importance" and described the mental qualities that were more desirable than beauty, and told what beauty of character meant. She spoke about personal neatness as a handmaid of beauty, and all the girls turned and gazed admiringly at me; and of the charm of animation, and they looked at Mabel Blossom; and of dignity of carriage and manner, and they gazed at Maudie Joyce. Before she got through she had made every girl there feel better—more comfortable, you know. Then she forbade us to make even the slightest criticism of one another's appearance in future. Every girl drew a long breath of relief, as if a heavy weight had been lifted from her heart. For it is indeed true that the more one loves one's dear friends the harder it is to have them tell one about one's faults. As a literary artist I really knew this all the time. But I had forgotten about it till the girls began to tell me my faults, and then it was too late.

That night, after the Great Silence fell, Kittie James crept along the halls to my room. Her sister had sent her a box that very day. Kittie had a chocolate cake in one hand and a jelly layer cake in the other, and she had to put them both down on the floor before she could open my door. The pockets of her bathrobe were filled with fudge. She sat on the edge of my bed and I sat up among the pillows, and we ate this nourishing food and talked in whispers. Kittie said she would have died in two weeks more if our beauty-work had gone on. She said she was never going to pursue beauty again, but she was going to make her character so lovely that the girls wouldn't mind how fat she was. It was a little hard to follow her noble resolutions because her mouth was full of chocolate cake. But, in spite of the cake, some things came out so clearly that I was afraid they would wake Adeline Thurston, who slept in the next room.

Kittie said that lately she had been thinking very seriously indeed about the ancient Greeks. She said that even yet she didn't really believe in them; but if there ever *had* been any, and if they really *had* pursued beauty, she was sure she knew exactly what had caused their decline and fall.

"Probably they told each other they were too fat and what was wrong with their features," Kittie said. "Of course that made the strong ones kill the weak ones, right off. Then the strong ones tried beauty-treatments and flesh-reduction and things like that for awhile—and just died of despair!"

I looked at Kittie with deep respect. At last I understood why George Morgan loved to talk to her. As I have oft said, she is not a brilliant student. But she has a way of thinking things out all by herself—and ever and anon she surprises one by the utterance of what Sister Irmingarde calls "a deep and vital truth."

Source: *May Iverson Tackles Life* (Harper & Brothers, 1912).

FROM
MAY IVERSON'S CAREER

"MY FIRST ASSIGNMENT"

(1914)

The Commencement exercises at St. Catharine's were over, and everybody in the big assembly-hall was looking relieved and grateful. Mabel Muriel Murphy had welcomed our parents and friends to the convent shades in an extemporaneous speech we had overheard her practicing for weeks; and the proud face of Mabel Muriel's father, beaming on her as she talked, illumined the front row like an electric globe. Maudie Joyce had read a beautiful essay, full of uplifting thoughts and rare flowers of rhetoric; Mabel Blossom had tried to deliver her address without the manuscript, and had forgotten it at a vital point; Adeline Thurston had recited an original poem; Kittie James had sung a solo; and Janet Trelawney had played the Sixth Hungarian Rhapsody on the piano.[1]

Need I say who read the valedictory? It was I—May Iverson—winner of the Cross of Honor, winner of the Crown, leader of the convent orchestra, and president of the senior class.[2] If there are those who think I should not mention these honors I will merely ask who would do it if I did not—and pause for a reply. Besides, young as I am, I know full well that worldly ambitions and triumphs are as ashes on the lips; and already I was planning to cast mine aside. But at this particular minute the girls were crying on one another over our impending parting, and our parents were coming up to us and saying the same things again and again, while Sister Edna was telling Mabel Muriel Murphy, without being asked, that she was not ashamed of one of us.

I could see my father coming toward me through the crowd, stopping to shake hands with my classmates and tell them how wonderful they were; and I knew that when he reached me I must take him out into the convent garden and break his big, devoted heart. At the thought of it a great lump came into my throat, and while I was trying to swallow it I felt his arm flung over my shoulder.

He bent down and kissed me. "Well, my girl," he said, "I'm proud of you."

That was all. I knew it was all he would ever say; but it meant more than anyone else could put into hours of talk. I did not try to answer, but I kissed him hard, and, taking his arm, led him downstairs, through the long halls and out into the convent garden, lovely with the scent of roses and honeysuckle and mignonette. He had never seen the garden before. He wanted to stroll through it and glance into the conservatories, to look at the fountain and visit the Grotto of Lourdes and stand gazing up at the huge cross that rises from a bed of passion-flowers.[3] But at last I took him into a little arbor and made him sit down. I was almost glad my delicate mother had not been able to come to see me graduate. He would tell her what I had to say better than I could.

When I have anything before me that is very hard I always want to do it immediately and get it over. So now I stood with my back braced against the side of the arbor, and, looking my dear father straight in the eyes, I told him I had made up my mind to be a nun.

At first he looked as if he thought I must be joking. Then, all in a minute, he seemed to change from a gallant middle-aged officer into a crushed, disappointed old man. He bowed his head, his shoulders sagged down, and, turning his eyes as if to keep me from seeing what was in them, he stared out over the convent garden.

"Why, May!" he said; and then again, very quietly, "Why, May!"

I told him all that was in my mind, and he listened without a word. At the end he said he had thought I wanted to be a newspaper woman. I admitted that I had felt that desire a year ago—when I was only seventeen and my mind was immature. He sat up in his seat then and looked more comfortable—and younger.

"I'll put my answer in a nutshell," he said. "You're too young still to know your mind about anything. Give your family and the world a chance. I don't want you to be a nun. I don't want you to be a newspaper woman, either. But I'll compromise. Be a newspaper woman for three years."

I began to speak, but he stopped me. "It's an interesting life," he went on. "You'll like it. But if you come to us the day you are twenty-one and tell us you still want to be a nun I promise that your mother and I will consent. Give us a chance, May." And he added, gently, "*Play fair.*"

Those two words hurt; but they conquered me. I agreed to do as he asked, and then we sat together, hand in hand, talking over plans, till the corners of the garden began to look mysterious in the twilight. Before we went back to the assembly-room it was understood that I was to go to New York in a week and begin my new career. Papa had friends there who would look after me. I was sure they would never have a chance; but I did not mention that to my dear father then, while he was still feeling the shock of decision.

When I was saying good-by to Sister Irmingarde six days later I asked her to give me some advice about my newspaper work. "Write of things as they are," she said, without hesitation, "and write of them as simply as you can."

I was a little disappointed. I had expected something inspiring—something in the nature of a trumpet-call. I suppose she saw my face fall, for she smiled her beautiful smile.

"And when you write the sad stories you're so fond of, dear May," she said, "remember to let your readers shed their own tears."

I thought a great deal about those enigmatic words on my journey to New York, but after I reached it I forgot them. It was just as well, for no one associated with my work there had time to shed tears.

My editor was Mr. Nestor Hurd, of the *Searchlight*. He had promised to give me a trial because Kittie James's brother-in-law, George Morgan, who was his most intimate friend, said he must; but I don't think he really wanted to. When I reported to him he looked as if he had not eaten or slept for weeks, and as if seeing me was the one extra trouble he simply could not endure. There was a bottle of tablets on his desk, and every time he noticed it he stopped to swallow a tablet. He must have taken six while he was talking to me. He was a big man, with a round, smooth face, and dimples in his cheeks and chin. He talked out of one side of his mouth in a kind of low snarl, without looking at anyone while he spoke.

"Oh," was his greeting to me, "you're the convent girl? Ready for work? All right. I'll try you on this."

He turned to the other person in the office—a thin young man at a desk near him. Neither of them had risen when I entered.

"Here, Morris," he said. "Put Miss Iverson down for the Ferncliff story."

The young man called Morris dropped a big pencil and looked very much surprised.

"But—" he said. "Why, say, she'll have to stay out in that house alone—all night."

Mr. Hurd said shortly that I couldn't be in a safer place. "Are you afraid of ghosts?" he asked, without looking at me. I said I was not, and waited for him to explain the joke; but he didn't.

"Here's the story," he said. "Listen, and get it straight. Ferncliff is a big country house out on Long Island, about three miles from Sound View. It's said to be haunted. Its nearest neighbor is a quarter of a mile away. It was empty for three years until this spring. Last month Mrs. Wallace Vanderveer, a New York society woman, took a year's lease of it and moved in with a lot of servants. Last week she moved out. Servants wouldn't stay. Said they heard noises and saw ghosts. She heard noises, too. Now the owner of Ferncliff, a Miss Watts, is suing Mrs. Vanderveer for a year's rent. Nice little story in it. See it?"

I didn't, exactly. That is, I didn't see what he wanted me to do about it, and I said so.

"I want you to take the next train for Sound View," he snarled, impatiently, and pulled the left side of his mouth down to his chin. "When you get there, drive out and look at Ferncliff to see what it's like in the daytime. Then go to the Sound View Hotel and have your dinner. About ten o'clock go back to Ferncliff, and stay there all night. Sit up. If you see any ghosts, write about 'em. If you don't, write about how it felt to stay there and wait for 'em. Come back to town tomorrow morning and turn in your story. If it's good we'll run it. If it isn't," he added, grimly, "we'll throw it out. See now?" I saw now.

"Here's the key of the house," he said. "We got it from the agent." He turned and began to talk to Mr. Morris about something else—and I knew that our interview was over.

I went to Sound View on the first train, and drove straight from the station to Ferncliff. It was almost five o'clock, and a big storm was coming up. The rain was like a wet, gray veil, and the wind snarled in the tops of the pine-trees in a way that made me think of Mr. Hurd. I didn't like the look of the house. It was a huge, gloomy, vine-covered place, perched on a bluff overlooking the Sound, and set far back from the road. An avenue of pines led up to it, and a high box-hedge along the front cut off the grounds from the road and the nearby fields. When we drove away my cabman kept glancing back over his shoulder as if he expected to see the ghosts.

I was glad to get into the hotel and have a few hours for thought. I was already perfectly sure that I was not going to like being a newspaper woman, and I made up my mind to write to papa the next morning and tell him so. I thought of the convent and of Sister Irmingarde, who was probably at vespers now in the chapel, and the idea of that assignment became more unpleasant every minute.[4] Not that I was afraid—I, an Iverson, and the daughter of a general in the army! But the thing seemed silly and unworthy of a convent girl, and lonesome work besides. As I thought of the convent it suddenly seemed so near that I could almost hear its vesper bell, and that comforted me.

I went back to Ferncliff at ten o'clock. By that time the storm was really wild. It might have been a night in November instead of in July. The house looked very bleak and lonely, and the way my driver lashed his horse and hurried away from the neighborhood did not make it easier for me to unlock the front door and go in. But I forced myself to do it.

I had filled a basket with candles and matches and some books and a good luncheon, which the landlady at the hotel had put up for me. I hurriedly lighted two candles and locked the front door. Then I took the candles into the living-room at the left of the hall, and set them on a table. They made two little blurs of light in which the linen-covered furniture assumed queer, ghostly shapes that seemed to move as the flames flickered. I did not like the effect, so I lighted some more candles.

I was sure the first duty of a reporter was to search the house. So I took a candle in each hand and went into every room, up-stairs and down, spending a great deal of time in each, for it was strangely comforting to be busy. I heard all sorts of sounds—mice in the walls, old boards cracking under my feet, and a death-tick that began to get on my nerves, though I knew what it was. But there was nothing more than might be heard in any other old house.

When I returned to the living-room I looked at my luncheon-basket—not that I was hungry, but I wanted something more to do, and eating would have filled the time so pleasantly. But if I ate, there would be nothing to look forward to but the ghost, so I decided to wait. Outside, the screeching wind seemed to be sweeping the rain before it in a rising fury. It was half past eleven. Twelve is the hour when ghosts are said to come, I remembered.

I took up a book and began to read. I had almost forgotten my surroundings when a noise sounded on the veranda, a noise that made me stop reading to listen. Something was out there—something that tried the knob of the door and pushed against the panels; something that scampered over to the window-blinds and pulled at them; something that opened the shutters and tried to peer in.

I laid down my book. The feet scampered back to the door. I stopped breathing. There followed a knocking at the door, the knocking of weak hands, which soon began to beat against the panels with closed fists; and next I heard a high, shrill voice. It seemed to be calling, uttering words, but above the shriek of the storm I could not make out what they were.

Creeping along the floor to the window, I pulled back one of the heavy curtains and raised the green shade under it half an inch. For a moment I could see nothing but the twisting pines. But at last I was able to distinguish something moving near the door—something no larger than a child, but with white hair floating round its head. It was not a ghost. It was not an animal. It could not be a human being. I had no idea what it was. While I looked it turned and came toward the window where I was crouching, as if it felt my eyes upon it. And this time I heard its words.

"Let me in!" it shrieked. "Let me in! Let me in!" And in a kind of fury it scampered back and dashed itself against the door.

Then I was afraid—not merely nervous—afraid—with a degrading fear that made my teeth chatter. If only I had known what it was; if only I could think of something normal that was a cross between a little child and an old woman! I went to the door and noiselessly turned the key. I meant to open it an inch and ask what was there. But almost before the door had moved on its hinges the thing outside saw it. It gave a quick spring and a little screech and threw itself against the panels. The next instant I went back and down, and the thing that had been outside was inside.

I got up slowly and looked at it. It seemed to be a witch—a little old, humpbacked witch—not more than four feet high, with white hair that hung in wet locks around a shriveled brown face, and black eyes gleaming at me in the dark hall like an angry cat's.

"You little fool!" she hissed. "Why didn't you let me in? I'm soaked through. And why didn't that bell ring? What's been done to the wire?"

I could not speak, and after looking at me a moment more the little old creature locked the hall door and walked into the living-room, motioning to me to follow. She was panting with anger or exhaustion, or both. When we had entered the room she turned and grinned at me like a malicious monkey.

"Scared you, didn't I?" she chuckled, in her high, cracked voice. "Serves you right. Keeping me out on that veranda fifteen minutes!"

She began to gather up the loose locks of her white hair and fasten them at the back of her head. "Wind blew me to pieces," she muttered.

She took off her long black coat, threw it over a chair, and straightened the hat that hung over one ear. She *was* a human being, after all; a terribly deformed human being, whose great, hunched back now showed distinctly through her plain black dress. There was a bit of lace at her throat, and when she took off her gloves handsome rings glittered on her claw-like fingers.

"Well, well," she said, irritably, "don't stand there staring. I know I'm not a beauty," and she cackled like an angry hen.

But it was reassuring, at least, to know she was human, and I felt myself getting warm again. Then, as she seemed to expect me to say something, I explained that I had not intended to let anybody in, because I thought nobody had any right in the house.

"Humph," she said. "I've got a better right here than you have, young lady. I am the owner of this house and everything in it—I am Miss Watts. And I'll tell you one thing"—she suddenly began to trot around the room—"I've stood this newspaper nonsense about ghosts just as long as I'm going to. It's ruining the value of my property. I live in Brooklyn, but when my agent telephoned me tonight that a reporter was out here working up another lying yarn I took the first train and came here to protect my interests."

She grumbled something about having sent her cab away at the gate and having mislaid her keys. I asked her if she meant to stay till morning, and she glared at me and snapped that she certainly did. Then, taking a candle, she wandered off by herself for awhile, and I heard her scampering around on the upper floors. When she came back she seemed very much surprised to hear that I was not going to bed.

"You're a fool," she said, rudely, "but I suppose you've got to do what the other fools tell you to."

After that I didn't feel much like sharing my supper with her, but I did, and she seemed to enjoy it. Then she curled herself up on a big divan in the corner and grinned at me again. I liked her face better when she was angry.

"I'm going to take a nap," she said. "Call me if any ghosts come."

I opened my book again and read for half an hour. Then

suddenly, from somewhere under the house, I heard a queer, muffled sound. "*Tap, tap, tap,*" it went. And again, "*Tap, tap, tap.*"

At first it didn't interest me much. But after a minute I realized that it was different from anything I had heard that night. And soon another noise mingled with it—a kind of buzz, like the whir of an electric fan, only louder. I looked at Miss Watts. She was asleep.

I picked up a candle and followed the noise—through the hall, down the cellar steps, and along a bricked passage. There the sound stopped. I stood still and waited. While I was staring at the bricks in front of me I noticed one that seemed to have a light behind it. I lowered my candle and examined it. Some plaster had been knocked out, and through a hole the size of a penny I saw another passage cutting through the earth like a little catacomb, with a light at the far end of it. While I was staring, amazed, the tapping began again, much nearer now; and I heard men's voices.

There were men under that house, in a secret cellar!

In half a minute I was standing beside Miss Watts, shaking her arm and trying to wake her. Almost before I was able to make her understand what I had seen she was through the front door and half-way down the avenue, dragging me with her.

"Where are we going?" I gasped.

"To the next house, idiot, to telephone to the police," she said. "Do you think we could stay there and do it?"

We left the avenue and came into the road, and as we ran on, stumbling into mud-holes and whipped by wind and rain, she panted out that the men were probably escaped convicts from some prison or patients from some asylum. I ran faster after that, though I hadn't thought I could. I wondered if I were having a bad dream. Several times I pinched myself, but I didn't wake up. Instead, I kept on running and stumbling and gasping, until I felt sure I had been running and stumbling and gasping for years and must keep on doing it for eons more. But at last we came to a house set far back in big grounds, and we raced side by side up the driveway that led to the front door. Late as it was, there were lights everywhere, and through the long windows opening on the veranda we could see people moving about.

Miss Watts gave the bell a terrific pull; someone opened the door, and we stumbled in. After that everything was a mixture of questions and answers and excitement and telephoning, followed by a long wait for the police. A man led Miss Watts and me into a room where a fire was burning, and left us to get warm and dry. When we were alone I asked Miss Watts if she thought they would keep us overnight. She stared at me.

"You won't have much time for sleep," she answered, almost kindly. "It will take you an hour or two to write your story."

It was my turn to stare, and I did it. "My story?" I asked her. "Tonight? What do you mean?"

She swung round in her chair and stared at me harder than ever. Then she cackled in her nastiest way. "And this is a New York reporter!" she said. "Why, you little dunce, you know you've *got* a story, don't you?"

"Yes," I answered, doubtfully. "But I'm to write it tomorrow, after I talk to Mr. Hurd."

Miss Watts uttered a squawk and then a squeal. "I don't know what fool sent you here," she snapped, "or what infant-class you've escaped from. But one thing I do know: You came here to write a Sunday 'thriller,' I suppose, which would have destroyed what little value my property has left. By bull-headed luck you've stumbled on the truth; and it's a good news story. It will please your editor, and it will save my property. Now, here's my point." She pushed her horrible little face close to mine and kept it there while she finished. "That story is coming out in the *Searchlight* tomorrow morning. I'd do it if I could, but I'm not a writer. So you're going to write it and telephone it into the *Searchlight* office within the next hour. Have I made myself clear?"

She had. I felt my face getting red and hot when I realized that I had a big story and had not known it. I wondered if I could ever live that down. I felt so humble that I was almost willing to let Miss Watts see it.

But before I could answer her there was the noise of many feet in the hall, with the voices of men. Then our door was flung open, and a young man came in, wearing a raincoat, thick boots covered with mud, and a wide grin. He was saving time by shaking the rain off his soft hat as he crossed the room to us. His eyes touched me, then passed onto Miss Watts as if I hadn't been there.

"Miss Watts," he said, "the police are here, and I'm going back to the house with them to see the capture. I'm Gibson, of the *Searchlight*."

Miss Watts actually smiled at him. Then she held out her skinny little claw of a hand. "A real reporter!" she said. "Thank Heaven! You know what it means to me to have this thing put straight. But how do you happen to be here?"

"Hurd sent me to look after Miss Iverson," he explained, glancing at me again. "He couldn't put her in a haunted house without a watch-dog, but, to do her justice, she didn't know she had one. I was in a summer-house on the grounds. I saw you leave and followed you here. Then I went up the road to meet the police."

He grinned at me, and I smiled a very little smile in return. I wasn't going to give him a whole smile until I found out how he was going to act about my story. Miss Watts started for the door.

"Come on," she said, with her hand on the knob.

The real reporter's eyes grew big. "Are *you* going along?" he gasped.

"Certainly I'm going along," snapped Miss Watts. "I'm going to see this thing through. And I'll tell you one thing right now, young man," she ended, "if you don't put the *facts* into your story I'm going to sue your newspaper for twenty-five thousand dollars."

He did not answer. His attention seemed to be diverted to me. I was standing beside Miss Watts, buttoning my raincoat and pulling my hat over my eyes again, preparatory to going out.

"Say, kid," said the real reporter, "you go back and sit down. You're not in this, you know. We'll come and get you and take you to the hotel after it's all over."

I gave him a cold and dignified glance. Then I buttoned the last button of my coat and went out into the hall. It was full of men. The real reporter hurried after me. He seemed to expect me to say something. So finally I did.

"Mr. Hurd told me to write this story," I explained, in level tones, "and I'm going to try to write it. And I can't write it unless I see everything that happens."

I looked at him and Miss Watts out of the corner of my eye as

I spoke, and I distinctly saw them give each other a significant glance. Miss Watts shrugged her shoulders as if she didn't care what I did; but the real reporter looked worried.

"Oh, well, all right," he said, at last. "I suppose it isn't fair not to let you in on your own assignment. There's one good thing—you can't get any wetter and muddier than you are." That thought seemed to comfort him.

We had a hard time going back, but it was easier because there were more of us to suffer. Besides, the real reporter helped Miss Watts and me a little when we stumbled or when the wind blew us against a tree or a fence. When we got near the house everybody moved very quietly, keeping close to the high hedge. We all went around to the back entrance. There the chief constable began to give his men orders, and the real reporter led Miss Watts and me into a grape-arbor, about fifty feet from the house.

"This is where we've got to stay," he whispered, pulling us inside and closing the door. "We can see them come out, and get the other details from Conroy, who's in charge."

The police were creeping closer to the house. Three of them took places outside while the rest went forward. First there was a long silence; then a sudden rush and crash—shouts and words that we didn't catch. Gleams of light flashed up for a minute—then disappeared. The men stationed outside the house ran toward the cellar. There was the flashing of more light, and at last the police came out with their prisoners—and the whole thing was over. There had not been a pistol-shot.

I was as warm as toast in my wet clothes, but my teeth were chattering with excitement, and I knew Miss Watts was excited, too, by the grip of her hand on my shoulder. The men came toward us through the rain on their way to the gate, and Mr. Conroy's voice sounded as if he had been running a race. But he hadn't. He had been right there.

"Well, Miss Watts, we've got 'em," he crowed. "A nice little gang of amachur counterfeiters. They've been visitin' you for 'most a year, snug and cozy; but I guess this is the end of your troubles."

Miss Watts walked out into the rain and, taking a policeman's electric bull's-eye, looked at the prisoners one by one.[5] I followed her and looked, too, while the real reporter talked to Mr. Conroy.

There were three counterfeiters, and they were all handcuffed and looked young. It could not have been very hard for six policemen to take them. One of them had blood on his face, and another was covered with mud, as if he had been rolled in it. Miss Watts asked the bloody one, who was also the biggest one, if his gang had really worked in a secret cellar at Ferncliff for a year. He said it had been there about ten months.

"Then you were there all winter?" Miss Watts asked him. "And you were so safe and comfortable that when the tenants moved in and you found they were all women, except a stupid butler, you decided to scare them away and stay right along?"

The man muttered something that seemed to mean that she was right. The real reporter interrupted, looking busy and worried again. "Miss Watts," he said, quickly, "can't we go right into your house and send this story to the *Searchlight* over your telephone? It's a quarter to one, and there isn't a minute to lose. The *Searchlight* goes to press in an hour. I've got all the facts," he added, in a peaceful tone.

Miss Watts said we could, and led the way into the house, while the counterfeiters and the police tramped off through the mud and rain. When we got inside, Miss Watts took us to the library and lit the electric lights, while the real reporter bustled about, looking busier than anyone I ever saw before. I watched him for a minute. Then I told Miss Watts I wanted to go into a quiet room and write my story. She and the real reporter looked at each other again. I was getting tired of their looks. The real reporter spoke to me very kindly, like a Sunday-school superintendent addressing his class.

"Now, see here, Miss Iverson," he said; "you've had a big, new experience and lots of excitement. You discovered the counterfeiters. You'll get full credit for it. Let it go at that, and I'll write the story. It's got to be a real story, not a kindergarten special."

If he hadn't said that about the kindergarten special I might have let him write the story, for I was cold and tired and scared. But at those fatal words I felt myself stiffen all over.

"It's my story," I said, with icy determination. "And I'm going to write it."

The real reporter looked annoyed. "But *can* you?" he protested. "We haven't time for experiments."

"Of course I can," I said. And I'm afraid I spoke crossly, for I was getting annoyed. "I'll write it exactly the way Sister Irmingarde told me to."

I sat down at the table as I spoke. I heard a bump and something that sounded like a groan. The real reporter had fallen into a chair. "Good Lord!" he said; and then for a long time he didn't say anything. Finally he began to fuss with his paper, as if he meant to write the story anyway. I wrote three pages and forgot about him. At last he muttered, "Here, let me see those," and his voice sounded like a dove's when it mourns under the eaves. I pushed the sheets toward him with my left hand and went on writing. Suddenly I heard a gasp and a chuckle. In another second the real reporter was standing beside me, grinning his widest grin.

"Why, say, you little May Iverson kid," he almost shouted, "this story is going to be good!"

I could hear Miss Watts straighten up in the chair from which she was watching us. She snatched at my pages, and he let her have them. I wanted to draw myself up to my full height and look at him coldly, but I didn't—there wasn't time. Besides, far down inside of me I was delighted by his praise.

"Of course it's going to be good," was all I said. "Sister Irmingarde told me to write about things as they are, and very simply."

He had my pages back in his hands now and was running over them quickly, putting in a few words here and there with a pencil. I could see he was not changing much. Then he started on a jump for the next room, where the telephone was, but stopped at the door. There was a queer look in his eyes.

"Sister Irmingarde's a daisy!" he muttered.

Then I heard him calling New York. "Gimme the *Searchlight*," he called. "Gimme the city desk. Hurry up! Say, Jack, this is Gibson, at Sound View. We've got a crackerjack of a story out here. No—the Iverson kid is doing it. It's all right, too. Get Hammond busy there and let him take it on the typewriter as fast as I read it. Ready? Here goes."

He began to read my first page.

Miss Watts got up and shut the door, and I bowed my thanks to her. The storm was worse than ever, but I hardly heard it. For a second his words had made me think of Sister Irmingarde. I felt sorry for her. She would never have a chance like this—to write a real news story for a great newspaper. The convent seemed like a place I had heard of, long ago.

Then I settled down to work, and for the next hour there was no sound in the room but the whisper of my busy pen and the respectful footsteps of Miss Watts as she reverently carried my story, page by page, to the chastened "real reporter."

Source: *May Iverson's Career* (Harper & Brothers, 1914).

"THE CRY OF THE PACK"

(1914)

Mr. Nestor Hurd, our "feature" editor, was in a bad humor. We all knew he was, and everybody knew why, except Mr. Nestor Hurd himself. He thought it was because he had not a competent writer on his whole dash-blinged staff, and he was explaining this to space in words that stung like active gnats. Really it was because his wife had just called at his office and drawn his month's salary in advance to go to Atlantic City.[1]

Over the little partition that separated his private office from the square pen where his reporters had their desks Mr. Hurd's words flew and lit upon us. Occasionally we heard the murmur of Mr. Morris's voice, patting the air like a soothing hand; and at last our chief got tired and stopped, and an office boy came into the outer room and said he wanted to see me.

I went in with steady knees. I was no longer afraid of Mr. Hurd. I had been on the *Searchlight* a whole week, and I had written one big "story" and three small ones, and they had all been printed. I knew my style was improving every day—growing more mature. I had dropped a great many amateur expressions, and I had learned to stop when I reached the end of my story instead of going right on. Besides, I was no longer the newest of the "cub reporters."[2] The latest one had been taken on that morning—a scared-looking girl who told me in a trembling voice that she had to write a special column every day for women. It was plain that she had not studied life as we girls had in the convent. She made me feel a thousand years old instead of only eighteen. I had received so much advice during the week that some of it was spilling over, and I freely and gladly gave the surplus to her. I had a desk, too, by this time, in a corner near a window where I could look out on City Hall Park and see the newsboys stealing baths in the fountain. And I was going to be a nun in three years, so who cared, anyway? I went to Mr. Hurd with my head high and the light of confidence in my eyes.

"'S that?" remarked Mr. Hurd, when he heard my soft foot-falls approaching his desk. He was too busy to look up and see. He was bending over a great heap of newspaper clippings, and the veins bulged out on his brow from the violence of his mental efforts. Mr. Morris, the thin young editor who had a desk near his, told him it was Miss Iverson. Mr. Morris had a muscular bulge on each jaw-bone, which Mr. Gibson had told me was caused by the strain of keeping back the things he wanted to say to Mr. Hurd. Mr. Hurd twisted the right corner of his mouth at me, which was his way of showing that he knew that the person he was talking to stood at his right side.

"'S Iverson," he began (he hadn't time to say Miss Iverson), "got 'ny money?"

I thought he wanted to borrow some. I had seen a great deal of borrowing going on during the week; everybody's money seemed to belong to everybody else. I was glad to let him have it, of course, but a little surprised. I told him that I had some money, for when I left home papa had given me—

He interrupted me rudely. "Don't want to know how much papa gave you," he snapped. "Want to know where 'tis."

I told him coldly that it was in a savings-bank, for papa thought—

He interrupted again. I had never been interrupted when I was in the convent. There the girls hung on my words with suspended breath.

"'S all right, then," Mr. Hurd said. "Here's your story. Go and see half a dozen of our biggest millionaires in Wall Street—Drake, Carter, Hayden—you know the list. Tell 'em you're a stranger in town, come to study music or painting. Got a little money to see you through—'nough for a year. Ask 'em what to do with it—how to invest it—and write what happens. Good story, eh?" He turned to Morris for approval, and all his dimples showed, making him look like a six-months-old baby. He immediately regretted this moment of weakness and frowned at me.

"'S all," he said; and I went away.

I will now pause for a moment to describe an interesting phenomenon that ran through my whole journalistic career. I always
went into an editor's room to take an assignment with perfect
confidence, and I usually came out of it in black despair. The
confidence was caused by the memory that I had got my past stories; the despair was caused by the conviction that I could not
possibly get the present one. Each assignment Mr. Hurd had
given me during the week seemed not only harder than the last,
but less worthy the dignity of a general's daughter. Besides, a new
and terrible thing was happening to me. I was becoming afraid—
not of work, but of men. I never had been afraid of anything before. From the time we were laid in our cradles my father taught
my brother Jack and me not to be afraid. The worst of my fear
now was that I didn't know exactly why I felt it, and there was no
one I could go to and ask about it. All the men I met seemed to be
divided into two classes. In the first class were those who were
not kind at all—men like Mr. Hurd, who treated me as if I were
a machine, and ignored me altogether or looked over my head or
past the side of my face when they spoke to me. They seemed
rude at first, and I did not like them; but I liked them better and
better as time went on. In the second class were the men who
were too kind—who sprawled over my desk and wasted my time
and grinned at me and said things I didn't understand and wanted
to take me to Coney Island.[3] Most of them were merely silly, but
two or three of them were horrible. When they came near me they
made me feel queer and sick. After they had left I wanted to
throw open all the doors and windows and air the room. There
was one I used to dream of when I was overworked, which was
usually. He was always a snake in the dream—a fat, disgusting,
lazy snake, slowly squirming over the ground near me, with his
bulging green eyes on my face. There were times when I was
afraid to go to sleep for fear of dreaming of that snake; and when
during the day he came into the room and over to my desk I
would hardly have been surprised to see him crawl instead of
walk. Indeed, his walk was a kind of crawl.

Mr. Gibson, Hurd's star reporter, whose desk was next to
mine, spoke to me about him one day, and his grin was not as
wide as usual.

"Is Yawkins annoying you?" he asked. "I've seen you actually

shudder when he came to your desk. If the cad had any sense he'd
see it, too. Has he said anything? Done anything?"

I said he hadn't, exactly, but that I felt a strange feeling of horror every time he came near me; and Gibson raised his eyebrows
and said he guessed he knew why, and that he would attend to it.
He must have attended to it, for Yawkins stopped coming to my
desk, and after a few months he was discharged for letting himself be "thrown down" on a big story, and I never saw him again.
But at the time Mr. Hurd gave me his Wall Street assignment I
was beginning to be horribly afraid to approach strangers, which
is no way for a reporter to feel; and when I had to meet strange
men I always found myself wondering whether they would be the
Hurd type or the Yawkins type. I hardly dared to hope they
would be like Mr. Gibson, who was like the men at home—kind
and casual and friendly; but of course some of them were.

Once Mrs. Hoppen, a woman reporter on the *Searchlight*,
came and spoke to me about them. She was forty and slender and
black-eyed, and her work was as clever as any man's, but it
seemed to have made her very hard. She seemed to believe in no
one. She made me feel as if she had dived so deep in life that she
had come out into a place where there wasn't anything. She came to
me one day when Yawkins was coiled over my desk. He crawled
away as soon as he saw her, for he hated her. After he went she
stood looking down at me and hesitating. It was not like her to
hesitate about anything.

"Look here," she said at last; "I earn a good income by attend-
ing to my own business, and I usually let other people's business
alone. Besides, I'm not cut out for a Star of Bethlehem.[4] But I just
want to tell you not to worry about that kind of thing." She
looked after Yawkins, who had crawled through the door.

I tried to say that I wasn't worrying, but I couldn't, for it wasn't
true. And someway, though I didn't know why, I couldn't talk to
her about it. She didn't wait for me, however, but went right on.

"You're very young," she said, "and a long way from home.
You haven't been in New York long enough to make influential
friends or create a background for yourself; so you seem fair
game, and the wolves are on the trail. But you can be sure of one
thing—they'll never get you; so don't worry."

I thanked her, and she patted my shoulder and went away. I

wasn't sure just what she meant, but I knew she had tried to be kind.

The day I started down to Wall Street to see the multimillionaires I was very thoughtful. I didn't know then, as I did later, how guarded they were in their offices, and how hard it was for a stranger to get near them. What I simply hated was having them look at me and grin at me, and seeing them under false pretenses and having to tell them lies. I knew Sister Irmingarde would not have approved of it—but there were so many things in newspaper work that Sister Irmingarde wouldn't approve of. I was beginning to wonder if there was anything at all she would approve; and later, of course, I found there was. But I discovered many, many other, things long before that.

I went to Mr. Drake's office first. He was the one Mr. Hurd had mentioned first, and while I was at school I had heard about him and read that he was very old and very kind and very pious. I thought perhaps he would be kind enough to see a strange girl for a few minutes and give her some advice, even if his time was worth a thousand dollars a minute, as they said it was. So I went straight to his office and asked for him, and gave my card to a buttoned boy who seemed strangely loath to take it. He was perfectly sure Mr. Drake hadn't time to see me, and he wanted the whole story of my life before he gave the card to anyone; but I was not yet afraid of office boys, and he finally took the card and went away with dragging steps.

Then my card began to circulate like a love story among the girls at St. Catharine's. Men in little cages and at mahogany desks read it, and stared at me and passed it onto other men. Finally it disappeared in an inner room, and a young man came out holding it in his hand and spoke to me in a very cold and direct manner. The card had my real name on it, but no address or newspaper, and it didn't mean anything at all to the direct young man. He wanted to know who I was and what I wanted of Mr. Drake, and I told him what Mr. Hurd had told me to say. The young man hesitated. Then he smiled, and at last he said he would see what he could do and walked away. In five or six minutes he came back again, still smiling, but in a pleasanter and more friendly manner, and said Mr. Drake would see me if I could wait half an hour.

I thanked him and settled back in my seat to wait. It was a very comfortable seat—a deep, leather-covered chair with big wide arms, and there was enough going on around me to keep me interested. All sorts of men came and went while I sat there; young men and old men, and happy men and wretched men, and prosperous men and poor men; but there was one thing in which they were all alike. Every man was in a hurry, and every man had in his eyes the set, eager look my brother Jack's eyes hold when he is running a college race and sees the goal ahead of him. A few of them glanced at me, but none seemed interested or surprised to see me there. Probably they thought, if they thought of it at all, that I was a stenographer trying to get a situation.

The half-hour passed, and then another half-hour, and at last the direct young man came out again. He did not apologize for keeping me waiting twice as long as he had said it would be.

"Mr. Drake will see you now," he said.

I followed him through several offices full of clerks and typewriters, and then into an office where a little old man sat alone. It was a very large office, with old rugs on the floor, and heavy curtains and beautiful furniture, and the little old man seemed almost lost in it. He was a very thin little old man, and he sat at a great mahogany desk facing the door. The light in his office came from windows behind and beside him, but it fell on my face, as I sat opposite him, and left his in shadow. I could see, though, that his hair was very white, and that his face was like an oval billiard-ball, the thin skin of it drawn tightly over bones that showed. He might have been fifty years old or a hundred—I didn't know which—but he was dressed very carefully in gray clothes almost as light in color as his face and hair, and he wore a gray tie with a star-sapphire pin in it. That pale-blue stone, and the pale blue of his eyes, which had the same sort of odd, moving light in them the sapphire had, were the only colors about him. He sat back, very much at his ease, his small figure deep in his great swivel-chair, the finger-tips of both hands close together, and stared at me with his pale-blue eyes that showed their queer sparks under his white eyebrows.

"Well, young woman," he said, "what can I do for you?"

And then I knew how old he was, for in the cracked tones of his voice the clock of time seemed to be striking eighty. It made me feel comfortable and almost happy to know that he was so old. I wasn't afraid of him anymore. I poured out my little story, which I had rehearsed with his clerk, and he listened without a word, never taking his narrow blue eyes from my face. When I stopped he asked me what instrument I was studying, and I told him the piano, which was true enough, for I was still keeping up the music I had worked on so hard with Sister Cecilia ever since I was eight years old. He asked me what music I liked best, and when I told him my favorite composers were Beethoven and De-bussy he smiled and murmured that it was a strange combina-tion.[5] It was, too, and well I knew it. Sister Cecilia said once that it made her understand why I wanted to be both a nun and a newspaper woman.

In a few minutes I was talking to Mr. Drake as easily as I could talk to George Morgan or to my father. He asked who my teach-ers had been, and I told him all about the convent and my years of study there, and how much better Janet Trelawney played than I did, and how severe Sister Cecilia was with us both, and how much I liked church music. I was so glad to be telling him the truth that I told him a great deal more than I needed to. I told him almost everything there was to tell, except that I was a news-paper reporter. I remembered not to tell him that.

He seemed to like to hear about school and the girls. Several times he laughed, but very kindly, and *with* me, you know, not *at* me. Once he said it had been a long time since any young girl had told him about her school pranks, but he did not sigh over it or look sentimental, as a man would in a book. He merely men-tioned it. We talked and talked. Twice the direct young secretary opened the door and put his head in; but each time he took it out again because nobody seemed to want it to stay there. At last I remembered that Mr. Drake was a busy man, and that his time was worth a thousand dollars a minute, and that I had taken about forty thousand dollars' worth of it already, so I gasped and apologized and got up. I said I had forgotten all about time; and he said he had, too, and that I must sit down again because we hadn't even touched upon our business talk.

So I sat down again, and he looked at me more closely than ever, as if he had noticed how hot and red my face had suddenly got and couldn't understand why it looked that way. Of course he couldn't, either; for I had just remembered that, though I had been a reporter for a whole week, I had forgotten my assignment! It seemed as if I would never learn to be a real newspaper woman. My heart went way down, and I suppose the corners of my mouth did, too; they usually went down at the same time. He asked very kindly what was the matter, and the tone of his voice was beautiful—old and friendly and understanding. I said it was because I was so silly and stupid and young and unbusiness-like. He started to say something and stopped, then sat up and began to talk in a very business-like way. He asked where my money was, and I told him the name of the bank. He looked at his watch and frowned. I didn't know why; but I thought perhaps it was because he wanted me to take it out of there right away and it was too late. It was almost four o'clock. Then he put the tips of his fingers together again, and talked to me the way the cashier at the bank had talked when I put my money in.

He said that the savings-bank was a good place for a girl's money—under ordinary conditions it was the best place. The interest would be small, but sure. Certain investments would, of course, bring higher interest, but no woman should try to invest her money unless she had business training or a very wise, experienced adviser back of her. Then he stopped for a minute, and it seemed hard for him to go on. I did not speak, for I saw that he was thinking something over, and of course I knew better than to interrupt him. At last he said that ordinarily, of course, he never paid any attention to small accounts, but that he liked me very much and wanted to help me and that, if I wished, he would invest my money for me in a way that would bring in a great deal more interest than the savings-bank would pay. And he asked if I understood what he meant.

I said I did—that he was offering to take entirely too much trouble for a stranger, and that he was just as kind as he could be, but that I couldn't think of letting him do it, and I was sure papa wouldn't want me to. He seemed annoyed all of a sudden, and his manner changed. He asked why I had come if I felt that way, and I began to see how silly it looked to him, for of course he didn't know I was a reporter getting a story on investments for women. I didn't know what to say or what to do about the money, either, for Mr. Hurd hadn't told me how to meet any offer of that kind.

While I was thinking and hesitating Mr. Drake sat still and looked at me queerly; the blue sparks in his eyes actually seemed to shoot out at me. They frightened me a little; and, without stopping to think any more, I said I was very grateful to him and that I would bring the money to his office the next day. Then I stood up and he stood up, too; and I gave him my hand and told him he was the kindest man I had met in New York—and the next minute I was gasping and struggling and pushing him away with all my strength, and he stumbled and went backward into his big chair, knocking over an inkstand full of ink, which crawled to the edge of his desk in little black streams and fell on his gray clothes.

For a minute he sat staring straight ahead of him and let them fall. Then he brushed his hand across his head and picked up the inkstand and soaked up the ink with a blotter, and finally turned and looked at me. I stared back at him as if I were in a nightmare. I was opposite him and against the wall, with my back to it, and for a moment I couldn't move. But now I began to creep toward the door, with my eyes on him. I felt some way that I dared not take them off. As I moved he got up; he was much nearer the door than I was, and, though I sprang for it, he reached it first and stood there quietly, holding the knob in his hand. Neither of us had uttered a sound; but now he spoke, and his voice was very low and steady.

"Wait a minute," he said. "I want to tell you something you need to know. Then you may go." And he added, grimly, "Straighten your hat!"

I put up my hands and straightened it. Still I did not take my eyes off his. His eyes seemed like those of Yawkins and the great snake in my dreams, but as I looked into them they fell.

"For God's sake, child," he said, irritably, "don't look at me as if I were an anaconda! Don't you know it was all a trick?" He came up closer to me and gave me his next words eye to eye and very slowly, as if to force me to listen and believe.

"I did that, Miss Iverson," he said, "to show you what happens to beautiful girls in New York when they go into men's offices asking for advice about money. Someone had to do it. I thought the lesson might come better from me than from a younger man."

His words came to me from some place far away. A bit of my

bit of Greek came, too—something about Homeric laughter.[6] Then next instant I went to pieces and crumpled up in the big chair, and when he tried to help me I wouldn't let him come near me. But little by little, when I could speak, I told him what I thought of him and men like him, and of what I had gone through since I came to New York, and of how he had made me feel degraded and unclean forever. At first he listened without a word; then he began to ask a few questions.

"So you don't believe me," he said once. "That's too bad. I ought to have thought of that."

He even wrung from me at last the thing that was worst of all—the thing I had not dared to tell Mrs. Hoppen—the thing I had sworn to myself no one should ever know—the deep-down, paralyzing fear that there must be something wrong in me that brought these things upon me, that perhaps I, too, was to blame. That seemed to stir him in a queer fashion. He put out his hand as if to push the idea away.

"No," he said, emphatically. "No, *no*! Never think that." He went on more quietly. "That's not it. It's only that you're a lamb among the wolves."[7]

He seemed to forget me, then to remember me again. "But remember this, child," he went on. "Some men are bad clear through; some are only half bad. Some aren't wolves at all; they'll help to keep you from the others. Don't you get to thinking that every mother's son runs in the pack; and don't forget that it's mighty hard for any of us to believe that you're as unsophisticated as you seem. You'll learn how to handle wolves. That's a woman's primer lesson in life. And in the meantime here's something to comfort you: Though you don't know it, you have a talisman. You've got something in your eyes that will never let them come too close. Now good-by."

It was six o'clock when I got back to the *Searchlight* office. I had gone down to the Battery to let the clean sea-air sweep over me.[8] I had dropped into a little chapel, too, and when I came out the world had righted itself again and I could look my fellow human beings in the eyes. Even Mr. Drake had said my experience was not my fault and that I had a talisman. I knew now what the talisman was.

Mr. Hurd, still bunched over his desk, was drinking a bottle of ginger ale and eating a sandwich when I entered. Morris, at his desk, was editing copy. The outer pen, where the rest of us sat, was deserted by everyone except Gibson, who was so busy that he did not look up.

"Got your story?" asked Hurd, looking straight at me for the third time since I had taken my place on his staff. He spoke with his mouth full. "Hello," he added. "What's the matter with your eyes?"

I sat down by his desk and told him. The sandwich dropped from his fingers. His young-old, dimpled face turned white with anger. He waited without a word until I had finished.

"By God, I'll make him sweat for that!" he hissed. "I'll show him up! The old hypocrite! The whited sepulcher!⁹ I'll make this town ring with that story. I'll make it too hot to hold him!"

Morris got up, crossed to us, and stood beside him, looking down at him. The bunches on his jawbones were very large.

"What's the use of talking like that, Hurd?" he asked, quietly. "You know perfectly well you won't print that story. You don't dare. And you know that you're as much to blame as Drake is for what's happened. When you sent Miss Iverson out on that assignment you knew just what was coming to her."

Hurd's face went purple. "I didn't," he protested, furiously. "I swear I didn't. I thought she'd be able to get to them because she's so pretty. But that's as far as my mind worked on it." He turned to me. "You believe me, don't you?" he asked, gently. "Please say you do."

I nodded.

"Then it's all right," he said. "And I promise you one thing now: I'll never put you up against a proposition like that again."

He picked up his sandwich and dropped the matter from his mind. Morris stood still a minute longer, started to speak, stopped, and at last brought out what he had to say.

"And you won't think every man you meet is a beast, will you, Miss Iverson?" he asked.

I shook my head. I didn't seem to be able to say much. But it seemed queer that both he and Mr. Drake had said almost the same thing.

"Because," said Morris, "in his heart, you know, every man wants to be decent."

I filed that idea for future reference, as librarians say. Then I asked them the question I had been asking myself for hours. "Do you think Mr. Drake really *was* teaching me a—a terrible lesson?" I stammered.

The two men exchanged a look. Each seemed to wait for the other to speak. It was Gibson who answered me. He had opened the door, and was watching us with no sign of his usual wide and cheerful grin.

"The way you tell it," he said, "it's a toss-up. But I'll tell you how it strikes me. Just to be on the safe side, and whether he lied to you or not, I'd like to give Henry F. Drake the all-firedest licking he ever got in his life."

"You bet," muttered Hurd, through the last mouthful of his sandwich. Mr. Morris didn't say anything, but the bunches on his jaw-bones seemed larger than ever as he turned to his desk.

I looked at them, and in that moment I learned the lesson that follows the primer lesson. At least one thing Mr. Drake had told me was true—all men were not wolves.

Source: *May Iverson's Career* (Harper & Brothers, 1914).

"THE CASE OF
HELEN BRANDOW"

(1914)

"'S Iverson," barked Nestor Hurd, over the low partition which divided his office from that of his staff, "c'm' here!"

I responded to his call with sympathetic haste. It had been a hard day for Mr. Hurd. Everything had gone wrong. Every reporter he had sent out seemed to be "falling down" on his assignment and telephoning in to explain why. Next to failures, our chief disliked explanations. "A dead man doesn't care a hang what killed him," was his terse summing up of their futility.

He was shouting an impassioned monologue into the telephone when I reached his side, and as a final exclamation-point he hurled the receiver down on his desk, upsetting a bottle of ink. I waited in silence while he exhausted the richest treasures of his vocabulary and soaked up the ink with blotters. It was a moment for feminine tact, and I exercised it, though I was no longer in awe of Mr. Hurd. I had been on the *Searchlight* a year, and the temperamental storms of my editors now disturbed me no more than the whirling and buzzing of mechanical tops. Even Mollie Merk had ceased to call me the "convent kid."[1] I had made many friends, learned many lessons, suffered many disappointments, lost many illusions, and taken on some new ones. I had slowly developed a sense of humor—to my own abysmal surprise. The memory of my convent had become as the sound of a vesper-bell, heard occasionally above the bugle-calls of a strenuous life. Also, I had learned to avoid "fine writing," which is why my pen faltered just now over the "bugle-calls." I knew my men associates very well, and admired most of them, though they often filled me with a maternal desire to stand them in a corner with their faces to the wall. I frequently explained to them what their wives or sweethearts really meant by certain things they had said. I was the recognized office authority on good form, Catholicism, and feminine psychology. Therefore I presented to Mr. Hurd's embittered glance the serene brow of an equal—even on occasions such as this, when the peace of the office lay in fragments around us.

At last he ceased to address space, threw the blotters into his waste-paper basket, and turned resentful eyes on me.

"Gibson's fallen down on the Brandow case," he snapped.

I uttered a coo of sympathy.

"The woman won't talk," continued Hurd, gloomily. "Don't believe she'll talk to anyone if she won't to Gibson. But we'll give her 'nother chance. Go 'n' see her."

I remained silent.

"You've followed the trial, haven't you?" Mr. Hurd demanded. "What d'you think of the case?"

I murmured apologetically that I thought Mrs. Brandow was innocent, and the remark produced exactly the effect I had expected. My chief gave me one look of unutterable scorn and settled back in his chair.

"Great Scott!" he groaned. "So you've joined the sobbing sisterhood at last![2] I wouldn't have believed it. 'S Iverson"—his voice changed, he brought his hand down on the desk with a force that made the ink-bottle rock—"that woman's as guilty as—as—"

I reminded him that the evidence against Mrs. Brandow was purely circumstantial.

"Circumstantial? 'Course it's circumstantial!" yelped Hurd. "She's too clever to let it be anything else. She has hidden every track. She's the slickest proposition we've had up for murder in this state, and she's young, pretty, of good family—so she'll probably get off. But she killed her husband as surely as you stand there, and the fact that he was a brute and deserved what he got doesn't make her any less guilty of his murder."

It was a long speech for Mr. Hurd. He seemed surprised by it himself, and stopped to glare at me as if I were to blame for the effort it had caused him.

"You know Davies, her lawyer, don't you?" he asked, more quietly.

I did.

"Think he'll give you a letter to her?"

I thought he would.

"'L right," snapped Mr. Hurd. "Go 'n' see her. If she'll talk, get an interview. If she won't, describe her and her cell. Tell how she looks and what she wears—from the amount of hair over her ears to the kind of polish on her shoes. Leave mawkish sympathy out of it. See her as she is—a murderess whose trial is going to make American justice look like a hole in a doughnut."

I went back to my desk thinking of his words. While I was pinning on my hat the door of Mr. Hurd's room opened and shut, and his assistant, Godfrey Morris, came and stood beside me.

"I don't want to butt in," he began, "but—I hope you're going on this assignment with an open mind, Miss Iverson."

That hurt me. For some reason it always hurt me surprisingly to have Godfrey Morris show any lack of faith in me in any way.

"I told Mr. Hurd," I answered, with dignity, "that I think Mrs. Brandow is innocent. But my opinion won't—"

"I know." Mr. Morris's ability to interrupt a speaker without seeming rude was one of his special gifts. "Hurd thinks she's guilty," he went on. "I think she's innocent. What I hope you'll do is to forget what anyone thinks. Go to the woman without prejudice one way or the other. Write of her as you find her."

"That," I said, "is precisely what I intend to do."

"Good!" exclaimed Morris. "I was afraid that what Hurd said might send you out with the wrong notion."

He strolled with me toward the elevator. "I never knew a case where the evidence for and against a prisoner was so evenly balanced," he mused. "I'm for her simply because I can't believe that a woman with her brains and courage would commit such a crime. She's too good a sport! By Jove, the way she went through that seven-hour session on the witness-stand the other day . . ." He checked himself. "Oh, well," he ended, easily, "I'm not her advocate. She may be fooling us all. Good-by. Get a good story."

"I'll make her confess to me," I remarked, cheerfully, at the elevator door. "Then we'll suppress the confession!"

"We'll give her a square deal, anyway," he called, as the elevator began to descend.

It was easy to run out to Fairview, the scene of the trial, easy to get the letter from Mr. Davies, and easiest of all to interview the friendly warden of the big prison and send the note to Mrs. Brandow in her cell when she had returned from court. After that the broad highway of duty was no longer oiled. Very courteously, but very firmly, too, Mrs. Brandow declined to see me. Many messages passed between us before I was admitted to her presence on the distinct understanding that I was not to ask her questions, that I was not to quote anything she might say; that, in short, I was to confine the drippings of my gifted pen to a description of her environment and of herself. This was not a heartening task. Yet when the iron door of Number 46 on the women's tier of the prison had swung back to admit me my first glance at the prisoner and her background showed me that Mr. Hurd would have at least one "feature" for the *Searchlight* the next morning.

On either side of Number 46 were typical white-painted and carbolic-scented cells—one occupied by an intoxicated woman who snored raucously on her narrow cot, the other by a wretched hag who clung to the bars of her door with filthy fingers and leered at me as I passed. Between the two was a spot as out of place in those surroundings as a flower-bed would seem on the stern brow of an Alpine glacier.

Mrs. Brandow, the newspapers had told the world, was not only a beautiful woman, but a woman who loved beauty. She had spent six months in Fairview awaiting her trial. All the members of the "good family" Mr. Hurd had mentioned had died young— probably as a reward of their excellence. She had no intimate friends—her husband, it was said, had made friendships impossible for her. Nevertheless, first with one trifle, then with another, brought to her by the devoted maid who had been with her for years, she had made herself a home in her prison.

Tacked on the wall, facing her small, white-painted iron bed, was a large piece of old Java print, its colors dimmed by time to dull browns and blues. On the bed itself was a cover of blue linen, and the cement floor was partly concealed by a Chinese rug whose rich tones harmonized with those of the print. Over the bed hung a fine copy of a Hobbema, in which two lines of trees stretched on and on toward a vague, far-distant horizon.[3] Near this a large framed print showed a great stretch of Scotch moors and wide, empty skies. A few silver-backed toilet articles lay on a small glass-covered hospital table. Against this unlooked-for background the suspected murderess, immaculate in white linen tailor-made garments, sat on a white-enameled stool, peacefully sewing a button on a canvas shoe.

The whole effect was so unprecedented, even to me after a year of the varied experiences which come to a New York reporter, that my sense of the woman's situation was wiped out by the tableau she made. Without intending to smile at all, I smiled widely as I entered and held out my hand; and Mrs. Brandow, who had risen to receive me, sent back an answering smile, cool, worldly, and understanding.

"It *is* a cozy domestic scene, isn't it?" she asked, lightly, reading my thoughts, "but on too small a scale. We're a trifle cramped. Take the stool. I will sit on the bed."

She moved the stool an inch, with a hospitable gesture which almost created an effect of space, and sat down opposite me, taking me in from head to foot with one straight look from black eyes in whose depths lurked an odd sparkle.

"You won't mind if I finish this?" she asked, as she picked up her needle. "I have only two more buttons."

I reassured her, and she bit off a piece of cotton and rethreaded her needle expertly.

"They won't let me have a pair of scissors," she explained, as she began to sew. "It's a wonder they lend me a needle. They tell me it's a special privilege. Once a week the guard brings it to me at this hour, and the same evening he retrieves it with a long sigh of relief. He is afraid I will swallow it and cheat the electric chair. He needn't be. It isn't the method I should choose."

Her voice was a soft and warm contralto, whose vibrations seemed to linger in the air when she had ceased to speak. Her manner was indescribably matter-of-fact. She gave a vigorous pull to the button she had sewed on and satisfied herself of its strength. Then she bit the thread again and began to secure the last button, incidentally chatting on, as she might have chatted to a friend over a cup of tea.

Very simply and easily, because it was my cue, but even more because I was immensely interested, I fell into her mood. We talked a long time and of many things. She asked about my work, and I gave her some details of its amusing side. She spoke of the books she had read and was reading, of places she had visited, and, in much the same tone, of her nights in prison, made hideous by her neighbors in nearby cells. As she talked, two dominating impressions strengthened in me momentarily: she was the most immaculate human being I had ever seen, and the most perfectly poised.

When she had sewed on the last button, fastening the thread with workman-like deftness, she opened a box of pipe-clay and whitened both shoes with a moist sponge.

"I don't quite know why I do all this," she murmured, casually. "I suppose it's the force of habit. It's surprising how some habits last and others fall away. The only wish I have now is that I and my surroundings may remain decently clean."

"May I quote that?" I asked, tentatively—"that, and what you have told me about the books you are reading?"

Her expression of indifferent tolerance changed. She regarded me with narrowed eyes under drawn, black brows. "No," she said, curtly. "You'll be good enough to keep to your bond. You agreed not to repeat a word I said."

I rose to go. "And I won't," I told her, "naturally. But I hoped you had changed your mind."

She rose also, the slight, ironic smile again playing about her lips. "No," she answered, in a gentler tone, "the agreement holds. But I don't wonder I misled you! I've prattled like a school-girl, and"—the smile subtly changed its character—"do you know, I've rather enjoyed it. I haven't talked to anyone for months but my maid and my lawyer. Mary's chat is punctuated by sobs. I'm like a freshly watered garden when she ends her weekly visits. And the charms of Mr. Davies's conversation leave me cold. So this has been"—she hesitated—"a pleasure," she ended.

We shook hands again. "Thank you," I said, "and good-by. I hope"—In my turn I hesitated an instant, seeking the right words. The odd sparkle deepened in her eyes.

"Yes?" she murmured. "You hope—?"

"I hope you will soon be free," I ended simply.

Her eyes held mine for an instant. Then, "Thank you," she said, and turned away. The guard, who had waited outside with something of the effect of a clock about to strike, opened the iron door, and I passed through.

Late that night, after I had turned in my copy and received in acknowledgment the grunt which was Mr. Hurd's highest tribute to satisfactory work, I sat at my desk still thinking of the Brandow case. Suddenly the chair beside me creaked as Godfrey Morris dropped into it.

"Just been reading your Brandow story. Good work," he said, kindly. "Without bias, too. What do you think of the woman now, after meeting her?"

"She's innocent," I repeated, tersely.

"Then she didn't confess?" laughed Morris.

"No," I smiled, "she didn't confess. But if she had been guilty she might have confessed. She talked a great deal."

Morris's eyes widened with interest. The day's work was over, and he was in a mood to be entertained. "Did she?" he asked. "What did she say?"

I repeated the interview, while he leaned back and listened, his hands clasped behind his head.

"She *was* communicative," he reflected, at the end. "In a mood like that, after months of silence, a woman will tell anything. As you say, if she had been guilty she might easily have given herself away. What a problem it would have put up to you," he mused, "if she *had* been guilty and *had* confessed! On the one hand, loyalty to the *Searchlight*—you'd have had to publish the news. On the other hand, sympathy for the woman—for it would be you who sent her to the electric chair, or remained silent and saved her."

He looked at me quizzically. "Which would you have done?" he asked.

It seemed no problem at all to me, but I gave it an instant's reflection. "I think you know," I told him.

He nodded. "I think I do," he agreed. "Just the same," he rose and started for his desk, "don't you imagine there isn't a problem in the situation. There's a big one."

He turned back, struck by a sudden idea. "Why don't you make a magazine story of it?" he added. "I believe you can write fiction. Here's your chance. Describe the confession of the murderess, the mental struggle of the reporter, her suppression of the news, and its after-effect on her career."

His suggestion hit me much harder than his problem. The latter was certainly strong enough for purposes of fiction.

"Why," I said, slowly, "thank you. I believe I will."

Before Mr. Morris had closed the door I was drawing a fresh supply of copy-paper toward me; before he had left the building I had written the introduction to my first fiction story; and before the roar of the presses came up to my ears from the basement, at a quarter to two in the morning, I had made on my last page the final cross of the press-writer and dropped the finished manuscript into a drawer of my desk. It had been written with surprising ease. Helen Brandow had entered my tale as naturally as she would enter a room; and against the bleak background of her cell I seemed to see her whole life pass before me like a series of moving-pictures which my pen raced after and described.

The next morning found me severely critical as I read my story. Still, I decided to send it to a famous novelist I had met a few months before, who had since then spent some of her leisure in good naturedly urging me to "write." I believed she would tell me frankly what she thought of this first sprout in my literary garden, and that night, quite without compunction, I sent it to her. Two days later I received a letter which I carried around in my pocket until the precious bit of paper was almost in rags.

"Your story is a corker," wrote the distinguished author, whose epistolary style was rather free.[4] "I experienced a real thrill when the woman confessed. You have made out a splendid case for her; also for your reporter. Given all your premises, things *had* to happen as they did. Offer the story to Mrs. Langster, editor of *The Woman's Friend*. Few editors have sense, but I think she'll know enough to take it. I inclose a note to her."

If Mrs. Appleton had experienced a thrill over my heroine's confession we were more than quits, for I experienced a dozen thrills over her letter, and long afterward, when she came back from a visit to England with new honors thick upon her, I amused her by describing them.[5] Within twenty-four hours after receiving her inspiring communication I had wound my way up a circular staircase that made me feel like an animated corkscrew, and was humbly awaiting Mrs. Langster's pleasure in the room next to her dingy private office. She had read Mrs. Appleton's note at once, and had sent an office boy to say that she would receive me in a few minutes. I gladly waited thirty, for this home of a big and successful magazine was a new world to me—and, though it lacked the academic calm I had associated with the haunts of literature in the making, everything in it was interesting, from the ink-spattered desks and their aloof and busy workers to the recurrent roar of the elevated trains that pounded past the windows.

Mrs. Langster proved to be an old lady, with a smile of extraordinary sweetness. Looking at her white hair, and meeting the misty glance of her near-sighted blue eyes, I felt a depressing doubt of Mrs. Appleton's wisdom in sending me to her with a work of fiction which turned on murder. One instinctively associated Mrs. Langster with organ recitals, evening service, and afternoon teas in dimly lighted rooms. But there was an admirable brain under her silver hair, and I had swift proof of the keenness of her literary discrimination; for within a week she accepted my story and sent me a check for an amount equal to the salary I received for a month of work. Her letter, and that of Mrs. Appleton, went to Sister Irmingarde—was it only a year ago that I had parted from her and the convent? Then I framed them side by side and hung them in a place of honor on my study wall, as a solace in dark hours and an inspiration in brighter ones. They represented a literary ladder, on the first rung of which I was sure I had found firm footing, though the upper rungs were lost in clouds.

Mrs. Langster allowed my story to mellow for almost a year before she published it; and in the long interval Helen Brandow was acquitted, and disappeared from the world that had known her.

I myself had almost forgotten her, and I had even ceased to look for my story in the columns of *The Woman's Friend*, when one morning I found on my desk a note from Mr. Hurd. It was brief and cryptic, for Mr. Hurd's notes were as time-saving as his speech. It read:

Pls. rept. immed.
    N. H.

Without waiting to remove my hat I entered Mr. Hurd's office. He was sitting bunched up over his desk, his eyebrows looking like an intricate pattern of cross-stitching. Instead of his usual assortment of newspaper clippings, he held in his hand an open magazine, which, as I entered, he thrust toward me.

"Here!" he jerked. "What's this mean?"

I recognized with mild surprise the familiar cover of *The Woman's Friend*. A second glance showed me that the page Mr. Hurd was indicating with staccato movements of a nervous forefinger bore my name. My heart leaped.

"Why," I exclaimed, delightedly, "it's my story!"

Mr. Hurd's hand held the magazine against the instinctive pull I gave it. His manner was unusually quiet. Unusual, too, was the sudden straight look of his tired eyes.

"Sit down," he said, curtly. "I want to ask you something."

I sat down, my eyes on the magazine. As Mr. Hurd held it, I could see the top of one illustration. It looked interesting.

"See here," Mr. Hurd jerked out. "I'm not going to beat around the bush. Did you throw us down on this story?"

I stared at him. For an instant I did not get his meaning. Then it came to me that possibly I should have asked his permission to publish any work outside of the *Searchlight* columns.

"But," I stammered, "you don't print fiction."

Mr. Hurd tapped the open page with his finger. The unusual quiet of his manner began to impress me. "*Is* it fiction?" he asked. "That's what I want to know."

Godfrey Morris rose from his desk and came toward us. Until that instant I had only vaguely realized that he was in the room.

"Hurd," he said, quickly, "you're in the wrong pew. Miss Iverson doesn't even know what you're talking about." He turned to me. "He's afraid," he explained, "that Mrs. Brandow confessed to you in Fairview, and that you threw us down by suppressing the story."

For an instant I was dazed. Then I laughed. "Mr. Hurd," I said, "I give you my word that Mrs. Brandow never confessed anything to me."

Mr. Hurd's knitted brows uncreased. "That's straight, is it?" he demanded.

"That's straight," I repeated.

Hurd dropped the magazine on the floor and turned to his papers. "'L right," he muttered, "don't let 't happen 'gain."

Mr. Morris and I exchanged an understanding smile as I picked up the magazine and left the room.

In the outer room I met Gibson. His grin of greeting was wide and friendly, his voice low and interested.

"Read your story last night," he whispered. "Say, tell me—*did* she, really?"

I filled the next five minutes explaining to Gibson. He looked relieved. "I didn't think there was anything in it," he said. "That woman's no murderess. But, say, you made the story read like the real thing!"

Within the next few days everybody on the *Searchlight* staff seemed to have read *The Woman's Friend*, and to be taking part in the discussion my story aroused. Those of my associates who believed in the innocence of Mrs. Brandow accepted the tale for what it was—a work of fiction. Those without prejudice were inclined to think there was "something in it," and at least half a dozen who believed her guilty also firmly believed that I had allowed an acute and untimely spasm of womanly sympathy to deprive the *Searchlight* of "the best and biggest beat in years." For a few days I remained pleasantly unconscious of being a storm-center; but one morning a second summons from Mr. Hurd opened my eyes to the situation.

"See here!" began that gentleman, rudely. "What does all this talk mean, anyway? They're saying now that you and Morris suppressed the Brandow confession between you. Jim, the elevator-boy, says he heard you agree to do it."

Godfrey Morris leaped to his feet and came toward us. "Good Lord, Hurd," he cried, fiercely, "I believe you're crazy! Why don't you come to me with this rot, if you're going to notice it, and not bother Miss Iverson? We joked about a confession, and I suppose Jim heard us. The joke was what suggested the magazine story."

"Well, *that's* no joke." Hurd spoke grudgingly, as if unwillingly impressed. "Suppose the woman had confessed," he asked me, suddenly—"would you have given us the story?"

I shook my head. "Certainly not," I admitted. "You forget that I had agreed not to print a word she said."

Hurd's expression of uncertainty was so funny that I laughed. "But she didn't," I added, comfortingly. "Do you think I'd lie to you?"

"You might." Hurd was in a pessimistic mood. "To save her, or—" A rare phenomenon occurred; he smiled—all his boyish dimples suddenly revealed—"to save Morris from losing his job," he finished, coolly.

I felt my face grow hot. Morris rushed to the rescue. "The only thing I regret in this confounded mess," he muttered, ignoring Hurd's words, "is the effect on Mrs. Brandow. *The Woman's Friend* has half a million readers. They'll all think she's guilty."

"Good job," said Hurd. "She *is* guilty!"

"Rot! She's absolutely innocent," replied Morris. "Why, even the fool jury acquitted her on the first ballot!"

I left them arguing and slipped away, sick at heart. In the sudden moment of illumination following Morris's words it had come to me that the one person to be considered in the whole episode was the person of whom I had not thought at all! I had done Helen Brandow a great wrong. Her case had been almost forgotten; somewhere she was trying to build up a new life. I had knocked out the new foundations.

It was a disturbing reflection, and the events of the next few days deepened my depression. Several reviewers commented on the similarity of my story to the Brandow case. People began to ask where Mrs. Brandow was, began again to argue the question of her innocence or her guilt. Efforts were made to find her hiding-place. The thought of the injury I had done the unhappy woman became an obsession. There seemed only one way to exorcise it, and that was to see or write to my "victim," as Hurd jocosely called her, make my confession, and have her absolve me, if she would, of any intent of injury.

On the wings of this inspiration I sought Mr. Davies, and, putting the situation before him, asked for his client's address.

"Of course I can't give you her address," he explained, mildly. "But I'll write to her and tell her you want it. Yes, yes, with pleasure. I know how you feel." He smiled reflectively. "She's a wonderful woman," he added. "Most remarkable woman I ever met—strongest soul." He sighed, then smiled again. "I'll write," he repeated; and with this I had to be content. I had done all that I could do. But my nerves began to feel the effect of the strain upon them, and it was a relief when I reached my home in Madison Square late one evening and found Mrs. Brandow waiting for me.

She was sitting in a little reception-room off the main hall of the building, and as I passed the door on my way to the elevator she rose and came toward me. She wore a thick veil, but something in me recognized her even before I caught the flash of her eyes through it, and noticed the characteristically erect poise of the head which every reporter who saw her had described.

"Mr. Davies said you wanted to talk to me," she began, without greeting me. "Here I am. Have I come at the wrong time?"

I slipped my hand through her arm. "No," was all I could say. "It was very good of you to come at all. I did not expect that." In silence we entered the elevator and ascended to my floor. As I opened the door with my latch-key and waited for her to go in I spoke again. "I can't tell you how much I've been thinking of you," I said.

She made no reply. We passed through the hall into my study, and while I turned on the electric lights she dropped into a big arm-chair beside a window overlooking the Square, threw back her veil, and slipped off the heavy furs she wore. As the lights flashed up we exchanged a swift look. Little more than a year had passed since our former meeting, but she seemed many years older and much less beautiful. There were new lines about her eyes and mouth, and the black hair over her temples was growing gray. I started to draw down the window-shades, for it was snowing hard, and the empty Square below, with a few tramps shivering on its benches, afforded but a dreary vista. She checked me.

"Leave them as they are," she directed, imperiously, adding as an afterthought: "Please. I like to be able to look out."

I obeyed, realizing now, as I had not done before, what those months of confinement must have meant to her. When I had removed my hat and coat, and lit the logs that lay ready in my big fireplace, I took a chair near her.

"First of all," I began, "I want to thank you for coming. And then—I want to beg your forgiveness."

For a moment she studied me in silence. "That's rather odd of you," she murmured, reflectively. "You know I'm fair game! Why shouldn't you run with the pack?"

My eyes, even my head, went down before that. For a moment I could not reply. Then it seemed to me that the most important thing in the world was to make her understand.

"Of course," I admitted, "I deserve anything you say. I did a horrible thing when I printed that story. I should never have offered it to an editor. My defense is simply that I didn't realize what I was doing. That's what I want to make clear to you. That's why I asked to see you."

"I see," she said, slowly. "It's not the story you're apologizing for. It's the effect."

"Yes," I explained, eagerly, "it's the effect. I hadn't been out of school more than a year when I came to you in Fairview," I hurried on. "I was very young, and appallingly ignorant. It never occurred to me that anyone would connect a fiction story with—with your case."

She looked at me, and with all the courage I could summon I gazed straight back into her strange, deep eyes. For a long instant the look held, and during it something came to me, something new and poignant, something that filled me with an indescribable pity for the loneliness I now understood, and for the courage of the nature that bore it so superbly. She would ask nothing of the world, this woman. Nor would she defend herself. People could think what they chose. But she would suffer.

I leaned toward her. "Mrs. Brandow," I said, "I wish I could make you understand how I feel about this. I believe it has made me ten years older."

She smiled. "That would be a pity," she said, "when you're so deliciously young."

"Is there anything I can do?" I persisted.

She raised her eyebrows. "I'm afraid not," she murmured, "unless it is to cease doing anything. You see, your activities where I am concerned are so hectic."

I felt my face burn. "You're very hard on me, but I deserve it. I didn't realize," I repeated, "that the story would suggest you to the public."

"Even though you described me?" she interjected, the odd, sardonic gleam deepening in her black eyes.

"But I didn't describe you as you are," I protested, eagerly. "I made you a blonde! Don't you remember? And I made a Western city the scene of the trial, and changed some of the conditions of the—" I faltered—"of the crime."

"As if that mattered," she said, coolly. "You described *me*—to the shape of my finger-nails, the buttons on my shoes." Suddenly she laughed. "Those dreadful buttons! I see them still in my dreams. It seems to me that I was always sewing them on. The only parts of me I allowed to move in the courtroom were my feet. No one could see them, under my skirt. I used to loosen a button almost every day. Then of course I had to sew them on. I had a sick fear of looking messy and untidy—of degenerating physically."

She faced the wide windows and the snow-filled sky. In my own chair, facing the fire, I also directly faced her.

"I'm going to Europe," she announced at last. "I'm sailing to-morrow morning—to be gone 'for good,' as the children say. That's why I came tonight." For a moment she sat in silence, wholly, restfully at her ease. Dimly I began to realize that she was enjoying the intimacy of the moment, the sense of human companionship, and again it came to me how tragically lonely she must be. She had no near friends, and in the minds of all others there must always be the hideous interrogation-point that stood between her and life. At best she had "the benefit of the doubt." And I had helped to destroy even the little that was left to her. I could have fallen at her feet.

"I'm going away," she added, "to see if there is any place for me in the life abroad. If there is I want to find it. If I were the sort of woman who went in for good works, my problem would be easier; but you see I'm not."

I smiled. I could not see her as a worker in organized charity, parceling out benefits tied with red tape. It was no effort, however, to picture her doing many human and beautiful kindnesses in her own way.

We talked of Europe. I had never been there. She spoke of northern Africa, of rides over Morocco hills, of a caravan journey from Tangier to Fez, of Algerian nights, of camping in the desert, of palms and ripe figs and of tropical gardens. It was fascinating talk in the purple lights of my driftwood fire, with a snow-storm beating at my windows. Suddenly she checked herself.

"I think, after all," she said, lightly, "you're rather good for me. You've done me good tonight. You did me good the day you visited me at Fairview. You were so young, so much in earnest, so much in love with life, and you saw so much with your big, solemn eyes. You gave me something new to think about, and I needed it. So—don't regret anything."

I felt the tears spring to my eyes.

She drew on her gloves and buttoned them slowly, still smiling at me.

"I might never even have seen your story," she went on, quietly, "if my maid had not brought it to me. I don't read *The Woman's Friend*." There was a hint of the old superciliousness in her tone and about her upper lip as she spoke. "On the whole, I don't think it did me any harm. The opinion of strangers is the least important thing in my little arctic circle. So, forget me. Good night—and good-by."

I kept her hand in mine for a moment. "Good-by," I said. "Peace be with you."

She drew her veil down over her face, and moved to the door. I followed and opened it for her. On the threshold she stopped and hesitated, looking straight at me; and in that instant I knew as surely as I ever knew anything in my life that now at last her guard was down—that from the fastness of her soul something horrible had escaped and was leaping toward me. She cast a quick glance up and down the outer hall. It was dim and empty. I hardly dared to breathe.

"There is one thing more," she said, and her words rushed out with an odd effect of breathlessness under the continued calm of her manner. "The only really human emotion I've felt in a long time is—an upheaval of curiosity."

I looked at her, and waited.

She hesitated an instant longer, then, standing very close to me, gripped my shoulders hard, her eyes deep in mine, her voice so low I hardly caught her meaning.

"Oh, wise young judge!" she whispered. "Tell me, before we part—*how did you know?*"

Source: *May Iverson's Career* (Harper & Brothers, 1914).

"THE REVOLT OF
TILDY MEARS"

(1914)

Every seat in the primitive town hall was occupied, and a somber
frieze of Dakota plainsmen and their sad-faced wives decorated
the rough, unpainted sides of the building. On boxes in the narrow aisles, between long rows of pine boards on which were
seated the early arrivals, late-comers squatted discontentedly,
among them a dozen women carrying fretful babies, to whom
from time to time they addressed a comforting murmur as they
swung them, cradle-fashion, in their tired arms.

The exercises of the evening had not yet begun, but almost
every eye in the big, silent, patient assemblage was fixed on a
woman, short and stout, with snow-white hair and a young and
vivid face, who had just taken her place on the platform, escorted
by a self-conscious official of the little town. Everyone in that
gathering had heard of Dr. Anna Harland; few had yet heard her
speak, but all knew what she represented: "new-fangled notions
about women"—women's rights, woman suffrage, feminism, unsettling ideas which threatened to disturb the peace of minds accustomed to run in well-worn grooves.[1] Many of the men and
women in her audience had driven twenty, thirty, or forty miles
across the plains to hear her, but there was no unanimity in the
expressions with which they studied her now as she sat before
them. In the men's regard were curiosity, prejudice, good-humored
tolerance, or a blend of all three. The women's faces held a different meaning: pride, affectionate interest, admiration tinged with
hope; and here and there a hint of something deeper, a wireless
message that passed from soul to soul.

At a melodeon on the left of the platform a pale local belle, who had volunteered her services, awaited the signal to play the opening chords of the song that was to precede the speaker's address.[2] In brackets high on the rough walls a few kerosene lamps vaguely illuminated the scene, while from the open night outside came the voices of cowboys noisily greeting late arrivals and urging them to "go on in an' git a change of heart!"

The musician received her signal—a nod from the chairman of the evening—and the next moment the voices of a relieved and relaxed audience were heartily swelling the familiar strains of "The Battle Hymn of the Republic."[3] As the men and women before her sang on, Dr. Harland watched them, the gaze of the brilliant dark eyes under her straight black brows keen and intent. Even yet she had not decided what she meant to say to these people. Something in the music, something in the atmosphere, would surely give her a cue, she felt, before she began to speak.

Sitting near her on the platform, I studied both her and her audience. The Far West and its people were new to me; so was this great leader of the woman's cause. But it behooved me to know her and to know her well, for I had accompanied her on this Western campaign for the sole purpose of writing a series of articles on her life and work, to be published in the magazine of which I had recently been appointed assistant editor. During our long railroad journeys and drives over hills and plains she had talked to me of the past. Now, I knew, I was to see her again perform the miracle at which I had not yet ceased to marvel—the transformation of hundreds of indifferent or merely casually interested persons into a mass of shouting enthusiasts, ready to enlist under her yellow banner and follow wherever she led.[4]

Tonight, as she rose and for a moment stood silent before her audience, I could see her, as usual, gathering them up, drawing them to her by sheer force of magnetism, before she spoke a word.

"My friends," she began, in the beautiful voice whose vibrating contralto notes reached every person in the great hall, "last Monday, at Medora, I was asked by a missionary who is going to India to send a message to the women of that land. I said to him, 'Tell them the world was made for women, too.'[5] Tonight I am here to give you the same message. The world is women's, too. The West is women's, too. You have helped to make it, you splendid,

pioneer women, who have borne with your husbands the heat
and burden of the long working-days. You have held down your
claims through the endless months of Western winters, while
your men were away; you have toiled with them in the fields; you
have endured with them the tragedies of cyclones, of droughts, of
sickness, of starvation. If woman's work is in the home alone, as
our opponents say it is, you have been most unwomanly. For you
have remained in the home only long enough to bear your children, to care for them, to feed them and your husbands. The rest
of the time you have done a man's work in the West. The toil has
been yours as well as man's; the reward of such toil should be
shared by you. The West is yours, too. Now it holds work for you
even greater than that you have done in the past, and I am here to
beg you to begin that work."

The address went on. In the dim light of the ill-smelling lamps I
could see the audience leaning forward, intent, fascinated. Even
among the men easy tolerance was giving place to eager response;
on row after row of the rough benches the spectators were already
clay in the hands of the speaker, to be molded, for the moment at
least, into the form she chose to give them. My eyes momentarily
touched, then fastened intently on a face in the third row on the
left. It was the face of a woman—a little, middle-aged woman of
the primitive Western type—her graying hair combed straight
back from a high, narrow forehead, her thin lips slightly parted,
the flat chest under her gingham dress rising and falling with emotion. But my interest was held by her eyes—brown eyes, blazing
eyes, almost the eyes of a fanatic. Unswervingly they rested on the
speaker's face, while the strained attention, the parted lips, the attitude of the woman's quivering little body betrayed almost uncontrollable excitement. At that instant I should not have been
surprised to see her spring to her feet and shout, *"Alleluia!"*[6]

A moment later I realized that Dr. Harland had seen her, too;
that she was, indeed, intensely conscious of her, and was direct-
ing many of her best points to this absorbed listener. Here was
the perfect type she was describing to her audience—the true
woman pioneer, who not only worked and prayed, but who read
and thought and aspired. The men and women under the flicker-
ing lights were by this time as responsive to the speaker's words
as a child to its mother's voice. They laughed, they wept, they

nodded, they sighed. When the usual collection was taken up they showed true Western generosity, and when the lecture was over they crowded forward to shake hands with the woman leader, and to exhaust their limited vocabulary in shy tributes to her eloquence. Far on the outskirts of the wide circle that had formed around her I saw the little woman with the blazing eyes, vainly endeavoring to force her way toward us through the crowd. Dr. Harland observed her at the same time and motioned to me.

"Will you ask her to wait, Miss Iverson?" she asked. "I would like to talk to her before she slips away." And she added, with her characteristic twinkle, "That woman would make a perfect 'Exhibit A' for my lecture."

I skirted the throng and touched the arm of the little woman just as she had given up hope of reaching the speaker, and was moving toward the door. She started and stared at me, almost as if the touch of my fingers had awakened her from a dream.

"Dr. Harland asks if you will wait a few moments till the others leave," I told her. "She is anxious to meet you."

The brown-eyed woman drew in a deep breath.

"Tha's whut I want," she exclaimed, ecstatically, "but it looked like I couldn't git near her."

We sat down on an empty bench half-way down the hall, and watched the human stream flow toward and engulf the lecturer. "Ain't she jest wonderful?" breathed my companion. "She knows us women better 'n we know ourselves. She knows all we done an' how we feel about it. I felt like she was tellin' them people all my secrets, but I didn't mind." She hesitated, then added dreamily, "It's high time men was told whut their women are thinkin' an' can't say fer themselves."

In the excited group around the speaker a baby, held high in its mother's arms to avoid being injured in the crush, shrieked out a sudden protest. My new acquaintance regarded it with sympathetic eyes.

"I've raised six of 'em," she told me. "My oldest is a girl nineteen. My youngest is a boy of twelve. My big girl she's lookin' after the house an' the fam'ly while I'm gone. I druv sixty miles 'cross the plains to hear Dr. Harland. It took me two days, an' it's jest about wore out my horse—but this is worth it. I ain't had sech a night sence I was a girl."

She looked at me, her brown eyes lighting up again with their queer, excited fires.

"My Jim he 'most fell dead when I told him I was comin'," she went on. "But I says to him, 'I ain't been away from this place one minute in twenty years,' I says. 'Now I guess you folks can git 'long without me fer a few days. For, Jim,' I says, 'ef I don't git away, ef I don't go somewhere an' have some change, somethin's goin' to snap, an' I guess it'll be me!'"

"You mean," I exclaimed, in surprise, "that you've never left your ranch in twenty years?"

She nodded.

"Not once," she corroborated. "Not fer a minute. You know whut the summers are—work, work from daylight to dark; an' in the winters I had t' hol' down the claim while Jim he went to the city an' worked. Sometimes he'd only git home once or twice the hull winter. Then when we begin to git on, seemed like 'twas harder than ever. Jim he kept addin' more land an' more stock to whut we had, an' there was more hands to be waited on, an' the babies come pretty fast. Lately Jim he's gone to Chicago every year to sell his cattle, but I ain't bin able to git away till now."

During her eager talk—a talk that gushed forth like a long-repressed stream finding a sudden outlet—she had been leaning toward me with her arm on the back of the bench and her shining eyes on mine. Now, as if remembering her "company manners," she sat back stiffly, folded her work-roughened hands primly in her lap, and sighed with supreme content.

"My!" she whispered, happily, "I feel like I was in a diff'rent world. It don't seem possible that only sixty miles out on the plains that ranch is right there, an' everything is goin' on without me. An' here I be, hearin' the music, an' all the folks singin' to-gether, an' that wonderful woman talkin' like she did! I feel"—she hesitated for a comparison, and then went on, with the laugh of a happy girl—"I feel like I was up in a balloon an' on my way to heaven!"

I forgot the heat of the crowded hall, the smell of the smoking lamps, the shuffle of hobnailed shoes on the pine floors, the wails of fretful babies. I almost felt that I, too, was floating off with this ecstatic stranger in the balloon of her imagination.

"I see," I murmured. "You're tired of drudgery. You haven't played enough in all these years."

She swung round again until she faced me, her sallow cheeks flushed, her eager, brilliant eyes on mine.

"I ain't played none at all," she said. "I dunno what play is. An' work ain't the only thing I'm tired of. I'm tired of everything. I'm tired of everything—except this."

Her voice lingered on the last two words. Her eyes left my face for an instant and followed the lecturer, of whose white head we obtained a glimpse from time to time as the crowd opened around her. Still gazing toward her, but now as if unseeingly, the plainswoman went on, her voice dropping to a lower, more confidential note.

"I'm sick of everything," she repeated. "Most of all, I'm sick of the plains and the sky—stretching on and on and on and on, like they do, as if they was no end to 'em. Sometimes when I'm alone I stand at my door an' look at 'em an' shake my fists an' shriek. I begun to think they wasn't anything but them nowhere. It seemed 's if the little town back East where I come from was jest a place I dreamed of—it couldn't really be. Nothin' *could* be 'cept those plains an' the cattle an' the sky. Then, this spring—"

She turned again to face me.

"I dunno why I'm tellin' you all this," she broke off, suddenly. "Guess it's because I ain't had no one to talk to confidential fer so long, an' you look like you understand."

"I do understand," I told her.

She nodded.

"Well, this spring," she went on, "I begun to hate everything, same as I hated the plains. I couldn't exactly hate my children; but it seemed to me they never did nothin' right, an' I jest had to keep tellin' myself they was mine, an' they was young an' didn't understand how they worried me by things they done. Then the hands drove me 'most crazy. They was one man—why, jes' to have that man pass the door made me feel sick, an' yet I hadn't nothin' again' him, really. An' finally, last of all, Jim—even Jim—"

Her voice broke. Sudden tears filled her eyes, quenching for the moment the sparks that burned there.

"Jim's a good man," she continued, steadily, after a moment's pause. "He's a good, hard-workin' man. He's good to me in his way, an' he's good to the children. But of course he ain't got much time for us. He never was a talker. He's a worker, Jim is, an' when night comes he's so tired he falls asleep over the fire. But everything he done always seemed pretty near right to me—till this spring."

Her voice flattened and died on the last three words. For a moment she sat silent, brooding, a strange puzzled look in her brown eyes. The crowd around Dr. Harland was thinning out, and people were leaving the hall. We could easily have reached her now, but I sat still, afraid to dam the verbal freshet that was following so many frozen winters.[7]

"This spring," she went on, at last, "it jest seems like I can't bear to have even Jim around." She checked herself and touched my arm timidly, almost apologetically. "It's a terrible thing to say, ain't it?" she almost whispered, and added slowly, "It's a terrible thing to *feel*. I can't bear to see him come into the room. I can't bear the way he eats, or the way he smokes, or the way he sets down, or the way he gits up, or the way he breathes. He does 'em all jest like he always has. They ain't nothin' wrong with 'em. But I can't bear 'em no more." She beat her hands together softly, with a queer, frantic gesture. Her voice took on a note of rising excitement. "I can't," she gasped. "I can't, I *can't*!"

I rose.

"Come," I said, cheerfully. "Dr. Harland is free now. I want you to talk to her. She can help you. She's a very wise woman."

A momentary flicker of something I did not recognize shone in my companion's eyes. Was it doubt or pity, or both?

"She ain't a married woman, is she?" she asked, quietly, as she rose and walked down the aisle by my side.

I laughed.

"No," I conceded, "she isn't, and neither am I. But you know even the Bible admits that of ten virgins five were wise!"[8]

Her face, somber now, showed no reflection of my amusement. She seemed to be considering our claims to wisdom, turning over in her mind the possibility of help from either of us, and experiencing a depressing doubt.

"Well, you're women, anyway," she murmured, at last, a pathetic note of uncertainty lingering in her voice.

"Will you tell me your name?" I asked, "so that I may introduce you properly to Dr. Harland?"

"Tildy Mears," she answered, promptly; then added, with stiff formality, "Mrs. James Mears of the X. X. M. Ranch."

We were already facing Dr. Harland, and I presented Mrs. Mears without further delay. The leader met her with the brilliant smile, the close hand-clasp, the warm, human sympathy which rarely failed to thrill the man or woman she was greeting. Under their influence Mrs. Mears expanded like a thirsty plant in a gentle shower. Within five minutes the two women were friends.

"You're at the hotel, of course," Dr. Harland asked, when she heard of the sixty-mile drive across the country. "Then you must have supper with Miss Iverson and me. We always want something after these long evenings, and I will have it sent up to our sitting-room, so that we can have a comfortable talk."

Half an hour later we were grouped around the table in the little room, and over the cold meat, canned peaches, lemonade, and biscuits which formed our collation Tildy Mears retold her story, adding innumerable details and intimate touches under the stimulus of the doctor's interest.[9] At the end of it Dr. Harland sat for a long moment in silent thought. Then, from the briskness with which she began to speak, I knew that she had found some solution of the human problem before us.

"Mrs. Mears," she said, abruptly, and without any comment on the other's recital, "I wish you would travel around with us for a fortnight. We're going to remain in this part of the state, and you would find our meetings extremely interesting. On the other hand, you could give me a great deal of help and information, and, though I cannot offer you a salary, I will gladly pay your expenses."

This was a plan very characteristic of Dr. Harland, to whom half-way measures of any kind made no appeal. I looked at Tildy Mears. For an instant, under the surprise of the leader's unexpected words, she had sat still, stunned; in the next, her eyes had flashed to us one of their ecstatic messages, as if she had grasped all the other woman's proposition held of change, of interest, of growth. Then abruptly the light faded, went out.

"I'd love to," she said, dully, "I'd jest *love* to! But of course it ain't possible. Why, I got to start home tomorrer. Jim," she gulped, bringing out the name with an obvious effort, "Jim expecks me back Sat'day night."

"Listen to me, Mrs. Mears"—Dr. Harland leaned forward, her compelling eyes deep in those of the Western woman—"I'm going to speak to you very frankly—as if we were old friends; as if we were sisters, as, indeed, we are."

Tildy Mears nodded. Her eyes, dull and tired now, looked trustfully back at the other woman.

"I feel like we are," she agreed. And she added, "You kin say anything you've a mind to."

"Then I want to say this."

I had never seen Dr. Harland more interested, more impressive. Into what she was saying to the forlorn little creature before her she threw all she had of persuasiveness, of magnetism, and of power.

"If you don't have a change," she continued, "and a very radical change, you will surely have a bad nervous breakdown. That is what I want to save you from. I cannot imagine anything that would do it more effectively than to campaign with us for a time, and have the whole current of your thoughts turned in a new direction. Why, don't you understand"—her deep voice was full of feeling; for the moment at least she was more interested in one human soul than in hundreds of human votes—"it isn't that you have ceased to care for your home and your family. It's only that your tortured nerves are crying out against the horrible monotony of your life. Give them the change they are demanding and everything else will come right. Go back and put them through the old strain, and—well, I'm afraid everything will go wrong."

As if something in the other's words had galvanized her into sudden action Mrs. Mears sprang to her feet. Like a wild thing she circled the room, beating her hands together.

"I can't go back!" she cried. "I can't go back! Whut 'll I do? Oh, whut 'll I do?"

"Do what I am advising you to do."

Dr. Harland's quiet voice steadied the hysterical woman. Under its calming influence I could see her pull herself together.

"Write Mr. Mears that you are coming with us, and give him our advance route, so that he will know exactly where you are all the time. If your daughter can manage your home for five days she can manage it for two weeks. And your little jaunt need not cost your husband one penny."

"I brought twenty dollars with me," quavered Tildy Mears.

"Keep it," advised the temporarily reckless leader of the woman's cause. "When we reach Bismarck you can buy yourself a new dress and get some little presents to take home to the children."[10]

Tildy Mears stopped her reckless pacing of the room and stood for a moment very still, her eyes fixed on a worn spot in the rug at her feet.

"I reckon I will," she then said, slowly. "Sence you ask me, I jest reckon I'll stay."

The next evening, during her remarks to the gathering she was then addressing, Dr. Harland abruptly checked herself.

"But there is someone here who knows more about that than I do," she said, casually, referring to a point she was covering. "Mrs. Mears, who is on the platform with me tonight, is one of you. She knows from twenty years of actual experience what I am learning from study and observation. She can tell you better than I can how many buckets of water a plainsman's wife carries into an unpiped ranch during the day. Will you tell us, Mrs. Mears?"

She asked a few questions, and hesitatingly, stammeringly at first, the panic-stricken plainswoman answered her. Then a woman in the audience spoke up timidly to compare notes, and in five minutes more Dr. Harland was sitting quietly in the background while Tildy Mears, her brown eyes blazing with interest and excitement, talked to her fellow plainswomen about the problems she and they were meeting together.

Seeing the success of Dr. Harland's experiment, I felt an increased respect for that remarkable woman. She had known that this would happen; she had realized, as I had not, that Tildy Mears could talk to others as simply and as pregnantly as to us, and that her human appeal to her sister workers would be far greater than any even Anna Harland herself could make. One night she described a stampede in words that made a slow chill run the length of my spine. Half an hour later she was discussing "hired hands," with a shrewd philosophy and a quaint humor that drew good natured guffaws from "hired hands" themselves as well as from their employers in the audience.

Within the next few days Tildy Mears became a strong feature of our campaign. Evening after evening, in primitive Dakota towns, her self-consciousness now wholly gone, she supplemented Dr. Harland's lectures by a talk to her sister women, so simple, so homely, so crudely eloquent that its message reached every heart. During the days she studied the suffrage question, reading and rereading the books we had brought with us, and asking as many questions as an eager and precocious child. Openly and unabashedly Dr. Harland gloried in her.

"Why, she's a born orator," she told me one day, almost breathlessly. "She's a feminine Lincoln. There's no limit to her possibilities. I'd like to take her East. I'd like to educate her—train her. Then she could come back here and go through the West like a whirlwind."

The iridescent bubble was floating so beautifully that it seemed a pity to prick it; but I did, with a callous reminder.

"How about her home?" I suggested—"and her children? and her husband?"

Dr. Harland frowned and bit her lip.

"Humph!" she muttered, her voice taking on the flat notes of disappointment and chagrin. "Humph! I'd forgotten them."

For a moment she stood reflecting, readjusting her plans to a scale which embraced the husband, the home, and the children of her protegee. Then her brow cleared, her irresistible twinkle broke over her face; she smiled like a mischievous child.

"I had forgotten them," she repeated. "Maybe"—this with irrepressible hopefulness—"maybe Tildy will, too!"

That Tildy did nothing of the kind was proved to us all too soon. Six days had passed, and the growing fame of Mrs. Mears as a suffrage speaker was attracting the attention of editors in the towns we visited. It reached its climax at a mass-meeting in Sedalia, where for an hour the little woman talked to an audience of several hundred, making all Dr. Harland's favorite points in her own simpler, homelier words, while the famous leader of the cause beamed on her proudly from the side of the stage.[11] After the doctor's speech the two women held an informal reception, which the Mayor graced, and to which the Board of Aldermen also lent the light of their presence. These high dignitaries gave most of their attention to our leader; she could answer any question they wished to ask, as well as many others they were extremely careful not to bring up. But the women in the audience, the babies, the growing boys and girls—all these turned to Tildy Mears. From the closing words of her speech until she disappeared within the hotel she was followed by an admiring throng. As I caught the final flash of her brown eyes before her bedroom engulfed her it seemed to me that she looked pale and tired. She had explained that she wanted no supper, but before I went to bed, hearing her still moving around her room, I rapped at her door.

"Wouldn't you like a sandwich?" I asked, when she had opened it. "And a glass of lemonade?"

She hesitated. Then, seeing that I had brought these modest refreshments on a tray, she stepped back and allowed me to pass in. There was an unusual self-consciousness in her manner, an unusual bareness in the effect of the room. The nails on the wall had been stripped of her garments. On the floor lay an open suitcase closely packed.

"Why!" I gasped. "Why are you packing? We're going to stay here over tomorrow, you know."

For an instant she stood silent before me, looking like a child caught in some act of disobedience by a relentless parent. Then her head went up.

"Yes," she said, quietly. "I'm packed. I'm goin' home!"

"Going home!" I repeated, stupidly. It seemed to me that all I could do was to echo her words. "When?" I finally brought out.

"To-morrer mornin'." She spoke almost defiantly. "I wanted to go tonight," she added, "but there wasn't no train. I got to go back an' start from Dickinson, where I left my horse."[12]

"But why?" I persisted. "Why? I thought you were going to be with us another week at least?"

"Well"—she drew out the word consideringly. Then, on a sudden resolve, she gave her explanation. "They was a man in the fourth row tonight that looked like Jim."

"Yes?" I said, and waited. "Was he Mr. Mears?" I asked, at last.

"No."

She knelt, and closed and locked the suit-case.

"He looked like Jim," she repeated, as if that ended the discussion.

For an instant the situation was too complicated for me. Then, in a flash of understanding, I remembered that only the week before I had been made suddenly homesick for New York by one fleeting glimpse of a man whose profile was like that of Godfrey Morris. Without another word I sought Dr. Harland and broke the news to her in two pregnant sentences.

"Mrs. Mears is going home tomorrow morning. She saw a man at the meeting tonight who looked like her husband."

Dr. Harland, who was preparing for bed, laid down the hair-brush she was using, slipped a wrapper over her nightgown, and started for Mrs. Mears's room. I followed. Characteristically, our leader disdained preliminaries.

"But, my dear woman," she exclaimed, "you can't leave us in the lurch like this. You're announced to speak in Sweetbriar and Mendan and Bismarck within the coming week."

"He looked jest like Jim," murmured Tildy Mears, in simple but full rebuttal. She was standing with her back to the door, and she did not turn as we entered. Her eyes were set toward the north, where her home was, and her children and Jim. Her manner dismissed Sweetbriar, Mendan, and Bismarck as if they were the flowers of last year.[13] Suddenly she wheeled, crossed the room, and caught Dr. Harland by the shoulders.

"Woman," she cried, "I'm homesick. Can't ye understand that, even ef you ain't got a home an' a husband ye been neglectin' fer days, like I have? I'm homesick." Patiently she brought out her refrain again. "The man looked jest like Jim," she ended.

She turned away, and with feverish haste put her case on a chair, and her jacket and hat on the case, topping the collection with an old pair of driving-gloves. The completeness of this preparation seemed to give her some satisfaction. She continued with more animation.

"I'm startin' early," she explained. "I told the hotel man soon's I come in to have me called at five o'clock. So I'll say good-by now. An' thank ye both fer all yer kindness," she ended, primly.

Dr. Harland laughed. Then, impulsively, she took both the woman's toil-hardened hands in hers.

"Good-by, then, and God bless you," she said. "My cure has worked. I'll comfort myself with that knowledge."

For a moment the eyes of Tildy Mears fell.

"You ben mighty good," she said. "You both ben good. Don't think I ain't grateful." She hesitated, then went on in halting explanation. "'S long's you ain't married," she said, "an' ain't got nothin' else to do, it's fine to travel round an' talk to folks. But someway sence I see that man tonight, settin' there lookin' like Jim, I realize things is different with us married women."

She drew her small figure erect, her voice taking on an odd suggestion of its ringing platform note.

"Talkin' is one thing," she said, tersely, "livin' is another thing. P'rhaps you ain't never thought of that. But I see the truth now, an' I see it clear."

Her peroration filled the little room, and like a swelling organ tone rolled through the open door and down the stairs, where it reached the far recesses of the hall below.[14] Her lean right arm shot upward in her one characteristic gesture, as if she called on high Heaven itself to bear witness to the wisdom of her words in this, her last official utterance.

"Woman's place," ended Tildy Mears, "is in the home!"

Source: *May Iverson's Career* (Harper & Brothers, 1914).

IV

COLLABORATION AND LITERARY ACTIVISM: JORDAN AS EDITOR AND ADVISER

In 1900, Jordan made a move from newspaper to magazine publishing when she was recruited for the position of editor of *Harper's Bazar*. As an experienced editor and journalist, and as an author of growing fame, she asserted a strong editorial voice, notably expressed in her editorial columns, which appeared at the beginning of each issue. Determined to modernize the magazine in light of significant shifts in both gender ideologies and the literary marketplace, she brought leadership and vision to her new role. During her tenure as editor (1900–1913), the *Bazar* expanded its literary offerings and books coverage and added more color plates and illustrations to its pages, for instance. Jordan devoted herself to retaining established writers from the *Harper's* universe (such as William Dean Howells and Mark Twain) while recruiting new voices into her pages (Charlotte Perkins Gilman, Henry James, and Mary Heaton Vorse, among scores of others). She also spearheaded multiple special projects, perhaps none so innovative (or cumbersome) as her work with Howells on the

1908 composite novel serialized in the magazine with separate chapters each written by a different author. Though described by Jordan as "a mess," *The Whole Family: A Novel by Twelve Authors* made Jordan's professional editorial acumen a public commodity beyond the field of magazine journalism.[1]

In 1913, Jordan moved on from *Harper's Bazar* to become a literary adviser to book publishers Harper & Brothers, a position from which she amplified the careers of many women writers, while continuing to publish fiction herself. One of Jordan's most significant projects during this period was National American Woman Suffrage Association (NAWSA) president Rev. Dr. Anna Howard Shaw's autobiography, *The Story of a Pioneer* (1915), selections from which appear here. Jordan admired Shaw (1847–1919), a trained physician, one of the first ordained female Methodist ministers in the US, and a longtime, close collaborator with Susan B. Anthony. In Jordan's own memoir, she described Shaw as "probably the best woman speaker America ever had."[2]

Jordan had edited and published Shaw's work prior to their collaboration on *The Story of a Pioneer*. Shaw's article "Why I Went into Suffrage Work" appeared in *Harper's Bazar* in September 1912; politically, the piece affirmed the necessity of women's financial independence and, editorially, it convinced Jordan that Shaw, though a transformative speaker, was a weak writer— who nonetheless deserved a book to tell her story.[3] Shaw initially resisted Jordan's suggestion that she write an autobiography, pleading her busy schedule as a lecturer during a decade of statewide campaigns to secure the ballot for women. When Shaw's agenda was derailed by a leg injury, Jordan shrewdly took advantage of the opportunity, working closely with Shaw on the project while the suffrage pioneer was recuperating at the McAlpin Hotel in Manhattan.

Every morning for three weeks, Jordan and her secretary, Charlotte Lambrecht, would visit Shaw in her hotel room. Drawing on her journalistic skills as an interviewer, Jordan asked Shaw questions and Lambrecht recorded the proceedings in shorthand. Correspondence between Shaw and Jordan from the period indicates mutual admiration and affection, as well as a shared acknowledgment that Jordan's editorial persistence made the book a reality, fostering its potential as a publicity tool for

NAWSA and the organization's state affiliates. Lambrecht typed and chronologically arranged her notes for Jordan, who created an outline, wrote the narrative, and read it, chapter by chapter, to Shaw for approval. It was published serially in *Metropolitan Magazine* before its release as a book, in which "with the Collaboration of Elizabeth Jordan" appeared on the title page.

Eager to credit her collaborator, Shaw once introduced Jordan at a party as "Miss Jordan, who wrote my book."[4] That their collaboration was a gesture of political solidarity and an affirmation of their shared status as public women becomes clear in the framing of Jordan's prose in the selections that follow, as well as in the trajectory of Jordan's career in the years immediately following the book's publication, when she became more directly involved in New York State suffrage politics.

"The Great Cause" outlines Shaw's awakening as an activist and her decision in 1885 to resign her position as a minister to take up full-time work "for suffrage, for temperance, for social purity."[5] Jordan's editorial and literary fingerprints are evident in the anecdotes marshaled to convey the import of Shaw's choice. Both a very young girl and an older male parishioner—a captain who speaks in dialect—express their devotion to Shaw's spiritual direction and attest to the impact she has had on them through her pulpit. Though Shaw is recounting events from the 1880s, they were being published for an audience of readers in the 1910s, when multiple state ballot initiatives were afoot, essentially asking men to vote to enfranchise women.

Jordan's infusion of the facts of Shaw's biography with the characters best positioned to make that case for the power of a woman's voice—a little girl and a gruff captain—reflects the deft use of narrative, punctuated by humor and wit, that hallmarked her journalism and her fiction, even as it anticipates her more hands-on participation in the 1917 (successful) statewide effort to secure votes for the women of New York. Elsewhere in the chapter, Shaw describes giving a suffrage talk to a group of cattlemen with whom she is snowbound on a train. They listen. These stories of her life function as a tool of persuasion and inspiration for potential allies, not simply polemic to rally her base.

Like Jordan's own memoir, Shaw's collaboratively authored autobiography is long on mentioning famous names (for example,

Ralph Waldo Emerson, Louisa May Alcott, William Lloyd Garrison, Julia Ward Howe) and shorter on details like dates and descriptive specifics of her encounters with such luminaries. In both instances, however, Shaw and Jordan are not so much namedropping as providing a historical record of the often-invisible labor of organizing and network-building that define activism and editorial work alike.

In "'Aunt Susan,'" Shaw—through Jordan's words—repeatedly illustrates the labor that underpinned her close relationship with Susan B. Anthony (who had died in 1906) as they tirelessly traveled the country lecturing and advocating together, ignoring both comforts and physical necessities in service to their mission. "To her failure was merely another opportunity," says Shaw of Anthony, a message that in the mid-1910s would have had particular meaning to New York suffragists such as Jordan.[6] In 1915, the Empire State Campaign to enfranchise women by referendum failed; two years later, the newly constituted New York State Woman Suffrage Party would enlist Jordan, a member of its "Contributors-editors Committee," to helm its publicity project during its second, successful campaign in 1917. The outcome of that undertaking was *The Sturdy Oak: A Composite Novel of American Politics*, a suffrage composite novel fashioned fully by Jordan's public persona as an editor and well-known literary figure in her own right. Today, it remains her best-known contribution to American literary culture. Jordan's engagement with the late suffrage movement was an inflection point in her career, pivotal to her identity as a public woman and literary activist.

FROM
THE STORY OF A PIONEER,
BY ANNA HOWARD SHAW WITH THE COLLABORATION OF ELIZABETH JORDAN

CHAPTER VII

"THE GREAT CAUSE"

(1915)

There is a theory that every seven years each human being undergoes a complete physical reconstruction, with corresponding changes in his mental and spiritual make-up. Possibly it was due to this reconstruction that, at the end of seven years on Cape Cod, my soul sent forth a sudden call to arms. I was, it reminded me, taking life too easily; I was in danger of settling into an agreeable routine. The work of my two churches made little drain on my superabundant vitality, and not even the winning of a medical degree and the increasing demands of my activities on the lecture platform wholly eased my conscience. I was happy, for I loved my people and they seemed to love me. It would have been pleasant to go on almost indefinitely, living the life of a country minister and telling myself that what I could give to my flock made such a life worthwhile.

But all the time, deep in my heart, I realized the needs of the outside world, and heard its prayer for workers. My theological and medical courses in Boston, with the experiences that accompanied them, had greatly widened my horizon. Moreover, at my invitation, many of the noble women of the day were coming to East Dennis to lecture, bringing with them the stirring atmosphere of the conflicts they were waging.[1] One of the first of these was my friend Mary A. Livermore;[2] and after her came Julia Ward Howe,[3] Anna Garlin Spencer,[4] Lucy Stone,[5] Mary F. Eastman,[6] and many others, each charged with inspiration for my people and with a special message for me, which she sent forth unknowingly and which I alone heard. They were fighting great battles, these women—for suffrage, for temperance, for social purity—and in every word they uttered I heard a rallying-cry. So it was that, in 1885, I suddenly pulled myself up to a radical decision and sent my resignation to the trustees of the two churches whose pastor I had been since 1878.

The action caused a demonstration of regret which made it hard to keep to my resolution and leave these men and women whose friendship was among the dearest of my possessions. But when we had all talked things over, many of them saw the situation as I did. No doubt there were those, too, who felt that a change of ministry would be good for the churches. During the weeks that followed my resignation I received many odd tributes, and of these one of the most amusing came from a young girl in the parish, who broke into loud protests when she heard that I was going away. To comfort her I predicted that she would now have a man minister—doubtless a very nice man. But the young person continued to sniffle disconsolately.

"I don't want a man," she wailed. "I don't like to see men in pulpits. They look so awkward." Her grief culminated in a final outburst. "They're all arms and legs!" she sobbed.

When my resignation was finally accepted, and the time of my departure drew near, the men of the community spent much of their leisure in discussing it and me. The social center of East Dennis was a certain grocery, to which almost every man in town regularly wended his way, and from which all the gossip of the town emanated. Here the men sat for hours, tilted back in their chairs, whittling the rungs until they nearly cut the chairs from under them, and telling one another all they knew or had heard about their fellow-townsmen. Then, after each session, they would return home and repeat the gossip to their wives. I used to say that I would give a dollar to any woman in East Dennis who could quote a bit of gossip which did not come from the men at that grocery. Even my old friend Captain Doane, fine and high-minded citizen though he was, was not above enjoying the mild diversion of these social gatherings, and on one occasion at least he furnished the best part of the entertainment. The departing minister was, it seemed, the topic of the day's discussion, and, to tease Captain Doane one young man who knew the strength of his friendship for me suddenly began to speak, then pursed up his lips and looked eloquently mysterious.[7] As he had expected, Captain Doane immediately pounced on him.

"What's the matter with you?" demanded the old man. "Hev you got anything agin Miss Shaw?"

The young man sighed and murmured that if he wished he could repeat a charge never before made against a Cape Cod minister, but—and he shut his lips more obviously. The other men, who were in the plot, grinned, and this added the last touch to Captain Doane's indignation. He sprang to his feet. One of his peculiarities was a constant misuse of words, and now, in his excitement, he outdid himself.

"You've made an incineration against Miss Shaw," he shouted. "Do you hear—*an incineration*! Take it back or take a lickin'!"

The young man decided that the joke had gone far enough, so he answered, mildly: "Well, it is said that all the women in town are in love with Miss Shaw. Has that been charged against any other minister here?"

The men roared with laughter, and Captain Doane sat down, looking sheepish.

"All I got to say is this," he muttered: "That gal has been in this community for seven years, and she 'ain't done a thing during the hull seven years that anyone kin lay a finger on!"

The men shouted again at this back-handed tribute, and the old fellow left the grocery in a huff. Later I was told of the "incineration" and his eloquent defense of me, and I thanked him for it. But I added:

"I hear you said I haven't done a thing in seven years that anyone can lay a finger on?"

"I said it," declared the Captain, "and I'll stand by it."

"Haven't I done any good?" I asked.

"Sartin you have," he assured me, heartily. "Lots of good."

"Well," I said, "can't you put your finger on that?"

The Captain looked startled. "Why—why—Sister Shaw," he stammered, "you know I didn't mean *that*! What I meant," he repeated, slowly and solemnly, "was that the hull time you been here you ain't done nothin' anybody could put a finger on!"

Captain Doane apparently shared my girl parishioner's prejudice against men in the pulpit, for long afterward, on one of my visits to Cape Cod, he admitted that he now went to church very rarely.

"When I heard you preach," he explained, "I gen'ally followed you through and I knowed where you was a-comin' out. But these young fellers that come from the theological school—why, Sister Shaw, the Lord Himself don't know where they're comin' out!"

For a moment he pondered. Then he uttered a valedictory which I have always been glad to recall as his last message, for I never saw him again.

"When you fust come to us," he said, "you had a lot of crooked places, an' we had a lot of crooked places; and we kind of run into each other, all of us. But before you left, Sister Shaw, why, all the crooked places was wore off and everything was as smooth as silk."

"Yes," I agreed, "and that was the time to leave—when everything was running smoothly."

All is changed on Cape Cod since those days, thirty years ago. The old families have died or moved away, and those who replaced them were of a different type. I am happy in having known and loved the Cape as it was, and in having gathered there a store of delightful memories. In later strenuous years it has rested me merely to think of the place, and long afterward I showed my continued love of it by building a home there, which I still possess.

But I had little time to rest in this or in my Moylan home, of which I shall write later, for now I was back in Boston, living my new life, and each crowded hour brought me more to do.[8]

We were entering upon a deeply significant period. For the first time women were going into industrial competition with men, and already men were intensely resenting their presence. Around me I saw women overworked and underpaid, doing men's work at half men's wages, not because their work was inferior, but because they were women. Again, too, I studied the obtrusive problems of the poor and of the women of the streets; and, looking at the whole social situation from every angle, I could find but one solution for women—the removal of the stigma of disfranchisement. As man's equal before the law, woman could demand her rights, asking favors from no one. With all my heart I joined in the crusade of the men and women who were fighting for her. My real work had begun.

Naturally, at this period, I frequently met the members of Boston's most inspiring group—the Emersons and John Greenleaf Whittier, James Freeman Clark, Reverend Minot Savage, Bronson Alcott and his daughter Louisa, Wendell Phillips, William Lloyd Garrison, Stephen Foster, Theodore Weld, and the rest.[9] Of them all, my favorite was Whittier. He had been present at my graduation from the theological school, and now he often attended our suffrage meetings. He was already an old man, nearing the end of his life; and I recall him as singularly tall and thin, almost gaunt, bending forward as he talked, and wearing an expression of great serenity and benignity. I once told Susan B. Anthony that if I needed help in a crowd of strangers that included her, I would immediately turn to her, knowing from her face that, whatever I had done, she would understand and assist me. I could have offered the same tribute to Whittier. At our meetings he was like a vesper-bell chiming above a battle-field. Garrison always became excited during our discussions, and the others frequently did; but Whittier, in whose big heart the love of his fellow-man burned as unquenchably as in any heart there, always preserved his exquisite tranquility.

Once, I remember, Stephen Foster insisted on having the word "tyranny" put into a resolution, stating that women were deprived of suffrage by the *tyranny* of men. Mr. Garrison objected, and the debate that followed was the most exciting I have ever heard. The combatants actually had to adjourn before they could calm down sufficiently to go on with their meeting. Knowing the stimulating atmosphere to which he had grown accustomed, I was not surprised to have Theodore Weld explain to me, long afterward, why he no longer attended suffrage meetings.

"Oh," he said, "why should I go? There hasn't been anyone mobbed in twenty years!"

The Ralph Waldo Emersons occasionally attended our meetings, and Mr. Emerson, at first opposed to woman suffrage, became a convert to it during the last years of his life—a fact his son and daughter omitted to mention in his biography. After his death I gave two suffrage lectures in Concord, and each time Mrs. Emerson paid for the hall.[10] At these lectures Louisa M. Alcott graced the assembly with her splendid, wholesome presence, and on both occasions she was surrounded by a group of boys. She frankly cared much more for boys than for girls, and boys inevitably gravitated to her whenever she entered a place where they were. When women were given school suffrage in Massachusetts, Miss Alcott was the first woman to vote in Concord, and she went to the polls accompanied by a group of her boys, all ardently "for the Cause."[11] My general impression of her was that of a fresh breeze blowing over wide moors. She was as different as possible from exquisite little Mrs. Emerson, who, in her daintiness and quiet charm, suggested an old New England garden.

Of Abby May[12] and Edna Cheney[13] I retain a general impression of "bagginess"—of loose jackets over loose waistbands, of escaping locks of hair, of bodies seemingly one size from the neck down. Both women were utterly indifferent to the details of their appearance, but they were splendid workers and leading spirits in the New England Woman's Club.[14] It was said to be the trouble between Abby May and Kate Gannett Wells, both of whom stood for the presidency of the club, that led to the beginning of the anti-suffrage movement in Boston.[15] Abby May was elected president, and all the suffragists voted for her. Subsequently Kate Gannett Wells began her anti-suffrage campaign. Mrs. Wells was the first anti-suffragist I ever knew in this country. Before her there had been Mrs. Dahlgren, wife of Admiral Dahlgren,[16] and Mrs. William Tecumseh Sherman.[17] On one occasion Elizabeth

Cady Stanton challenged Mrs. Dahlgren to a debate on woman suffrage, and in the light of later events Mrs. Dahlgren's reply is amusing.[18] She declined the challenge, explaining that for anti-suffragists to appear upon a public platform would be a direct violation of the principle for which they stood—which was the protection of female modesty! Recalling this, and the present hectic activity of the anti-suffragists, one must feel that they have either abandoned their principle or widened their views.

For Julia Ward Howe I had an immense admiration; but, though from first to last I saw much of her, I never felt that I really knew her. She was a woman of the widest culture, interested in every progressive movement. With all her big heart she tried to be a democrat, but she was an aristocrat to the very core of her, and, despite her wonderful work for others, she lived in a splendid isolation. Once when I called on her I found her resting her mind by reading Greek, and she laughingly admitted that she was using a Latin pony, adding that she was growing "rusty." She seemed a little embarrassed by being caught with the pony, but she must have been reassured by my cheerful confession that if *I* tried to read either Latin or Greek I should need an English pony.[19]

Of Frances E. Willard, who frequently came to Boston, I saw a great deal, and we soon became closely associated in our work.[20] Early in our friendship, and at Miss Willard's suggestion, we made a compact that once a week each of us would point out to the other her most serious faults, and thereby help her to remedy them; but we were both too sane to do anything of the kind, and the project soon died a natural death. The nearest I ever came to carrying it out was in warning Miss Willard that she was constantly defying all the laws of personal hygiene. She never rested, rarely seemed to sleep, and had to be reminded at the table that she was there for the purpose of eating food. She was always absorbed in some great interest, and oblivious to anything else. I never knew a woman who could grip an audience and carry it with her as she could. She was intensely emotional, and swayed others by their emotions rather than by logic; yet she was the least conscious of her physical existence of anyone I ever knew, with the exception of Susan B. Anthony. Like "Aunt Susan," Miss Willard paid no heed to cold or heat or hunger, to privation or fatigue.[21] In their relations to such trifles both women were disembodied spirits.

Another woman doing wonderful work at this time was Mrs. Quincy Shaw, who had recently started her day nurseries for the care of tenement children whose mothers labored by the day.[22] These nurseries were new in Boston, as was the kindergarten system she also established. I saw the effect of her work in the lives of the people, and it strengthened my growing conviction that little could be done for the poor in a spiritual or educational way until they were given a certain amount of physical comfort, and until more time was devoted to the problem of prevention. Indeed, the more I studied economic issues, the more strongly I felt that the position of most philanthropists is that of men who stand at the bottom of a precipice gathering up and trying to heal those who fall into it, instead of guarding the top and preventing them from going over.

Of course I had to earn my living; but, though I had taken my medical degree only a few months before leaving Cape Cod, I had no intention of practicing medicine. I had merely wished to add a certain amount of medical knowledge to my mental equipment. The Massachusetts Woman Suffrage Association, of which Lucy Stone was president, had frequently employed me as a lecturer during the last two years of my pastorate. Now it offered me a salary of one hundred dollars a month as a lecturer and organizer. Though I may not have seemed so in these reminiscences, in which I have written as freely of my small victories as of my struggles and failures, I was a modest young person. The amount seemed too large, and I told Mrs. Stone as much, after which I humbly fixed my salary at fifty dollars a month. At the end of a year of work I felt that I had "made good"; then I asked for and received the one hundred dollars a month originally offered me.

During my second year Miss Cora Scott Pond and I organized and carried through in Boston a great suffrage bazaar, clearing six thousand dollars for the association—a large amount in those days.[23] Elated by my share in this success, I asked that my salary should be increased to one hundred and twenty-five dollars a month—but this was not done. Instead, I received a valuable lesson. It was freely admitted that my work was worth one hundred and twenty-five dollars, but I was told that one hundred was the limit which could be paid, and I was reminded that this was a good salary for a woman.

The time seemed to have come to make a practical stand in defense of my principles, and I did so by resigning and arranging an independent lecture tour. The first month after my resignation I earned three hundred dollars. Later I frequently earned more than that, and very rarely less. Eventually I lectured under the direction of the Slaton Lecture Bureau of Chicago, and later still for the Redpath Bureau of Boston.[24] My experience with the Redpath people was especially gratifying. Mrs. Livermore, who was their only woman lecturer, was growing old and anxious to resign her work. She saw in me a possible successor, and asked them to take me on their list. They promptly refused, explaining that I must "make a reputation" before they could even consider me. A year later they wrote me, making a very good offer, which I accepted. It may be worthwhile to mention here that through my lecture-work at this period I earned all the money I have ever saved. I lectured night after night, week after week, month after month, in "Chautauquas" in the summer, all over the country in the winter, earning a large income and putting aside at that time the small surplus I still hold in preparation for the "rainy day" every working-woman inwardly fears.[25]

I gave the public at least a fair equivalent for what it gave me, for I put into my lectures all my vitality, and I rarely missed an engagement, though again and again I risked my life to keep one. My special subjects, of course, were the two I had most at heart—suffrage and temperance. For Frances Willard, then President of the Woman's Christian Temperance Union, had persuaded me to head the Franchise Department of that organization, succeeding Ziralda Wallace, the mother of Gen. Lew Wallace; and Miss Susan B. Anthony, who was beginning to study me closely, soon swung me into active work with her, of which, later, I shall have much to say. But before taking up a subject as absorbing to me as my friendship for and association with the most wonderful woman I have ever known, it may be interesting to record a few of my pioneer experiences in the lecture-field.

In those days—thirty years ago—the lecture bureaus were wholly regardless of the comfort of their lecturers. They arranged

a schedule of engagements with exactly one idea in mind—to get
the lecturer from one lecture-point to the next, utterly regardless
of whether she had time between for rest or food or sleep. So it
happened that all-night journeys in freight-cars, engines, and ca-
booses were casual commonplaces, while thirty and forty mile
drives across the country in blizzards and bitter cold were equally
inevitable. Usually these things did not trouble me. They were
high adventures which I enjoyed at the time and afterward loved
to recall. But there was an occasional hiatus in my optimism.

One night, for example, after lecturing in a town in Ohio, it
was necessary to drive eight miles across country to a tiny railroad station at which a train, passing about two o'clock in the
morning, was to be flagged for me. When we reached the station
it was closed, but my driver deposited me on the platform and
drove away, leaving me alone. The night was cold and very dark.
All day I had been feeling ill, and in the evening had suffered so
much pain that I had finished my lecture with great difficulty.
Now toward midnight, in this desolate spot, miles from any
house, I grew alarmingly worse. I am not easily frightened, but
that time I was sure I was going to die. Off in the darkness, very
far away, as it seemed, I saw a faint light, and with infinite effort
I dragged myself toward it. To walk, even to stand, was impossible; I crawled along the railroad track, collapsing, resting, going
on again, whipping my willpower to the task of keeping my brain
clear, until after a nightmare that seemed to last through centuries I lay across the door of the switch-tower in which the light
was burning. The switchman stationed there heard the cry I was
able to utter, and came to my assistance. He carried me up to his
signal-room and laid me on the floor by the stove; he had nothing
to give me except warmth and shelter; but these were now all I
asked. I sank into a comatose condition shot through with pain.
Toward two o'clock in the morning he waked me and told me my
train was coming, asking if I felt able to take it. I decided to make
the effort. He dared not leave his post to help me, but he signaled
to the train, and I began my progress back to the station. I never
clearly remembered how I got there; but I arrived and was helped
into a car by a brakeman. About four o'clock in the morning I
had to change again, but this time I was left at the station of a
town, and was there met by a man whose wife had offered me

hospitality. He drove me to their home, and I was cared for. What I had, it developed, was a severe case of ptomaine poisoning, and I soon recovered; but even after all these years I do not like to recall that night.[26]

To be "snowed in" was a frequent experience. Once, in Minnesota, I was one of a dozen travelers who were driven in an omnibus from a country hotel to the nearest railroad station, about two miles away.[27] It was snowing hard, and the driver left us on the station platform and departed. Time passed, but the train we were waiting for did not come. A true Western blizzard, growing wilder every moment, had set in, and we finally realized that the train was not coming, and that, moreover, it was now impossible to get back to the hotel. The only thing we could do was to spend the night in the railroad station. I was the only woman in the group, and my fellow-passengers were cattlemen who whiled away the hours by smoking, telling stories, and exchanging pocket flasks. The station had a telegraph operator who occupied a tiny box by himself, and he finally invited me to share the privacy of his microscopic quarters. I entered them very gratefully, and he laid a board on the floor, covered it with an overcoat made of buffalo-skins, and cheerfully invited me to go to bed. I went, and slept peacefully until morning. Then we all returned to the hotel, the men going ahead and shoveling a path.

Again, one Sunday, I was snowbound in a train near Faribault, and this time also I was the only woman among a number of cattlemen.[28] They were an odoriferous lot, who smoked diligently and played cards without ceasing, but in deference to my presence they swore only mildly and under their breath. At last they wearied of their game, and one of them rose and came to me.

"I heard you lecture the other night," he said, awkwardly, "and I've bin tellin' the fellers about it. We'd like to have a lecture now."

Their card-playing had seemed to me a sinful thing (I was stricter in my views then than I am today), and I was glad to create a diversion. I agreed to give them a lecture, and they went through the train, which consisted of two day coaches, and brought in the remaining passengers. A few of them could sing, and we began with a Moody and Sankey hymn or two and the appealing ditty, "Where is my wandering boy tonight?" in which they all joined with special zest.[29] Then I delivered the lecture, and they listened attentively. When I had finished they seemed to think that some slight return was in order, so they proceeded to make a bed for me. They took the bottoms out of two seats, arranged them crosswise, and one man folded his overcoat into a pillow. Inspired by this, two others immediately donated their fur overcoats for upper and lower coverings. When the bed was ready they waved me toward it with a most hospitable air, and I crept in between the overcoats and slumbered sweetly until I was aroused the next morning by the welcome music of a snow-plow which had been sent from St. Paul to our rescue.[30]

To drive fifty or sixty miles in a day to meet a lecture engagement was a frequent experience. I have been driven across the prairies in June when they were like a mammoth flower-bed, and in January when they seemed one huge snow-covered grave—my grave, I thought, at times. Once during a thirty-mile drive, when the thermometer was twenty degrees below zero, I suddenly realized that my face was freezing. I opened my satchel, took out the tissue-paper that protected my best gown, and put the paper over my face as a veil, tucking it inside of my bonnet. When I reached my destination the tissue was a perfect mask, frozen stiff, and I had to be lifted from the sleigh. I was due on the lecture platform in half an hour, so I drank a huge bowl of boiling ginger tea and appeared on time. That night I went to bed expecting an attack of pneumonia as a result of the exposure, but I awoke next morning in superb condition. I possess what is called "an iron constitution," and in those days I needed it.

That same winter, in Kansas, I was chased by wolves, and though I had been more or less intimately associated with wolves in my pioneer life in the Michigan woods, I found the occasion extremely unpleasant. During the long winters of my girlhood, wolves had frequently slunk around our log cabin, and at times in the lumber-camps we had even heard them prowling on the roofs. But those were very different creatures from the two huge, starving, tireless animals that hour after hour loped behind the cutter in which I sat with another woman, who, throughout the whole experience, never lost her head nor her control of our frantic horses.[31] They were mad with terror, for, try as they would, they could not outrun the grim things that trailed us, seemingly not trying to gain on us, but keeping always at the same distance, with a patience that was horrible. From time to time I turned to look at them, and the picture they made as they came on and on is one I shall never forget. They were so near that I could see their eyes and slavering jaws, and they were as noiseless as things in a dream. At last, little by little, they began to gain on us, and they were almost within striking distance of the whip, which was our only weapon, when we reached the welcome outskirts of a town and they fell back.

Some of the memories of those days have to do with personal encounters, brief but poignant. Once when I was giving a series of Chautauqua lectures, I spoke at the Chautauqua in Pontiac, Illinois. The State Reformatory for Boys was situated in that town, and, after the lecture the superintendent of the Reformatory invited me to visit it and say a few words to the inmates. I went and spoke for half an hour, carrying away a memory of the place and of the boys which haunted me for months. A year later, while I was waiting for a train in the station at Shelbyville, a lad about sixteen years old passed me and hesitated, looking as if he knew me. I saw that he wanted to speak and dared not, so I nodded to him.

"You think you know me, don't you?" I asked, when he came to my side.

"Yes'm, I do know you," he told me, eagerly. "You are Miss Shaw, and you talked to us boys at Pontiac last year. I'm out on parole now, but I 'ain't forgot. Us boys enjoyed you the best of any show we ever had!"

I was touched by this artless compliment, and anxious to know how I had won it, so I asked, "What did I say that the boys liked?"

The lad hesitated. Then he said, slowly, "Well, you didn't talk as if you thought we were all bad."

"My boy," I told him, "I don't think you are all bad. I know better!"

As if I had touched a spring in him, the lad dropped into the seat by my side; then, leaning toward me, he said, impulsively, but almost in a whisper:

"Say, Miss Shaw, *some of us boys says our prayers!*"

Rarely have I had a tribute that moved me more than that shy confidence; and often since then, in hours of discouragement or failure, I have reminded myself that at least there must have been something in me once to make a lad of that age so open up his heart. We had a long and intimate talk, from which grew the abiding interest I feel in boys today.

Naturally I was sometimes inconvenienced by slight misunderstandings between local committees and myself as to the subjects of my lectures, and the most extreme instance of this occurred in a town where I arrived to find myself widely advertised as "Mrs. Anna Shaw, who whistled before Queen Victoria"! Transfixed, I gaped before the billboards, and by reading their additional lettering discovered the gratifying fact that at least I was not expected to whistle now. Instead, it appeared, I was to lecture on "The Missing Link."

As usual, I had arrived in town only an hour or two before the time fixed for my lecture; there was the briefest interval in which to clear up these painful misunderstandings. I repeatedly tried to reach the chairman who was to preside at the entertainment, but failed. At last I went to the hall at the hour appointed, and found the local committee there, graciously waiting to receive me. Without wasting precious minutes in preliminaries, I asked why they had advertised me as the woman who had "whistled before Queen Victoria."

"Why, didn't you whistle before her?" they exclaimed in grieved surprise.

"I certainly did not," I explained. "Moreover, I was never called 'The American Nightingale,' and I have never lectured on 'The Missing Link.' Where *did* you get that subject? It was not on the list I sent you."

The members of the committee seemed dazed. They withdrew to a corner and consulted in whispers. Then, with clearing brow, the spokesman returned.

"Why," he said, cheerfully, "it's simple enough! We mixed you up with a Shaw lady that whistles; and we've been discussing the missing link in our debating society, so our citizens want to hear your views."

"But I don't know anything about the missing link," I protested, "and I can't speak on it."

"Now, come," they begged. "Why, you'll have to! We've sold

all our tickets for that lecture. The whole town has turned out to hear it."

Then, as I maintained a depressed silence, one of them had a bright idea.

"I'll tell you how to fix it!" he cried. "Speak on any subject you please, but bring in something about the missing link every few minutes. That will satisfy 'em."

"Very well," I agreed, reluctantly. "Open the meeting with a song. Get the audience to sing 'America' or 'The Star-spangled Banner.' That will give me a few minutes to think, and I will see what can be done."

Led by a very nervous chairman, the big audience began to sing, and under the inspiration of the music the solution of our problem flashed into my mind.

"It is easy," I told myself. "Woman is the missing link in our government. I'll give them a suffrage speech along that line."

When the song ended I began my part of the entertainment with a portion of my lecture on "The Fate of Republics," tracing their growth and decay, and pointing out that what our republic needed to give it a stable government was the missing link of woman suffrage. I got along admirably, for every five minutes I mentioned "the missing link," and the audience sat content and apparently interested, while the members of the committee burst into bloom on the platform.

Source: Anna Howard Shaw, with the Collaboration of Elizabeth Jordan, *The Story of a Pioneer* (Harper & Brothers, 1915).

CHAPTER IX

" 'AUNT SUSAN' "

(1915)

(excerpt)

In *The Life of Susan B. Anthony* it is mentioned that 1888 was a year of special recognition of our great leader's work, but that it was also the year in which many of her closest friends and strongest supporters were taken from her by death.[1] A. Bronson Alcott was among these, and Louisa M. Alcott, as well as Dr. Lozier; and special stress is laid on Miss Anthony's sense of loss in the diminishing circle of her friends—a loss which new friends and workers came forward, eager to supply.[2]

"Chief among these," adds the record, "was Anna Shaw, who, from the time of the International Council in '88, gave her truest allegiance to Miss Anthony."[3]

It is true that from that year until Miss Anthony's death in 1906 we two were rarely separated; and I never read the paragraph I have just quoted without seeing, as in a vision, the figure of "Aunt Susan" as she slipped into my hotel room in Chicago late one night after an evening meeting of the International Council. I had gone to bed—indeed, I was almost asleep when she came, for the day had been as exhausting as it was interesting. But notwithstanding the lateness of the hour, "Aunt Susan," then nearing seventy, was still as fresh and as full of enthusiasm as a young girl. She had a great deal to say, she declared, and she proceeded to say it—sitting in a big easy chair near the bed, with a rug around her knees, while I propped myself up with pillows and listened.

Hours passed and the dawn peered wanly through the windows, but still Miss Anthony talked of the Cause—always of the Cause—and of what we two must do for it. The previous evening she had been too busy to eat any dinner, and I greatly doubt whether she had eaten any luncheon at noon. She had been on her feet for hours at a time, and she had held numerous discussions with other women she wished to inspire to special effort. Yet, after it all, here she was laying out our campaigns for years ahead, foreseeing everything, forgetting nothing, and sweeping me with her in her flight toward our common goal, until I, who am not easily carried off my feet, experienced an almost dizzy sense of exhilaration.

Suddenly she stopped, looked at the gas-jets paling in the morning light that filled the room, and for a fleeting instant seemed surprised. In the next she had dismissed from her mind the realization that we had talked all night. Why should we not talk all night? It was part of our work. She threw off the enveloping rug and rose.

"I must dress now," she said, briskly. "I've called a committee meeting before the morning session."

On her way to the door nature smote her with a rare reminder, but even then she did not realize that it was personal. "Perhaps," she remarked, tentatively, "you ought to have a cup of coffee."

That was "Aunt Susan." And in the eighteen years which followed I had daily illustrations of her superiority to purely human weaknesses. To her the hardships we underwent later, in our Western campaigns for woman suffrage, were as the airiest trifles. Like a true soldier, she could snatch a moment of sleep or a mouthful of food where she found it, and if either was not forthcoming she did not miss it. To me she was an unceasing inspiration—the torch that illumined my life. We went through some difficult years together—years when we fought hard for each inch of headway we gained—but I found full compensation for every effort in the glory of working with her for the Cause that was first in both our hearts, and in the happiness of being her friend. Later I shall describe in more detail the suffrage campaigns and the National and International councils in which we took part; now it is of her I wish to write—of her bigness, her many-sidedness, her humor, her courage, her quickness, her sympathy, her understanding, her force, her supreme common-sense, her selflessness; in short, of the rare beauty of her nature as I learned to know it.

Like most great leaders, she took one's best work for granted, and was chary with her praise; and even when praise was given it usually came by indirect routes.[4] I recall with amusement that the highest compliment she ever paid me in public involved her in a tangle from which, later, only her quick wit extricated her. We were lecturing in an especially pious town which I shall call B——, and just before I went on the platform Miss Anthony remarked, peacefully:

"These people have always claimed that I am irreligious. They will not accept the fact that I am a Quaker—or, rather, they seem to think a Quaker is an infidel. I am glad you are a Methodist, for now they cannot claim that we are not orthodox."

She was still enveloped in the comfort of this reflection when she introduced me to our audience, and to impress my qualifications upon my hearers she made her introduction in these words:

"It is a pleasure to introduce Miss Shaw, who is a Methodist minister. And she is not only orthodox of the orthodox, but she is also my right bower!"

There was a gasp from the pious audience, and then a roar of laughter from irreverent men, in which, I must confess, I lightheartedly joined. For once in her life Miss Anthony lost her presence of mind; she did not know how to meet the situation, for she had no idea what had caused the laughter. It bubbled forth again and again during the evening, and each time Miss Anthony received the demonstration with the same air of puzzled surprise. When we had returned to our hotel rooms I explained the matter to her. I do not remember now where I had acquired my own sinful knowledge, but that night I faced "Aunt Susan" from the pedestal of a sophisticated worldling.

"Don't you know what a right bower is?" I demanded, sternly.

"Of course I do," insisted "Aunt Susan." "It's a right-hand man—the kind one can't do without."

"It is a card," I told her, firmly—"a leading card in a game called euchre."[5]

"Aunt Susan" was dazed. "I didn't know it had anything to do with cards," she mused, mournfully. "What must they think of me?"

What they thought became quite evident. The newspapers made countless jokes at our expense, and there were significant smiles on the faces in the audience that awaited us the next night. When Miss Anthony walked upon the platform she at once proceeded to clear herself of the tacit charge against her.

"When I came to your town," she began, cheerfully, "I had been warned that you were a very religious lot of people. I wanted to impress upon you the fact that Miss Shaw and I are religious, too. But I admit that when I told you she was my right bower I did not know what a right bower was. I have learned that, since last night."

She waited until the happy chortles of her hearers had subsided, and then went on.

"It interests me very much, however," she concluded, "to realize that everyone of you seemed to know all about a right bower, and that I had to come to your good, orthodox town to get the information."

That time the joke was on the audience.

Miss Anthony's home was in Rochester, New York, and it was said by our friends that on the rare occasions when we were not together, and I was lecturing independently, "all return roads led through Rochester." I invariably found some excuse to go there and report to her. Together we must have worn out many Rochester pavements, for "Aunt Susan's" pet recreation was walking, and she used to walk me round and round the city squares, far into the night, and at a pace that made policemen gape at us as we flew by. Some disrespectful youth once remarked that on these occasions we suggested a race between a ruler and a rubber ball—for she was very tall and thin, while I am short and plump. To keep up with her I literally bounded at her side.

A certain amount of independent lecturing was necessary for me, for I had to earn my living. The National American Woman Suffrage Association has never paid salaries to its officers, so, when I became vice-president and eventually, in 1904, president of the association, I continued to work gratuitously for the Cause in these positions. Even Miss Anthony received not one penny of salary for all her years of unceasing labor, and she was so poor that she did not have a home of her own until she was seventy-five. Then it was a very simple one, and she lived with the utmost economy. I decided that I could earn my bare expenses by making one brief lecture tour each year, and I made an arrangement with the Redpath Bureau which left me fully two-thirds of my time for the suffrage work I loved.

This was one result of my all-night talk with Miss Anthony in Chicago, and it enabled me to carry out her plan that I should accompany her in most of the campaigns in which she sought to arouse the West to the need of suffrage for women. From that time on we traveled and lectured together so constantly that each of us developed an almost uncanny knowledge of the other's mental processes. At any point of either's lecture the other could pick it up and carry it on—a fortunate condition, as it sometimes became necessary to do this. Miss Anthony was subject to contractions of the throat, which for the moment caused a slight strangulation. On such occasions—of which there were several—she would turn to me and indicate her helplessness. Then I would repeat her last sentence, complete her speech, and afterward make my own.

The first time this happened we were in Washington, and "Aunt Susan" stopped in the middle of a word. She could not speak; she merely motioned to me to continue for her, and left the stage. At the end of the evening a prominent Washington man who had been in our audience remarked to me, confidentially:

"That was a nice little play you and Miss Anthony made tonight—very effective indeed."

For an instant I did not catch his meaning, nor the implication in his knowing smile.

"Very clever, that strangling bit, and your going on with the speech," he repeated. "It hit the audience hard."

"Surely," I protested, "you don't think it was a deliberate thing—that we planned or rehearsed it."

He stared at me incredulously. "Are you going to pretend," he demanded, "that it wasn't a put-up job?"

I told him he had paid us a high compliment, and that we must really have done very well if we had conveyed that impression; and I finally convinced him that we not only had not rehearsed the episode, but that neither of us had known what the other meant to say. We never wrote out our speeches, but our subject was always suffrage or some ramification of suffrage, and, naturally, we had thoroughly digested each other's views.

It is said by my friends that I write my speeches on the tips of my fingers—for I always make my points on my fingers and have my fingers named for points. When I plan a speech I decide how many points I wish to make and what those points shall be. My mental preparation follows. Miss Anthony's method was much the same; but very frequently both of us threw over all our plans at the last moment and spoke extemporaneously on some theme suggested by the atmosphere of the gathering or by the words of another speaker.

From Miss Anthony, more than from anyone else, I learned to keep cool in the face of interruptions and of the small annoyances and disasters inevitable in campaigning. Often we were able to help each other out of embarrassing situations, and one incident of this kind occurred during our campaign in South Dakota. We were holding a meeting on the hottest Sunday of the hottest month in the year—August—and hundreds of the natives had driven twenty, thirty, and even forty miles across the country to hear us. We were to speak in a sod church, but it was discovered that the structure would not hold half the people who were trying to enter it, so we decided that Miss Anthony should speak from the door, in order that those both inside and outside might hear her. To elevate her above her audience, she was given an empty dry-goods box to stand on.

This makeshift platform was not large, and men, women, and children were seated on the ground around it, pressing up against it, as close to the speaker as they could get. Directly in front of Miss Anthony sat a woman with a child about two years old—a little boy; and this infant, like everyone else in the packed throng, was dripping with perspiration and suffering acutely under the blazing sun. Every woman present seemed to have brought children with her, doubtless because she could not leave them alone at home; and babies were crying and fretting on all sides. The infant nearest Miss Anthony fretted most strenuously; he was a sturdy little fellow with a fine pair of lungs, and he made it very difficult for her to lift her voice above his dismal clamor. Suddenly, however, he discovered her feet on the dry-goods box, about on a level with his head. They were clad in black stockings and low shoes; they moved about oddly; they fascinated him. With a yelp of interest he grabbed for them and began pinching them to see what they were. His howls ceased; he was happy.

Miss Anthony was not. But it was a great relief to have the child quiet, so she bore the infliction of the pinching as long as she could. When endurance had found its limit she slipped back out of reach, and as his new plaything receded the boy uttered shrieks of disapproval. There was only one way to stop his noise; Miss Anthony brought her feet forward again, and he resumed the pinching of her ankles, while his yelps subsided to contented murmurs. The performance was repeated half a dozen times. Each time the ankles retreated the baby yelled. Finally, for once at the end of her patience, "Aunt Susan" leaned forward and addressed the mother, whose facial expression throughout had shown a complete mental detachment from the situation.

"I think your little boy is hot and thirsty," she said, gently. "If you would take him out of the crowd and give him a drink of water and unfasten his clothes, I am sure he would be more comfortable."

Before she had finished speaking the woman had sprung to her feet and was facing her with fierce indignation.

"This is the first time I have ever been insulted as a mother," she cried; "and by an old maid at that!" Then she grasped the infant and left the scene, amid great confusion. The majority of those in the audience seemed to sympathize with her. They had not seen the episode of the feet, and they thought Miss Anthony was complaining of the child's crying. Their children were crying, too, and they felt that they had all been criticized. Other women rose and followed the irate mother, and many men gallantly followed them. It seemed clear that motherhood had been outraged.

Miss Anthony was greatly depressed by the episode, and she was not comforted by a prediction one man made after the meeting.

"You've lost at least twenty votes by that little affair," he told her.

"Aunt Susan" sighed. "Well," she said, "if those men knew how my ankles felt I would have won twenty votes by enduring the torture as long as I did."

The next day we had a second meeting. Miss Anthony made her speech early in the evening, and by the time it was my turn to begin all the children in the audience—and there were many— were both tired and sleepy. At least half a dozen of them were crying, and I had to shout to make my voice heard above their uproar. Miss Anthony remarked afterward that there seemed to be a contest between me and the infants to see which of us could make more noise. The audience was plainly getting restless under the combined effect, and finally a man in the rear rose and added his voice to the tumult.

"Say, Miss Shaw," he yelled, "don't you want these children put out?"

It was our chance to remove the sad impression of yesterday, and I grasped it.

"No, indeed," I yelled back. "Nothing inspires me like the voice of a child!"

A handsome round of applause from mothers and fathers greeted this noble declaration, after which the blessed babies and I resumed our joint vocal efforts. When the speech was finished and we were alone together, Miss Anthony put her arm around my shoulder and drew me to her side.

"Well, Anna," she said, gratefully, "you've certainly evened us up on motherhood this time."

That South Dakota campaign was one of the most difficult we ever made. It extended over nine months; and it is impossible to describe the poverty which prevailed throughout the whole rural community of the State. There had been three consecutive years of drought. The sand was like powder, so deep that the wheels of the wagons in which we rode "across country" sank half-way to the hubs; and in the midst of this dry powder lay withered tangles that had once been grass. Everyone had the forsaken, desperate look worn by the pioneer who has reached the limit of his endurance, and the great stretches of prairie roads showed innumerable canvas-covered wagons, drawn by starved horses, and followed by starved cows, on their way "Back East." Our talks with the despairing drivers of these wagons are among my most tragic memories. They had lost everything except what they had with them, and they were going East to leave "the woman" with her father and try to find work. Usually, with a look of disgust at his wife, the man would say: "I wanted to leave two years ago, but the woman kept saying, 'Hold on a little longer.'"

Both Miss Anthony and I gloried in the spirit of these pioneer women, and lost no opportunity to tell them so; for we realized what our nation owes to the patience and courage of such as they were. We often asked them what was the hardest thing to bear in their pioneer life, and we usually received the same reply:

"To sit in our little adobe or sod houses at night and listen to the wolves howl over the graves of our babies. For the howl of the wolf is like the cry of a child from the grave."

Many days, and in all kinds of weather, we rode forty and fifty miles in uncovered wagons. Many nights we shared a one-room cabin with all the members of the family. But the greatest hardship we suffered was the lack of water. There was very little good water in the state, and the purest water was so brackish that we could hardly drink it.[6] The more we drank the thirstier we became, and when the water was made into tea it tasted worse than when it was clear.

When we reached the Black Hills we had more of this genuine campaigning.[7] We traveled over the mountains in wagons, behind teams of horses, visiting the mining-camps; and often the gullies were so deep that when our horses got into them it was almost impossible to get them out. I recall with special clearness one ride from Hill City to Custer City.[8] It was only a matter of thirty miles, but it was thoroughly exhausting; and after our meeting that same night we had to drive forty miles farther over the mountains to get the early morning train from Buffalo Gap. The trail from Custer City to Buffalo Gap was the one the animals had originally made in their journeys over the pass, and the drive in that wild region, throughout a cold, piercing October night, was an unforgettable experience.[9] Our host at Custer City lent Miss Anthony his big buffalo overcoat, and his wife lent hers to me. They also heated blocks of wood for our feet, and with these protections we started. A full moon hung in the sky. The trees were covered with hoar-frost, and the cold, still air seemed to sparkle in the brilliant light.[10] Again Miss Anthony talked to me throughout the night—of the work, always of the work, and of what it would mean to the women who followed us; and again she fired my soul with the flame that burned so steadily in her own.

It was daylight when we reached the little station at Buffalo Gap where we were to take the train. This was not due, however, for half an hour, and even then it did not come. The station was only large enough to hold the stove, the ticket-office, and the inevitable cuspidor.[11] There was barely room in which to walk between these and the wall. Miss Anthony sat down on the floor. I had a few raisins in my bag, and we divided them for breakfast. An hour passed, and another, and still the train did not come. Miss Anthony, her back braced against the wall, buried her face in her hands and dropped into a peaceful abyss of slumber, while I walked restlessly up and down the platform. The train arrived four hours late, and when eventually we had reached our destination we learned that the ministers of the town had persuaded the women to give up the suffrage meeting scheduled for that night, as it was Sunday.

This disappointment, following our all-day and all-night drive to keep our appointment, aroused Miss Anthony's fighting spirit. She sent me out to rent the theater for the evening, and to have some hand-bills printed and distributed, announcing that we would speak. At three o'clock she made the concession to her seventy years of lying down for an hour's rest. I was young and vigorous, so I trotted around town to get somebody to preside, somebody to introduce us, somebody to take up the collection, and somebody who would provide music—in short, to make all our preparations for the night meeting.

When evening came the crowd which had assembled was so great that men and women sat in the windows and on the stage, and stood in the flies. Night attractions were rare in that Dakota town, and here was something new. Nobody went to church, so the churches were forced to close. We had a glorious meeting. Both Miss Anthony and I were in excellent fighting trim, and Miss Anthony remarked that the only thing lacking to make me do my best was a sick headache. The collection we took up paid all our expenses, the church singers sang for us, the great audience was interested, and the whole occasion was an inspiring success.

The meeting ended about half after ten o'clock, and I remember taking Miss Anthony to our hotel and escorting her to her room. I also remember that she followed me to the door and made some laughing remark as I left for my own room; but I recall nothing more until the next morning when she stood beside me telling me it was time for breakfast. She had found me lying on the cover of my bed, fully clothed even to my bonnet and shoes. I had fallen there, utterly exhausted, when I entered my room the night before; and I do not think I had even moved from that time until the moment—nine hours later—when I heard her voice and felt her hand on my shoulder.

After all our work, we did not win Dakota that year, but Miss Anthony bore the disappointment with the serenity she always showed. To her a failure was merely another opportunity, and I mention our experience here only to show of what she was capable in her gallant seventies. But I should misrepresent her if I did not show her human and sentimental side as well. With all her detachment from human needs she had emotional moments, and of these the most satisfying came when she was listening to music. She knew nothing whatever about music, but was deeply moved by it; and I remember vividly one occasion when Nordica sang for her, at an afternoon reception given by a Chicago friend in "Aunt Susan's" honor.[12] As it happened, she had never heard Nordica sing until that day; and before the music began the great artiste and the great leader met, and in the moment of meeting became friends. When Nordica sang, half an hour later, she sang directly to Miss Anthony, looking into her eyes; and "Aunt Susan" listened with her own eyes full of tears. When the last notes had been sung she went to the singer and put both arms around her. The music had carried her back to her girlhood and to the sentiment of sixteen.

"Oh, Nordica," she sighed, "I could die listening to such singing!"

Another example of her unquenchable youth has also a Chicago setting. During the World's Fair a certain clergyman made an especially violent stand in favor of closing the Fair grounds on Sunday. Miss Anthony took issue with him.

"If I had charge of a young man in Chicago at this time," she told the clergyman, "I would much rather have him locked inside the Fair grounds on Sunday or any other day than have him going about on the outside."

The clergyman was horrified. "Would you like to have a son of yours go to Buffalo Bill's Wild West Show on Sunday?" he demanded.

"Of course I would," admitted Miss Anthony. "In fact, I think he would learn more there than from the sermons preached in some churches."

Later this remark was repeated to Colonel Cody ("Buffalo Bill"), who, of course, was delighted with it. He at once wrote to Miss Anthony, thanking her for the breadth of her views, and offering her a box for his "Show." She had no strong desire to see the performance, but some of us urged her to accept the invitation and to take us with her. She was always ready to do anything that would give us pleasure, so she promised that we should go the next afternoon. Others heard of the jaunt and begged to go also, and Miss Anthony blithely took every applicant under her wing, with the result that when we arrived at the box-office the next day there were twelve of us in the group. When she presented her note and asked for a box, the local manager looked doubtfully at the delegation.

"A box only holds six," he objected, logically.

Miss Anthony, who had given no thought to that slight detail, looked us over and smiled her seraphic smile.

"Why, in that case," she said, cheerfully, "you'll have to give us two boxes, won't you?"

The amused manager decided that he would, and handed her the tickets; and she led her band to their places in triumph. When the performance began Colonel Cody, as was his custom, entered the arena from the far end of the building, riding his wonderful horse and bathed, of course, in the effulgence of his faithful spot-light. He rode directly to our boxes, reined his horse in front of Miss Anthony, rose in his stirrups, and with his characteristic gesture swept his slouch-hat to his saddle-bow in salutation. "Aunt Susan" immediately rose, bowed in her turn and, for the moment as enthusiastic as a girl, waved her handkerchief at him, while the big audience, catching the spirit of the scene, wildly applauded. It was a striking picture—this meeting of the pioneer man and woman; and, poor as I am, I would give a hundred dollars for a snapshot of it.

On many occasions I saw instances of Miss Anthony's prescience—and one of these was connected with the death of Frances E. Willard. "Aunt Susan" had called on Miss Willard, and, coming to me from the sick-room, had walked the floor, beating her hands together as she talked of the visit.

"Frances Willard is dying," she exclaimed, passionately. "She is dying, and she doesn't know it, and no one around her realizes it. She is lying there, seeing into two worlds, and making more plans than a thousand women could carry out in ten years. Her brain is wonderful. She has the most extraordinary clearness of vision. There should be a stenographer in that room, and every word she utters should be taken down, for every word is golden. But they don't understand. They can't realize that she is going. I told Anna Gordon the truth, but she won't believe it."[13]

Miss Willard died a few days later, with a suddenness which seemed to be a terrible shock to those around her.

Of "Aunt Susan's" really remarkable lack of self-consciousness we who worked close to her had a thousand extraordinary examples. Once, I remember, at the New Orleans Convention, she reached the hall a little late, and as she entered, the great audience already assembled gave her a tremendous reception. The exercises of the day had not yet begun, and Miss Anthony stopped short and looked around for an explanation of the outburst. It never for a moment occurred to her that the tribute was to her.

"What has happened, Anna?" she asked at last.

"You happened, Aunt Susan," I had to explain.

Again, on the great "College Night" of the Baltimore Convention, when President M. Carey Thomas of Bryn Mawr College had finished her wonderful tribute to Miss Anthony, the audience, carried away by the speech and also by the presence of the venerable leader on the platform, broke into a whirlwind of applause. In this "Aunt Susan" artlessly joined, clapping her hands as hard as she could. "This is all for you, Aunt Susan," I whispered, "so it isn't your time to applaud."

"Aunt Susan" continued to clap. "Nonsense," she said, briskly. "It's not for me. It's for the Cause—the Cause!"

Miss Anthony told me in 1904 that she regarded her reception in Berlin, during the meeting of the International Council of Women that year, as the climax of her career. She said it after the unexpected and wonderful ovation she had received from the German people, and certainly throughout her inspiring life nothing had happened that moved her more deeply.

For some time Mrs. Carrie Chapman Catt, of whose splendid work for the Cause I shall later have more to say, had cherished the plan of forming an International Suffrage Alliance.[14] She believed the time had come when the suffragists of the entire world could meet to their common benefit; and Miss Anthony, always Mrs. Catt's devoted friend and admirer, agreed with her. A committee was appointed to meet in Berlin in 1904, just before the meeting of the International Council of Women, and Miss Anthony was appointed chairman of the committee. At first the plan of the committee was not welcomed by the International Council; there was even a suspicion that its purpose was to start a rival organization. But it met, a constitution was framed, and officers were elected, Mrs. Catt—the ideal choice for the place— being made president. As a climax to the organization, a great public mass-meeting had been arranged by the German suffragists, but at the special plea of the president of the International Council Miss Anthony remained away from this meeting. It was represented to her that the interests of the Council might suffer if she and other of its leading speakers were also leaders in the suffrage movement. In the interest of harmony, therefore, she followed the wishes of the Council's president—to my great unhappiness and to that of other suffragists.

When the meeting was opened the first words of the presiding officer were, "Where is Susan B. Anthony?" and the demonstration that followed the question was the most unexpected and overwhelming incident of the gathering. The entire audience rose, men jumped on their chairs, and the cheering continued without a break for ten minutes. Every second of that time I seemed to see Miss Anthony, alone in her hotel room, longing with all her big heart to be with us, as we longed to have her. I prayed that the loss of a tribute which would have meant so much might be made up to her, and it was. Afterward, when we burst in upon her and told her of the great demonstration the mere mention of her name had caused, her lips quivered and her brave old eyes filled with tears. As we looked at her I think we all realized anew that what the world called stoicism in Susan B. Anthony throughout the years of her long struggle had been, instead, the splendid courage of an indomitable soul—while all the time the woman's heart had longed for affection and recognition. The next morning the leading Berlin newspaper, in reporting the debate and describing the spontaneous tribute to Miss Anthony, closed with these sentences: "The Americans call her 'Aunt Susan.' She is our 'Aunt Susan,' too!"

Throughout the remainder of Miss Anthony's visit she was the most honored figure at the International Council. Every time she entered the great convention-hall the entire audience rose and remained standing until she was seated; each mention of her name was punctuated by cheers; and the enthusiasm when she appeared on the platform to say a few words was beyond bounds. When the Empress of Germany gave her reception to the officers of the Council, she crowned the hospitality of her people in a characteristically gracious way. As soon as Miss Anthony was presented to her the Empress invited her to be seated, and to remain seated, although everyone else, including the august lady herself, was standing. A little later, seeing the intrepid warrior of eighty-four on her feet with the other delegates, the Empress sent one of her aides across the room with this message: "Please tell my friend Miss Anthony that I especially wish her to be seated. We must not let her grow weary."

In her turn, Miss Anthony was fascinated by the Empress. She could not keep her eyes off that charming royal lady. Probably the thing that most impressed her was the ability of her Majesty as a linguist. Receiving women from every civilized country on the globe, the Empress seemed to address each in her own tongue—slipping from one language into the next as easily as from one topic to another.

"And here I am," mourned "Aunt Susan," "speaking only one language, and that not very well."

At this Berlin quinquennial, by the way, I preached the Council sermon, and the occasion gained a certain interest from the fact that I was the first ordained woman to preach in a church in Germany. It then took on a tinge of humor from the additional fact that, according to the German law, as suddenly revealed to us by the police, no clergyman was permitted to preach unless clothed in clerical robes in the pulpit. It happened that I had not taken my clerical robes with me—I am constantly forgetting those clerical robes!—so the pastor of the church kindly offered me his robes.

Now the pastor was six feet tall and broad in proportion, and I, as I have already confessed, am very short. His robes transformed me into such an absurd caricature of a preacher that it was quite impossible for me to wear them. What, then, were we to do? Lacking clerical robes, the police would not allow me to utter six words. It was finally decided that the clergyman should meet the letter of the law by entering the pulpit in his robes and standing by my side while I delivered my sermon. The law soberly accepted this solution of the problem, and we offered the congregation the extraordinary tableau of a pulpit combining a large and impressive pastor standing silently beside a small and inwardly convulsed woman who had all she could do to deliver her sermon with the solemnity the occasion required.

Source: Anna Howard Shaw, with the Collaboration of Elizabeth Jordan, *The Story of a Pioneer* (Harper & Brothers, 1915).

Acknowledgments

Our thanks to Erin Dooling, Christine Lenahan, Sophia Pandelidis, and Riane Lumer who assisted in compiling Jordan's writings, transcribing articles from microfilm, double-checking transcriptions, deciphering difficult-to-read words, and identifying references that required endnotes, among other tasks. Their work on this edition was made possible by the Undergraduate Research Fellowship Program at Boston College. We would also like to thank the staff at Boston College's O'Neill Library for valuable assistance. Our gratitude goes to Brooke Kroeger for contributing the foreword and for her continued support of our research; Karen Roggenkamp for providing crucial materials and for her important work on Jordan; and Sharon Harris for sharing the vast knowledge she has accrued while working on a biography of Jordan. Thank you also to Elif Armbruster, Thomas Augst, Julia Bogiages, Mary Chapman, Patricia Crain, Kimberly Chabot Davis, Ellen Gruber Garvey, Maia McAleavey, Elizabeth McHenry, Victoria Olwell, Claudia Stokes, and Ilyon Woo. And finally, thank you to the team at Penguin, especially our editor Elizabeth Vogt and cover designer Michelle Thompson, for making our "dream classics project" a reality.

Notes

I: NEWSPAPER WOMAN: SEEING "THE WORLD"

1. "write each story as [if it were] fiction": Elizabeth Garver Jordan, *Three Rousing Cheers* (New York: D. Appleton-Century Co., 1938), p. 49.
2. "combined the best features of the stunt age with sound writing": Ishbel Ross, *Ladies of the Press: The Story of Women in Journalism by an Insider* (New York: Harper & Brothers, 1936), p. 178.
3. "shed their own tears": Jordan, *Three Rousing Cheers*, p. 37.
4. "two Lizzie Bordens": Elizabeth Garver Jordan, "This Is the Real Lizzie Borden," *New York World*, June 18, 1893, p. 15; see p. 107 in this volume.
5. when women are accused of violent crimes: As evidence of the cultural fascination with women's violent criminality, Borden's story has been the subject of multiple retellings and adaptations, from nursery rhymes ("Lizzie Borden took an axe / And gave her mother forty whacks / When she saw what she had done / She gave her father forty-one") to feminist interpretations. American choreographer Agnes de Mille created a ballet adaptation, *Fall River Legend*, that debuted in 1948; in the 1960s, composer Jack Beeson and writer Richard Plant created an opera *Lizzie Borden: A Family Portrait in Three Acts*. A number of literary interpretations, including Evan Hunter's *Lizzie* (1984) and Elizabeth Engstrom's *Lizzie Borden* (1990), explore Borden's potential motive and other aspects of her identity, including her sexuality. Sharon Pollock's 1981 play *Blood Relations* interprets Borden's story in a social commentary that is also a reflection on the playwright's own experience as battered wife, while noted feminist fiction writer Angela Carter's story "The Fall River Axe Murders" emphasizes Borden's physical constriction and discomfort while menstruating. Borden's life has been the subject of both television movies (notably 1974's *The*

Legend of Lizzie Borden and 2014's *Lizzie Borden Took an Ax*) and slasher-style B movies. Most recently, Riley Sager's popular thriller *The Only One Left* (Dutton, 2023) took its inspiration from the Borden murders. For more, see Ann Schofield, "Lizzie Borden Took an Axe: History, Feminism and American Culture." *American Studies* vol. 34, no. 1 (Spring, 1993), pp. 91–103.

6. **her journalistic prowess:** Jordan was one of a small number of women journalists—including Anna Page Scott (also of the *New York World*) and Amy Robsart (of the *Boston Post*)—covering the trial. See Cara Robertson, *The Trial of Lizzie Borden* (New York: Simon & Schuster, 2019), pp. 92–93, 96.

7. **"the newspaper woman of the twentieth century":** Elizabeth G. Jordan, "What It Means to Be a Newspaper Woman," *Ladies' Home Journal* 16, no. 2 (January 1899): 8; see p. 128 in this volume.

"A MOUNTAIN PREACHER"

1. **Wise, Lee, Scott and Letcher counties:** Counties in the Appalachian Mountains.

2. **Reed:** Thomas Brackett Reed (1839–1902) was a Republican politician who served as Speaker of the House of Representatives from 1889 to 1891 and then from 1895 to 1899. In 1896, Reed ran for president and lost the Republican nomination to William McKinley.

3. **McKinley:** William McKinley (1843–1901) was the twenty-fifth president of the United States. McKinley served from 1897 until 1901, when he was assassinated. Prior to his term, he served as a Republican congressman and was responsible for the Tariff Act of 1890, which caused fierce debate between Democrats and Republicans.

4. **Big Stone Gap:** A town in Virginia whose early development was due to the coal industry.

5. **negro guide:** Now an outdated term, "negro" referred to Black or African American people and was not necessarily used in a derogatory sense.

6. **delf cups:** A variation on Delft, this refers to a cup with a blue-on-white design.

7. **"janders":** Jaundice.

8. **"Pollock's Pomes":** This may be a reference to Edward Pollock's *Poems* published in 1876. Pollock's poems were popular but con-

sidered poor imitations of work by more accomplished poets such as Edgar Allan Poe.

9. **Stedman or Aldrich:** Edmund Clarence Stedman (1833–1908) and Thomas Bailey Aldrich (1836–1907) were American poets.

"JESSIE ADAMSON'S SUICIDE"

1. **troth:** A term for faith or loyalty.
2. **Eldorado:** Usually written as El Dorado, the term refers to a place of gold and riches and is associated with sixteenth- and seventeenth-century European myths about the Americas, specifically South America.
3. **Fortunate Isles:** Fortunate Isles were islands in the Atlantic Ocean where the heroes of Greek mythology were said to live in a winterless paradise.
4. **burin:** A tool used for engraving.
5. **Midas:** In Greek mythology, King Midas was known for his wealth because everything he touched turned into gold.
6. **the old, old story:** A reference to a nineteenth-century hymn "Tell me the old, old story."
7. **bromide of potassium:** Potassium bromide was a salt used as a sedative and anticonvulsant in the nineteenth century.
8. **roof-tree:** The beam that lays atop the sloping parts of a roof.

"THE HAPPIEST WOMAN IN NEW YORK"

1. **L roads:** Shorthand for the elevated railroad.
2. **the woman reporter of THE WORLD:** As the author of this article, Jordan is referring to herself in the third person.
3. **Dutch table:** A type of table with extension leaves that slide out.
4. **stuff dress:** Stuff refers to the kind of material used to make the dress and usually means it was made of something other than silk or another expensive fabric.
5. **indolent ulcer:** A sore that fails to heal as expected.
6. **The Elevated Railroad:** A railroad that ran through Manhattan on tracks above street level.
7. **Pulitzer Building:** Home to the New York *World*, the Pulitzer Building was the tallest building in New York City upon its completion in 1890.
8. **"Ach, Gott":** "Oh God!" Note that the rest of the German translations appeared in the original *World* article.

"A STRANGE LITTLE EAST SIDE GIRL"

1. **"queer":** In its nineteenth-century usage, queer meant strange, odd, or different. At the time, it did not necessarily have associations with sexual identity.
2. **"Petit Daniel":** "Petit Daniel" may be a reference to a character from the nineteenth-century French children's book *Daniel* by Jeanne Marcel.
3. **Bowery:** A street and neighborhood in lower Manhattan.
4. **a WORLD man:** The reference to "a WORLD man" suggests that this particular "True Stories of the News" article was written by a male reporter, which is a possibility. However, Jordan has taken credit for the entire "True Stories of the News" series, and Barbara Belford's *Brilliant Bylines* specifically attributes this piece to her. If the article is indeed authored by Jordan, there are a number of explanations; for example, Karen Roggenkamp suggests that Jordan could be assuming a male persona. Jordan could also be using "man" in the generic sense of the word to refer to herself, or the figure of "a WORLD man" could be a different individual than the reporter who wrote this piece. For further discussion of this issue and Jordan's "True Stories" stories in general, see Karen Roggenkamp, "Elizabeth Jordan, 'True Stories,' and Newspaper Fiction in Late-Nineteenth-Century Journalism," *Literature and Journalism: Inspirations, Intersections, and Inventions from Ben Franklin to Stephen Colbert*, ed. Mark Canada (New York: Palgrave Macmillan, 2013), pp. 119–141.
5. **Father Drumgoole's:** Drumgoole was an Irish Catholic priest who ran a home for orphaned and homeless children in New York City in the nineteenth century.

"PUT YOURSELF IN HIS PLACE"

1. **lares and penates:** Home and household possessions.
2. **Hoffman House:** A fancy hotel located at Broadway and Twenty-fifth Street in New York City.
3. **Little Lord Fauntleroy's:** Little Lord Fauntleroy is the title character of a popular 1885 novel by children's book author Frances Hodgson Burnett.
4. **croup:** Common among children, croup is an infection of the upper airway that makes breathing difficult.
5. **"gasfitter":** Prior to the advent of electricity, gasfitters installed gas lamps and other gas appliances.

6. **in bad odor:** An English idiom meaning that one is regarded with disapproval.

"THE SILVER LINING OF THE CLOUD"

1. **pathetic story was told in Wednesday's WORLD:** This is a reference to the previous article, "Put Yourself in His Place."

"THE CASE OF LIZZIE BORDEN"

1. **Lizzie D. Borden:** The article erroneously lists the initial "D" for her middle name. Lizzie Borden's middle name was Andrew, after her father, Andrew Borden.
2. **Choctaw Indian squaw:** Squaw is a derogatory term used to refer to Native American women. Because the Choctaw were known to be fierce warriors, this reference uses negative stereotypes about purported Native American savagery to emphasize the violence of the crime.
3. **penurious:** Stingy.
4. **niggardly:** Stingy.
5. **dinner:** In the nineteenth century, it was fairly customary to eat a meal called dinner in the early afternoon.
6. **held in abeyance:** The information was temporarily suspended by the prosecution, presumably so that the lawyers could reveal it at the trial.
7. **sinkers:** Weights that are attached to a fishing line to keep it anchored.
8. **Marion:** Marion is a town in Massachusetts located on Buzzards Bay.
9. **peradventure:** Beyond any doubt or uncertainty.
10. **Boisgobey school of French novels:** Refers to the work of French writer Fortuné Hippolyte Auguste Abraham-Dubois (1821–1891), who published under the pen name Fortuné du Boisgobey and was a popular nineteenth-century crime novelist.
11. **prussic acid:** Hydrogen cyanide, a colorless chemical compound that is usually fatal when ingested.
12. **the Manchester girl:** Bertha Manchester was murdered in Fall River five days before the trial of Lizzie Borden began. She was found dead in her kitchen in a similar state as the Bordens, which raised suspicions that the same person could be responsible for both crimes. In 1894, Jose Correa de Mello was convicted of

Manchester's murder. The murders appear to be unconnected as he was not in Fall River at the time of the Bordens' murders.

13. **the Whitechapel murderer or the murderers in London:** The Whitechapel murders were a series of unsolved murders of women that took place in London beginning in 1888 and were attributed to the notorious serial killer Jack the Ripper.

14. **Taunton Jail:** Lizzie Borden was held in a jail in Taunton, Massachusetts, prior to her trial.

"LIZZIE'S DARK DAY"

1. **Wilkie Collins:** Collins (1824–1889) was an English novelist best known for his mystery novel *The Woman in White* (1859), one of the most famous examples of sensation fiction.

2. **turnouts:** A turnout is a carriage.

3. **coupe:** An enclosed carriage.

4. **reefer jacket:** A double-breasted jacket, usually made of wool to supply warmth.

5. **the attack of grip:** Influenza (usually spelled "grippe").

6. **the bar:** The railing that separates those directly involved in the trial proceedings from the spectators.

7. **Mr. Adams:** Melvin O. Adams (1850–1920) was an attorney and part of Lizzie Borden's legal defense team.

8. **inquest:** An initial inquiry in which a judge surveys the facts about an incident, usually a death, in order to determine if it was a crime.

9. **bromo-caffeine:** A medical remedy used for headaches and mental fatigue.

10. **depredators:** A depredator is one who attacks and plunders.

11. **Gov. Robinson:** George Robinson (1834–1896) was a former Massachusetts governor who served as Lizzie Borden's defense attorney.

12. **Maggie (Bridget):** Refers to the Bordens' Irish servant, Bridget Sullivan. Lizzie and her sister, Emma, referred to Bridget as "Maggie," the name of their previous Irish servant. For a discussion of ethnicity in the Borden case, see Joseph Conforti, *Lizzie Borden on Trial: Murder, Ethnicity, and Gender* (Lawrence, KS: University of Kansas Press, 2016).

13. **Bedford cord:** A durable fabric similar to corduroy. The fabric is named after the town of New Bedford, a textile manufacturing center where the Borden trial happened to be taking place.

"MISS BORDEN'S HOPE"

1. **calico and cambric:** Different kinds of cotton fabric.
2. **basques:** A close-fitting bodice that extends over the hips and was worn by women in the Victorian era.
3. **gores:** The front triangular section of a skirt.
4. **cut-biases:** A bias cut refers to a way of cutting fabric diagonally so that it drapes softly over curves of the body.
5. **demi-trains:** A short train at the back of a skirt or dress.
6. **bell-skirts:** A bell-shaped skirt.

"THIS IS THE REAL LIZZIE BORDEN"

1. **the real Lizzie Borden:** For a detailed account of the Borden trial, see Cara Robertson, *The Trial of Lizzie Borden* (New York: Simon and Schuster, 2019).
2. **French kid boots:** Boots made of leather from a goat's skin that are either manufactured in France or resemble leather originally manufactured in France.
3. **French twist:** A woman's hairstyle in which the hair is coiled and secured at the back of the head.
4. **Irish nose:** Lizzie Borden was not Irish. Jordan is playing with imagery here, not reporting facts. In creating a picture of her subject for the reader, she suggests that Borden's nose resembles that of someone who is ethnically Irish.
5. **scolding locks:** Strands of hair that refuse to stay in place.
6. **cut:** Refers to an illustration made for a newspaper in the nineteenth century. The article included a close-up sketch (or cut) of Lizzie Borden's mouth.
7. **physiognomy:** Now considered a pseudoscience, physiognomy is the study of facial features as indicative of character and/or ethnic origin.
8. **farmer's satin:** A type of durable fabric usually made from cotton and wool.
9. **crepe:** A lightweight fabric.
10. **haircloth:** A stiff fabric.
11. **pompon:** An alternative spelling of pompom, a decorative ball made of wool and often used on hats.
12. **Chimney Corner Companion:** A book compilation that advertised itself as a "selection of the most interesting, amusing, and authentic descriptions and anecdotes of men, manners, and things taken from the best sources in English literature."

13. **Scott, Thackeray, and Dickens:** These are the names of three of the best-known nineteenth-century novelists, Sir Walter Scott (1771–1832), William Makepeace Thackeray (1811–1863), and Charles Dickens (1812–1870). Scott was Scottish and Thackeray and Dickens were British.

"THE NEWSPAPER WOMAN'S STORY"

1. **Max O'Rell:** Pen name for the French journalist Leon Paul Blouet (1847–1903), who published a book called *A Frenchman in America* in 1891.
2. **Monsieur Blouet's:** Refers to Max O'Rell, which was the pen name of French journalist Leon Paul Blouet. See previous note.
3. **These women:** The names mentioned are those of successful women journalists. For more on women in journalism history, see Ishbel Ross, *Ladies of the Press: The Story of Women in Journalism by an Insider* (New York: Harper & Bros., 1936) and Brooke Kroeger, *Undaunted: How Women Changed American Journalism* (New York: Knopf, 2023).
4. **modistes:** Stylish dressmakers.
5. **"space-work":** A newspaper reporter who did space-work was paid according to how much space their copy filled in print.
6. **Olive Schreiner:** Schreiner (1855–1920) was a South African writer known for her feminist views. Her 1892 short story "The Policy In Favor of Protection," which is subtitled "Was it Right?—Was it Wrong?," features a journalist as the main character.
7. **page story:** A story that appears on the front page of the newspaper.
8. **quinine capsules:** A drug used to treat malaria.
9. **The Koch lymph cure:** A cure for tuberculosis named for German physician Robert Koch and developed in 1890. The cure was subsequently proven to be ineffective.
10. **Blackwell's Island:** An island in Manhattan's East River that housed several institutions in the nineteenth century, including a hospital, a prison, and an insane asylum. It is now known as Roosevelt Island and is primarily residential.
11. **"phthisis":** Another word for tuberculosis.

"WHAT IT MEANS TO BE A NEWSPAPER WOMAN"

1. "galleys": Final proofs of an article.
2. mawkish: Sentimental or silly, used in a pejorative sense.
3. nervous dyspepsia: A nervous stomach.
4. abroad: Abroad here refers to being out and about in different areas, not necessarily to being in a foreign country.
5. "perquisites": Perks.
6. passes: In this context, the word "passes" likely refers to romantic overtures.
7. "build heads": Crafts headlines.

II: THE CITY ROOM AND BEYOND: EARLY NEWSPAPER FICTIONS AND MAGAZINE STORIES

1. "the first emotional expression of the woman reporter": "Cosmopolitan Literary Juggling," *Life*, April 7, 1898, p. 299.

"RUTH'S HERRICK'S ASSIGNMENT"

1. cuts: An illustration.

"A POINT OF ETHICS"

1. "prig": Someone who acts like they are morally superior to others.
2. "Park Row": A street in New York City also referred to as "Newspaper Row" because the major newspaper buildings were located there in the nineteenth and early twentieth centuries.
3. "on space": Work paid according to how much space the copy filled in print.

"A ROMANCE OF THE CITY ROOM"

1. dwarf bookcase: A small bookcase, usually about three feet in height.
2. clew: Archaic spelling of "clue."

3. **concomitant:** A natural accompaniment; in this case, the note with the roses.
4. **"'Pleasures of Life'":** A book by Sir John Lubbock (1834–1913) in which he shares his philosophy for leading a good life.
5. **"For the spring, the spring is coming":** These are the lyrics to a song called "The Swallows" popularized by soprano Evangeline Florence at the turn of the twentieth century.
6. **jacqueminots:** A kind of rose.
7. **"consumptive":** Affected with a wasting disease, usually tuberculosis.
8. **"Algiers":** The capital of Algeria.

"MISS VAN DYKE'S BEST STORY"

1. **Tammanyites:** Political supporters of Tammany Hall, the main political machine of the Democratic Party in the nineteenth century. Tammany Hall was usually associated with political corruption.
2. **Wigwam:** Tammanyites notoriously appropriated Native American words and customs, naming their meeting space after the domed dwellings used by many Indigenous tribes. The organization itself was named for Chief Tamanend, a Lenni-Lenape leader who signed a peace treaty with William Penn in the late seventeenth century.
3. **"Tenderloin":** New York City's red-light district in the nineteenth and early twentieth centuries.
4. **"corker":** Slang for something outstanding.
5. **red paint:** Makeup (that is, rouge and lipstick).
6. **"Tenderfoot":** A newcomer or novice.
7. **sobriquet:** Nickname.
8. **"author of 'The Deceased Wife's Sister'":** This is a reference to novelist William Clark Russell (1844–1911). Russell's 1874 novel, *The Deceased Wife's Sister*, marked an early success in his career due to its sensational content.

"BETWEEN DARKNESS & DAWN"

1. **"Die Zauberflöte":** The German opera *The Magic Flute* by Wolfgang Amadeus Mozart.
2. **Apostles' Creed:** A Catholic prayer professing faith in God.
3. *fin de siècle*: End of the nineteenth century.
4. **mignonette:** A herbaceous plant with fragrant flowers.

"IN THE CASE OF HANNAH RISSER"

1. **Forsyth Street:** A street on the Lower East Side of Manhattan.
2. **cripple:** An outdated term for someone with a physical disability, usually one that prevents them from walking.
3. **A little Jewish society:** A Jewish philanthropic association.
4. **Rip Van Winkle:** "Rip Van Winkle" (1819) is a short story by Washington Irving in which the main character, Rip Van Winkle, falls asleep for twenty years and awakes to a changed world.
5. **brougham:** A horse-drawn carriage.
6. **pigeon-English:** Usually spelled "pidgin," this phrase refers to a grammatically simplified form of English used by non-native speakers.
7. ***"Ach Gott!"* she gasped. *"Gott sei dank!"*:** German for "Oh God!" and "Thank God!"

"MRS. WARBURTON'S THEORIES"

1. **portières:** A curtain hanging in a doorway.
2. **"gum shoes":** A shoe made of rubber.
3. **"According to her theory":** The theories attributed to Mrs. Warburton closely resemble those of women's rights activist Charlotte Perkins Gilman, author of *Women and Economics* (1898) and many other works of feminist nonfiction. Gilman also wrote fiction with feminist themes such as the well-known short story "The Yellow Wallpaper" (1892).
4. **rather yellow as to his journalism:** Refers to yellow journalism, a kind of sensationalized journalism popularized during the late nineteenth century as a means of attracting readers and increasing circulation.
5. **Delft:** A style of blue-on-white pottery that originated in the Netherlands.
6. **"The Walkürie":** A German opera by Richard Wagner, loosely based on Norse mythology.
7. **"Belleek cup":** Belleek is a kind of pottery that originated in Belleek, Ireland.
8. ***"quart d'heure"*:** A quarter of an hour, or fifteen minutes.
9. **"guyed":** Ridiculed.
10. ***"mon Dieu"*:** French exclamation meaning "My god!"
11. ***"certainement"*:** French for "certainly."
12. ***"vraiment"*:** French for "truly."

13. *"fille"*: French for "maid."
14. *"maintenant"*: French for "now."
15. *"oui"*: French for "yes."
16. hassock: A footstool.
17. filliped: Flicked a small object.

III: THE NEW WOMAN COMES OF AGE: MAY IVERSON AND THE SEEDS OF #METOO

"THE VOICE OF TRUTH"

1. St. Catharine's: The fictional convent school that the character May Iverson attends. It was modeled on St. Mary's in Milwaukee, the convent school that Jordan attended.
2. Horace Greeley: Greeley (1811–1872) was a journalist who founded the *New York Tribune*. He died a month after the death of his wife, hence the reference to dying of a broken heart.
3. Juliet: A reference to the teenage character in William Shakespeare's tragedy *Romeo and Juliet*.
4. the way the mother pelican does: This is a reference to the false belief that mother pelicans pierced their breasts to feed their young.
5. "organ": A periodical that represents the views of an organization.
6. Ignominy: Public shame or disgrace.
7. Henry James: James (1843–1916) was an American novelist known for his experimental literary style that straddled realism and modernism.
8. "Parsifal": An 1882 opera by Richard Wagner. It was performed at the Metropolitan Opera House in New York in 1903.
9. Iroquois Theatre fire: In 1903, a fire in Chicago's Iroquois Theatre killed over six hundred people.
10. Ethel Barrymore: Barrymore (1879–1959) was a famous American actress who was born and raised in Philadelphia.
11. "Cousin Kate": A 1903 play by Hubert Henry Davies.
12. President Roosevelt: Theodore Roosevelt (1858–1919) served as President of the United States from 1901–1909.
13. Schenectady: A city in New York.

"WHAT DREAMS MAY COME"

1. **as Shakespeare says:** This is a reference to the famous lines from Shakespeare's *As You Like It*: "All the world's a stage, / And the men and women merely players."

2. **Sarah Underhill Worthington:** A fictional writer created by Jordan who appears in other May Iverson stories.

3. **Charles Dudley Warner:** Warner (1829–1900) was an American writer and intellectual.

4. **minims:** The smallest, referring to the youngest girls at the convent.

5. **Madame Duse:** Eleonora Duse (1858–1924), a famous Italian actress.

6. **Sarah Bernhardt:** Bernhardt (1844–1923) was a famous French actress.

7. **Margaret Sangster:** Sangster (1838–1912) was an American editor and writer. She was the editor of *Harper's Bazar* in the 1890s. She was succeeded by Elizabeth Jordan, who took over as editor in 1900.

8. **Henry Van Dyke:** Van Dyke (1852–1932) was a Presbyterian minister and author whose work was known for its religious themes and with whom Jordan worked as an editor.

9. **Ethel Barrymore:** Barrymore (1879–1959) was a famous American actress.

10. **Mr. Henry James and Mr. William Dean Howells:** James (1843–1916) and Howells (1837–1920) were famous American writers with whom Jordan collaborated over the course of her career.

11. **Marconi:** Guglielmo Marconi (1834–1937) was an Italian inventor known for developing a wireless telegraph.

12. **A. Henry Savage Landor:** Landor (1865–1924) was an English painter, explorer, and anthropologist.

13. **Mark Twain:** Twain is the pen name of Samuel Clemens (1835–1910), a famous American writer and humorist with whom Jordan worked as an editor.

14. **Dr. Grace Peckham Murray:** Murray (1848–1933) was an American physician known for her work on women's health.

15. **Margaret Deland:** Deland (1857–1945) was a realist American novelist whose fiction dealt with social and religious issues and with whom Jordan worked as an editor.

16. **Mrs. Humphry Ward:** British novelist Mary Augusta Ward (1851–1920), who published under her husband's name, was a founding president of Britain's Women's National Anti-Suffrage League.

17. **Harry Lehr:** Henry Symes Lehr (1869–1929) was a Gilded Age socialite known as "America's Court Jester."

18. **Marianna Wheeler:** Wheeler (?–1931) was a turn-of-the-twentieth-century writer known for her advice books about how to care for babies and raise children.
19. **Welsh-rabbits:** Also known as Welsh rarebit, a dish consisting of hot cheese sauce over toasted bread.
20. **"creepers":** A one-piece outfit worn by infants.
21. **take the black veil:** In Catholicism, a way of indicating that someone has become a nun (that is, wears a black veil).

"WOMAN SUFFRAGE AT ST. CATHARINE'S"

1. **sharper than a serpent's tooth:** This is a reference to a line from Shakespeare's *King Lear*: "How sharper than a serpent's tooth it is / To have a thankless child!"
2. **Mrs. Pankhurst:** Emmeline Pankhurst (1858–1928) was a British activist and leading suffragist who traveled to the United States in the early twentieth century to lecture on women's rights.
3. **fed through tubes:** When suffrage activists were imprisoned, some went on hunger strikes and were subsequently force-fed by the authorities using feeding tubes.
4. **antis:** A term used to refer to anti-suffragists.
5. **"not single spies, but in battalions":** The quotation is from Shakespeare's *Hamlet*: "When sorrows come, they come not single spies, / But in battalions."
6. **"clouded with a doubt," like King Arthur's:** The reference is to a line from the nineteenth-century poem "Morte d'Arthur" ("The Passing of Arthur") by Alfred, Lord Tennyson.
7. **a man I read about somewhere:** The Greek orator Demosthenes was said to overcome his speech impediment by practicing speaking with pebbles in his mouth.
8. **like the boy on the burning deck:** This is likely a reference to the poem "Casabianca" (1826) by Felicia Hemans.
9. **"It is Thou":** This is a reference to a poem by Rumi, a thirteenth-century Persian poet, Islamic scholar, and Sufi mystic.
10. **it wasn't a tiger:** This is a reference to Frank Stockton's 1882 short story "The Lady, or the Tiger?"

"I INTRODUCE BEAUTY CULTURE"

1. **wedge:** Dental wedges were used to shift teeth and fix other irregularities.

2. **Greek fillet:** A fillet was a narrow band worn to encircle the head. It originated in classical antiquity—hence, the adjective "Greek."

3. **Byron and Keats and Tennyson:** Lord Byron (1788–1824), John Keats (1795–1821), and Alfred, Lord Tennyson (1809–1892) were famous English poets associated with Romanticism.

4. **"From Silken Samarcand to cedar'd Lebanon":** These are lines from the poem "The Eve of St. Agnes" (1820) by John Keats.

"MY FIRST ASSIGNMENT"

1. **Sixth Hungarian Rhapsody:** A musical composition by Franz Liszt (1811–1886).

2. **the Cross of Honor, winner of the Crown:** Student awards. When Elizabeth Jordan graduated from St. Mary's, she was awarded the Cross of Honor, as she describes in her autobiography, *Three Rousing Cheers*.

3. **Grotto of Lourdes:** A Catholic shrine replicating the grotto in Lourdes, France, where apparitions of Our Lady of Lourdes were seen in 1858.

4. **vespers:** Evening prayer service.

5. **policeman's electric bull's-eye:** A kind of lantern often used by police on patrol.

"THE CRY OF THE PACK"

1. **Atlantic City:** A resort city in New Jersey known for gambling and entertainment.

2. **"cub reporters":** New or inexperienced newspaper reporters.

3. **Coney Island:** A seaside area of Brooklyn, New York, with leisure attractions including a famous amusement park.

4. **"Star of Bethlehem":** The star in the nativity story that leads the wise men to Christ's birth.

5. **Beethoven and Debussy:** German composer Ludwig von Beethoven (1770–1827) and French composer Claude Debussy (1862–1918).

6. **Homeric laughter:** Irrepressible laughter.

7. **"lamb among the wolves":** This saying originated with a biblical verse, "Behold, I am sending you out like sheep among wolves. Therefore be as shrewd as snakes and as innocent as doves" (Matthew 10:16).

8. **Battery:** The area at the southern end of Manhattan.

9. **"whited sepulcher":** A biblical reference to a person who appears good on the outside but turns out to be wicked inside.

"THE CASE OF HELEN BRANDOW"

1. **Mollie Merk:** A fictional character who is introduced prior to this chapter in *May Iverson's Career*. Mollie Merk is described as "Mr. Hurd's most sensational woman reporter—the one who went up in air-ships and described her sensations, or purposefully fell in front of trolley-cars to prove that the fenders would not work" (Elizabeth Jordan, *May Iverson's Career*, Harper & Brothers, 1914, p. 68). Merk is modeled on girl stunt reporters such as Nellie Bly (1864–1922).

2. **sobbing sisterhood:** "Sob sister" was a term coined in 1907 for female reporters who specialized in "sob stories," using emotional sentimentality to create human interest. It was often used in a derogatory (and sexist) sense.

3. **a Hobbema:** A painting by Dutch landscape painter Meindert Hobbema (1638–1709).

4. **corker:** Slang for something outstanding.

5. **If Mrs. Appleton had experienced:** Mrs. Appleton is based on Jordan's friend, the novelist Gertrude Atherton (1857–1948). In *Three Rousing Cheers*, Jordan describes asking Atherton for feedback on her early short story "Ruth Herrick's Assignment." Atherton responded with the following note: "Your story is a corker. I experienced a real thrill when the woman came out with her confession. I have sent the story to the editor of the *Cosmopolitan*. God alone knows what editors will do, but this one seems to have better judgment than most and I think he will take it" (Elizabeth Jordan, *Three Rousing Cheers*, New York: D. Appleton-Century Co, 1938, p. 110).

"THE REVOLT OF TILDY MEARS"

1. **Dr. Anna Harland:** The character of Dr. Anna Harland is based on Rev. Dr. Anna Howard Shaw (1847–1919), a prominent suffrage leader. Shaw received her medical degree from Boston University and was one of the first ordained female Methodist ministers in the United States. See pp. 337–72 of this volume for additional context.

2. **melodeon:** A small organ.

3. **"The Battle Hymn of the Republic":** A popular nineteenth-century patriotic song written by Julia Ward Howe (1819–1910).

4. **yellow banner:** Yellow was an emblematic color for the suffrage movement.

5. **Medora:** A city in North Dakota.

6. *"Alleluia"*: A Latin phrase meaning "praise God" used in Christianity.
7. **freshet:** Flooding from a stream or river due to heavy rain or melted snow.
8. **"of ten virgins five were wise":** This is a reference to the Parable of the Wise and Foolish Virgins in the Book of Matthew.
9. **collation:** A light, informal meal.
10. **"Bismarck":** Capital city of North Dakota.
11. **Sedalia:** A city in Missouri.
12. **"Dickinson":** A city in North Dakota.
13. **Sweetbriar and Mendan and Bismarck:** Cities in North Dakota.
14. **peroration:** The conclusion of a speech.

IV: COLLABORATION AND LITERARY ACTIVISM: JORDAN AS EDITOR AND ADVISER

1. **"a mess":** See Jordan, *Three Rousing Cheers*, p. 280.
2. **"probably the best woman speaker America ever had":** See Jordan, *Three Rousing Cheers*, p. 332.
3. **Shaw's work:** Anna Howard Shaw, "Why I Went into Suffrage Work," *Harper's Bazar* 46, no. 9 (September 1912): 440.
4. **"Miss Jordan, who wrote my book":** See Jordan, *Three Rousing Cheers*, p. 336.
5. **"for suffrage, for temperance, for social purity":** Anna Howard Shaw, with the Collaboration of Elizabeth Jordan, *The Story of a Pioneer* (New York: Harper & Brothers, 1915), p. 147; see p. 341 of this volume.
6. **"To her failure was merely another opportunity":** Shaw, *The Story of a Pioneer*, p. 204; see p. 357 of this volume.

CHAPTER VII: "THE GREAT CAUSE"

1. **East Dennis:** A town in Cape Cod, Massachusetts, where Shaw served as minister of the Wesleyan Methodist Church from 1878 to 1885.
2. **Mary A. Livermore:** Livermore (1820–1905) was an American journalist and woman's rights activist.
3. **Julia Ward Howe:** Howe (1819–1910) was a writer and suffragist, known for writing the "Battle Hymn of the Republic."
4. **Anna Garlin Spencer:** Spencer (1851–1931) was a Unitarian minister and the first woman ordained in Rhode Island.

5. **Lucy Stone:** Stone (1818–1893) was a leading suffragist and aboli-
   tionist. Along with Julia Ward Howe, she founded the American
   Woman Suffrage Association (AWSA). Because she did not change
   her name after she married, feminist women who kept their
   maiden names became known as Lucy Stoners.
6. **Mary F. Eastman:** Eastman (1833–1908) was an American suffragist.
7. **Captain Doane:** The Doane family resided in Cape Cod for multiple generations and were among the town of East Dennis's most
   prominent citizens.
8. **Moylan:** A town in Pennsylvania where Shaw lived from 1908
   until her death in 1919 at the age of seventy-two.
9. **the Emersons and John Greenleaf Whittier:** The figures listed here
   were prominent intellectuals, writers, and activists based in the
   Boston area. "The Emersons" refers to Transcendentalist thinker
   and writer Ralph Waldo Emerson (1803–1882) and his wife, Lid-
   ian Jackson Emerson (1802–1892). Whittier (1807–1892) was best
   known as a poet. James Freeman Clark (1810–1888) and Minot
   Savage (1841–1918) were ministers. Bronson Alcott (1799–1888)
   was a philosopher and reformer; his daughter, Louisa May Alcott
   (1832–1888), was a famous novelist, best remembered now as the
   author of *Little Women* (1868). Wendell Philips (1811–1884),
   William Lloyd Garrison (1805–1879), Stephen Symonds Foster
   (1809–1881), and Theodore Weld (1803–1895) were best known as
   abolitionists.
10. **Concord:** A town in Massachusetts where many of the Transcen-
    dentalists were based.
11. **school suffrage:** In some areas of the United States, women had the
    right to vote in school-related elections, even when they could not
    vote in local, state, and national elections.
12. **Abby May:** Abigail May Alcott (1840–1879) was a suffragist and
    the mother of novelist Louisa May Alcott.
13. **Edna Cheney:** Edna Dale Littlehale Cheney (1824–1904) was a
    nineteenth-century American writer and reformer based in Boston.
14. **New England Woman's Club:** One of the earliest women's clubs in
    the United States, it was founded in Boston in 1868. The nineteenth-
    century women's club movement brought middle-class women to-
    gether to discuss a variety of topics and provided opportunities for
    learning.
15. **Kate Gannett Wells:** Wells (1838–1911) was a prominent anti-
    suffragist.
16. **Mrs. Dahlgren, wife of Admiral Dahlgren:** Madeleine Vinton
    Dahlgren (1825–1898) was an anti-suffragist.

17. **Mrs. William Tecumseh Sherman:** Eleanor Boyle Ewing Sherman (1824–1888) was the wife of General William Tecumseh Sherman, leader of the Union Army during the Civil War.

18. **Elizabeth Cady Stanton:** A leading suffragist. With her long-time collaborator Susan B. Anthony, Stanton (1815–1902) founded the National Woman Suffrage Association (NWSA) in 1869. In 1890, the NWSA would merge with the rival American Woman Suffrage Association (AWSA) to form the National American Woman Suffrage Association (NAWSA).

19. **pony:** Translation of a foreign-language text, often used illicitly by students.

20. **Frances E. Willard:** Best-known as president of the Woman's Christian Temperance Union, Willard (1839–1898) was also a prominent suffragist.

21. **"Aunt Susan":** Suffrage leader Susan B. Anthony (1820–1906) was affectionately referred to as "Aunt Susan" by fellow suffragists.

22. **Mrs. Quincy Shaw:** Shaw (Pauline Agassiz Shaw; 1841–1917) was a suffragist, philanthropist, and reformer.

23. **Cora Scott Pond (Pope):** Pond (1856–?) was a fellow suffragist.

24. **Bureau of Boston:** Lecture bureaus that facilitated arrangements for speakers.

25. **"Chautauquas":** An educational movement in the United States especially popular in the late nineteenth and early twentieth centuries. Often held during the summer in rural communities, Chautauquas would bring in speakers to give lectures on a variety of topics.

26. **ptomaine poisoning:** A type of food poisoning.

27. **omnibus:** Another word for a bus.

28. **Faribault:** A city in Minnesota.

29. **Moody and Sankey hymn:** Ira David Sankey (1840–1908) was a gospel singer who worked with Dwight L. Moody (1837–1899), an evangelist. Together, they composed and popularized a number of nineteenth-century American hymns.

30. **St. Paul:** A city in Minnesota.

31. **cutter:** A horse-drawn sleigh.

CHAPTER IX: " 'AUNT SUSAN' "

1. **In *The Life of Susan B. Anthony*:** *The Life of Susan B. Anthony* refers to *The Life and Work of Susan B. Anthony* by Ida Husted Harper (Bowen-Merrill, 1899), which was published in two volumes.

2. **Dr. Lozier:** Clemence Sophia Harned Lozier (1813–1888) was an American physician who founded the New York Medical College and Hospital for Women. Lozier was active in the woman's suffrage movement.

3. **"International Council":** The International Council of Women, founded in 1888, advocated human rights for women across national boundaries.

4. **chary:** Cautiously reluctant.

5. **"euchre":** A card game in which each player plays one card, known as a "trick," and the player with the highest value card wins the trick. The highest trump card is the jack and is known as the Bower.

6. **brackish:** Salty.

7. **Black Hills:** A mountain range in western South Dakota.

8. **Hill City to Custer City:** Cities in South Dakota.

9. **Buffalo Gap:** A town in South Dakota.

10. **hoar-frost:** A feathery frost.

11. **cuspidor:** A cuspidor, or spittoon, was a large receptacle for spitting into, often used by men when chewing tobacco. Cuspidors were found in train stations, hotels, banks, and saloons in nineteenth-century America.

12. **Nordica:** Lillian Nordica (1857–1914), a famous opera singer.

13. **Anna Gordon:** Anna Adams Gordon (1853–1931) was involved with the Woman's Christian Temperance Union and served as Willard's personal secretary.

14. **Carrie Chapman Catt:** Catt (1859–1947) was a leading American suffragist. She served as president of the National American Woman Suffrage Association after Shaw and founded the League of Women Voters.